CADOGAN
ISLAND GUIDES

MALTA
GOZO & COMINO

P9-CLQ-363

Cadogan Books Ltd
Letts House, Parkgate Road,
London SW11 4NQ

The Globe Pequot Press
6 Business Park Drive, PO Box 833,
Old Saybrook, Connecticut 06475–0833

Copyright © Simon Gaul September 1993
Illustrations © Anna Grima

Book design by Animage
Cover design by Ralph King
Cover illustration by Povl Webb
Maps © Cadogan Guides, drawn by Thames Cartographic Ltd
Macintosh: Alexander Manolatos
Index: David Lee

Editing: Brenda Eisenberg and Vicki Ingle
Proofing: Wilson Peters
Managing Editor: Vicki Ingle
Series Editor: Rachel Fielding

A catalogue record for this book is available from the British Library
ISBN 0–947754–44–X

Library of Congress Cataloging-in-Publication-Data

Gaul, Simon
Malta/Simon Gaul
p. cm. -- (Cadogan guides)
'A Voyager Book.'
ISBN 1–56440–178–2
1. Mata -- Guidebooks. I. Title. II. Series.
DG988.8.G38 1993
914.58'504 -- dc20   93-11608 CIP

Typeset in Weidemann and produced on
Apple Macintosh with Quark XPress, Photoshop,
Freehand and Word software.

Printed and bound in great Britain by Redwood Books,
Trowbridge, Wiltshire on
Selkirk Opaque supplied by
McNaughton Publishing Papers Ltd.

Mgarr Harbour, Gozo

For my late father and his Maltese friend and sailing companion,
Gerrado Zammit. Unknowingly, they both helped to write this book.

About the Author

Simon Gaul was born in London thirtysomething years ago and spent much of
his childhood happily, but idly, sailing the shores of the Maltese islands and the
central Mediterranean. More recently he drove from London to Beijing just as
the Soviet Union collapsed (for which he accepts no blame). As well as being a
director of the Travel Bookshop in London, he writes children's books and is a
contributor to various publications. He is a half-competent sailor and pilot and
before sailing the Atlantic in 1994 intends to devote time to cooking *risottos*
and finishing the novel which this book interrupted.

Acknowledgements

A guide book is erroneously credited solely to the author, whereas the credit
belongs to all those who played a part in its realization.

In London. Industrial-sized thanks to my editor Vicki Ingle whose forebear-
ance, skill, encouragement, patience and rotten
time-keeping were invaluable. At Cadogan,
thanks to everyone especially Bill
Colegrave, Rachel Fielding for
bravely commissioning the
book, Brenda Eisenberg for

copy-editing and Alex Manolatos for glueing it all together. Thanks also to Sarah Anderson, Sophie Kington and all at The Travel Bookshop; to Sammy Portelli of Air Malta for finding airplane seats; and to Lotte Lorimer, my long-suffering PA.

In Malta. Thanks to Anna Grima whose illustrations shed much-needed light on the text and to Diane Camilleri for her proof-reading. Dr Michael Refalo, the Tourism Secretary and the NTOM were most helpful—Louis Azzopardi's voluminous address book solved many problems. Thanks to Tony Pace, Michael Galea, Walter Zahra, Stephen Spiteri, Dr Zammit-Maempel, Fathers Michael Zammit and Victor Camilleri, and literally dozens of sacristans and priests whose knowledge proved very helpful. Ron Agius of Progress Press, the Virtu Steamship Co., Paul Mercieca of Manduca Mercieca Accountants, Sapienzas Bookshop and Pierre at the Morris Bookshop all lent a hand. Air Malta's generosity with airline tickets is very gratefully acknowledged.

Finally, thanks to those friends who provided alcohol and anecdotes, books and introductions, *risottos* and shelter, and anything else I've forgotten: Michael and Petra Bianchi, Mark Hilpern, Brian and Jeff Mizzi, my stepmother Angela and brother Xavier, CT, Kathy, T-Bone, Tony, Sammy, Philip Nicholson, and my Suzuki jeep which somehow sped me safely over 4,000 km. The last word can only go to my wife Harriett, who contrived to deliver our son Hamilton mid-way through Part IX.

Please help us keep this guide up to date

We have done our best to ensure that the information in this guide is correct at the time of going to press. But timetables and facilities are constantly changing; standards and prices in hotels and restaurants fluctuate; bars and nightclubs come and go. We would be delighted to receive any comments concerning existing entries or omissions, as well as suggestions for new features. All contributors will be acknowledged in the next edition and will receive a copy of the Cadogan Guide of their choice.

Contents

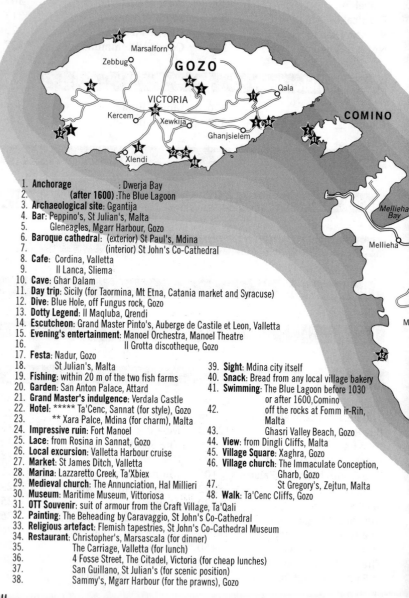

1. **Anchorage**: Dwerja Bay
2. **(after 1600)**: The Blue Lagoon
3. **Archaeological site**: Ggantija
4. **Bar**: Peppino's, St Julian's, Malta
5. Gleneagles, Mgarr Harbour, Gozo
6. **Baroque cathedral**: (exterior) St Paul's, Mdina
7. (interior) St John's Co-Cathedral
8. **Cafe**: Cordina, Valletta
9. Il Lanca, Sliema
10. **Cave**: Ghar Dalam
11. **Day trip**: Sicily (for Taormina, Mt Etna, Catania market and Syracuse)
12. **Dive**: Blue Hole, off Fungus rock, Gozo
13. **Dotty Legend**: Il Maqluba, Qrendi
14. **Escutcheon**: Grand Master Pinto's, Auberge de Castile et Leon, Valletta
15. **Evening's entertainment**: Manoel Orchestra, Manoel Theatre
16. Il Grotta discotheque, Gozo
17. **Festa**: Nadur, Gozo
18. St Julian's, Malta
19. **Fishing**: within 20 m of the two fish farms
20. **Garden**: San Anton Palace, Attard
21. **Grand Master's indulgence**: Verdala Castle
22. **Hotel**: ***** Ta'Cenc, Sannat (for style), Gozo
23. ** Xara Palce, Mdina (for charm), Malta
24. **Impressive ruin**: Fort Manoel
25. **Lace**: from Rosina in Sannat, Gozo
26. **Local excursion**: Valletta Harbour cruise
27. **Market**: St James Ditch, Valletta
28. **Marina**: Lazzaretto Creek, Ta'Xbiex
29. **Medieval church**: The Annunciation, Hal Millieri
30. **Museum**: Maritime Museum, Vittoriosa
31. **OTT Souvenir**: suit of armour from the Craft Village, Ta'Qali
32. **Painting**: The Beheading by Caravaggio, St John's Co-Cathedral
33. **Religious artefact**: Flemish tapestries, St John's Co-Cathedral Museum
34. **Restaurant**: Christopher's, Marsascala (for dinner)
35. The Carriage, Valletta (for lunch)
36. 4 Fosse Street, The Citadel, Victoria (for cheap lunches)
37. San Guillano, St Julian's (for scenic position)
38. Sammy's, Mgarr Harbour (for the prawns), Gozo
39. **Sight**: Mdina city itself
40. **Snack**: Bread from any local village bakery
41. **Swimming**: The Blue Lagoon before 1030 or after 1600, Comino
42. off the rocks at Fomm ir-Rih, Malta
43. Ghasri Valley Beach, Gozo
44. **View**: from Dingli Cliffs, Malta
45. **Village Square**: Xaghra, Gozo
46. **Village church**: The Immaculate Conception, Gharb, Gozo
47. St Gregory's, Zejtun, Malta
48. **Walk**: Ta'Cenc Cliffs, Gozo

The Best of Malta and Gozo

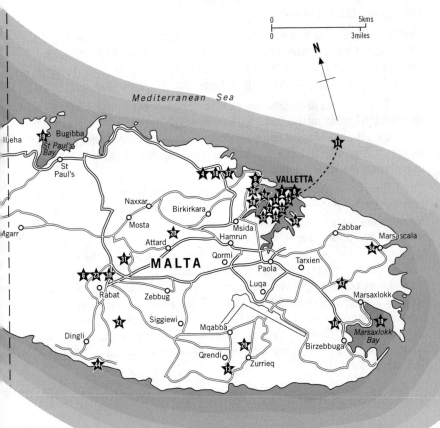

Basic Geography

The islands which constitute the Republic of Malta lie almost dead-centre of the Mediterranean: Sicily is just 93 km to the north, North Africa 288 km to the south, Gibraltar 1,826 km to the west and Alexandria 1,510 km to the east. The archipelago consists of three principal inhabited islands: Malta, Gozo and Comino; and three uninhabited islets, Cominotto, Filfla and St Paul's Island.

Malta, the largest landmass, covers 246 sq km with 136 km of coastline; the sister island, **Gozo**, is approximately 13.5 by 7 km and has 43 km of coastline; and tiny **Comino** covers only 2.5 sq km. Combined, the islands are no bigger than the Isle of Wight; Malta itself is no bigger than Martha's Vineyard.

The total population of the islands—the fourth-highest per square kilometre in the world, is approximately 358,000, of whom 26,000 are Gozitan. In addition there are 580,000 Maltese nationals dotted throughout the world, predominantly in Australia and North America. The language is Malti but nearly everyone speaks English and Italian.

The islands are primarily sedimentary rock, two-thirds being the soft pale honey-coloured globigerina limestone from which the majority of local stone buildings are made. The landscape is unremarkable, neither flat nor hilly, with moderate contours and open valleys. From the air it can look barren, especially in summer, redeemed only by the pinks, reds and whites of the oleander bushes. The limestone buildings and the dry-stone walls built to protect crops from the extremes of the weather don't flatter the landscape either, but in spring it is surprisingly verdant. Gozo, only 5 km away, is perennially greener due to its clay soil and hillier, more compact contours. None of the islands have mountains, rivers or natural minerals. The highest point on Malta is Dingli Cliffs at 260 m above sea level: Gozo's little summit is the hill at Ta'Dbiegi (194 m).

You are lucky if you travel to Malta by boat. That's how the Phoenician traders, in their small rounded vessels, first encountered the archipelago nearly three thousand years ago. Today, the stirring bastions of the fortress capital Valletta skim welcomingly into view out of the hazy Mediterranean light, but time has barely altered the landfall.

Introduction

From the air, the archipelago is the last splutter of Europe before Africa, and the bare limestone topography hints at the arid sands 300 km beyond. Flying north from Africa, the islands are like a tentative toe-print from the outsize body of the dark continent as it stretches towards Europe. That's Malta: an untethered outcrop at the crossroads of the Mediterranean; a devoutly Roman Catholic country, but with Allah as its name for the father of Christ.

Think of Malta, and two very different ideas may come to mind: "an unconscionably romantic history', to quote Evelyn Waugh, and, more prosaically, a holiday destination under a baking sun. The Order of St John ruled supreme here for nearly 270 years, and its crusading knights, "the flower of European aristocracy', left part of the magic of their era in towering fortifications, stately *palazzos*, and noble baroque churches and cathedrals whose walls are adorned still with the art of Caravaggio, Antoine de Favray and Mattia Preti; a disproportionately grand legacy for such a small island. In addition, just about every major player in European history—from Count Roger the Norman, to Napoleon, to Hitler—has squabbled over this isolated but valuable piece of real estate, and left a mark in some corner. The only visitors who came in peace were St Luke and St Paul, who planted the banner of Christianity.

For travellers today, not even the spell cast by the knights can soften the unforgiving, even cruel, landscape. In the long months of summer the islands lie quietly shimmering, like a mirage, refreshed only by the famously clear waters of the rocky coast. For those who don't wish to griddle themselves under the relentless sun, there are over 350 churches to snoop around, walks along the cliffs, terrific swimming, diving and sailing, and the monumental remains of prehistoric sites older than Stonehenge and the Pyramids.

Nevertheless, you have to be selective about when and what you explore. Traipsing through the dagger-like shadows of Mdina in August, when the temperature exceeds 35°C, is not everyone's idea of fun. Moreover, some of the islands' physical heritage is not worth visiting at all, having disintegrated or been devoured by the tourist industry. Visit in late May or September for a less aggressive climate; or, for a gentler Mediterranean atmosphere altogether, bypass overbuilt Malta for its small sister island, Gozo. In mid-September the Gozitans shed the protective scales they acquire during the lunacy of high summer, and parts of the island are still, if only just, becalmed in the gentler and less touristy waters of the 1950s.

The islanders, both Maltese and Gozitan (and there is a difference you will discover), are an energetic, industrious and wealthy people. Short and stocky, loud and proud, but with an open and warm nature, they can en masse resemble a cast of amphetamine-fueled characters from a cartoon. Yet, for a much-invaded people they are almost naïvely welcoming, and the only timidity you may find is on Gozo.

But, of course, the-times-they-are-a-changing. The current dilemma is the ugly face of commercialism. Since independence in 1964, Malta has fluttered towards tourism like a moth towards light. In 1992, just under a million people visited the islands—that's almost three times their combined population. Only now, and possibly too late, are the authorities trying to take their holiday destination "up market'; with the marketing men doing everything in their power to lose the reputation (and unprintable sobriquets) the islands earned in the 1970s. New services, communications and hotels have been built, and tariffs have, inevitably and markedly, risen.

One of the few things that hasn't changed, so far, is the cheeky grin the Maltese always sport, except when behind the wheel of a car. Beware, their driving is anything but Catholic.

Travel

By Air

For such a small country Malta has a surprisingly large number of direct flights from most of the capital cities of Europe to the new **Malta International Airport** (MIA) at **Luqa** 9 km from Valletta. The national airline, **Air Malta**, has a modern fleet and an impeccable safety record.

From the UK

Air Malta runs the only scheduled service with 13 flights a week from **Heathrow** rising to 14 in the peak summer months (June–September). There is a scheduled daily service from **Gatwick** and 4 flights a week from **Manchester**. Flight time is approximately 3 hours. Contact **Air Malta**, 314–16 Upper Richmond Road, Putney, London SW15 6TU, © (081) 785 3177 for reservations and information on fares—Super Pex, Pex, Eurobudget and Business Class. The only unrestricted return fare is a hefty £478 (Business Class).

Malta is principally a holiday destination and there is a *smorgasbord* of **charter flights** available: **Air Malta**, **Britannia**, **Monarch**, **Air 2000** and **Airtours International** fly round the clock (literally) from Heathrow, Gatwick, Manchester and *16* other airports in the UK, depending on the time of year. Beware of trying to book seats only in high summer. Prices can be absurdly low, £69 return at the time of writing. The travel pages of the Sunday broadsheets and your local travel agent will offer the best choice (*see also* pp. 6–7).

From Europe, North Africa and Beyond

Air Malta runs regular services to 21 European cities and a further 8 routes (including Dublin, Geneva, Madrid and, ironically, Istanbul) will be added to the network in mid-1993. These are reciprocated by some of the national carriers including **Lufthansa**, **Swissair** and **Alitalia**. In addition, Air Malta has introduced new services to Catania and Palermo in Sicily: 16 and 5 flights weekly, respectively, in summer. Air Malta also flies twice a week from Cairo. **Tuninter** has a twice-weekly service to Tunis from Malta. While the UN sanctions against Libya remain in force both Air Malta's and **Libyan Arab Airways'** direct flights to Tripoli and Benghazi are suspended.

Malta is destinational but a few airlines offload passengers and refuel en route to evocative-sounding places like Accra, Cape Verde Islands, Casablanca, Cotonou, Lome, Luanda, Lusaka and Montevideo, all of which are served by

Aeroflot which stops here outbound from the CIS. Check with Aeroflot's Malta office (*see below*) for the latest schedules. **Balkan Airways** flies weekly to Sofia, and **CSA** does likewise to Prague in summer. **Biman Bangladesh Airways** has a weekly service to Dhaka (check with Air Malta locally).

From Canada, the US and Australia

London and Rome are used as hubs to Malta from both continents. The Air Malta offices listed below will recommend carriers and advise on fares.

Air Malta Offices

Australia: 7 offices. Head office: 10th level, 403 George Street, Sydney NSW 2000, ✆ (02) 2391722; reservations, ✆ (2) 2903306.

Canada: Toronto: 388 Bay Street, 130 Bloor Street West, ✆ (416) 9252311. Also, Ottawa, Montreal and Vancouver.

Egypt: Nile Hilton Commercial Centre, Suite 34, Tahrir Square, Cairo, ✆ (2) 756022/3.

France: 37 Rue Lafayette, 75009. Paris, ✆ (1) 48743956.

Germany: Muenchenerstrasse 49, 6000. Frankfurt, ✆ (69) 239076.

Holland: Singel 540, 1017 AZ. Amsterdamn ✆ (20) 6246096.

Italy: Via Barbarini 50, 00187. Rome, ✆ (6) 4883106.

Switzerland:1-216 Terminal B, CH8058. Zurich Airport, ✆ (1) 816012/3.

USA: World Air Transportation Consultants, 475 Sansome St, Suite 840, San Francisco, California, 94111, ✆ (415) 36 22 929.

Flight Information in Malta

Flight Enquiries: MIA ✆ 249600/697800.

Do not leave it until the last minute to check in for your return flight. All carriers are merciless about bumping you from planes they have overbooked; even on a full Business Class ticket your legal redress is almost non-existent. This problem is most pronounced in summer, so arrive 90 minutes prior to the scheduled departure time. The 10-minute Gozo Helicopter airlink flies directly to MIA, but add a further 10 minutes for luggage.

Principal Airlines

Aeroflot: Regency House, Republic St, Valletta, ✆ 232641.

Air Malta: 280 Republic St, Valletta, ✆ 238282, 224444.

Alitalia: Suite 19, Valletta Buildings, South St, Valletta, ✆ 234454.

Austrian Airlines: Apt 5, 19 Tigne Sea Front, Sliema, ✆ 343444/5.

Libyan Arab Airlines: Valletta Buildings, South St, Valletta ✆ 222735.

Lufthansa: Palazzo Marina, 143 St Christopher St, Valletta, ✆ 241178.

PTM Int: (Balkan and CSA), Regency Hse, Republic St, Valletta, ✆ 238483.

Swissair: 6 Zachary St, Valletta, ✆ 244159.

Tuninter: First Floor, MIA, Luqa, ✆ 882920/5.

By Sea

From Europe

The route is via Sicily or southern Italy. The Italian line **Tirrenia** (c/o: **Serena Holidays**, 40–2 Kenway Road, London SW5 ORA, ✆ (071) 244 8422; or **S. Mifsud & Son**, 311 Republic Street, Valletta, Malta, ✆ 232211) operate a car ferry from Naples, Reggio di Calabria, Catania and Syracuse. Departs **Naples** Thursday 2030, arrives Malta 2130 Friday. £95.60 per car (up to 4.5 m) and £82.50 per person in a 2nd-class cabin *one way* in summer (1 June–30 Sept). **Reggio di Calabria**, **Catania** and **Syracuse** crossings are on a Tuesday, Friday and Sunday, a round-robin beginning at Reggio di Calabria. Fares are one-way: dep. Reggio 0830, car £63.40, £45.40 per person; dep. Catania 1300 and Syracuse 1630, car £59.60, £40.40 per person from both ports; the ferry docks in Malta at 2130. Out-of-season fares are approximately 20% cheaper.

The Gozo Channel Company, c/o Multitours, 7 Denbigh Street, London SW1V 2HF, ✆ (071) 821 7000 operates a twice-weekly car ferry service from April to September—increasing to 4 times a week in the summer peak period—from Sa Maison to Pozzallo in southeast Sicily.

Sea Malta, Flagstone Wharf, Marsa, Malta, ✆ 232230/9 plies a passenger-only service between Malta and Tripoli daily at 1800; £135 one-way. It also has a cargo vessel which departs Marseilles on a Monday, stops in Livorno on a Tuesday, and docks in Malta on a Friday. Fares one-way from either embarkation point: car £105, passenger £95, and a special customs clearance charge of £48 is levied (if you are a 'wannabe' truckdriver this is *the* way to get to Malta).

The Virtu Steamship Company, 3 Princess Elizabeth Terrace, Ta'Xbiex Malta, ✆ 317088 (UK agent Multitours), runs a Malta–Tripoli service, and a high-speed catamaran to Catania, Pozzallo and Licata in Sicily for passengers only (*see* pp. 335–6).

There is a Lm4 tax when departing Malta by sea; this does not apply to private yachts.

From the UK

The 38-hour **train** journey as far as Syracuse encompasses many treats: cross-Channel ferries, at least two changes, the (inevitable) delays on Italian trains, a diet of railway food, and forced intimacies with complete strangers. For supple under-26-ers who purchase an Interail card, it makes more sense. Whatever you do, reserve a *couchette* and bring your own small pillow. Strangely, **coach travel** is a less masochistic alternative. In summer **National Coaches** will take you as far as Rome, non-stop. Departures: Monday, Wednesday and Friday at 1200, arriving in Rome at 2100—in time for supper. The following morning it's a train or a plane for all points south. The train is a very economical, but tiring, 12-hour journey with a change at Messina for Syracuse. Air Malta and Alitalia have 20 flights a week from Rome to MIA between them in summer. The flight is just over an hour.

Tickets

British Rail European Travel Centre, Victoria Station, London SW1, ℂ (071) 834 2345 will handle all the bookings. The 2nd-class fare is £122 one way or £202 for a 2-month return. Add £20 for a *couchette*, an Italian supplement and the cost of the Syracuse–Malta ferry. **Wasteels Travel**, 121 Wilton Road, London SW1V 1JZ, ℂ (071) 834 7066 also issues Italian train tickets and the excellent value Italian railcards. **Interail** cards enable you to scoot around the whole of Europe for a month (£249 from travel agents and main-line stations).

Eurolines ℂ (071) 730 0202 or **Eurolines/National Express**, 52 Grosvenor Gardens, London SW1 0AU, ℂ (071) 730 8235. London–Rome costs £139 return and a 2nd-class rail fare on the Rome–Syracuse leg is approximately £32, one way. **The Italian Tourist Office**, 1 Princes Street, London W1R 8AY, ℂ (071) 408 1254 has more general information.

By Car from the UK

This is a more viable alternative, not least because you will not be at the mercy of Italian timetables. The journey is about 2,150 km and can be done in 2 days, but it is more enjoyable to linger. If you have had enough of driving by the time you reach **Naples**, the weekly ferry service to Malta can be a pleasant start to a holiday; reserve a berth for the night crossing in summer. Otherwise, car ferries go from Reggio di Calabria or Catania and Syracuse in Sicily (*see* p. 4).

Checklist: Car Log book (for Italy and Malta), **Green Card** (for Switzerland and Malta), full UK **driving licence**, basic **spares** (clutch cable, fan belt, radiator hose), **First Aid kit**. The best **maps** for France are *Michelin*, and for Italy *Touring Club Italiano*.

Tour Operators and Specialist Travel Agents

Malta features in most tour operators' programmes; the shoulder booking periods (April and October) are becoming increasingly popular for those who wish to avoid the glaring summer heat. Variations on the standard 'two-week' package are listed below. The **National Tourist Office of Malta** (NTOM) has comprehensive information on the island's cultural and sporting events.

NTOM

UK: Mappin House, Suite 300, 4 Winsley Street, London W1N 7AR, ✆ (071) 323 0506.

USA: Permanent Mission of Malta to the UN, 249 East 35th Street, New York, NY 10016, ✆ (212) 725 2345/9.

France: 9, Cite de Trevise, 75009 Paris, ✆ (1) 48000379.

Tour Operators

Airtours plc (general, self-catering), Wavell House Holcombe Road, Helmshore, Rossendale, Lancashire BB4 4NB, ✆ (0706) 240033.

Aquasun Holidays (general, diving), 41 Crawford Street, London W1H 1HA, ✆ (071) 258 3555.

Belleair Holidays (general, tickets only), 314–16 Upper Richmond Road, London SW15 6TU, ✆ (081) 785 3266.

Cadogan Travel (general), 9–10 Portland Street, Southampton, Hampshire, ✆ (0703) 332551.

Enterprise and Sovereign Holidays (general), Groundstar House, London Road, Crawley, West Sussex RH10 2TB, ✆ (0293) 560777.

Gozo Holidays (Gozo), Dunny Lane, Chipperfield, Hertfordshire WD4 9DQ, ✆ (0923) 262059.

HF Holidays (walking), Imperial House, Colindale, London NW9 5AL, ✆ (081) 905 9556.

Highway Holidays (heritage, religious), 3 Winchester Street, Whitchurch, Hampshire. RG18 7AH, ✆ (0256) 895966.

Holts Battlefield Tours (heritage, disabled), 15 Market Street, Sandwich, Deal, Kent CT20 1AZ, ✆ (0304) 612248.

Inter-Church Travel (religious), Saga Building, Middleburg House, Folkstone, Kent CT20 1BL, ✆ (0303) 857535.

Meon Villa Holidays (Gozo farmhouses, villas), Meon House, College Street, Petersfield, Hampshire, ℗ (0730) 268411.

Multitours (Maltatours UK) (general, flights only), 7 Denbigh Street, London SW1V 4RR, ℗ (071) 821 7000.

Martin Randall (architectural, heritage), 10 Barley Mow Passage, Chiswick, London W4 4PH, ℗ (081) 994 6477.

Owners Abroad (general, flights only), Royal Buildings, 2 Mosley Street, Picadilly, Manchester, M2 3AB, ℗ (061) 831 7000.

Prestige Holidays (non-package, specialist), Prestige House, 14 Market Place, Ringwood, Hampshire BH24 1JA, ℗ (0425) 480400.

Raymond Cook Holidays (religious, painting, walking), Bedfordia House, Prebend Street, Bedford MK40 1QG, ℗ (0234) 349512.

St Paul's Tours (in the steps of St Paul), 164 Chelsworth Road, Felixstowe, Suffolk 1PU 8UJ, ℗ (0394) 282198.

Saga Holidays (over-60s), Saga Building, Middleburg House, Folkstone, Kent CT20 1BL, ℗ (0303) 8577000.

Sport Tours (marathon running), 91 Walkden Road, Manchester, M28 5DQ ℗ (061) 703 8161.

Sportsman's Travel (diving, all sports), PO Box 269 Brentwood, Essex CM15 8NR, ℗ (0277) 264444.

Tour Operators in Eire

747 Travel (general), 82 Aungier Street, Dublin 2, ℗ (1) 780099.
Abbey Sun (general), Ha'penny Court, 36–7 Lower Ormond Quay, Dublin 1, ℗ (1) 727711.

Entry Formalities

Visas and Immigration

Entry **visas** are not required by anyone holding a passport from the US, Europe, Australia, Japan, or certain African and South American countries. People requiring visas should apply to the Malta consul in their respective countries. Sojourns are limited to 3 months but extensions are readily granted if an application is made at **Police Headquarters** in Floriana before the 3 months are up. Employment is prohibited. British temporary passports are valid.

Malta does itself a disservice with its tedious **immigration formalities**. Wherever you are from you will have to complete an entry card before handing your passport to an unsmiling official, who will verify your probity before thumping an illegible stamp in your passport. The time-consuming process can grate, especially when two or more flights arrive simultaneously. Should Malta's EC application be granted, this unwelcoming anachronism will in all probability cease.

Customs

The officers are vigilant. Malta is a small country and any imported 'nasty' such as food bacteria or rabies would have a devastating effect (certain foodstuffs are often banned). You can bring in personal items such as radios, cameras and video cameras, although sometimes the Customs officer will need to be convinced that you are not going to flog the item in question and leave without it—imports attract high duty. The duty-free allowance per adult is 200 cigarettes or equivalent, one bottle of spirits, one bottle of wine and a 'reasonable quantity' of perfume. A gift for a Maltese resident exceeding Lm2 in value is dutiable and should be declared—eat the box of chocolates on the plane.

If you arrive at the Pinto Wharf docks **by car** Customs officers will note your vehicle's serial numbers. You will be asked to sign a declaration stating that you will be liable for duty (65% for those of EC origin and 85% for others) on *their* valuation of your car and its constituent parts. The full duty can be demanded from those unfortunate enough to have had their car stolen or written off in an accident.

Non-residents can bring as much **foreign currency** into the country as they wish, but any sum larger than £1,000 should be declared on arrival to avoid problems on departure. The maximum amount of the local decimal currency, the *Liri* (Lm), that can be imported is Lm50; Lm25 is the maximum that can be exported. Hang onto your **exchange receipts** as you will need them to retrieve your own currency; trying to cash even modest amounts of *liri* overseas is an uphill struggle. There is a 24-hour **foreign exchange bureau** at MIA (*see also* pp. 31-3).

Getting Around

By Air

Malta–Gozo

The demise of the communist bloc brought a long-awaited Malta–Gozo airlink—a Soviet-built Mi-8, 20-seat helicopter flown by ex-communist bloc pilots under the auspices of **Malta Air Charter**, © 824330. The 12-minute trip along the southwest coast from MIA at Luqa to the Gozo Heliport midway between Mġarr and Victoria is a great improvement on the 2-hour journey overland which can be uncomfortable and irksome, especially in summer. Ask your hotel or agent in Gozo to arrange a taxi to meet you at the heliport, or you will have to take a short hike to the main road and catch a bus into Victoria.

The service operates 12 times a day in the peak season (1 July–26 Sept) and 10 times a day during the shoulder season (15 April–30 June and 27 Sept–25 Oct), from 0400 to 1920. In winter, check times. **Tickets** can be booked by your hotel or Air Malta © 882920/5, or at the Gozo Heliport © 557905/561301. **Check in** 10 minutes before departure time. The **baggage allowance** is 30 kg per passenger. **Fares:** open return Lm18; day return Lm15; one-way Lm10; children (2–12) 50% fare and infants 10%. There are also two **sightseeing trips**, of 20 or 40 minutes, Lm12 and Lm20 respectively, and the helicopter is available for charter.

By Sea

Malta–Gozo

Gozo Channel Co: © 580435/6; timetable © 556016; Gozo office © 556114.

The state-controlled company enjoys a monopoly on the extremely lucrative Malta–Gozo run; on a cost per mile basis it's 2.5 times more expensive than a full Business Class air fare. The service carries nearly 2 million people and 400,000 cars a year on four lovingly maintained ro-ro rust buckets of north European provenance. Somewhat unfairly, tourists have to pay 50% more than the Maltese: return fares (whether embarking at Ċirkewwa or Sa Maison) are Lm3.50 per car, Lm1.50 per person, children (3–12) 50c.

The principal shuttle route is from **Ċirkewwa** on the northwestern tip of Malta to **Mġarr Harbour** in Gozo. The 5-km journey takes 25 minutes and operates approximately once every 90 minutes, day and night, in **summer**. At peak season most daytime crossings can be crowded, so if you are planning to take a car, arrive half an hour before the scheduled sailing time. In **winter** the night service is infrequent. For those who do not wish to cross Malta by car, the largest and most luxurious ferry, the *Għawdex*, sails for Mġarr from **Sa Maison** in Pieta Creek on the outskirts of Valletta. The sailing lasts about 1¼ hours and there is a daily service at 1330 in summer.

Timetables change frequently; copies are available free from most hotels, NTOM offices and travel agents. **Tickets** cannot be booked in advance, and under a new system you can purchase your ticket *only* in Mġarr.

The Gozo Channel Co. also operates a good passenger-only **Hovermarine** service 4 times a day between **Mġarr** and **Sliema**; on some trips it stops at **Comino** and **Sa Maison**. This hybrid hovercraft is quick, clean, efficient, air conditioned and good value, but it runs only in summer when it's calm, and can be a noisy and unsettling contraption the morning after a *festa*. By Hovermarine, the average journey from Mġarr to Sliema shrinks to just 30 minutes. Fare: Lm1 one way.

To Comino

Getting to Comino is more problematic. Apart from the infrequent **Hovermarine**, the only scheduled service is run by the **Comino Hotel**, ℂ 529827/9, from March to November when the hotel is open. The hotel's boat has 6–7 departures a day from both Ċirkewwa and Mġarr Harbour, beginning at dawn and ending at dusk. Return fare: Lm1.50 from either embarkation point.

From **Marfa** (1.5 km before you get to Ċirkewwa) a charming old reprobate known as 'Gozo Charlie' motors to Comino all day long in April–October. His boat, the unregal *Royal 1*, chugs from Marfa every hour on the hour. The Lm2 return fare can be purchased on board. **Cruise boats** make the trip to Comino every day (*see below*). When the Comino Hotel is shut, try the **fishermen** in Mġarr Harbour.

Sliema–Valletta

The Marsamxetto Ferry, ℂ 335689/338981, is the least aggravating way of getting to Valletta from Sliema. The 100-seat boat, her topsides painted a distinctive blue and white, beetles back and forth across the creek from the **Ferries** in Sliema to the Valletta **bastions**. The journey takes 5 minutes and runs approximately every 40 minutes from 0745–1815 Monday–Saturday. Fares are 35c each way and 15c for the under-16s and over-60s.

Pleasure Cruises

Three companies run cruises around the islands and to specific destinations. **Captain Morgan Cruises**, ℂ 331961/336981/343373, offers more variations on a theme than either of the others. Its large 11-vessel fleet ranges from a giant *luzzu* to a brand new submarine, *Lampuka*, which dives down to snoop around a wreck for 45 minutes. All excursions depart from the **Ferries** in Sliema except for the submarine (from Ċirkewwa) and the 'Sea-Below' (from Buġibba). The most popular trips are the **Harbour Cruise** (Lm3.25), the **Comino/Blue Lagoon Day-Cruise** (Lm7.50), and the **submarine dive** (Lm16.95). There are concessions for children and some fares include free pick-up from your hotel.

Boat Charters

The Maltese islands have many tucked-away coves and bays that are best reached by boat, and a handful of professional skippers who will take you swimming or fishing wherever you want to go. Prices are in the region of Lm90 per day for a crewed boat and (generally) a buffet lunch and soft drinks.

Lady Kirsti, Nautica Marine, 21 Msida Road, Gzira, ✆ 338253.

Fernandes, ✆ 342209/346861.

Heidi, call Loretu in Gozo, ✆ 552531.

The Malta Cruising School, c/o S&D Yachts, 8 Marina Court, Guiseppe Cali Street, Ta'Xbiex ✆ 331515/320577/339908.

Fishermen will also sometimes oblige if you can track one down. They will rarely go out for a full day and price is a matter of personal, and probably drawn-out, negotiation. Try Marsascala and Marsaxlokk in Malta, and Marsalforn and Mġarr Harbour in Gozo.

For **self-drive boats** try **Oki-KO-Ki Boat Hire Co.**, near the Cavalieri Hotel in St Julian's, ✆ 339831, which hires out craft from dinghys to speedboats. Age restrictions apply and a hefty deposit is required. The principal marine **brokers and agents** are listed under 'Yachting' (pp. 45–8).

By Bus

Enquiries: ✆ 441765/486927.

Buses have been the only means of public transport on Malta since the 11 km of railway shut in 1931. The pale green and chrome diesel buses are rudimentary pieces of equipment with no air conditioning, meagre suspension, threadbare seating and sometimes grumpy drivers; in other words they are no different from most European transit systems. All vehicles have been christened with names as diverse as *Elvis Presley* and *St Paul* on their shiny bonnets. Nearly all terminate in the village square or by the village church. If you want a bus to stop, wave frantically, as if shipwrecked, from the roadside bus-stop; if you are inside, ring the clanky bell. Fares are cheap (6–13c); the service generally runs from 0600–2300, but check (there isn't anything as prosaic as a printed timetable).

In Malta, the main terminus is outside **Valletta** at **City Gate**, where the buses orbit the large Triton fountain and from which tentacular routes spread across the island; just about every village is served, albeit infrequently. Nearly all buses originate and return to Valletta, so cross-routing can be a problem.

Bus Routes

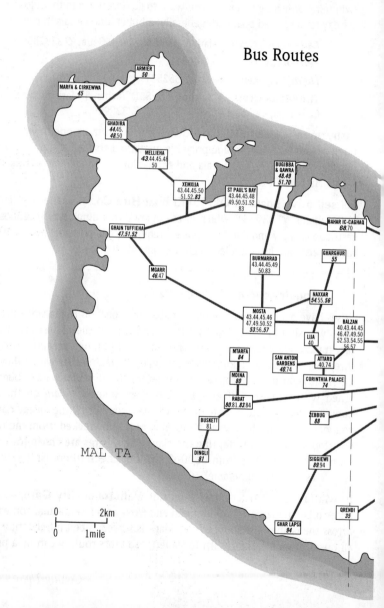

ARMIER
50

MARFA & CIRKEWWA
45

GHADIRA
44.45.
48.50

MELLIEHA
43.44.45.48
50

XEMXIJA
43.44.45.50
51.52.*83*

ST PAUL'S BAY
43.44.45.48
49.50.51.52
83

BUGIBBA
& QAWRA
48.49
51.70

BAHAR IC-CAGHAQ
68.70

GHAJN TUFFIEHA
47.51.52

BURMARRAD
43.44.45.49
50.83

GHARGHUR
55

MGARR
46.47

NAXXAR
54.55.*56*

MOSTA
43.44.45.46
47.49.50.52
53.56.*57*

BALZAN
40.43.44.45
46.47.49.50
52.53.54.55
56.57

LIJA
40

MTARFA
84

SAN ANTON
GARDENS
40.74

ATTARD
40.74

MDINA
80

CORINTHIA PALACE
74

RABAT
80.81.*83*.84

BUSKETT
81

ZEBBUG
88

DINGLI
81

SIGGIEWI
89.94

QRENDI
35

GHAR LAPSI
94

MAL TA

0   2km

0   1mile

12

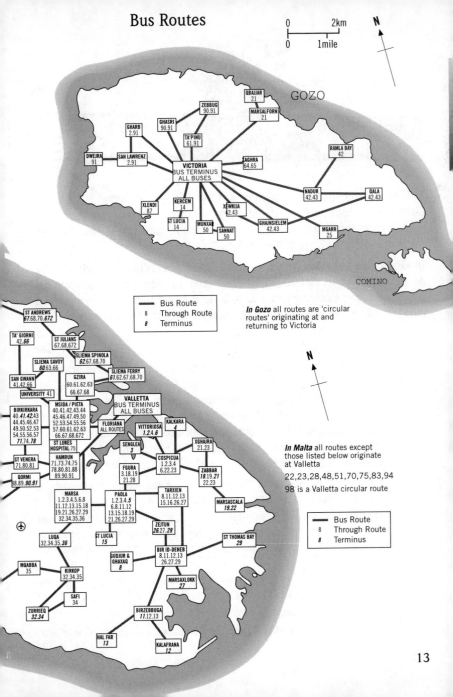

There is a helpful information booth at City Gate which helps to translate numbers into destinations (which are *not* marked on the buses). If in doubt, ask—the Maltese have an encyclopaedic knowledge of the routes.

In Gozo, buses are grey with a red stripe. The terminus is in **Victoria** (Rabat). As all roads lead to Victoria, you have to change there when cross-routing. Buses meet most incoming ferries up to 2030 at Mġarr Harbour. Don't expect a fluid service in Gozo; it's geared to the local working and school hours.

By Car

The Maltese are car mad, although to witness the way many of them drive you wouldn't know it. There are about 130,000 cars for a population of 355,000. When a significant percentage of this number is out in force (as on Sundays), the 1,300 km of roads (an impressive statistic for an island only 27 km long) can appear all too meagre. Add three more disturbing facts: Malta does *not* yet have any form of mandatory MOT or vehicle test; no drink-driving and no seat-belt laws. All this can lead to problems that even Mad Max would find daunting.

- Be careful at **roundabouts**. Maltese drivers are very indecisive as to right of way—it's the code of the jungle not the highway that counts.

- If you are involved in an **accident** do *not,* under any circumstance, move your car one millimetre until the police arrive to take measurements and adjudicate, even if the result is a noisy jam. If you do, your car-rental insurance may be made void.

- Driving the wrong way down a one-way street is conventional practice and has its roots in the national love of gambling.

- No one *ever* indicates, uses a mirror or acknowledges a courtesy.

- Don't worry about **traffic lights**: there is only one set in Malta, at Msida, and it is only sporadically obeyed during the congested rush hours (0730–0830 and 1600–1730).

- Drive on the **left** (as in the UK) and give way to the right.

- The **speed limits** are never policed or adhered to, but out of interest they are: 64 kph, and 40 kph in built-up areas.

- A familiar sight (and one to be avoided) is piles of scrap metal (in reality, 30-year-old Ford Populars and the like) that belch blue smoke as they struggle to maintain 30 kph in the wrong lane. Occasionally, they career out of control as an ancient but vital component disintegrates.

There are three **breakdown** companies: RMF © 235464, **MTC** © 320349/248933 and **CAA** © 829374. Only a few rental firms include breakdown cover; if yours doesn't, your thumb should get you back to the garage.

Garages open Monday–Friday, 0800–1800 (1900 in summer and on Saturdays) and on Sundays on a roster basis. **Petrol** costs about 28c per litre and **diesel** 18c per litre. **Unleaded petrol** is available at a handful of garages.

Malta has taken energetic steps to modernize its infrastructure, but the quality of the **roads** is still pretty terrible—an agglomeration of undulations, tyre-devouring pot-holes, malicious reverse camber and poor-quality tarmac, all conspire to make driving uncomfortable and potentially hazardous. None of the roads is numbered, few are properly lit, and after the rains all have the holding qualities of an ice rink. Nevertheless, impressive improvements are under way, such as the new Santa Vennera bypass and tunnel system—Malta's own spaghetti junction—which opened in September 1992. The road network links all the towns and villages with Valletta, and, antiquated heaps notwith-standing, it should take no more than an hour to drive from one end of Malta to the other.

Parking can be a hassle of migraine-inducing proportions, especially in Valletta, and at the weekends in St Julian's. Try not to park illegally as the police have a quick-fire approach to violations: a Lm5 fine. A dearth of traffic signs often makes chosing a space a gamble, and protesting to an officer won't get you anywhere. If you do find a slot in a car park, tip the attendant 10–20c when you leave.

Names and Signs

Malti is an unsophisticated language of connections and derivatives, and many place names are everyday words. For example: *ramla* = sandy bay, *marsa* = harbour, *qala* = small cove, *baħar* = sea or bay, *għar* = cave, *blata* = rock, *xagħra* = stony ground, *nadur* = look-out. *Triq* means street, *San* prefixes a saint's name and *Triq Il-Kbira* is the high or main street. *Misrah* means square, as does *piazza*.

As many of the major tourist roads have both Malti and English **names**, this guide uses the English spelling, although in the smaller villages the street names are invariably just in Malti. The Maltese have an infuriating habit of re-naming their streets, especially after politicians; the late Nationalist prime minister, Georg Borg Olivier, heads the current crop. Again, ask if you get lost; local knowledge always supercedes the local honours system.

Road signs are poor and do not display distances, but slowly are being replaced. Navigating anywhere other than to a major town can sometimes be trying, but you will reach your destination in the end; you can't fail. Malta is an island after all. Tourist sights are posted in white with green letters. Signs or graffiti bearing the legend **RTO** deal with the hunters' right to shoot birds during the *kaċċa*. It's not uncommon to see country road signs peppered with shot, having been used, presumably, for target practice.

Hire Cars

If the above has not put you off hiring a car (it shouldn't), the major companies are represented at the airport and in the major tourist locations. The local car hire companies, with tantalizing names like the Alcapone Car Hire Co., are just as good and often 10–20% cheaper.

Excellent vehicles from small family jeeps to Group A cars cost, from the major companies, Lm12.50 and Lm6 per day, respectively. The rates published are for 7 days or more in peak season, and it sometimes pays to ignore these tariffs especially with the smaller companies. A credit card imprint will be taken as a deposit. If you have a specific requirement, it is advisable to request it in advance.

You will have to be over 25 and under 70 and to have held a full driving licence for 12 months; a few companies will hire to those outside these parameters. **Insurances** vary but all have mandatory third-party fire and theft cover. Moving your car after an accident may invalidate your insurance.

All hire cars have distinctive, yellow registration plates. These are not to single you out as prey for local drivers (although it will sometimes feel that way), and may ensure that very minor infractions are waved on. **Chauffeur-driven** cars are expensive, and all are funereal Mercedes or Volvos; Wembley's has the largest fleet.

Hertz (Gzira), © 314635-7. **Avis** (Msida), © 225986-8. **Eurodollar** (Blata l-Bajda), © 233116-7. **Europcar** (Ħamrun), © 238745/245038.

Good local firms: Alcapone (Mellieħa), © 572477. **Unicar** (Gzira), © 342584/5. **Percius** (Lija), © 447564. **Wembley's** (St Andrew's), © 370451/2. **Windsor** (Msida and Sliema), © 330046/346921. **Gozo–Mayjo** (Victoria), © 556678.

By Motorcycle and Bicycle

People who think the Maltese islands are flat have never cycled them. The prevailing road and traffic conditions make cycling a recommended pastime only for the very skillful or the very brave, and certainly not for children. **Motorcycles** and scooters are available for hire at approximately Lm6 per day, decreasing to Lm4 out of season. A crash helmet is obligatory and apart from holding a driving licence you have to be over 21 and leave a deposit.

Hollywood Rent-a-Car, Sliema, © 318704/343686 or **Astra**, Qawra, © 575171, can also help with locating **pedal cycles**. In **Gozo** try Grace opposite the Marsalforn Hotel, © 561503.

By Taxi and Karrozin

Maltese cabs only really serve the visitor. Cabs are clean white chariots of varying vintages; a few are old Mercedes with huge ivory-coloured steering-wheels belonging to the glory days of soft suspension. All have two things in common: red number plates and shut-off meters (asking for them to be switched on is pointless). On the whole, drivers are not interested in advancing Maltese tourist relations and the well-intentioned government tariffs are merely laughed at. Taxis are to be found on ranks in the larger towns. If there are plenty of cars but no drivers peer into each car—one of them will be host to the card-game. You should ask, haggle, then agree the fare *before* getting in. Tipping is rarely offered or expected. The fare from the Airport to Valletta, Sliema and St Paul's Bay should be no more than Lm4, Lm5 and Lm7, respectively. Most taxis are private but the largest company, **Wembley's** in St Julian's, © 332074/345454, operates a very reliable 24-hour service.

Karrozin are horse-drawn carriages that have plied their trade since 1856. They are a good way to see the sights, especially in Valletta. The four-person canopied bench-seats are high up, and children enjoy the ride. *Karrozin* can be found outside most main tourist attractions. Haggle with all your skill before alighting, the Maltese who use the *karrozin* on Sundays do.

Walking—other than on a pavement in a town—can be frightening. Very few roads have sidewalks and drivers display a blind disregard for pedestrians. If you do venture onto the roads, walk in single file *facing* the oncoming traffic and as close in as possible. Avoid walking on unlit roads at night, but only on account of the driving.

Malta, Gozo and Comino are blessed with a varied and rugged **countryside** that provides excellent **rambles** to peaceful out of the way places, especially in spring. Some of the most rewarding spots can only be reached on foot. Avoid walking over cultivated land or through crops, and do remember a sun hat and water. If you see one of the few indigenous snakes, it will *not* be deadly.

The Maltese are very friendly, providing they are not behind a wheel. Ask anyone for directions if you get lost.

Travellers With Disabilities

Maltese pavements, where they exist, tend to be narrow and uneven—difficult if you are frail or in a wheelchair. Entrances to many shops and hotels can also be tricky, but the more modern ones have implemented the government's policy of improving access where possible. Bus transport is impossible, but all other modes including the Gozo ferry are available. The principal archaeological sites (except the Hypogeum) can be seen with help, and major churches have wheelchair access; but the Museum of Fine Arts, the upper floors of the Grand Master's Palace and St John 's Co-Cathedral are inaccessible.

Few things remain constant in Malta and therefore check with either the **NTOM**, or the **National Commission for the Handicapped**, St Joseph's High Road, Santa Venera, © 487789. Both provide advice and a list of hotels. The newly refurbished **Hotel Phoenicia** in Floriana has two rooms designed specifically for disabled visitors. **The Paola Rehabilitation Centre**, Corradino, Paola, Malta, © 693863/692221, will organize wheelchair hire for a Lm5 donation and a Lm10 deposit, for two weeks.

Practical A–Z

19

At the height of **summer** do not be fooled by the sea breeze, the *Majjistral*, which comes predominantly from the northwest; during July and August areas of high pressure sit over the central and southern Mediterranean basin and Malta bakes like a brick under cloudless skies. In May and September the dry, hot *sirocco* blows in from North Africa, bringing with it the reddish Saharan sand and inducing a state of torpidity. They say in Sicily—the wind's next stop—that if it blows continuously for more than five days all crimes of passion should be forgiven.

The **winters** tend to be mild but can sometimes be very wet. The first rains come in October or November and if they persist until January the islands can be as uncomfortable and damp as a cellar. The *gregale* is an aggressive winter wind which blows down from the northeast across the Adriatic into Malta, and is justly feared by fishermen and yachtsmen alike. The local newspaper, *The Times*, publishes a very reliable land and sea forecast on page 5.

In the shoulder season, despite the still-warm days, it gets dark at about 1800 in the spring and autumn.

Communications

Post

In **Malta** the main post office is in the Auberge d'Italie, Merchants Street, Valletta. In addition to normal services it provides a philatelic service and an expedited datapost service. In **Gozo** the post office at 129 Republic Street, Victoria offers the same services. *See* Opening Hours, pp. 32–3. *Poste restante* is available only at the main post offices and then only if written application is made in advance to the postmaster-general at the General Post Office in Valletta. There is a *poste restante* for pleasure yachts (*see* Yachting, pp. 45–8).

The local post is reliable. Letters costs 4c; stamps are available from most newsagents. A letter posted to the UK or USA should take 4 days or 6 respectively, and cost 10c to the UK (cards and letters) and 14c to the USA (a card is 12c). Reminders of the British colonial influence are the red post-boxes; one or two wall-mounted boxes in the villages bear Queen Victoria's insignia, *VR*.

DHL International, DHL House, Hompesch Street, Fgura, © 800148/9. **EMS Data Post**, the General Post Office, Valletta, © 224421.

Telephones

International country code: 356. Calls from Gozo to Malta require the prefix 8.

Until quite recently a completed **international call** was cause to rejoice, but the government has replaced the crackling, bakelite antiques with a new digital system, and now calls to anywhere in the world are simple and hiss-free. **Telemalta** has offices in **Malta** at Luqa Airport, Ħamrun, Mdina, Qawra, Sliema and St Paul's Bay, Valletta. The main office in St Julian's (Mercury House, St George's Road) is open 24 hours a day. In **Gozo** the only Telemalta office is in Republic Street, Victoria but there are two booths, one at the Mġarr tourist office, the other in Xlendi. In emergencies the police station in Marsalforn will oblige. Making an overseas call from any of the Telemalta offices is appreciably cheaper than from your hotel. Cheap rate is from 2100–0800 and all day on Sunday. A handful of international boxes exist; some take coins, others the new **Telecard** which is available in two denominations, Lm5 and Lm2.50, from any of their offices. In most cases your hotel will help out with international telegram, telex and fax requests. Public facilities are only available from the Valletta, St Julian's and Luqa Airport offices and the Victoria office, Gozo. There is no local telegram service.

Local calls are easier. The barman and the shopkeeper have replaced the almost non-existent local phone-box (you will see the iron remnants from the British colonial days, few of which work). Local calls to anywhere within the islands of *any duration* are charged at a flat rate of 5c. You will be charged 10–20c. Just walk into any establishment and ask.

An excellent mobile **cellular** service called **Telecell** covers the islands and extends 30 km out to sea. Telecell hires portable phones for periods of a day to a year against a credit card deposit. Contact Telecell, Msida House, Birkirkara, © 493074/482820. Hire charges for the phone itself start at Lm5 per day but decrease to Lm3 after 30 days. Local and international calls are charged at 12.5c a unit. Note, however, that you cannot call a Telecell phone from a shop-keeper's or local payphone. Through **Vodaphone**, those who possess portable cellular phones in the UK can sign on for the duration of their stay in Malta, provided they bring their portable handsets.

Police: ℗ 191

Malta Police Headquarters, Floriana, ℗ 224002.
Gozo Police Headquarters, Victoria, ℗ 562040–3.
The Armed Forces of Malta, ℗ 824212–4.

Since independence in 1964, tourism in Malta has developed at a breakneck speed and has brought tremendous benefits, but there is no hiding from its side-effects. Young men and women, who even 10 years ago would have been content to remain in their towns and villages, now want to be a part of the new and changing Malta, and cracks have appeared in the hitherto granite-firm foundations of family life. This has resulted in a degree of envy and a sour tension; envy is manifested in an increasing number of burglaries, while tension is burnt off through violence in certain tourist areas such as Paceville. Hot-blooded stabbings and shootings, while uncommon, are no longer unheard of. Visitors are seldom, if ever, caught up in this petty violence which is rooted in *machismo*, and mostly over women. The police, while undermanned, have managed to subtly increase their presence; as yet there is no sign of a diminution of respect for them.

But you will not see beggars or alms-takers anywhere; nor will you be accosted into buying goods. The Maltese look after their poor, elderly and infirm. The streets are safe day and night from dangers and hooliganism and mugging are as rare as good drivers.

The *pulizija* are for the most part unarmed, and wear a blue uniform almost identical to that of the UK police. Every village has a station, even if it is staffed only by one man, that is open 24 hours a day; but in the smaller villages it will sometimes be left unmanned. Any crime should be reported at once to the police *and* to your consulate. A strong line is taken against drugs, however 'soft'. If you are involved in a motoring incident do *not* move your car until the police have arrived to take details.

The **Armed Forces of Malta** are responsible, among other duties, for patrolling the seas with boats and helicopters, mainly to ensure dope-dealers use Sicily and not Malta; they also rescue unfortunate yachtsmen.

Electricity

Voltage is 220–240 AC 50 cycles. Sockets are UK standard, with three square pins. Lights have both bayonet and screw fittings. Power surges and failures are rare, but bring a surge protector for computers, etcetera.

Government representatives are there to help should you find yourself in trouble with the local police or even be in search of that elusive manufacturer of powder compacts. Definitely seek their assistance in the event of a lost passport or a serious illness.

Australia: (High Commission), Ta'Xbiex Terrace, Ta'Xbiex, ℂ 338201.

Canada: J.M. Demajo, 103 Archbishop Street, Valletta, ℂ 233121–7.

France: Villa Seminia, 12 Sir Temi Zammit Street, Ta'Xbiex, ℂ 331107/335856.

Germany: Il Piazetta, Entrance B, 1st Floor, Tower Road, Sliema, ℂ 336531/336520.

Italy: 5 Vilhena Street, Floriana ℂ 233157–9.

Switzerland: M. Lowell, 6/7 Zachary Street, Valletta, ℂ 244159.

UK: (High Commision), 7 St Anne Street, Floriana, ℂ 233134–8.

USA: Development House, St Anne Street, Floriana, ℂ 243653/240424–5.

Entertainment and Nightlife

Bars are divided into two distinct sorts: the village bar which is a microcosm of local life and intrigue, and bars aimed at the tourist market which tend to have a maximum three-year life span. In the second type you could be anywhere from Hong Kong to Gambia—with homogenized decor, copy-cat music and lager in a familiar bottle. They are a ritual meeting and courting ground for most age groups, tourists and Maltese alike. Friday and Saturday nights can be a real crush, and areas such as **Paceville** in St Julian's should be treated with a degree of caution. Parking can also be a nightmare around bars that are currently 'in'.

For **nightlife** read discos. Some hotels have their own 'disco' but rotating mirror balls are usually the peak of their sophistication. A handful make their own grade: Paceville and St George's Bay feature two of the busiest and most high-tech clubs which are open all year: **Styx II** and **AXIS**. The best open-air discos are **Ta' Giuanpula** in the middle of nowhere on the Rabat to Siġġiewi road and **Il-Grotta** in Gozo on the Xlendi road. For **jazz**, try **BJ's** in Paceville.

The Casino on Dragonara Point (adm. Lm2) was the summer residence of the Marquis Scicluna family until 1964, and is a beautifully proportioned classical villa on an attractive promontory. In summer the dress code is 'smart-casual', otherwise a jacket and tie are required. If you are not a gambler you can dine. **The Manoel Theatre**, ℂ 246389/222618, is one of the oldest and smallest theatres in Europe. It is Malta's national theatre and the island's main venue for drama and concerts. The season runs Oct–May. Sadly, only a few of the traditional 'fleapit' **cinemas** remain in Sliema, Valletta and Victoria (Gozo). A new cineplex with six screens has opened in St George's Bay. The papers have listings for both films and plays.

If you consider **tenpin bowling** entertainment, there is an excellent alley (and a roller rink), the **Eden Super Bowl**, in St George's Bay. Game charges are Lm1 and shoe hire 30c. Open 1000—0030. Call ℂ 319888/341196 to book a lane.

Festas and Public Holidays

Every village has at least one feast or *festa* in honour of its patron and favourite saint on a specific day each year. The majority of *festas* take place from May to September, the most popular being the Assumption on 15 August. The villagers (aided by their parish priest, church and band clubs) plot the celebrations, make the fireworks and petards, and gather in all their flamboyant finery for a weekend of noise, drinking and nougat. The day after is called '*xalata*, meaning 'a pleasure outing', and is for hangovers and picnics. Try to catch at least one. Each village's principal *festa* is listed in the text, and national *festas* and holidays are listed below. (*See also* Topics, pp. 79–80.)

Almost everything shuts down on **public holidays**. A few restaurants and bars stay open, buses run reduced services, taxis and ferries run as normal and a pharmacy will be open somewhere. Be warned, roads and beaches are crowded.

January 1:   **New Year's Day**

February: The **Valletta Carnival** held over 3 days hails the end of winter and the coming of spring; adults and children run amok in fancy dress among carnival floats. Gozo has a similar carnival a few days later. **St Paul's Shipwreck**, Valletta is on the **10th**.

March: **St Joseph** and **Freedom Day** are on the **19th** and **31st** respectively.

April: Nearly all the larger towns have their own Good Friday and Easter Sunday processions and celebrations.

May 1:   **Worker's Day.**

June 7:   **Sette Guigno.** The **L-Imnarja** *festa* on **29** June celebrates the end of the harvests and quickly turns into a jamboree of picnics, wine, music and dance in the gardens of Buskett. Donkey and horse races are also held the next day in nearby Rabat.

August 15:   Seven villages and Victoria celebrate the **Assumption**, also referred to as *Santa Marija*.

September 8: **Victory Day** signals the end of the Great Sieges both of 1565 and 1940–3 with, among other celebrations, traditional boat races and a regatta in the Grand Harbour; **21st: Independence Day**.

December 8: *Festa* of the **Immaculate Conception**; **13th: Republic Day**; **Christmas Day**.

Food and Drink

Over 150 years of British colonial rule have left their mark—though thankfully its culinary influence is no longer omnipresent. Sometimes a menu will give you that stomach-tightening *deja vu* of yester-year school lunches, but the star turns of British cooking such as fish and chips are not hard to locate.

Maltese cooking is the product of many kitchens: southern Italy, Sicily, Greece and North Africa. It has evolved as a simple culinary experience, made from produce that has been readily available, including hardy vegetables that thrive in the warm but harsh climate. Nothing goes to waste; the same ingredients are to be found in many different dishes. Favourites include *minestra*, a thick soup eaten all year round made from eight or more vegetables, three or four pulses and a pasta, and allowed to cook for at least 3 hours. *Timpana*, a Sicilian dish by origin, is macaroni with minced meat, livers, tomatoes and eggs, baked under a topping of pastry—not for the weight-conscious. *Bragoli* is rolled beef stuffed with bacon, parsley, breadcrumbs and hard-boiled eggs.

Fish is traditionally eaten on Wednesdays and Fridays, and is best purchased on those days. Grouper (*cerna*), amberjack (*accola*), bream (*sargu*), swordfish (*pixxispad*) and a small dorado (*lampuka*) which makes a superb pie, are all available. With the end of summer comes the *lampuki* season when you'll often find fishermen on street corners selling their fresh catch.

Meat, especially home-reared lamb and pork, has always been popular with the Maltese, but does not appear on many restaurant menus. An old and near-extinct tradition revolves around the Sunday roast. The lady of the household would prepare her meat on a bed of potatoes and onions, and season it with pepper and coarse sea-salt. Having covered it with a cloth she would march the dish across the square to the baker, who would tag it and put it in his cavernous oven with all the other villagers' food. Progress has curtailed this custom but traditional Sunday aromas can occasionally be sniffed in more remote villages. Fresh vegetables from the courgette, aubergine and marrow family are always eaten with meat. A traditional Maltese meal might end with fresh fruit such as figs or peaches, or *ġejniet*, a delicious light goat's cheese sprinkled with ground peppercorns.

National Dishes

Cominotto used to be overrun with **rabbits** (*fenek*)—not anymore, they must have ended up in the the national dish (*see* Topics, p. 78). *Hobż biz-żejt* is local bread which is rubbed with tomatoes until it turns pink, and then topped with tomatos, capers, olive oil and seasoning. *Pastizzi* are oval pockets of flakey pastry—about three-bite size—stuffed with either a light ricotta cheese, or a grim mushy pea concoction; both varieties are served warm. If you return home before sunrise you will find a few bars open and men sipping glasses of sweet white tea while chomping *pastizzi*. Go and join them, it'll staunch the impending hangover. Locally baked **bread** is a real treat. The traditional crusty loaf is the staple of the local diet. Buy one piping hot from any baker before 1130 and it will be a miracle if your loaf makes it home intact. *Ftira*, another scrummy local bread, is harder to find; it looks like a huge sun-tanned Polo mint—soaked in pungent olive oil and chopped tomatoes, it's delicious.

Drink

Alas, local commercially produced **wine** is not up to much. There is a story—probably apocryphal—that as the founder of one of the local wineries lay on his deathbed, he croaked to his two sons to approach. 'Listen well', he whispered, 'I must tell you', he paused to gather his last gasp, 'it is also possible to make wine from grapes'. The moral for the unwary visitor is that even a modest amount can make you feel as if you are circling the airport; treat it with caution.

Marsovin, the largest of the local vintners, imports white and red grapes from both Italy and France, and produces excellent wines that are considerably cheaper than their imported counterparts, which carry a high levy.

Soft drinks producers revel in the fact that more non-alcoholic drinks are consumed per head in Malta than almost anywhere else in the world. All major brands are available and most are bottled locally. With either ecological or financial foresight, they only come in bottles and seem to taste better for it.

Simmonds Farsons, the island's main brewer, produces Cisk an excellent lager and an ale called Hop Leaf. The company also produces a popular fizzy drink peculiar to Malta called Kinnie, which looks like yesterday's cold tea but tastes better. Marsovin brew Lowenbrau locally and the Coca-Cola Company sells Stella Artois. Other leading brands of beer are imported but are more expensive. All internationally known brands of **spirits** are widely available and are consumed in unbelievable quantities. The General Soft Drinks Company (Coke) makes the only local liqueur, **Tamakari**, a weird blend of oranges and herbs.

Eating Out

Malta has a phenomenal number of licensed catering establishments, 680 at the last count (excluding hotel restaurants). Those mentioned in the text are current, but in Malta, chefs transfer their allegiences as quickly as footballers. Where possible, sound local establishments are featured (you won't be allowed to miss the tourist ones), and many different palates are catered for.

The Maltese tend to have lunch at home, so apart from those in hotels only a handful of restaurants in tourist locations open at mid-day. The evenings are for eating out—the curtain does not even rise on the night's entertainment until 8 pm, and as in Italy this follows on from the evening *passegiata*. The Maltese, like all Latins, abhor solitude or even dining *à deux*—the preserve of honeymooning tourists. The curtain only falls when the last person has left, normally around 4 am.

As a general rule, **stay with the fish**. More often than not you will be shown the day's catch (check for clear eyes and red gills). Imported meat such as veal has usually been the victim of brutal attempts at tenderizing. **Vegetarians** will survive: many establishments will run up special dishes, and pizzas are available everywhere. **Standards** of catering, decor and service have risen markedly, along with the variety of kitchens—from Malay to Russian and everything in between—but so too have prices. Frankly, some establishments have slapped on major-city prices but don't deliver the goods.

Price Categories

The following categories are used throughout the guide and are based on **a three-course dinner for two with an imported bottle of wine plus tax**. (The 10% levy is on all restaurant bills. It's *not* a service charge, which is normally left to your discretion, 7.5–10% being acceptable).

Expensive:	Lm23+
Inexpensive:	Lm8–15
Moderate:	Lm15–23
Cheap:	Lm8 or less

The Gay Scene

The gay scene is somewhat difficult to find. Certain bars and cafés are favourites but, like everything else in Malta, they change; ask around. Unfortunately, at the time of writing no public or private helplines or contact organisations exist.

Health

Emergencies: Police ℭ 191, Fire ℭ 199, Ambulance ℭ 196.
St Luke's Hospital, Gwardamanga, ℭ 241251/247860/234101.
The Gozo General Hospital, Victoria, ℭ 556851.

There are no inoculation requirements for Malta. Your hotel will be able to provide an English-speaking doctor at short notice. The islands have a reciprocal arrangement with the UK and Australian health services. Visitors from elsewhere are advised to take out separate health insurance that covers repatriation. Check the small print in your life or health policy if you plan to go diving, parasailing, etcetera.

St Luke's Hospital is Malta's principal hospital; Gozo has its own, the **General Hospital**. While neither is up to certain American or British technological standards, they do provide competent care. St Philip's, a private hospital operated by a British concern is due to open in Santa Venera 1994.

Larger towns, like Mosta, have **clinics** that deal with lesser emergencies. For minor complaints there is a rota of doctors who hold surgeries at the larger pharmacies. All pharmacies are flagged with green neon crosses and 12 are open on Sundays and public holidays; a list is published in *The Times* on Saturdays and Sundays. Most stock international medicines, including diabetic products and contraceptives. Should you fall foul of 'Mediterranean tummy', though it's highly unlikely, rest for 36 hours on a diet of bread and water before gobbling fistfuls of pills; diarrhoea is very dehydrating. There has been a handful of cases of AIDS.

Water

The water is safe to drink but it simply doesn't taste very pleasant, like delicately salted crushed aluminium. Four brands of bottled 'table' water are available everywhere at a very reasonable cost. Mineral water is imported and most known brands are available.

Things That Bite

Apart from the ubiquitous mosquito there is nothing on land that will do you any harm; snakes are not common and, like spiders, **not poisonous**. Some of the local wild dogs are unsavoury, and Manoel Island has a motley pack of beasts, but rabies is not a problem. If a Mediterranean ecological disaster is flavour of the summer, a few non-poisonous jelly fish may fetch up in the coastal waters.

Libraries

The national library, the **Bibliotheca**, Republic Square, Valletta, ✆ 224338, houses a plethora of source material including the archives of the Order of St John. *Open to the public except Wed and Sun.* The **public lending library** is in **Beltissebh**, next door to the police headquarters in Floriana, ✆ 224044/243473/240703. UK library tickets are valid. **Gozo** has its own reference and lending libraries in Victoria: Vajringa Street and St Francis Square, ✆ 556200 and 553729 respectively. *Closed Wed and Sun but open Wed Oct–May.*

Living and Working in Malta

Conditions imposed on immigrants are none too onerous: a minimum remitted income of Lm6,000, a flat tax rate of 15%, and a residence that is either purchased for over Lm20,000 or rented for over Lm1,200 p.a.. Death duty is only chargeable on an immigrant's Maltese estate. Further information can be obtained from the **Ministry of Finance**, Floriana, ✆ 236306.

Business and offshore tax and company registration questions should be addressed to **Malta International Business Authority** (MIBA), Palazzo Spinola, St Julian's, ✆ 344230/3 or any of the major international accountancy partnerships.

The following **cultural centres** may prove useful:

> **The British Council**, 89 Archbishop Street, Valletta, ✆ 224707.
>
> **Alliance Francaise**, 108 St Thomas Street, Floriana, ✆ 220701/238456.
>
> **The American Center**, Development House, St Anne Street, Floriana, ✆ 241240/233080.
>
> **The German-Maltese Circle**, Messina Palace, 141 St Christopher Street, Valletta, ✆ 246967.
>
> **The Italian Cultural Institute**, 'Vecchia Cancelleria', Piazza San Giorgio, Valletta, ✆ 221462.

Media

Forests of tall aerials give you more than a hint of the role **television** plays in Maltese life. The broadcasting authority has been independent of government control since it first went on the air in 1962. **Television Malta** (TVM) broadcasts news, soccer, and Anglo-US imports for 6 hours a day; except for the imports all programmes are in Malti. **CNN** broadcasts every morning on the TVM channel in English. A 33-channel cable franchise has just begun a trial operation but the champions of the air waves will undoubtedly remain the deregulated **Italian TV stations**. In addition to broadcasting football, these numerous channels have circumvented the last vestige of church censorship in Malta: their absurd blue-tinged late-night quiz shows are immensely popular.

Radio is booming—literally. There are nine local radio stations, all of which play a mix of pop spiced with BBC news reports. *Voice of the Mediterranean*, run jointly by Malta and Libya, broadcasts news and current affairs 2–4 hours a day in Arabic and Malti. Global short-wave stalwarts such as the *BBC World Service* and *Voice of America* can also be found. Frequencies for all but the latter are published in *The Times*. **Newspapers** are prolific with three dailies, three weeklies and three Sundays. The principal English-language papers are *The Times, The Independent* and *The Sunday Times*. In all the local papers politics are invariably centre stage. **UK and European** newspapers are available late in the afternoon on the day of publication; UK Sunday papers are available on Sunday mornings. The only US papers available are *The International Herald Tribune* and, rather more spasmodically, *USA Today*. *Time* and *Newsweek* are punctual. In **Gozo** all foreign papers, except the UK Sundays, are a day late. *Welcome, the Holiday Guide* is a useful fortnightly publication available from newsagents for 20c.

Money

The Malta *lira* (**Lm**) is pegged to a basket of currencies that includes the ECU and the US dollar, and is a soft currency not traded on any international exchange. In common with many economies dependent on tourism (about 27% GNP in Malta), the currency is prisoner to very strict exchange controls.

The currency is decimal and divided into *liri* and *cents*. Notes: Lm20, Lm10, Lm5, Lm2. Coins: Lm1, 50c, 25c, 10c, 5c, 2c, 1c. There is a further subdivision from cents into *mils*, but these are rarely seen or used. Inflation is tame.

At the time of writing, to buy one Malta *lira* (also known as the *pound*) you will have to give £1.71 or US$2.54. Try not to leave Malta—unless of course you intend to return—with any local currency at all. British high street banks will more than likely tell you to take it elsewhere, like back to Malta.

Cash and traveller's cheques can be exchanged at banks and hotels. Maltese hotels indulge in the worldwide custom of overcharging for this privilege, so the bank will be your best bet. Whenever you change money, keep the receipt: you will need it to get your hard currency back. As with all countries that have a controlled currency, a **black market** does exist, though no one would ever admit to it publicly. It is an accepted way of life and easy to tap into, but given the miserly premium it's just not worth the hassle. Some shops will take foreign currency at a marginally firmer rate than the banks.

American Express, **Diners**, **Mastercard/Access**, and **Visa** are accepted in most of the larger establishments. **Eurocheques** to the value of Lm90 can be cashed each day at banks and the majority of shops and hotels.

Banks

There are three principal retail banks. **Mid Med** (the old Barclays Bank International), the **Bank of Valletta** and the much smaller **Lombard Bank**. You'll never be far from a bank: there are over a hundred branches and Mid Med has recently installed 24-hour foreign currency machines in the principal tourist areas. Mid Med will provide cash against your Visa card and the Bank of Valletta will provide the same cashing facilities against your Visa and Mastercard/Access cards. You need to show your passport for all transactions other than exchanging cash. Avoid having money wired; 'unfortunate delays' in the labyrinthine central banking system are not uncommon.

American Express has an office situated at 14 Zachery Street, Valletta, ℂ 232141, which provides cashing and travel facilities for Amex card- and traveller's cheque-holders. **Thomas Cook** is at Il-Piazzetta, Tower Road, Sliema, ℂ 344225/7. **Coppini**, an independent foreign exchange dealer, has a head office at 58 Merchants Street, Valletta and branches in Sliema, Qawra and St Julian's.

Queues can be tiresome and there aren't any specific times to avoid (see below *Opening Hours*).

Museums

The national museums (as distinct from those associated with individual churches, like St John's Co-Cathedral) cover archaeology, fine arts, the megalithic sites and maritime history. Until 1 January 1993 entry was a modest 15c but the government has inexplicably sextupled the entrance fee to Lm1 (under-16s, 25c). There are **concessions**: Sunday entrance is free and an all-day pass is Lm3. This is impracticable, except for Valletta or Gozo; the pass can be purchased at the first museum you visit. National museums are closed on public holidays and the Hypogeum at Hal Saflieni is closed indefinitely (*see below*, Opening Hours).

Opening Hours

Winter: 1 Oct–14 June
Summer: 15 June–30 Sept

Malta follows the great Mediterranean tradition of the *siesta*, a 3-hour mid-day break that has cemented family life for generations. Lunch is taken at home, rarely at restaurants, and in summer white-collar employees work shorter hours. Very few shops are open on a Sunday and everything is hermetically shut on public holidays (*see* pp. 24–5).

Shops

Food shops 0700–1230 and 1600–1900. Some non-essential shops stay open 0900–1900.

Banks

Winter 0830–1245 Mon–Fri; Tues and Fri afternoon only 1430–1600; Sat 0830–1200. **Summer** 0800–1245 Mon–Fri; Fri afternoon only 1430–1600;

Sat 0800–1130. There is a 24-hour branch of the Bank of Valletta at Luqa Airport (closed Christmas and New Year's Day). In larger towns **foreign exchange** departments remain open outside these hours, normally 1600–1900 in summer and 1500–1800 in winter. Mid Med has a few machines in the principal tourist areas.

Pharmacies

0800–1230 and 1530–1900.

Government Offices

Winter 0745–1230 and 1315–1715 Mon–Fri. **Summer** 0730–1330 Mon–Fri.

Commercial Offices

0830–1230 and 1530–1730. In the summer months many offices are either closed from 1245 or have a skeleton staff.

Museums

Winter 0815–1700 Mon–Sat and 0815–1615 on Sundays. **Summer** 0745–1400, 7 days a week. **In Gozo** timetables can be a little erratic—subtract or add 15–30 minutes.

Cathedrals and Churches

The two cathedrals in Valletta and Mdina, Mosta church, the cathedral in Victoria and the church in Xewkija in Gozo all have similar hours to the museums. As a general rule the larger parish churches open every day from 0600–1030 and again in the afternoon from about 1630–1900. Each village keeps its own idiosyncratic hours.

Post Offices

Open 0800–1245 Mon–Sat. The main post office in Valletta remains open 0800–1830 Mon–Sat in **winter**, and 0730–1800 in **summer**. **Telemalta**: 0830–2300; the office in Valletta closes at 1830, in St Julian's it is open 24 hours including public holidays.

Markets and Vans

Any time around dawn to about 1200. Many of the fruit vans will have disappeared by noon, except in the main tourist areas where their tail-gates remain down for most of the day.

Packing

Take as little as possible in the summer months. Simple **cotton clothes** are ideal for the heat. There is no need for bold sartorial statements, Malta is not a 'jacket and tie' country unless you are attending a function or mass on Sundays. Some churches such as Ta' Pinu require long-sleeved shirts and long trousers; for the majority, commonsense and respect is all that is required.

If you go outside the peak season a cotton **sweater or jacket** will suffice for the evenings. For the winter, depending upon your constitution, you should take one woollen **sweater** or a range of **thermals**. Women should take note that Malta is a very Catholic country and skimpy clothes are not only frowned upon but considered disrespectful.

It's a good idea to take all necessary **prescription medicines, high-factor sun creams, mosquito repellent,** a **hat, sun glasses** and **driving licence**. Note down your relevant **passport details**, and **traveller's cheque and credit card numbers**. A stout pair of **walking shoes** is a good idea if you plan to do any country walking; a **torch** for some of the gloomier church paintings is worth considering. And for anyone umbilically attached to the clipped intonations of the World Service, a short-wave **radio** is a good idea.

Photography

Larger format camera film and video film are available from camera shops. Black-and-white film will be available somewhere on the island but not readily. If you want to show Mdina in a *chiaroscuro* mood, in which incidentally it is at its best, bring your own supply. Leading brands of 35-mm colour print and transparency film are everywhere. A roll of 36 prints will cost you Lm6 to process (nearly double the UK equivalent) at any of Kodak's quick-developing centres. If you like photographing churches don't forget a wide-angle lens: baroque façades were not designed for a 35-mm SLR camera.

The Maltese and especially the farmers, fishermen and their families are a proud and secretive people. Ask permission if you wish to include them in a composition (or be extremely subtle if you don't).

Religious Affairs

Malta is a devoutly Roman Catholic country with over 357 churches. Nearly all services are held in Malti though there are 15 churches in which mass can be celebrated in English. Places of worship for other denominations:

Church of Scotland, Methodist and Free Churches: St Andrew's Scots Church on the corner of South Street and Old Bakery Street, Valletta.

Anglican: St Paul's Anglican Pro-Cathedral, Independence Square, Valletta; Holy Trinity Church, Rudolphe Street, Sliema.

Synagogue: Spur Street, Valletta.

Greek Orthodox: St George's, 83 Merchants Street, Valletta.

Evangelical Church of Germany: St Andrew's Scots Church, Valletta.

Mosque: Corradino Hill, Paola.

At **St Barbara's** in Republic Street services are in **French and German** and at **St Catherine of Italy** in Victory Square, Valletta, mass is said in **Italian**. For further information, contact either the church directly or your consular official. Times of services are advertised in the Malta *Sunday Times*.

Shopping

There will always be a siege mentality in Malta. Nothing is wasted, stocks are normally high, and if you can't find what you want, however esoteric, someone somewhere will make it for you.

Food

Local products are essentially organic and pesticide-free. Vans of fruit and veg are the travelling greengrocers, each with their own 'patch'. All the best produce is fresh from smallholdings and will have gone by 1130. Measurements are metric, and you should expect a few cents mark-up in price for the privilege of being a tourist. **Butchers** normally follow shop hours and are tucked away in side streets. Surprisingly, **fish** is harder to track down. Go to Azzopardi on the Mosta Road, **St Paul's Bay**, or in the the covered market in **Valletta**. In Gozo try the fishermen in **Mġarr Harbour** who will sometimes oblige. **Valletta Fish Market**, Barriera Wharf is a wholesale market, open from 0430–0600. Each town and village has its own super-market varying in size from 10-product hole-in-the-wall establishments to the **Dolphin Supermarkets** in Paceville and Balzan, where you will be able to find anything from garden furniture to Marmite (but still buy your fresh produce from the vans).

Markets

Markets thrive from Monday to Friday. Apart from food (including fish sometimes, but not meat) there will be clothes, fabric, extraordinary china figures, a plethora of household items and hundreds of punk-coloured buckets. Do not expect orderly queues—eye contact with the vendor is what counts. **Valletta's** main market takes place on Sunday in **St James's Ditch**, but there is a daily market in **Merchants Street**. Behind the Grand Master's Palace is an indoor market that affords a full choice of

Sampaki in high season

fresh fish, meat, poultry and vegetables (open Mon–Sat 0500–1900, except Wednesdays when it closes at 1400).

Victoria, Gozo, has its own open-air market beneath the citadel, in the piazza _It-Tokk_. The usual stalls of T-shirts, bolts of cloth and brooms are to be found as well as good cheap straw hats (Lm1); in the maze of streets running off the square you will find the fresh produce.

Clothes

While the shopping is not the via Condotti, an Italian influence does prevail, through what is imported. All the usual chains (both UK and Italian) are represented but at prices higher than you would expect. _Espadrilles_ are a bargain at Lm1.20 and are to be found in most tourist areas, as is the avoidable totem, the flourescent T-shirt. Gozo is famed for its **lace** and is still the best place to buy it. Sometimes it's difficult to tell the difference between hand- and machine-made work, so ask and be convinced before you hand over your cash; inevitably, proper handmade lace will be more expensive. The small village of **Sannat** has long been the centre of this intricate and ancient craft, where you will still find women (the elderly and the very young) sitting in the shade of the doorways working with their bobbins (_see_ pp. 314–15).

Crafts and Souvenirs

There is a crafts centre and a crafts village in Malta, and a crafts village in Gozo. **Ta'Qali**, a disued World War II airfield in the centre of Malta is the largest of the three. Here in the original RAF nissen huts there is an exhaustive array of local handicrafts and craftsmen displaying their skills—potters, lacemakers, wrought-iron forgers and Mdina glass-blowers, who will make you a vase or a doorstop while you watch. Chunky knitwear and jewellery are also for sale. Aspiring knights or fancy dress fanatics can even buy a full suit of armour. Entrance is free: quality and prices are generally okay.

Ta'Qali Crafts Village, Ta' Qali, Malta.

Malta Crafts Centre, St John's Square, Valletta.

Ta'Dbiegi Crafts Village, between Gharb and St Lawrenz, Gozo.

Sports and Activities

Beaches

The mean sea temperature in July, August and September is 23°C. The coastline of the islands is not pitted with long stretches of sandy beach, but the waters are exceptionally clear; it's the water itself that has always been important to the Maltese, not how or from where you enter it. A 'beach', therefore, can be sand, rock, a concrete lido, even a boat-ladder or a diving-board. The only thing it cannot be is the steps into a fresh-water swimming-pool; 'sweet water' as they call it has none of the properties of sea water, only a lot of chemicals.

There are 11 sandy beaches on Malta, two on Gozo and two (just) on Comino. Nearly all have been corralled by hotels but they are open to the public. The only private beach in Malta belongs to the Comino Hotel in San Nicklaw Bay. Conventional sand beaches offer safety, ease of access, facilities for those with families, but not necessarily the best swimming. They also attract the biggest crowds, especially at weekends.

The sandiest beach in **Malta** is **Għadira** or Mellieħa Bay on the northeast coast. The island's shores to the **north** and **northeast** are calmer and less steep than those to the south or west. Along these coasts from Sliema to Ramla are countless **beach clubs** or **lidos**, all of which offer access to the sea, bars and shelter. They charge an entrance fee (Lm1.50–Lm2) and are often allied to an hotel. Should your idea of exercise be the creak of a right elbow joint, the occasional opening of an eyelid and inhaling the aroma of coconut oil, look no further. On the **northwest** coast as far as **Ġnejna and Fomm Ir-Riħ Bay** is a hotchpotch of sandy beaches, smooth cream-coloured rocks and little coves. The only method of entering the water on the **southwest** coast up to **Għar Lapsi** is by boat-ladder. The sea under the sheer cliffs of **Dingli** is deep and sometimes rough. To the **south**, Island Bay, St Peter's Pool and St Thomas's Bay are well known spots—access can be tricky, and St Peter's Pool is best reached by boat.

In **Gozo** the sandiest beach is **Ir-Ramla** (if you count red sand as sand). Other good places to swim in Gozo are Mġarr ix-Xini, San Blas, Qala Point and the tiny Għasri Valley. **Comino** has a 10-m handkerchief of sand in the **Blue Lagoon**. This can hardly be called a beach but if you swim there before or after the pleasure-cruises invade, it can fairly be described as sublime. The public beach in Santa Marija Bay, with its few trees, is pleasant and less populous.

A few words of **caution**: people will tell you that the currents and undertow around the islands are minimal; it's not true, especially of the northwest coast and the Malta–Gozo channel. Gozo may look close from Comino, but don't even think of trying to swim it. The Maltese possess a prolific arsenal of speed boats, a few owned by idiots and show-offs, and it's a rare season when a bather is not struck, so keep a look out. If snorkelling, swim with a marker-buoy. Do not swim off rocks when it is rough: a wave will probably splatter you against them.

Diving and Snorkelling

Emergencies: © 824212–4

Diving off the coast of Malta is superb—with clear warm waters, nothing to devour you, and highly competent instructors and guides. The coastal waters of Malta are well known among the diving fraternity. This has resulted in an infrastructure in which the novice can easily be trained. Every school has to be licensed and has equipment for hire. If you already have an internationally accepted diving certificate the **Department of Health**, 15 Merchants Street, Valletta, © 224071, will issue you with a C-card permit on production of your log-book, medical certificate, two photos and Lm1. If you would like to learn, the school will arrange everything; the courses last for a minimum of five days and cost from Lm90, including equipment hire.

The skilled cave- and night-diver will feel at home in the caves and grottoes along the coastline, home to groupers, rays, lobsters and octopuses. Some of the best sites in the archipelago are: Anchor Bay, Aħrax Point, Ċirkewwa, Għar Lapsi, and Qawra Point in Malta; Dwerja Point and Fungus Rock in Gozo; the Santa Marija Caves and Irqieqa Point around Comino. **Snorkellers** will enjoy the waters' clarity, but should always tow an **inflatable red marker-buoy** to warn off the lunatic fringe of speedboat-owners. Equipment is for sale in any tourist location.

The **NTOM** has a list of schools and recommended dive sites (*see below*). Spear-fishing is forbidden, as is removing any ancient booty you may unearth. St Luke's Hospital has a **decompression** chamber and the Armed Forces of Malta has a rescue helicopter and patrol boats.

For more information contact the **British Subaqua Club** at 16 Upper Woburn Place, London WC1H 0QU, © (071) 387 9302, or the **Association of Professional Diving Schools**, Msida Court, 61/2 Msida Sea Front, © 336441.

Malta: Cresta Quay Diving Centre, St George's Bay, St Julian's, ✆ 310743; **Dive Systems**, 48 Gzira Road, Gzira, ✆ 317137; **Maltaqua**, Mosta Road, St Paul's, ✆ 571873.

Gozo: Frankie's Diving Centre, Mġarr Road, Xewkija, ✆ 551315.

Comino: Tony's Diving, Comino Hotel, ✆ 529822–5.

Fishing

In Malta fishing is neither sport nor recreation, but a way of life. You don't need a licence to fish in Maltese waters but spear-fishing is prohibited. Wherever you see a sea wall you will find a man with an impossibly long rod, bait and very few fish, if any, at his side. Onshore fishing is an end-of-the-day therapy—most of the fish are found in the deeper waters of the Malta–Sicily channel. To fish for swordfish, dentici or even lampuka, seek the help of a fisherman who will know where to look. Try Marsaxlokk Bay or St Paul's Bay on Malta, or Mġarr and Marsalforn on Gozo (*see* Boat Charters, p. 11). You won't find the great ocean sailfish in the saline Mediterranean, but occasionally shark sightings occur way out to sea. All this does is encourage glory-seeking Italians to depart Mġarr laden with buckets of offal in vain pursuit.

Football

The premier national league comprises 10 teams and competes from August to June. Matches are generally played on weekends and in the afternoons. The impressive National Stadium (17,000 seats) at Ta'Qali hosts the international matches as well as premier league matches. The teams all have evocative throwback second names like, Tigers, Hotspurs and Rovers.

Football is akin to a religion and is treated with reverence, albeit raucous, and has none of the mindless violence that hallmarks English football. If the team near where you are staying wins a match, however inconsequential, expect parades of cars bearing team colours and blaring horns. Postpone any notion of sleep. **Malta Football Association**, ✆ 222697, provides information.

Horse Riding

Riding is available, unaccompanied or accompanied, near the Marsa and throughout Malta and Gozo. Schools include: **Darmanin Riding School**, the Marsa, ✆ 235649; **Mellieħa Holiday Centre Riding School** ✆ 573901; **L. Spiteri Riding School**, ✆ 556254 in Gozo. Fees are around Lm3 per hour.

This was added to the sporting calendar in 1992 and is held in June. Expect four days of expensive and noisy razzamatazz. Contact **The Royal Malta Yacht Club**, Couvre Porte, Manoel Island, ✆ 333109.

The Marsa Sports Club

The Marsa is where the Turks made their encampment during the Great Siege of 1565. Since 1901 it has been home to the majority of Malta's land-based recreations. The club is open Mon–Fri 0900–2100, closes at 1700 at weekends. Temporary membership is available to visitors on a daily, weekly or monthly basis which includes use of the bar and restaurant. Initial contact should be made through your hotel or directly to **the Marsa Sports Club (MSC)**, ✆ 233851/232842/230664.

Horse-Racing. The Marsa Racing Club, Racecourse Street, Marsa, ✆ 224800/223802, holds a meeting every Sunday afternoon from October to May. Trotting races are the more thrilling and outnumber the flat by seven to one. There can be as many as nine races on the card. In Malta racing ranks a close second to football, and the theatre of a trotting race has to be seen to be believed—remember the Maltese are passionate gamblers.

Golf. Oscar Wilde described golf as 'a good walk ruined', which is a little unfair to the flat 18-hole, par-68 course situated within the racetrack of the Marsa. The shortish fairways are green, and so presumably are the greens when you reach them—there are over 50 sand bunkers. The sixth and only named tee is called 'the maid's bedroom' and no one will say why. Clubs are available for hire at Lm2, and a round costs Lm8 including day membership to the MSC. A weekly pass and membership is Lm40. Open on Mon, Wed, and Fri from 0730 and in the afternoons only on Tue, Thurs, Sat and Sun.

Tennis. The club has 17 all-weather courts that cost Lm2 per 90 minutes and Lm4 for the three floodlit courts which can be hired until 2200 in summer. It is advisable to book if you wish to play in the late afternoon or at weekends.

Squash. Five courts. Lm1.20 for 45 minutes; again book if you want to play after 1630.

Archery. The national sport of Bhutan and has a strong following in Malta. Matches are played at the Marsa. The **Archery Federation**, © 445060/487871.

Polo. The game has regained some of its colonial cachet with those who can afford it, the Coca-Cola Cup being the grail. It's fun to spectate, even if the horsemanship does ape that of the Marx Brothers in 'A Day at the Races'. Free for spectators.

Other Activities. The Marsa also has a **cricket** pitch (spectating at the twice-weekly matches is free), a large **swimming-pool** (adm. is 50c a day), an 18-hole **mini-golf** course (a round is 40c for children and 60c for adults), **table tennis**, 2 **snooker** tables (40c a game) and a low-tech **gym**.

Parasailing

Adapted boats lift you 35 m into the air, and you cruise around for eight minutes praying the cable won't break. Try St Julian's, St Paul's and Mellieħa Bay.

Shooting

The *kaċċa* is a very unsavoury part of Maltese sporting life. *Kaċċatur* or hunters are responsible for the deaths (by shooting, netting, caging or trapping) of nearly 4 million birds a year. The great mediterranean sea eagle and the peregrine falcon are among the many species which are now extinct in the islands (*see* Topics, pp. 80–82). The true sporting side of shooting can be found at **Malta Shooting Federation**, Bidnija (limits of Mosta), © 412506, where trap, I.S.U. and skeet are harmlessly shot at.

Running

The Malta Marathon is run from Mdina to Sliema over the statutory 26 miles in February. For questions regarding entry contact Mr. E. Attard, **Malta Marathon Committee**, 56 Autumn Street, Mosta, © 432402.

Water Polo

The sport is the summer's football—an exciting and, in Malta, noisy game. Matches are played, out of the anger of the sun, in the late afternoon. Contact the **Amateur Swimming Association**, © 236033.

Water-skiing

Skiing is nearly as easy as it looks, mono-skiing is not. The ideal time is very early in the morning or an hour or two before sunset when the sea is usually oily calm and empty. Facilities are available from any hotel that has a beach, or from the larger sandy beaches. A current fad with children aged 10 upwards is being towed on a massive inflatable 'sausage' that is ridden like a horse (but seats five or six) until it overturns and tips them into the sea amid yelps of delight. Rides cost approximately Lm1.50 for 10 minutes.

Windsurfing

This would become the national summer sport if someone could dream up a team angle to it. The Maltese possess all the right ingredients: the sea, nautical skills, a reckless attitude to speed, and verve. Proof of this is the annual Malta to Sicily (Pozzallo) windsurfing race, the world's longest. The event takes place in May and the record to beat is just under six hours. Details from **Wishbone Windsurfing Promotions**, 193 St Albert's Street, Gzira, © 314956. For the somewhat less ambitious, tuition and boards can be found on the larger beaches and at some hotels. National Championships are held in September and October.

Other Sports

For information on other sports and sporting events, including the **International Air Rally**, **motor-racing**, **martial arts**, **badminton**, **hockey** and **basketball**, contact the **NTOM** in Valletta (*see* p. 43).

Time

Malta is on **Central European Time** (CET) and is therefore one hour ahead of GMT. Dial 195 for a time check.

Toilets

Invariably the public toilets are spotlessly clean; nearly all have a legacy of sound-swooshing British plumbing in vitreous china bowls. Almost every village has a matched pair and quite a few underground, often in the square. There's sometimes an attendant— it's considered polite to leave a few cents.

Tourist Information

Government tourist offices are on the whole ecologically unfriendly places: forests of glossy brochures depicting impossibly attractive couples. The **NTOM** (National Tourist Office of Malta) is a welcome exception. Its information is useful and spare, covers most aspirations, and succeeds without loading you with sheaves of paper. Your hotel will have maps (Mid Med Bank offers **free maps**), eating and activity suggestions. Should you wish to discover the whereabouts of the Malta Ornithological Society (64/5 St Lucia Street,

Valletta, © 230684), or simply where to find a cheap hotel in Gozo, the offices will help out.

The **NTOM** headquarters is 280 Republic Street, Valletta © 238282. Its principal office for tourist information is in Freedom Square, Valletta © 237747, 100 m from the bus terminus inside the City Gate. **Sliema:** corner of Tower Road and Bisazza Street, © 313409. **Buġibba:** Bay Square, © 577382 (summer only). **St Julian's:** Main Street, Balluta Bay © 342671/2. **MIA:** the Arrivals Hall, © 249600 ext. 6073/4). The **Air Malta** information desk next door will have any relevant flight information.

Gozo has two offices: a small one in Mġarr Harbour, © 553343, 150 m from where the ferry disembarks, and a bigger office in Republic Street, Victoria © 558106/557407.

*In small villages where there is no tourist office, go to the **police station**, where they will be able to help out.*

Where to Stay

In a country which derives nearly 30% of its GNP from tourism there is, predictably, the full spectrum of accommodation available—from self-catering studios to 5-star hotel suites. Malta has adopted the World Tourism Organisation (WTO) internationally-recognized **'star' system**, which unfortunately does not tell the whole story, being based upon amenities and open to 'creative' interpretation by hotel operators, tourist organisations and managements. Tour operators have further confused the issue by doling out their own 'stars'. Furthermore, there is no recognition in the WTO's grading system for imaginative and sympathetic architecture, or lack thereof.

During the past seven years the government has worked at making the Maltese islands a more up-market tourist destination. To that end the only new building permits being issued are for 5-star hotels in Malta and Gozo, while existing hotels are being encouraged to upgrade.

In this guide official star ratings and government classifications are included but accommodation is organised by price.

Luxury:	5★ Lm40+
Expensive:	4★ Lm25–39
Moderate :	3★ Lm12–24
Inexpensive:	1–2★/Guest Houses Lm5–11

There are 127 registered hotels in Malta, 10 in Gozo, and 1 in Comino. At the time of writing only six are 5★; the majority have 3★ and 2★. It is generally safe to assume that a 5★ hotel will have hot and cold running everything and a 1★ will have clean respectable accommodation—there aren't any 'black holes' in Malta. Only the independent traveller or the businessman will have to pay rack rates as 'bed stock' is invariably sold to package-holiday companies at substantial discounts. If you are staying for longer than a week outside the peak season, a friendly haggle with the proprietor will often be rewarding. Tariffs are quoted per night in the high season and some include half board.

Holiday Complexes, Aparthotels, Guest Houses and Self-Catering

Self-catering of any description sold through recognised tour operators and holiday companies has to be licensed by the government and is divided into four classes, with Class I having the most amenities. There are 121 holiday complexes in total with facilities from studio rooms to 3- and 4-bedroom apartments. There is a wide selection in the brochures of the bigger tour operators and nearly all are along the northern coast in St Julian's, St Andrew's, Buġibba, Qawra and Mellieħa. A few properties are to be found inland in less conventional tourist locations. Facilities differ but most of the tatty operations are being cleaned up or denied licences.

Villas and Farmhouses

The yen for privacy and the individual tastes of a fickle market have added to the number and quality of properties available, especially on Gozo. Again, those on offer through tour operators for short holiday periods have to be licensed. **Farmhouses** are rural old stone houses that once housed families of goats, and tend to have character. **Villas** are likely to be more contemporary and made from yet-to-be-weathered local stone. Both usually have their own pools. You will find more villas in Malta; in Gozo there are more farmhouses. The leading operator in the UK is **Meon** (*see* Travel Agents pp. 6–7), which represents Gozo Farmhouses Ltd with over 20 farmhouses, modernized to an exceptional standard.

Hostels

Malta is an affiliated member of the Youth Hostels Association (YHA) and an up-to-date list can be obtained from the YHA equivalent in your country or from the **YHA**, 17 Tal-Borg Street, Paola, © 693957. There are five hostels in Malta and one on Gozo. The **NTOM** will furnish you with a further list of accommodation at affordable rates if the limited hostel space is taken up in the summer.

Camping

The islands don't have a recognized **campsite**, but a few hardy north European backpackers call Ramla Bay in Gozo home for the summer.

Timeshare

Malta escaped the great **timeshare** scam, as perpetrated in the Canary Islands. But, if you hang around Bay Square in unappealing Buġibba for a nano-second, relentless touts with improbable lines in chat will swoop down like vultures and bite into your credit cards if given half the chance. For legitimate (and honourable) timeshare in Malta contact the **Central Mediterranean Timeshare Association**, Ramla Bay Hotel, Ramla, © 573521.

Women Travellers

You will need both parts of your bikini. Nude and topless bathing in public or in private lidos is against the law. Laws do not exist to dictate what clothes you may go walking or shopping in, but anything less than shorts and shirt may mean you are politely asked to dress by the police.

Maltese men have been flattered all their lives by mothers, aunts and grand-mothers, so expect them to have an inflated idea of their own attributes. In keeping with most Latin races they tend to behave in a playful but harmless manner. If this offends you, one or two tough verbal rebukes should send them scurrying, otherwise invent a nearby husband. Pharmaceutical products for women and cosmetics are available in pharmacies and some supermarkets.

If you are travelling with **children** most English and Italian brand-named baby foods are available. A babysitter will cost Lm1.50–Lm2 per hour; enquire at your hotel.

Yachting Information

Position: the European Datum for the Grand Harbour Breakwater: 35° 54'.18 N – 14° 31'.5 E; for Marsamxett Harbour: 35° 54'.35 N – 14° 30'.6 E.

For thousands of years mariners have sought refuge in Malta's greatest asset, her natural deep-water harbours; the Grand Harbour, for commercial shipping (except for Kalkara Creek), lies to the southeast of the Valletta peninsula, and the Marsamxett Harbour, for pleasure yachts, lies to the northwest of it.

Marsamxett Harbour comprises three creeks; Lazzaretto, Msida and Sliema. The former two have been adapted into modern marinas. The present capacity in **Msida Creek** is for 700 yachts up to 18 m in length on 15 serviced pontoons. The smaller stern-to quays of **Ta'Xbiex** and **Lazzaretto** are reserved for yachts longer than 18 m. In addition there are 114 berths in the newly created **Mġarr Marina** in Gozo for boats up to 16m in length. All the services come under the **Malta Maritime Authority** whose administrative office is: Msida Marina, Msida, ✆ 235711/235713. The Harbour Master is John Farrugia who invariably can be found at the Yacht Centre on neighbouring Manoel Island.

Arrival and Departure Procedures

Before arriving fly the 'Yellow Duster' ('Q'flag) and a courtesy flag. The visitors' berths are in Lazzaretto Creek and if they are occupied drop anchor in the creek and take all the ship's papers, crew list and passports to Customs and Immigration. Then contact the Harbour Master on VHF channel 9 or go to the Yacht Centre office on Manoel Island. Anchoring within the confines of the creek is only permitted until a berth has been allocated. If in any doubt contact Valletta Port Control or Malta Radio, which monitor VHF channels 9, 12 and 16.

Customs and Immigration

The offices are on Manoel Island and are open 0730–1630 in summer and 0745–1715 in winter. The ship's Master will need to report there immediately after berthing and 24 hours before departure with all ship's and crew papers. If you are accompanied by a **pet**, drop anchor in Lazzaretto Creek and do *not* bring it ashore. The authorities are very helpful here and usually visit and clear arriving vessels expeditiously.

Berthing Fees

A 14–18-m vessel on a serviced pontoon (inc. water and electricity) in summer is Lm46 per week. The comparable rate for an 18-m vessel in Lazzaretto Creek is Lm2.55 per metre per week, with water and electricity extra. If you wish to stay for a longer period it is advisable to write and request a berth for the specific period that you wish to stay.

Yacht Centre Facilities

There are two centres, one in Msida and the other just over the bridge on Manoel Island. International telephones, showers and public conveniences, and a *poste restante* for ships' mail, are all available.

Weather Forecasts

Broadcast daily by Valletta Port Control (Valletta Radio) on VHF channel 12. On MW, the frequencies are 2182 kHz and 2625 kHz. Forecasts are four times a day at 0803, 1203, 1803 and 2303 in summer and in winter one hour earlier; or © 220310 for the Weather Ansaphone. The forecasts are valid for 50 nautical miles around Malta and are usually reliable. The Department of Civil Aviation publish an excellent land and sea forecast daily on page 5 of *The Times*.

Winds

The prevailing wind is the northwesterly *majjistral* (mistral). The southerly and torpid *xlokk* (sirocco) blows mostly in late September and sometimes in late spring. The *tramuntana* from the north hardly blows at all. The most feared is the northeasterly winter wind, the *gregale*. It blows down through the Adriatic from the cold mountains above; a blow usually lasts at least three days and brings with it terrible seas and high winds. Avoid.

Bunkering, Gas and Duty-Free

Duty-free stores will be sealed on board a foreign-registered vessel until departure; a charge is made for the attendance and services of the Customs officer. For bunkering fuels contact Falzon Service Station © 442763 or a broker/agent. Gas bottles can be refilled (approx. Lm4 for 10 kg bottle) at any of the principal chandleries (*see below*).

A Few Regulations

- The maximum speed in any creek and both harbours is 5 knots.
- No vessel is to be moved from one position to another without prior permission.
- Oil or garbage is not to be disposed of in harbour.
- Fees are to be paid 24 hours before intended departure.
- A vessel can anchor for the night in any of the many bays and inlets anywhere in the archipelago.
- Filfla island is out of bounds.

The Royal Malta Yacht Club

The club is situated at Couvre Port, Manoel Island, © 333109/331131. The Secretary will have information on its racing calendar and the Comino Regatta in June. Members of recognized yacht clubs around the world can avail themselves of the club's facilities; check with the Secretary.

Repairs, Chandleries and Brokers

Manoel Island Yacht Yard in Manoel Island is the largest and most reputable in the central Mediterranean, © 334453/4. Its UK office is at Malta Drydocks, 6 Charterhouse Buildings, Goswell Street, London EC1M 7AN © (071) 253 5433. Kalkara Boatyard Co., Kalkara Wharf, Kalkara © 781306 has a 55-ton haul-out crane on its wharf in the eponymous creek in the Grand Harbour. Bezzina Ship Yard, 1–3 Church Wharf, Marsa, © 244613/234411, can accommodate yachts up to 65 m in its docking facilities, also in the Grand Harbour.

The Chandleries

RLR, **Gauci Borda**, **Nautica**, **International Marine** and **Medcomms** are all to be found in Ta'Xbiex and Msida and have just about every gizmo you don't need.

Principal Agents and Brokers

Eddie Woods, **Trader Marine**, Msida Seafront, © 346470/313019; Roland Darmanin, **S & D Yachts**, 8 Marina Court, Guiseppe Cali Street, Ta'Xbiex, © 339908; or Christian Ripard, **RLR**, 156 Ta'Xbiex Seafront, © 331563/335591.

History

The Death of Dragut Rais from the painting by Guiseppe Cali

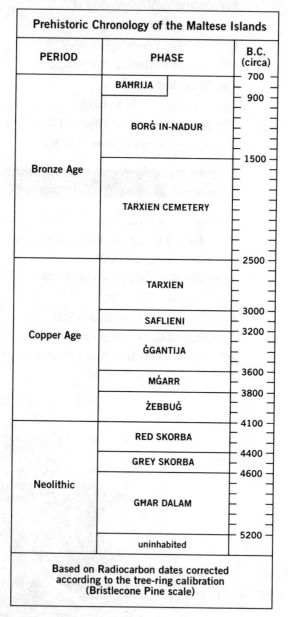

Prehistoric Chronology of the Maltese Islands		
PERIOD	**PHASE**	**B.C. (circa)**
Bronze Age	BAĦRIJA	— 700 —
		— 900 —
	BORĠ IN-NADUR	
		— 1500 —
	TARXIEN CEMETERY	
		— 2500 —
Copper Age	TARXIEN	
		— 3000 —
	SAFLIENI	— 3200 —
	ĠGANTIJA	
		— 3600 —
	MĠARR	— 3800 —
	ŻEBBUĠ	
Neolithic	RED SKORBA	— 4100 —
	GREY SKORBA	— 4400 —
		— 4600 —
	GĦAR DALAM	
	uninhabited	— 5200 —

Based on Radiocarbon dates corrected according to the tree-ring calibration (Bristlecone Pine scale)

Prehistory: *c.* 5,000–*c.* 800 BC

Malta is rich with prehistoric remains. The first period of its prehistory began when the islands became separated from Sicily and the continental European landmass, at the very beginning of the current Holocene era, 10,000–12,000 years ago. The first human inhabitation of the archipelago probably occurred some 7,000 years ago in the **Neolithic** period; there are early pottery relics from the **Skorba** phases in the Museum of Archaeology, Valletta.

The most active settlements established themselves during the long **Temple** phase of the **Copper Age**, which lasted from *c.* 4,100 BC to *c.* 2,500 BC. Man then would have been no more than a simple subsistence farmer who garnered his vital materials, such as obsidian, from neighbouring Sicily. Yet this civilisation constructed the great structures like Ġgantija on Gozo. The last phase in the Copper Age, the **Tarxien Phase** when the structures at Tarxien were built, was the most elaborate. (As the Tarxien Phase was ending *c.* 2,600 BC the Great Pyramid was constructed—up to 1,000 years *after* Ġgantija.) The Temple phase, with its idolatrous **'Fat' divinities** (possibly symbolizing fertility), came to an abrupt and possibly fiery end soon after. Theories for the sudden disappearance of this clever and religious culture range from invasion to mass suicide. There is no evidence of the subsequent, far less artistic and skilled inhabitants having had any connection with the peoples of the Temple phase—they appeared as if from another civilisation.

The third and last period in Malta's prehistory is the **Bronze Age**. (Bronze, a man-made alloy fused out of molten lead, copper and tin, came to Malta from the eastern Mediterranean.) Its discovery revolutionized weaponry, habitation and agriculture here as elsewhere. Little is known of the civilization that occupied the islands over this 1,700-year period until *c.* 800 BC; similar pieces of

'The Sleeping Lady' from the Hypogeum

pottery, weapons and jewellery have been found as far afield as Greece and southern Italy. The **Tarxien Cemetery** phase (during which Stonehenge was built in Britain) marked the introduction of cremation. During the later **Borġ in-Nadur** and **Baħrija** phases man began to display his more hostile intentions, building fortified hilltop settlements and beginning to move about the island. (The cart ruts which line parts of the island date from the Baħrija phase.) By 800–700 BC a primitive society capable of self-sufficiency seems to have evolved, but also appeared ready to embrace new ideas brought by the larger exploring cultures of the Near East.

Phoenician and Carthaginian periods: *c.* 800–218 BC

The **Phoenicians** were bold yet peaceful traders from the Near and Middle East, what is roughly Lebanon today. From *c.* 1200 BC they began plying their routes through the Mediterranean, exporting Tyrian purple cloth, timber and jewellery while in pursuit of treasures like tin from the rich seams of Cornwall. By 800 BC they had established trading outposts in Birgu (Vittoriosa) and the Grand Harbour. It was at this time that Malta was first christened: *maleth*, which is Phoenician for 'a place of shelter, or haven', and it's from the Phoenician language that Malti has evolved.

With the ascendancy of **Carthage** in North Africa during the 6th century BC, the Phoenician hold waned. Malta became a vital naval base for the Carthaginians just as Sicily had been for their enemy, the Greeks, 200–300 years earlier. The Romans first sacked Malta in 257 BC during the First Punic War. Thereafter, the Carthaginians reoccupied the islands until the Second Punic War in 218 BC when the Roman consul Tiberius Sempronious finally ended their colonization.

The Roman Period: 218 BC–AD 318

The Romans left more of a mark than the previous incumbents; they brought prosperity, albeit under a Roman yoke, during their 536-year occupation but left scant archaeological remains. Malta settled into a European base, one it has never really left, and the island became famous for its honey, cloth and sailcloth. Despite the wholesale pillaging by the **Roman Praetor Verres** (73–71 BC) the island enjoyed peace as a Roman adjunct to Sicily; both Julius Caesar and Augustus invoked laws aimed at helping their colonies, and during Hadrian's reign (AD 117–38) Malta and Gozo were made *municipia*.

The single-most important occurrence during Rome's occupation was **St Paul's** arrival, however unplanned, in AD 60. He and St Luke sowed the seeds of **Christianity**, and converted **Roman Governor Publius** who subsequently became the first bishop of Malta.

The Byzantine and Arab Periods: AD 318–1090

The dark ages are particularly murky in Malta's case. Very little is known of those who occupied the islands or how they were governed. After the division of the Roman Empire into Eastern and Western Empires in AD 395, Malta fell under Constantinople (Byzantium) in the east. There is no written or physical evidence to support the theory that the north European Vandals or the Goths settled the islands.

The **Arab** *caliphs* deposed the Byzantines in AD 870, 168 years after the death of the Prophet Mohammed. Initially it was a peaceful period, with Christians and Moslems living amicably together. The Maltese adopted aspects of Arab culture (many converted to Islam), including their language and agricultural skills, and together they carried on the earnest trade of slaving. Yet, Arabic heritage is scant on the islands: essentially they reduced the walls of Mdina, and fortified Birgu (Vittoriosa).

The Medieval Period: 1090–1530

Norman 1090–1194, Swabian (Germans) 1194–1266, Angevin (French) 1266–1283, Aragonese and Castilian (Spanish) 1283–1530.

Medieval, in historical terms, usually refers to the 1,000-year period from the abdication of Romulus Augustulus in AD 476 to the fall of Constantinople and the Turkish Empire in 1453. Malta's medieval period is far shorter but extends to the arrival of the Order of St John in 1530.

Count Roger the Norman took the islands from the Arabs in 1090, annexing them to his recent conquest of Sicily, just 24 years after his fellow countryman, William, conquered England. (Folklore tells how Roger, needing the help of the Maltese citizens, tore his quartered red-and-white banner in half, thus creating the Maltese flag of today.) He immediately introduced a tri-partite feudal system of State, Church and Nobility, all subject to the whim of the ruling fief. Thus, providing the taxes were paid, Malta now enjoyed a hitherto unknown degree of independence; and in spite of their Christian overlord the people remained basically Moslem. The country only began to adopt European mores after a genealogical dispute between the Normans and Swabians made the **Swabian** Frederick II (head of the House of Hohenstaufen) King Frederick I of Sicily in 1197 as well as Holy Roman Emperor.

As the new Holy Roman Emperor, Frederick paid little attention to Malta, using it at one time as a penal colony—in 1223 he shipped the entire population of the Italian town of Celano to Malta after its feudal lord committed high treason. Towards the end of his 53-year reign (1197–1250) he indulged in his own brand of 'ethnic cleansing' by expelling Moslems from the islands for ever.

Mercifully, the **Angevin** rule of Malta lasted a mere 17 years. In 1266 Manfred, the last of the Swabian kings was killed in battle by Charles of Anjou, brother of Louis IX and King of France. Thus the Kingdom of Sicily, and therefore Malta, passed to the **French**. This was unfortunate, for as a ruler Charles was half tyrannical despot, half simply mad. He was defeated at sea off Malta by Peter of Aragon's fleet the year after the calamitous uprising of 1282, known as the **Sicilian Vespers**; Peter of Aragon was then crowned King of Sicily by a grateful people.

Under the **Aragonese**, Malta remained a fief and not a part of the crown's land; it became no more than an outsize gaming chip, passed around, mortgaged and bartered among Spanish nobles. The patent disregard the Aragonese had for the overtaxed and exploited islands and its people led to an increase in the already frequent corsair slaving raids. However the first Maltese noble was created under the Aragonese in 1350, and towards the end of the 14th century both Malta and Gozo established a local governing body, the *Università*, the head of which, the *Hakem* or Captain of the Rod, was appointed by the Sicilian monarch. How effective it was at dealing with anything other than local matters is debatable; feudal overlords were rarely interested in the plight of serfs.

In 1412 the Aragonese line became extinct, and the islands passed to the **Castilian** Spanish, but very little changed—the island was still mostly pawn or prey. On one occasion in 1419, and at the request of the *Università*, Alphonso V raised a wine tax to pay for a fort on Comino in an attempt to stem the corsair raids. But having collected the money he absconded with it, and the very next year hocked the islands to the Sicilian Don Antonio Cardona for 30,000 gold florins. Eight years later in 1428, **Alphonso V** visited Malta and accepted that the islands would forever remain in the royal domain. In 1436, 10 new parishes were formed, but until and after the arrival of the Order of St John in 1530, the islands continued to be plagued by famine, North African corsairs, Turks and pestilence.

The Sovereign Military and Hospitaller Order of St John of Jerusalem of Rhodes and Malta.

The Constitution

The **Convent** or official seat (be it in Acre, Rhodes or Malta), held the corpus of the Order. Three principal ranks existed within the Order to mirror its three principal vocations: the military, the religious and the medical—the **Knights of Justice**, the **conventual chaplains** and the **servants-at-arms**. At the head presided the **grand master**, freely elected for life by his fellow knights within three days of his predecessor's death.

A **Knight of Justice** not only had to be of noble Catholic birth but also had to deliver 'proofs' of his maternal and paternal purity, with from 4 to 16 quarterings. (The Italians were the least strict, with four quarterings lest the 'proofs' revealed too much illegitimacy; while the Teutonic temperament of the Germans forbade admittance even to papal and royal bastards, who were allowed in the other *langues*.) Having been accepted as a novice, a young knight would reside in the *auberge* or hall of residence of his *langue*, and serve a total of five years at the Convent. During these years he had to serve in at least six *caravans* (tours of duty), two a year, in the galleys. Upon the completion of his novitiate the young nobleman attended his investiture at the feet of the grand master. Only after the solemn mass at which he swore oaths of Obedience, Poverty and Chastity, did he receive his eight-pointed cross on a black mantle (symbolising the camel's skin worn by the Order's patron saint, John the Baptist) and become a Knight of Justice. Further down the hierarchy, the **conventual chaplains** who served in the galleys, hospitals and churches had only to prove they were of legitimate and gentle birth and unconnected with 'any vile mechanic business'. **Servants-at-arms** simply had to show legitimate birth and were allowed to serve in a military or secretarial capacity. Furthermore, the grand master held within his gift honorary ranks such as **Knight of Grace**.

Apart from the conventual church, hospital and other public buildings of this sovereign state, the Convent accommodated what was initially the eight *langues* of knights: of Provence, Auvergne, France, Italy, Aragon, Castile et Leon (which was once a part of Aragon), Germany and England. Each had its own *auberge*. (After Henry VIII's reformation in 1540 the English *langue* disbanded.) At the head of each *langue* was the ***pilier***, who also held a high-ranking post within the Order. For example, the pilier of the Italian *langue* was also the admiral of the fleet and the pilier of Provence was the Order's treasurer. Each *langue* owned properties in its territory and the revenues paid to the Order were called *responsions*. A knight was bound by statute to leave four-fifths of his entire wealth to the Order, but was free to dispose of his *quint* or one-fifth. Thus the Order grew wealthy from the coffers of European aristocracy.

A newly-created knight was at liberty to return to his own country or to remain in the Convent and become eligible to vie for promotion and a position in any of the Order's more than 500 *commanderies*. The larger of these were called **priories** and the smaller **bailiwicks** and ***commanderies***. The heads of the *commanderies* held corresponding ranks of priors, bailiffs and commanders. If, on the other hand, a knight chose to return to his own estates he must, if summoned by the grand master in times of threat, make immediate haste to the aid of the Convent.

The **grand master** enjoyed the status and prerogatives of a ruling sovereign. He presided over four separate governing councils responsible for all financial, judicial, religious and military matters. The supreme governing and legislative authority lay in the **Chapter-General**. Headed by the grand master, it comprised the *piliers* of each *langue*, the bishop, and other senior distinguished knights, or Knights Grand Cross and could only be convened by either the Pope or the grand master.

The Order still exists today under Grand Master Andrew Bertie, a Scot, and it maintains its seat in Rome as well as an embassy in Valletta. It concentrates on charitable and hospitalling works around the world.

History of the Order Before 1530

The Order of St John of Jerusalem, the oldest chivalric Order, was established in 1048 by a group of pious Italian merchants from Amalfi. Its sole purpose was to provide a nursing hospital for the increasing number of pilgrims visiting the Holy Sepulchre in Jerusalem, then a part of the Caliphate of Egypt. It was not until 1099, after the successful **First Crusade** had wrested Jerusalem back, that the nursing brothers began to assume a military role. In 1104 King Baldwin I of Jerusalem offered them land, and in 1113 Pope Paschal II formally recognised the constitution of the Knights Hospitallers in a bull and conferred upon them papal protection. (The original Bull is in the Bibliotheca in Valletta.)

Under their first leader, the Frenchman Raymond du Puy (1125–58), the transformation from hospitaller to warrior was made, and the knights went into battle wearing their distinctive tunics of a white cross emblazoned against a scarlet background—'the white cross of peace in the bloodstained field of war'. In the 12th and 13th centuries they fought alongside the various kings of Jerusalem during the **Second and Third Crusades**. In the course of the bloody Third Crusade of 1191, Richard Coeur de Lion took Acre, 130 km from Jerusalem on the shores of the east Mediterranean, and the Order established itself there for nearly a hundred years. But the rear-guard action the Christians waged against the forces of Islam was ultimately doomed: the knights were defeated at Acre in 1291 in the last battle of the Crusades and sought refuge in Cyprus, a sojourn that lasted until they captured Rhodes in 1310.

For nearly 200 years the Order of St John fortified **Rhodes** and harried the Turks with needling consistency. The pot-pourri of inter-married European royalty nurtured its growth (after the suppression of the Knights Templars the mercenary aristocrats of St John were the only effective force preventing Islam from infiltrating westwards). Consequently its wealth and status grew, it developed a navy and strengthened its internal organization. After the fall of Byzantine Constantinople to the Turkish Sultan, Mahomet II in 1453, the **Turks** turned their attention to Rhodes. Their first attempt at invasion in 1480 was repulsed, but the second in 1522 succeeded following a fierce six-month siege. Grand Master L'Isle Adam extracted terms for an honourable surrender from the young Turkish Sultan, Suleyman I (son of Selim the Grim), also known as Suleyman the Magnificent. On 1 January 1523 the grand master, 180 knights and upwards of 4,000 Rhodians set sail like refugees for an unknown destination.

For nearly eight years **Grand Master L'Isle Adam** knocked on the doors of Europe's rulers. Henry VIII promised the Order 20,000 crowns and Pope Clement VIII gave it temporary refuge in Viterbo. Eventually the shrewd and self-motivated Charles V, Emperor of Spain, offered them permanent sanctuary in **Malta**, providing they also assumed the burdensome defence of Tripoli. The Order sent a delegation to recce the island, and received a dismal report: infertile, barren, lacking in water, marauded by corsairs, difficult to defend and populated by 12,000 impoverished people. But, with no alternative in sight, L'Isle Adam accepted the territories as the Order's perpetual sovereign domain. The annual rent was none too steep: a peregrine falcon to be presented annually on All Saints' Day to Charles V's Sicilian viceroy. The **Act of Donation** was signed in April 1530 (it too is in the Bibliotheca's archives in Valletta), and the Order dropped anchor in the Grand Harbour in October of that year.

The Order's Reign in Malta: 1530–1798

Alphonso V's promise in 1428 to maintain Malta as part of the Spanish Empire in perpetuity was broken by his descendant Charles V. In the same way, the Order quickly forswore L'Isle Adam's promise to the Maltese to uphold their interests and nobility. For the Order, Malta was initially somewhere to regroup before attempting to retake the verdant island of Rhodes. But a series of Christian defeats shattered all the knights' illusions and they proceeded to make Malta as safe and congenial a home as possible.

In the ensuing 25 years, while the Maltese aristocracy sulked in Mdina and the knights fortified Birgu, the **Turks** had virtually free run of the central Mediterranean. **Dragut Rais**, Suleyman's *de facto* mercenary, kept up his marauding ways and in one attack in 1551 depopulated Gozo, hauling 5,000 into slavery. Later that same year, the Order ignominiously lost its unwanted base at Tripoli to Dragut Rais and Sinan Pasha. Morale was at a very low ebb by the time **de la Valette** assumed the magistracy in 1557. Two years later in a catastrophic attempt to capture Dragut's base, the island of Djerba off the North African coast, the Order and its Christian allies lost over half their fleet; the forces of Islam effectively had won the battle for the central Mediterranean. All that stood in their way was a puny garrison on the obscure sandstone rock of Malta.

The Great Siege of 1565

> *"If the Turks should prevail against the Isle of Malta it is uncertain what further peril might follow to the rest of Christendom."*

> Queen Elizabeth I, 1565

In the theatre of Christian-Moslem attrition that gripped the Mediterranean during the 16th century, Malta, with its vanguard of chivalrous knights, was centre stage. **Grand Master de la Valette** was a perspicacious man: sooner or later, he surmised, the now septuagenarian **Suleyman the Magnificent** would wish to extinguish the Order before he died (something Suleyman regretted not doing 43 years earlier at Rhodes).

On the morning of 18 May 1565 the finest Moslem forces, marshalled from every corner of Suleyman's empire, hove into view over the horizon. A formidable armada of 181 ships under the command of Admiral Piali contained a mighty army (in excess of 35,000 warriors) under the command of Mustapha Pasha. De la Valette had been able to muster 541 knights and servants-at-arms, a brave but untrained Maltese militia of about 4,500 and a regiment of 1,200 Spanish and Italian foot soldiers; with the other conscripts and slaves his forces totalled 8,500–9,000 men in all. His request to the Sicilian viceroy, Don Garcia de Toledo, for 15,000 reinforcements went initially unheeded. De la Valette had time enough to poison the island's few water wells and harvest the crops before he and his Maltese subjects shut the gates of Birgu, L'Isla and Mdina on that late spring morning and settled down to wait.

From the very first day of the campaign, the Turks were hampered by the fiercest of military enemies: bad luck, petty jealousies and a split command. Suleyman had foolishly divided the command between **Admiral Piali** and **Mustapha Pasha**. Fortunately for the knights, Suleyman's military mentor and long-time scourge of Malta, **Dragut Rais**, was delayed in North Africa. With a long summer ahead Admiral Piali argued against Mustapha Pasha's wise strategy of attacking Mdina and Birgu overland from the south. Piali demanded the safe haven of Marsamxetto for his prized fleet, an obsession which bedevilled the entire campaign, and which meant storming **Fort St Elmo** first.

When the octogenarian Dragut Rais finally arrived on 2 June with his own band of 1,500 mercenaries, he found a disastrous plan hindered in its execution by a quarrelling and split command. Quickly he galvanized the Turkish troops and, knowing it was too late to withdraw from the attack on St Elmo, established further gun enplacements. The siege of Fort St Elmo carried on relentlessly until, after 31 days of continuous bombardment, it fell on 23 June, the eve of the feast of John the Baptist, the Order's patron saint. Vignettes of the brutality of the siege emerged: the fanatical, hashish-fueled *Iayalar* warriors were slaughtered in such numbers in their repeated assaults on the fort that their corpses became bridges of putrefying flesh; Mustapha Pasha beheaded four knights and placed their torsos on crosses to float across the Grand Harbour; in retaliation de la Valette fired the heads of Turk prisoners from his cannons. Most disastrous of all (for the Turks) was Dragut Rais's accidental death from a rock splinter, which marked the turning-point of the siege, in which no quarter was asked, nor ever given.

The Turks continued to pound away at **Forts St Angelo and St Michael** during the sweltering summer months; the capture of St Elmo at the cost of 8,000 men had just been a Phyrric victory. Finally, on 7 September, the meagre and long overdue relief force of 8,000 men arrived from the dilatory viceroy of Sicily, Don Garcia de Toledo. The rout of the Turks was completed the following day in a final bloody pitched battle in the shallows of St Paul's Bay. The Turks had lost 30,000 men and of the original 9,000-strong Christian garrison just 600 were standing and able to bear arms. But the toll went far beyond the horror of the mere death count. For the Turkish Empire it marked the beginning of the end; the loss of prestige was immense and its subsequent defeat by the Holy Alliance forces at the Battle of Lepanto in 1571, where 197 of its ships were destroyed, was one from which they were never to recover. Suleyman the Magnificent died in battle the following year while besieging an Hungarian city, both Mustapha Pasha and Piali returned to Levant and were spared, and Don Garcia faded ignominiously from history. De la Valette died peacefully three years later in his chapel in Fort St Angelo, feted as a hero by all Europe.

After the Great Siege: 1565–1798

> "The knights neglected to live, but were prepared to die, in the service of Christ."
>
> Edward Gibbon (1737–94)

The Order had locked the forces of Islam in their eastern Mediterranean basin, and in the euphoric aftermath of the Great Siege contemporary Maltese history begins. In a fit of grateful munificence the Pope and the crowned heads of Europe, including a protestant Queen Elizabeth I, showered the already wealthy Order with financial rewards. Within six years the knights' new fortified city, **Valletta**, was built.

Prosperity came to Malta during the Order's subsequent 233-year reign: new agricultural skills were learnt and new industries created; the population increased fivefold to 100,000; it became a trading post and Europe's largest slave market; and the rich knights spent famously on towns, palaces and defences. Perversely, the Order's victory over its Islamic enemy—its *raison d'être* for so long—combined with subsequent affluence, brought about a cancer which led to its downfall.

A Succession of Grand Masters

Grand Master de la Valette died in 1568, leaving **Grand Master del Monte** (1568–72) to inaugurate the new city in 1571. His successor, the very pious and aged **Grand Master de la Cassiere** (1572–81), was perhaps the first to identify the hazards that lay ahead for a religious Order without a real enemy. Offended by the spread of Protestantism, he tried to reaffirm the monastic traditions and counter the exuberant and unmonastic behaviour of the young knights who had replenished the Order's ranks. In desperation he turned to the Pope, who saddled the Order with an **inquisitor** in an attempt to stamp out those who chose not to obey their vows of Obedience, Poverty and Chastity. De la Cassiere still found time to build and pay for **St John's Co-Cathedral** and the **Sacra Infermeria**. After his death in Rome he was succeeded by one of the more colourful grand masters, the French **de Verdalle** (1581–95), who was the first to take his sovereign position to heart and to enjoy its trappings. Resolutely hedonistic, he interpreted the enlightenment of his people to mean extra candles at his lavish banquets. He reigned supremely yet shrewdly and was able to marry his lavish tastes with the more tempered ones of his church: he built for himself the **Verdala Castle**, commissioned his own galley for privateering and still ingratiated himself with Pope Sixtus V who appointed him a cardinal (the only one in the Order's history). But his 14-year reign was unsettled: he curtailed the powers of the *Università*, endured factional disputes between the different *langues*, reacted to a new Turkish threat by building the two Cavaliers of St John and St James in Valletta, and stood by while 15 percent of the population was wiped out by bubonic plague. **Grand Master Garzes** (1595–1601) was the opposite—a humble peace-loving man who cared for the poor. His suit of armour is on display in the Palace Armoury.

By the time that **Alof de Wignacourt** (1601–22) assumed the magistracy, Valletta's population was the same as it is today, and the much-needed aqueduct from Rabat to Valletta was one of the many projects he undertook. The 21-year reign of this tall handsome man was marked by humility and compassion. He founded the *Monte di Rendenzione degli Schiavi* to ransom Christian slaves and built the island's most impressive forts, St Lucian, St Thomas and St Mary's, to guard against the still–prevalent corsair raids. His magnificent suit of armour is displayed in the Palace Armoury and his portrait hangs in the Grand Master's Palace (a Caravaggio portrait of him is in the Louvre). **Grand Master Vasconcellos** (1622–3) was all but dead when he succeeded de Wignacourt; well into his eighties, he only lasted a matter of months. Another Frenchman with opulent, almost corrupt tastes, was **de Paule** (1623–36) who built the **San Anton Palace** as a summer retreat for hosting none-too-religious gatherings. Fearing a Turkish invasion he commenced the building of the Floriana Lines and, despite his high living, he too reigned until ripe: he died aged 84.

In spite of the constant threat of a major Turkish invasion the 17th century was essentially one of peace for Malta. In 1614 the last Turkish raid took place, and

from then on only the piratical incursions of the Barbary corsairs had to be toler-
ated. But it was not so for Europe: France and Spain were at war, creating
problems for the neutral Order and the *langues* of those countries, while Venice
was locked in a fierce struggle with the Turks. Pug-faced **Grand Master
Lascaris** (1636–57) brought a strong measure of puritanism to an idle Order
and began the building of defences known as the Margherita Lines. He too
hung onto power, eventually relinquishing it at the age of 97. The deterrent
effect of the Valletta fortifications helped maintain the peace and as the century
progressed subsequent grand masters strategically reinforced the coastline,
thereby encouraging the Maltese to settle the countryside. Lascaris's Spanish
successor, **De Redin** (1657–60) built a series of towers, many of which still
stand. **Grand Master Gessan** reigned for a matter of weeks in 1660. The
Spanish **Cotoner brothers**, Raphael (1660–63) and Nicolas (1663–80)
commenced, and were nearly bankrupted by, the construction of vast defences
known as the Cottonera Lines; they also improved the Sacra Infermeria after a
plague which left 12,000 dead. More famously, the brothers commissioned the
splendid baroque vault frescoes by **Mattia Preti** in St John's Co-Cathedral.
Cotoner's Neopolitan successor **Grand Master Caraffa** (1680–90), was a
spritely 66 when elected and was part of the European Alliance which defeated
the Turks and forced the abdication of Sultan Mohammed IV. In 1693, during
the reign of Alof **de Wignacourt's** nephew, Adrien (1690–97), a cataclysmic
earthquake destroyed much of Ionian Sicily, Malta and Gozo. The Aragonese
Grand Master Perellos (1697–1720) rebuilt the Cathedral in Mdina, one of
the finest examples of the local baroque idiom. Apart from displaying an artistic
flair (he acquired the exquisite Gobelin tapestries in the Grand Master's Palace
and those in St John's Co-Cathedral), this cultured and good-looking man
modernized the Order's navy. His reign ushered in, what proved to be for the
Order, a fateful 18th century.

The Decline of the Order

By the time of Perellos's death in 1720, the Order had shifted imperceptibly
into final decline. Womanizing, drinking, duelling and an unparalled ostentation had fully supplanted the ideals founded in the Holy Lands; its
consciousness of militant catholicism had expired and its very fabric had
become a sham. The knights were now an embarrassing anachronism to all
save their equally morally bankrupt protectors, the Popes in Rome. They had
become an exotic central Mediterranean police force. Their navy helped to
good effect in the Venetian-Turkish war of 1715–18, but mostly it just roamed
the sea in search of a diminishing stock of corsairs.

Pope Alexander VII was once an inquisitor in Malta. His nephew, **Grand Master Zondadari** (1720–2), succeeded Perellos and attempted to develop the islands into an *entrepôt* for trade. His two-year reign was followed by 14 years under the aristocratic Portuguese **de Vilhena**. This wealthy and popular aesthete zealously built many magnificent buildings such as Fort Manoel, the Manoel Theatre, and the Palazzo Vilhena. When de Vilhena died in 1736, King Philip V of Spain's son, the Bourbon Charles VIII, united Naples and Sicily and crowned himself the autonomous king of the newly created Kingdom of the Two Sicilies; so Spain no longer had direct administration over what was in effect Malta's breadbasket, Sicily. Following the uneventful reign of the Majorcan **Ramon Despuig** (1736–41) was the long 32-year reign of another Iberian, the Portuguese **Grand Master Pinto** (1741–73). The pompous but crafty Pinto assumed more regal airs and traits than the kings of England and France combined, and it was during his tenure at the Grand Master's Palace that the Order's death-knell sounded and went unheard. His self-aggrandizement knew no bounds: for evidence look at either the evocative portrait by de Favray in the sacristy at St John's Co-Cathedral or the strikingly ebullient façade he commissioned for his Auberge de Castile et Leon. Pinto was not a man to be content with mere titles, so he tried to acquire Corsica from the Genoese in 1763; this shrewd ruse was designed to reduce Malta's dependence on Sicily, and also to enhance his standing with those whom he considered his peers, the monarchs of Europe. Despite much haggling, a price could not be agreed upon and the French bought it in 1768, just one year before the Order's nemesis, **Napoleon Bonaparte**, was born there. Pinto's despised Spanish successor, **Grand Master Ximenes** (1773–5), struggled along for only two years; his legacy after a third of a century of Pinto's despotism was an empty treasury and an understandably resentful population. Following a commonplace disagreement between the Order and the Maltese clergy there was a feeble but nevertheless symbolic rebellion in 1775, known as '**the Priest's Revolt**'; Ximenes executed the ringleaders. Later that year, but too late to save the Order, the wise and cautious French aristocrat **de Rohan** (1775–97) was elected to the magistracy. He immediately convened a Chapter-General, the first since de Paule's reign 144 years earlier, and put in place a new municipal code, laws and statutes to alleviate tension; the ordinary Maltese had grown weary of their self-destructive and arrogant rulers. Financially and spiritually impoverished, the Order received its final blow in 1789 with the **French Revolution**. De Rohan, a staunch royalist, financed **Louis XVI's** unsuccessful flight to Varrenes from France in 1791, which resulted in the confiscation of all the Order's French *commanderies* the next year; the *langues* of Auvergne,

France and Provence contributed three-quarters of the Order's finances. The reforming and decent de Rohan died in 1797, convinced he would be the last grand master to reign in Malta.

Again, and unwittingly, Malta found itself at the centre of the Mediterranean stage. Turmoil and war lay in store for Europe and the empires of Austria, France, the Two Sicilies, Russia and Britain, and America all watched each other nervously throughout the last decade of the 18th century. For Malta the situation was unique—while on previous occasions the island itself had been prized, its value now was stategic and lay in keeping the island out of the hands of the enemy, whoever that was. In 1797 a compliant, even simple German—the first in the Order's history—**von Hompesch** (1797–98) was elected. Strapped for cash, this kindly man foolishly accepted Tsar Paul I's offer of 72 *commanderies* to found a Russian Orthodox *langue*. Napoleon was enraged at this move, and while en route to his Egyptian campaign, he anchored his incredible armada of 472 ships and 50,000 soldiers off the Grand Harbour; on 9 June 1798 he requested permission to water his ships. While an understandably intimidated von Hompesch vacillated, a fifth column of French knights brought months of subversive scheming into play. Two days later, and with few shots fired at or from the greatest fortifications in Europe, von Hompesch was 'persuaded' to capitulate ignominiously. Terms were agreed aboard Napoleon's flagship *L'Orient*: the Order would be given three days to pack its possessions and leave, but the French knights were free to stay. The aggrieved and now deserted Maltese meanwhile, were treated by the French to the same empty promises with regard to their own status as they had been many times before. Von Hompesch was given sanctuary in Russia, and as a force—nursing, religious or military—the Order was spent.

Ironically, the knights had fortified and defended themselves into provocation and near extinction; the better and more lavish the defences, the more coveted the island. It was a prize England would not allow France to keep for long.

The French: 1798–1800

'I would rather see the British on the heights of Montmartre than in Malta.'

Napoleon

Napoleon stayed six days, about half as long as the average tourist's sojourn. But during that time he and his governor, **General Vaubois**, descended like a plague of republicanizing super-locusts; they despoiled churches, defaced escutcheons, looted *palazzos*, created havoc and basically stole anything that wasn't nailed to the floor. The Maltese population looked on helplessly.

Napoleon left with 268 years-worth of accumulated treasures and all the silver *L'Orient* could hold (Nelson sunk it and its cache of plunder two months later in the Battle of the Nile). General Vaubois remained in charge of a timorously small garrison of 4,000 men. His first mistake, apart from promulgating unpopular new laws, was to upset the clergy. In the wake of an attempt to auction the treasures of the Carmelite church in Mdina, the oppressed Maltese spontaneously killed a French officer and began an uprising on 2 September 1798.

Vaubois and his garrison retreated into Valletta, and ironically the Maltese were the only ones ever to lay siege to de la Valette's fortress city. Assistance came from the Portuguese navy and the **British**, who were busily repairing their warships after Nelson's earlier victory at the Battle of the Nile; together their ships blockaded the harbours while the Anglo-Maltese forces attended to the landward front. Dispirited as he was by Napoleon's defeat in Egypt, it still took until 5 September 1800 for General Vaubois to be starved into surrender. In October, Captain Alexander Ball assumed temporary administrative responsibility for the islands on behalf of the British.

British Colonial Rule from 1800

"Well, when the great cauldron of war is seething, and the nations stand round it striving to fish out something to their purpose from the mess, Britannia always has a great advantage in her trident. Malta is one of the titbits she has impaled with that awful implement."

James Russell Lowell, 1854

The Treaty of Amiens of 1802 forged a fragile peace between France and England. It was agreed that the Maltese islands should be restored to the Order, a compromise both war-weary countries felt able to tolerate. But the astonished Maltese wanted none of it: a bankrupt and essentially leaderless Order could not offer the islands the stability they would have as a British colony. The recently knighted Sir Alexander Ball prevaricated (as the Order waited impatiently in Sicily), while trying to canvass support in London for Britain's *de facto* occupation of Malta.

For 12 years Malta was in limbo as a quasi-British protectorate. The island's future was not officially clarified until Napoleon's abdication and the subsequent Treaty of Paris in 1814 when they were formally added to George III's growing list of colonial possessions. Malta's first British governor was Sir Thomas Maitland, known as 'King Tom' on account of his imperious manner. One of his first acts was to abolish the *Università* and bring certain laws in line with British jurisprudence.

For Malta the 19th century was uneventful, the islands simply reflecting the fluctuating fortunes of Britain and her empire. Similarly, the economy was inextricably linked to the naval base and garrison. The **Crimean War** (1854–6) brought a degree of prosperity, as did the opening of the Suez Canal in 1869. Defence spending increased with the new dock in French Creek and the construction of the Victoria Lines. By the closing decades of the century Malta had become an important and flourishing coaling station for the imperial steamships plying between Britain and India. As the century progressed the islands were slowly 'anglicized' and English joined Italian as the spoken language (Malti was still a local dialect).

Internal affairs were also of a roller-coaster nature. Ultimate authority rested in London, via the governor, but the beginning of the 19th century saw a flame lit under an erstwhile dormant Maltese political consciousness. The first of many attempts at giving the Maltese a restricted degree of autonomy was in 1835; further efforts were made in 1849 and 1887. All of the implemented local constitutions were argued over between London, Malta and the governor and subsequently revoked.

At the turn of the 20th century the population approached 185,000. **World War I** saw the island return to its hospitaller roots when it became the 'nurse of the Mediterranean' and tended 25,000 sick and wounded from the Dardenelles. Economic and political tensions in an island ever vulnerable to the vicissitudes of war culminated in riots on 7 June 1919 when four Maltese were shot by British troops. A new diarchic constitution was introduced in 1921: with a local Maltese government for Maltese affairs and an imperial one for foreign and military decisions, and a system of proportional representation (which still prevails today). However, after hiccuping through many trying coalitions and local dissensions the constitution was again revoked by the British in 1930. It was restored two years later only to have its mandate finally withdrawn in 1933—certain strata of Maltese society were undecided whether their allegiance lay with a conservative Britain or with a burgeoning fascist Italy.

"To Honour her brave People I award the George Cross to the Island Fortress of Malta to bear witness to a Heroism and a Devotion that will long be famous in History."

King George VI, 15 April 1942

The second Great Siege of Malta was to be a more drawn out and severe test of human resolve than the Turkish attempt in 1565. Both sieges were waged on Malta because it had the misfortune to be a strategic cog in the grand design of the oppressors at the time. 400 years on, the strategy of siege warfare had not changed: bomb the enemy mercilessly, cut off supplies and hope to starve the besieged into surrender. Although both campaigns ultimately failed, the Axis powers came perilously close to victory in the summer of 1942.

On 10 June 1940 **Mussolini** and his Italian army joined **Hitler's** war effort. By dawn the following morning Italian bombers were over Malta and the first casualties were incurred: in 1940 there were 211 air-raid warnings, a modest foretaste of what lay in store.

Almost the sum total of their preparedness on 11 June was a few anti-aircraft guns, the antiquated guns of HMS *Terror* lying in Pieta Creek and four  Gloucester Gladiator bi-planes. Three of the planes nicknamed *Faith*, *Hope* and *Charity* flew, the fourth was cannibalized for spares. (*Faith*, the sole survivor, is on display in the War Museum in Valletta.) On that day the governor, Lieutenant General Sir William Dobbie, immediately implemented war restrictions on the population of 250,000 civilians and 30,000 military.

N5520 'FAITH' sole surviving Gladiator

The Allied command had been divided over the fortress island's fate in the event of war; the Army and RAF favoured mass evacuation, while the Royal Navy, with a 145 years experience of Malta's strategic importance, advocated staying put; the Royal Navy's vote was carried solely due to **Winston Churchill's** influence. Nonetheless, the procrastination meant that Malta was ill-equipped to deal with the realities of modern aerial and marine warfare.

In the new year of **1941**, the Italians were being routed in North Africa. In London the War Office had noted that Malta could be an effective base for offensive strikes against Axis shipping. But so too did the Axis high command: crack squadrons of the German *Luftwaffe* were stationed in Sicily and with the sinking of HMS *Illustrious,* en route to the Allies' Mediterranean naval base at Alexandria, the conflict intensified. Mussolini's dispirited army of 130,000 were taken prisoner in February, the month **Field Marshal Rommel** assumed command of the North African campaign. Throughout the spring and summer the Allies used Malta like an aircraft carrier to harry Rommel's supply lines, but after the fall of Crete at the end of May, the Malta–Alexandria supply line was almost cut off; the base for the convoys of supplies to the besieged island was then switched to Gibraltar.

Hitler's ultimately fatal invasion of Russia on 22 June, and the subsequent redeployment of the *Luftwaffe* gave Malta a respite from the thrice-daily air raids; the total for 1941 was 963. In the autumn and winter months of that year Malta reached the peak of its disruptive powers and more Axis shipping was destroyed than ever before.

Rommel, despite the supply deprivations, enjoyed considerable success in the early months of **1942**. Scenting a victory in the desert, the Axis command deployed more aircraft in Sicily; Malta had simply to be bombed and starved into submission. By the end of February 1942, *The Times* of Malta (the newspaper did not miss one day of publication throughout the siege) reported that there had been 80 days of almost continuous alert. In January and February alone there were 499 air raid alerts and during six weeks of March and April 6,700 tons of bombs fell; Malta endured 157 days of continuous bombing (London had 57 during the 'Blitz'). From January to June (and for a long time thereafter), rationing was way below life-sustaining levels; the staple provisions for a family of two adults and three children for *one month* was: four 300-g tins of corned beef, four 100-g tins of fish, 330 g of rice, 2.75 kg of sugar and a daily bread ration of 1,375 g; powdered milk, flour, fruit or eggs just did not exist.

It was during this maelstrom of bombs and splintering limestone, when ammunition, food, and kerosene were as scarce as typhoid, scurvy and amoebic dysentery were commonplace, that King George VI staged a morale-boosting coup; Malta and its population were awarded the **George Cross**, the highest British civilian award, on 15 April 1942.

In May, an ailing Governor (now) Lord Dobbie was replaced by Field Marshal Viscount Gort VC. One of Dobbie's last actions in office was to prepare an inventory of the remaining rations and set an August 'target date' when Malta would have to surrender unless a substantial convoy arrived. Ultimately, and ironically, it was the Allies' catastrophic loss of Tobruk to Rommel in June which saved Malta; the Axis high command blinked and scotched the planned invasion of Malta, 'Operation Herkules'. During this momentary lapse of concentration, the Allies were able to assemble the convoy which was to save the island, 'Operation Pedestal'. Of the 14 heavily guarded merchantmen, only five made it into the Grand Harbour. (It became known as the *Santa Marija* convoy after the venerated 15 August *festa* to the Assumption when the final ship, the US oiler *Ohio*, limped into port.) Its comparative success forced the Axis powers to accept that Malta could and would now survive. Two months later, Rommel's February 1941 statement to Berlin, 'Without Malta, the Axis will end by losing control of North Africa', came true. The Axis lost the battle of El Alamein and with it North Africa. The cost to Malta had been enormous: from 1941 to 1942 alone there were 2,994 air raid alerts (an average of over four a day), 30,000 buildings were destroyed, hundreds of thousands of tons of shipping were lost, as were many thousands of civilian and servicemen's lives.

There were better tidings in **1943**. The Allies took Tripoli in January, and the final surrender of the Axis forces in North Africa came in May. Air raids still continued, though infrequently, and rations were very marginally increased. King George VI visited Malta and the Allies prepared for the planned invasion of Sicily, 'Operation Husky'; once again the island became a strategic aircraft carrier for over 30 squadrons of aircraft. Following the success of 'Operation Husky', Mussolini's downfall and the surrender of the Italian navy, Malta's role in World War II slipped into the shade, as the Allies' cloud began to blanket a hitherto Axis Europe.

After World War II to Independence in 1964

The British Government donated £30 million to help compensate the Maltese for the extensive war damage. The inventiveness demanded by the war years had turned many simple farmers into semi-skilled manual workers. The combination of compensation and new skills provided a base for the post-war expansion. In September 1947 a new constitution, similar to the 1921 diarchal one, was introduced along with the vote for women. In the same year the flow of emigrants to North America and Australia began; today Maltese emigrants total one and a half times the island's entire population.

By the late 1950s the famous dockyards were economically unviable and had begun to outlive their usefulness to the British. In the 1962 elections the two principal parties (the Malta Labour Party and the Nationalist Party), both placed independence for Malta in their manifesto; when the population voted in favour, the Colonial Secretary in London had no alternative but to take heed. Malta was granted independence on 21 September 1964 but signed a 10-year Mutual Defence Agreement and remained a part of the British Commonwealth.

From 1964 to the Present

From 1972 NATO and the British maintained a military presence which finally ended in 1979. Malta became a **democratic republic** in 1974 and today the islands are neutral and non-aligned.

Malta joined the United Nations in 1964 and the Council of Europe in 1965. But with the demise of British colonial rule came a real need to establish an economy that could survive on its own (the only British financial involvement was the 'rent' paid for military installations and the money its servicemen spent locally). **Tourism** became an obvious target for development.

Politically the internal situation has been and is split almost equally between the ruling **Nationalist Party** and the **Malta Labour Party**. The five-yearly elections are always closely run and passionately contested. Each party has been in power for similar periods since independence, with the Labour Party under **Mr Dom Mintoff** ruling continuously (and sometimes fractiously with Britain) for the period 1971–87. The Nationalist Party under **Mr Eddie Fenech Adami** is currently midway through its second five-year term.

Malta's eventful history has been punctuated with occupying peoples, both friend and foe. It has shown that the Maltese were always ready to acknowledge a *seigneur*, from the Arabs to the British. Yet in spite of its hard-won independence the country still yearns to belong; by belonging it feels its national voice will be heard. The republic currently has an application lodged with Brussels for full membership of the EC, the outcome of which is as yet undecided.

Topics

Driving

Local drivers have **seven golden rules**.

1. Wheels and a semblance of movement are enough to classify something as a vehicle. Age, condition and size of rustholes are immaterial.

2. Exclusive ownership of the road is included in the hire-purchase agreement.

3. Vehicles are fertility symbols and 200-decibel stereos are part of the mating ritual.

4. Once behind the wheel you are immortal. (Many roadside shrines attest to the fallacy of this belief.)

5. Noise is in direct proportion to speed.

6. Courtesy is a small township in the Australian Outback.

7. The Highway Code is something the Axis cracked in 1944; it has no bearing on driving in Malta.

A vehicle designed to suit local roads and driving conditions would by necessity look like a Heath Robinson contraption, and incorporate the best design attributes of an armoured personnel carrier, a tractor and an amphibious vehicle. There would be three models: the 'Christian', the 'Lion' and the 'Gladiator'. The last, a two-wheeled vehicle, would do away with all safety features due to the infinitesimally brief life expectancy of its owner, and would resemble at 150 kph a malevolent, unsilenced, prewar lawnmower. The volume-selling everyday model, the **Lion**, would be powered by carcinogenic, 12-cylinder turbo-diesel. Standard features would include an on/off accelerator switch (flat out or stationery), hooks for dice, a 120-decibel airhorn, a 7-m TV aerial and seating that converts into a divan. There would be no indicators, silencers or seat belts. Decals, the width of stripes, length and colour of fluff for seat covers, etcetera, would be at the purchaser's discretion. Similar in most ways to the Lion but bigger, the **Christian** would be able to accommodate three generations of *two* families, while the untuned sewing-machine motor would ensure a top speed of 20 kph. It's expected the Christian would be used exclusively on Sundays. Manufacturers could expect healthy sales in other countries: Turkey, Iran, Belgium and almost the entire African Continent.

Of Churches

Venturing off the beaten track onto the even more beaten secondary tracks, you will encounter three contrasting insights into the Maltese and their sometimes bewildering relationship with their Church.

Non Gode Immunita Ecclesiastica. A small marble tablet set into stone walls by the main door of many wayside chapels eloquently demonstrates how 'economical' interpretation of legal loopholes isn't a late 20th-century phenomenon. Until the beginning of the 19th century the ecclesiastical authorities had temporal jurisdiction over all church buildings to the complete exclusion of the civil authorities. Wily criminals soon cottoned onto this, and in times of imminent arrest many hapless villains sought sanctuary in a nearby chapel. Understandably, the ecclesiastical authorities became concerned and withdrew these rights of sanctuary in respect of certain churches by affixing the *Non Gode* legends.

After Malta had become a British colony in the early 19th century, the British refused to tolerate the Church's compromise with this old custom, which still enabled old lags to seek refuge in *unmarked* buildings. So in 1828 Governor Sir Frederic Ponsonby proclaimed the end of rights to asylum, 'for wicked and profligate men have often been tempted to commit murders, robberies and other atrocious crimes in the hope of escaping punishment by taking refuge in such places.'

Clocks. Many village churches have a clock affixed to one of their usual twin baroque towers (invariably it was the only clock the villagers had). Aesthetically a second clock was needed to achieve the all-important symmetry of the building, but often by the time the new church had been completed (sometimes 30 years after work had begun) the parishioners' goodwill (and their pocketbooks) had long been exhausted. Frequently, the dilemma was resolved by painting a second *trompe l'œil* clockface. All have their hands set steadfastly a few minutes before midnight—the devil's witching hour.

Nicci. These are similar to wall-mounted cash-dispensers, only in reverse: money is deposited and favours are promised. You will see them in the unlikeliest of places—where roads meet, or in dead-end streets and around blind corners. Each has its own saint, and is often further adorned by a small altar. Prayers are said here and money dropped into the embedded and locked box. In return there are heavenly rewards in the here-after, but such rewards are entirely dependent on how much money is given. Lm10 could ensure you a whole week in heaven.

The Maltese Cross

While the Order of St John was still in Acre (in the mid-13th century), the eight-pointed cross, known as the Maltese Cross, replaced the Order's simple insignia of a white cross on a scarlet background—'the white cross of peace in the blood-stained field of war'.

The knights' new insignia enshrined in its four principal arms the Christian tenets of Prudence, Justice, Temperance and Fortitude. The eight points of the cross's four arms represent the Beatitudes as taught by Christ in the Sermon on the Mount. The whiteness of the cross symbolizes the purity required by those who would live, fight and die in the service of the Christian faith.

Dom Mintoff

It all seems so long ago now, a generation or more. In fact it was only in 1984 that Dom Mintoff, the leader of the Malta Labour Party (MLP), resigned as the country's longest-serving prime minister.

He was born to a poor family, in Cospicua in 1916 when the Three Cities were a proletariat backyard of British colonial rule. Malta was then a fortress island, its fate tied to the waning British empire. His socialist views (like those of many) were formed within the Three Cities and the sweaty lee of the Royal Navy's dockyards. The cold mantle of arrogance worn by the British didn't help to foster good relations either.

Between the wars he trained as an architect and engineer in Malta, and in 1939 he won a Rhodes Scholarship to Oxford University. Upon his return he contested the postwar election in 1947, and the MLP won. At the time, his party had a pro-British stance—a *fin d'empire* British cheque book was helping to rebuild the island after the devastations of World War II. Furthermore, the 31-year-old Dom (now Minister of Works) had married an English woman. In 1955, after a factional dispute within the MLP, (still a pro-British party) he became Prime Minister on a mandate for full integration with Britain.

Oddly enough, if one fact is to be remembered about Mintoff's foreign policy (apart from the fact that he didn't *actually* have one) it is his taunting and vociferous dislike of the British—the roots of which surely lay in the integration issue. Mintoff adopted the notion of integration with Britain after it was first espoused some years before by Lord Strickland: the Maltese islands were to become, in effect, just another set of parliamentary constituencies sending MPs to the House of Commons at Westminster. In today's more politically aware times his proposal smacks of incomprehensible naivety. Yet Britain, nervous of the rumblings of Arab nationalism coming from Nasser, appeared to countenance the idea. Much against the wishes of his long-time adversaries, the Catholic Church, a referendum was tabled for 1956. The result was conclusive: 74.83% of the those who had cast votes ticked the box for full integration with Britain. But, the powers in Whitehall fudged the issue and turned the proposal down, saying that the vote did not take into account the wishes of those who had not voted! Loss of face and honour were very important to Mintoff and amid the pervading aroma of betrayal, a stalemate ensued. He resigned in 1958 and the British suspended the Maltese constitution.

In the bitter aftermath of the debacle, the issue was no longer integration: it was independence or bust. Mintoff now seemed more determined than ever to make Malta over to the Maltese. He wanted to take the people away from the insensitive assertiveness of the British, and out of their state of surpressive ignorance perpetrated by the Church. But the general election of 1962 was a disaster for the MLP, and it was the right-wing Nationalist Party that ushered in independence in 1964. (Although a greater percentage of the population actually voted at the subsequent independence referendum, only 50.68% voted for independence.)

For nine years Mintoff remained as Leader of the Opposition, albeit anything but quietly. It was during this fallow period, and his subsequent premiership in the 1970s, that the dangerous side of his talents began to manifest itself. As a leader he was hated and worshipped in equal measure; in that respect alone he was out of the Reagan–Thatcher mould. Mintoff possessed the two most seductive qualities a politician can: he was both truly charismatic and a forceful orator—a pied piper figure whose clarion call of Malta for the Maltese was followed by the people. But if you weren't for him you were against him, (apathy and neutrality were not the hallmarks of his era) and sadly he polarized a nation. The MLP was re-elected in 1971 and remained in power until 1987. In March 1979 Mintoff was finally to achieve a somewhat Phyrric victory when the last British warship sailed out of the Grand Harbour. Malta now belonged to the Maltese, and then only did he seem content, a life's work done.

Whatever has and will be said about him, even his fiercest detractors acknowledge he was a skilled and maverick politician; he courted controversy and didn't mind being cut off from an overbearing Church he despised, any more than he minded going to London to demand more money with forceful ultimatums. He'd flirt with the Soviets or be in cahoots with the palpably deranged Colonel Qaddafi, just as readily as he would beg aid from the Italians. Any action was acceptable providing *he* saw it as fulfilment of *his* ideals for Malta; ironically, his singlemindedness was his blind spot.

During the 16 years or more the MLP governed, unsavoury and undemocratic governments like China and North Korea provided aid, labour and training; hospitals and schools were needlessly shut, taxes were burdensomely high, and the Church was baited like a bear in a pit. Worst of all, corruption flourished; it wasn't the benign back-scratching of South American nations, either. *Everything* required a permit in socialist Malta and there was almost a published tariff of bribes. All this appeared to be lost in Mintoff's blind spot. As a man of humble tastes, he incorrectly presumed his ministers were too. An instinctive player, he rarely watched his own back let alone anyone else's.

The legacy of his long years in office was contradiction and oddity. Malta was left with little or no debt but with little or no ability to move forward either; the island's infrastructure had been woefully neglected. Yet while Mintoff and Malta accumulated more column inches of international press comment than many a country a hundred times larger, living standards for the poor *did* rise, and the islands *were* returned to the Maltese.

He knew (and didn't mind) that his resignation as prime minister in 1984—midway through a term of office—would leave a power vacuum. His untimely departure wasn't on account of a tawdry sex scandal *à l' Anglaise*, nor an Italian financial *tangenti*; he had simply had enough. And after 30 years in politics he knew his own, and his party's chances of re-election in the evolutionary 1980s were slim. As far as he was concerned, his deputy prime minister could be the fall guy (he was), and the MLP could lose the next election under a different leader (they did, two and a half years later, in 1987).

A Little More About Local Politics

Malta is a very politically aware nation. The islands have approximately one elected representative (MP) per 5,000 of population. (Duplicate that in Britain or America and you would have 11,700 MPs in the House of Commons or 50,000 Members of Congress: chaos would reign and no law would ever be passed.)

The Maltese political system is very similar to the British one. There are two principal parties: the right-wing Nationalist Party and the more left-wing Malta Labour Party. MPs are elected to a single House of Representatives in free democratic elections in five-year cycles on a proportional representation basis. All are fiercely contested and decided by the smallest of margins, and the somewhat overloaded system functions well, despite an aura of self-importance.

The idea of 'the career politician' is an alien phenomenon (an MP's salary is Lm2,800 per annum rising to the dizzy summit of Lm6,500 for the prime minister). Here, parliament is not a congenial social club, or an ivory tower in which to languish. Rewards are more intangible and come from the reverence shown by their followers; walk through any village and at least one street will be named after a politician—it's an honours system in all but name.

The importance of politics in Malta has increased ever since the end of the last war, while the Church's erstwhile iron grasp over the conscience of the population (priests would 'advise' their congregation how to vote) has simultaneously diminished. Surprisingly at first, the post-independence generation seemed to approve of the contraction of Malta's power and wealth, but there is no mystery behind the politicizing of the nation. The search by a vulnerable and much-invaded island race for a national and international voice, independence in 1964, and declaration as a neutral republic in 1974 has helped to keep politics on everyone's mind. A somewhat less apparent, but probably no less important, reason for its ascendancy can be spotted in every village. The *zuntier* (forecourt) of the parish church is the traditional end-of-day meeting place, somewhere for the men to sit and talk. Never far away, there were (and still are) the political clubs or *każin*; the blue banners of the Nationalist Party and the red ones of the Malta Labour Party winking invitingly from their ever-open doors. The clubs (together with their bars) pulled people off the church's *zuntier* and into their sphere of influence.

Every day at the most basic level, the Maltese are kept in close touch with their politicos and their antics. Their breakfast time diet of newsprint is prolific: they digest three daily and four Sunday newspapers, and politics is never off the front page. The local TV and radio stations gleefully report on even the most tedious events. It's no wonder that at the last general election (1992) the discussion of politics was actually *outlawed* in bars throughout the islands for the entire duration of the campaign. But recently a new spectre has risen. It has been mooted that each village should elect a council and a mayor. The day looms when every street in the islands is adorned with a political plaque.

- Rabbit Stew -

1 Rabbit cleaned and cut in pieces.
½ bottle of red wine.
2 carrots diced.
1 onion finely chopped.
2 bay leaves.
1 tin peeled tomatos
3 tablespoons tomato paste.

Marinade Rabbit overnight.

Fry Rabbit pieces in with garlic until browned & remove from pan.

Fry onions and carrots until golden, add the tomato paste and peeled tomatos, bay leaves and the wine marinade.

Add Rabbit pieces and simmer for 1½ hrs

Serve with vegetables and fresh local bread or with Spaghetti.

The Eye of Osiris

On either side of the high prow of every Maltese fishing boat or *luzzu* you will see an inky oval blob, the reverentially painted open and ever-watchful Eye of Osiris, a simple superstition to ward off evil spirits. Catholic names and shrines also found on board show how the strands of the island's different cultures entwine.

Osiris (with his wife Isis and son Horus) is one of a trinity of ancient Egyptian gods. First deified as the god of fertility in the Nile delta regions of upper Egypt more than 4,000 years ago, Osiris developed a second role as god of the dead after his brother Seth murdered him and dumped his body in the Nile. His wife Isis recovered his body, but Seth found it and cut it up into 14 pieces and scattered them to the winds. Vigilant Isis searched for and found his phallus and thus enabled Osiris to became god of eternal life for the dead in the under-world, where he reigned as king and judge. Their son Horus, however, was a sky god, often depicted as a falcon, whose eyes were the moon and the sun. Wishing to revenge his father's death, Horus engaged his uncle Seth in a fierce fight and slayed him. During the struggle Horus's left eye, his moon eye, was damaged (thereby explaining the phases of the moon). It is the all-seeing restored eye of Horus combined with the knowledge of eternal life offered by his father Osiris, that has become the talisman from which evil spirits shy away.

The *Festa*

If you can, try to imagine a film set in a Maltese *piazza* in front of an illuminated and well-dressed baroque church; families dressed in all their finery are milling about in a bustle of unco-ordinated activity. The bunting and pennants quiver gratefully in the breeze, and the lights are respectfully dimmed to a soft Mediterranean dusk. Suddenly, there are several explosive cracks like mortar fire; the young jump like rabbits, while the elderly stoically grip their chests. Now, study the scene a little closer, and you will perceive that the many Laurel-and-Hardy-style directors appear to be reading from a biblical script (that easily could have been written by Groucho Marx) as a solemn procession appears. There is a frightful din as the band strikes up, and decorations and lighting are supplanted by a seemingly endless and deafening display of gunpowder pyrotechnics, Las Vegas style. Moreover, the scene seems to gather momentum as the hours roll into the black night.

If your mind's eye is capable of drawing such a dysfunctional picture, you know how a *festa* might appear. But it's only on the surface that the gathering looks anarchic. In reality the villagers' *festa*, held annually in honour of their patron saint, is painstakingly prepared, rehearsed and anticipated—the high point of the year.

The history of the village *festa* dates back to the later years of the Order of St John, when celebrations were encouraged on thin pretexts as an unsophisticated method of diverting the peasant's mind away from his lot. It was under the British in the mid- and late 19th century that local celebrations really started to flourish and civic band clubs (the communities' glue) began to form. Today the *festa* is an important social occasion when families reunite from all over the islands, and the prestige of the village and its clubs are vested in the event's outcome. (Some would say, rather cynically, that it's also a time when the Church can reassert its authority.)

The *festa* lasts a weekend, building throughout Saturday, to climax on Sunday. Weeks of volunteer work—spring-cleaning the village, fund-raising, decorating the streets, reverential hanging of red damask and chandeliers in the church, polishing the statues that are to be carried solemnly through the streets—are over. Sometime after dawn on Saturday the brutal noise of the petards heralds the start of the party.

Throughout the celebrations the Maltese, making the boldest of sartorial statements (the women wear *all* their jewellery), will mooch in and out of relatives' and friends' houses, sing songs and occasionally pause to listen to the less-than-euphonious brass bands, lose teeth to vicious and sweet *qubbajt* (nougat), chomp on *mqaret* (vile-looking hot fritters stuffed with crushed dates), and drink too much. The two high points are the high mass when the bells are rung with as much rhythm as free verse, and the evening firework displays which signal the end of the day's festivities. The startling fireworks are homemade; catherine-wheels whirr like a hypnotist's eyes, and the rocket-tails cascade in exploding rainbows; it's a very unusual year when someone does not blow themselves to pieces in the preceding weeks. But the Maltese have very few cares at *festa* time, and the following Monday, *'xalata*, is the day for hangovers, picnics and lazing by the beach.

If one singular aspect stands out in all the noise, gunpowder, and incense of the *festas* its the unsophisticatedness of it all—that's what makes them entirely unique. They are traditional and simple celebrations to which all are invited.

Festas usually run through the long evenings of June, July, August and September. Many villages have a secondary festa; *only the primary ones are noted in the text.*

The *Kaċċa*

Most nations have their bloodsports: in England, 'the unspeakable pursue the uneatable', in Spain they thrust cold steel between the eyes of healthy bulls, in Japan they relentlessly pursue whales and in Malta they engage in the wholesale slaughter of birds. But the British fox is classed as vermin and, evidently, needs to be culled; in the traditional Spanish bullfight the animal has a chance to defend itself, and at least there is *some* honour in the final duel; and in Japan the whales once provided food and a living for isolated communities. However unpalatable and tenuous these arguments are, they *do* have an element of economic, social or conservation responsibility. Furthermore, set seasons or quotas are adhered to.

In Malta the *kaċċa*, or the hunt, has now become killing simply for the sake and thrill of it, and the 'seasons' are so abused that they no longer have any meaning. In mitigation the worn out plea to, 'look at other countries' is trotted out by the hunters, but their principal self-justification rests with tradition—the knights hunted in the islands for 268 years. In reality there is no excuse for the atrocities, and the practices of the lawless minority continue to bring international condemnation on Malta. The island's three principal bird sanctuaries are no longer inviolate—even rats are 'hunted' around the government rubbish dumps.

The single-most disturbing aspect of all is the shooting of migratory birds—whether internationally protected or not—as they fly between habitats. If you walk by Dingli Cliffs in spring when the birds migrate north from Africa, the dawn chorus sounds, without hyperbole, like Beirut of old. Many practices have gone way beyond the boundaries of sportsmanship: semi-automatic shotguns are used and speedboats driven by the *kaċċatur*, the hunters, wait out at sea for the exhausted birds *before* they even reach landfall.

Malta does not have a legal requirement in which the 'bag' is recorded, therefore estimates of birds trapped, netted or shot can be misleading. Nevertheless, figures published in 1992 (and disputed by the Malta Association for Hunting and Conservation) suggest that among the long list of those shot, killed or trapped is an astonishing *annual* bag of 3 million finches, 500,000 thrushes, 500,000 swallows, 135,000 turtle doves, 80,000 golden orioles and 50,000 birds of prey—an average of 12 birds for every man, woman and child on the islands. (There are no figures at all for those birds caught in illegal drift-nets which you will sometimes come across by the cliffs.) With few exceptions the birds are inedible and the Maltese are not great poultry eaters. So what happens to them? The larger and rarer species are left with the taxidermist, to appear later as possessions on a mantlepiece, while small birds like finches are either shot at for target practice (like road signs) or end up trapped in minute cages.

To the average holiday-maker or businessman passing through it seems obvious that the time has come to outlaw the *kaċċa*, or at the very least curb and police it. Unfortunately, the authorities (who collect revenues from guns, ammunition, etcetera) are either unable or unwilling to grasp the nettle. Even the minority, *macho* wannabe-Hemingways go scott-free while drawing unwanted attention to those who do only hunt permitted prey within the seasons. Evidently, the hunting lobby is just too powerful in the precariously balanced war of attrition that is local politics. Until Malta's breadwinner, the tourist industry, is very seriously affected nothing will be done; 'green' tourists and certain conferences already boycott the islands but they are a tiny number compared with a large market.

The migration seasons, March–May and September–November, are the periods when the unsavoury customs of the *kaċċatur* are at their most pronounced. Unlike Japan where it is highly unlikely that you will stumble across a whaling fleet, in Malta it's impossible during these months not to be concerned or intimidated, or both, in parts of the countryside. Try to avoid, especially in the mornings or early evenings, Dingli, Buskett, Wardija, Delimara, the deserted areas near to Ħaġar Qim and any of the exposed cliffs in Malta and Gozo. Comino is a policed sanctuary.

De la Valette and Dragut Rais

Leaders sometimes epitomize the era in which they live. The 16th century with its religious polarization and brutal warfare brought together two adversaries of similar mettle: the Christian knight Jean Parisot de la Valette, and the Muslim corsair, Dragut Rais, known as 'The Drawn Sword of Islam'.

Jean Parisot de la Valette was born in 1494, 'issue of the first hereditary Counts of Toulouse of ancestors who had fought in the Albigensian wars and in the Crusades with St Louis'. He joined the Order of St John (variously described as 'the most remarkable body of religious warriors the world has ever seen' and 'a foreign legion of militant Christians'), at the age of 20 and never returned to his native France, dedicating his life to the Order.

Described by the Abbé de Brantôme as 'a very handsome man, tall, calm and unemotional', he was just 28 when the Order was defeated at Rhodes in 1522 by the Turks and their young sultan, Suleyman the Magnificent. Born in the same year as de la Valette, and together with Dragut, Suleyman was to be his archenemy. During the Order's subsequent wilderness years, before it was offered Malta in 1530, de la Vallette observed as Grand Master L'Isle Adam begged for aid from monarchs across Europe. It was then that he acquired the traits that came to symbolize his subsequent magistracy: a bearing which commanded respect and inspiration, patience, iron discipline, rigid observance of vows, a nose for politics and an almost fanatical hatred of Moslems. It was said 'the seal of a hero was on his brow' and furthermore that de la Valette was 'capable of converting a Protestant or of governing a kingdom'.

By the time he was elected grand master in 1557 at the age of 63, he had served in all the important positions within the Order, and had even had the unique distinction of being General of the Galley's, a sinecure of the Italian *langue*. And it was during one summer *caravan* that the centuries-old Christian-Muslim confict caused the two warriors to meet.

In the summer of 1541 de la Valette was wounded during a sea engagement and his ship, *San Giovanni*, was sunk. Dragut was an officer on board the corsair Kust Aly's ship, and it was he who ensured that de la Valette's wounds were properly treated. De la Valette spent more than year chained to an oar as a galley slave until an exchange of prisoners secured his release. In an extraordinary parallel, some years later Dragut was captured and he too was tethered to the rowing benches; fate had again thrown the two men together for a second and last time. 'Dragut, it's the custom of war', de la Valette is said to have remarked as Dragut pulled on the oar, to which a smiling Dragut replied, 'and a change of fortune!'

De la Valette knew Suleyman the Magnificent would one day try to complete the annihilation of the Order after his uncustomary moment of clemency at Rhodes in 1522, and in the warm May of 1565 the Turkish fleet appeared off Malta and what became known as the Great Siege began in earnest. Throughout the siege the now 70-year-old grand master led from the front. The Christian footsoldier and diarist Fransisco Balbi who fought in the siege wrote, 'If it had not been for the constant foresight and preparations made by the grand master, not one of us would have survived.'

With the Muslim enemy routed and Suleyman's expansion into the central Mediterranean halted, plaudits and wealth were heaped on him and the Order. De la Valette lived for a further three years and died a peaceful death in 1568 in the chapel at Fort St Angelo after a day's hunting in the *boshetto*. He is buried in the crypt of St John's Co-Cathedral in the city which bears his name.

The Latin inscription on his tomb, composed by his English secretary Sir Oliver Starkey, reads: 'Here lies La Valette, worthy of eternal honour. He who was once the scourge of Africa and Asia, and the shield of Europe, whence he expelled the barbarians by his holy arms is the first to be buried in this beloved city, whose founder he was.'

If the central Mediterranean had mainstay industries at all in the 15th and 16th centuries it was piracy and slavery. Rounding up Christian slaves to sell or ransom was a highly profitable wheeze for the corsairs whose nesting-ground was the north coast of Africa, the Barbary Coast. At the turn of the 16th century the most skilled and feared practitioners were the brothers Barbarossa, Khaired-din, known as 'Redbeard' and Horuk, and it was with them that **Dragut Rais** learnt his trade.

He was born to an Anatolian peasant family in 1485 in the little village of Charabalac in Turkey. His fate was sealed when as a child the province's governor took him to Egypt where he later enlisted in the military as a bombardier. But he soon tired of the conventions of the army corps and went to sea as a gunner on a pirate vessel and later 'acquired' a *galliot* of his own. Dragut's exploits reached the ears of the wily Barbarossa brothers who persuaded him to fall in with them at their newly captured base of Algiers in 1529 when he was 44. He sailed as lieutenant of their squadron until 1546 when Redbeard died and the mantle of 'christian scourge' fell easily upon Dragut's shoulders; by now he was a maverick tactician of audacious cunning with an encyclopedic knowledge of the Mediterranean.

In 1551, tired of lone piracy and thirsting for war, Dragut put his acumen and galleys at the service of the Turkish sultan, Suleyman the Magnificent. His first campaign as a new admiral in the Turkish navy was to capture the Order's outpost in Tripoli with Sinan Pasha. The battle was swift and decisive (he 'built a pyramid of Christian bones'), and a grateful Suleyman then confirmed him as governor of Tripoli. In the same year he carried off the entire population of Gozo in an act of revenge for the death of his brother who had been killed there in 1544 during one of his numerous raids on the islands.

Dragut was 80 years old when he arrived in Malta on 2 June, just three weeks after the Great Siege of 1565 had commenced. Not even his tactical skill could reverse the disastrous miscalculations of the Turkish commanders and 16 days later on 18 June he was killed accidentally by a splinter of rock thrown up by a cannon ball. Eleven years earlier in what proved to be a self-fulfilling prophecy, Dragut had remarked after his brother's death, 'I have felt in this island, the shadow of the wing of death. One of these days it is written that I, too, shall die in the territory of the knights'. The death of one of de la Valette's arch-enemies boosted the flagging morale of the besieged, and Francisco Balbi recorded it thus: 'Dragut laid low, his brains spattered from his mouth, nostrils and ears … de la Valette was very pleased at this'. His tomb can still be seen in Tripoli and, in Malta, Dragut Point is where he 'left his name with his life'; but perhaps the most fitting epitaph for one of the greatest warriors of the 16th century was written by the French historian Jurien de la Gravière in 1887: '*Il est mort sans déclin, dernière faveur de la fortune pour un homme qu'elle avait toujours gâté.*' ('He died on the up, the last stroke of luck for a man who was always spoilt.')

Valletta and the Three Cities

Grand Harbour, Valletta, Senglea, and Vittoriosa have all the ingredients of the picturesque—ancient buildings, fortifications, narrow and precipitous streets, national costume, local religious festivals, and an unconscionably romantic history.

Evelyn Waugh, *Labels*, 1930

As European capitals go **Valletta** is a rarity—it's only just 420 years old. The city is not therefore a place of impacted civilizations that bears the trace of its country's history in its architecture. To the contrary it was actually a *planned* city.

Around Valletta

Valletta was named after Grand Master de la Valette and was devised, in the wake of his victory against the Turks in the Great Siege of 1565, with two aims: to be a Christian fortress able to withstand the forces of Islam (a deterent in itself) and to be a congenial home for the aristocratic flower of Europe, the chivalrous Order of the Knights of St John. Consequently, within its bastion walls it acquired all the trappings of a capital city, most of which remain—parliament, the judiciary and government; plus offices of the larger private enterprises. Yet, for all its fine architecture and noble birth Valletta lacks character and soul. Neither has it avoided late 20th-century phenomena such as unemployment, drugs-related problems and a diminishing population. To most Maltese it is just *Il Belt*, literally 'the city'; a place to work or somewhere to find something unobtainable elsewhere. The city empties at sunset (the best restaurant only opens for two evenings a week) and many even go home during the long lunch-hours.

For the visitor, however, Valletta is impressive: somewhere you can be truly subjective and can get away with it. It can become what you want it to be: an historically seductive fortress built by crusading knights in shining armour, a commercial centre that looks like a miniature Manhattan with its skyscrapers cheese-wired off, or simply a city with an incredible cathedral, fascinating baroque architecture, and museums and cafés to linger in.

Across the Grand Harbour from the Valletta promontory is the area known as the **Three Cities** variously called, Senglea, Cospicua and Vittoriosa, the original home of the Order. Until they built Valletta, the Three Cities were the island's *de facto* capital, and the area bore the brunt of the Great Sieges of both 1565 and 1941–3.

A tightly knit working-class community lives in the narrow streets and there is soul in the Three Cities, but not much else. The government's efforts in marketing the area have been extensive, but apart from the new **Maritime Museum** there are few conventional attractions to offer anyone not interested in the early history of the Order in Malta. But if you walk through Vittoriosa in the late afternoon after having visited Valletta, it will pull each into sharper focus.

Valletta

Valletta is a schizophrenic city. By day it's a thriving and bustling capital: idle dissenters loiter outside the law courts, lawyers and businessmen lean on the bar of the Café Cordina having their morning fix of *espresso*, housewives rummage around **Merchant Street market** for bargains, and tourists jostle unsurely up and down **Republic Street**. The splendours of **St John's Co-Cathedral**, the displays in the **Museum of Archaeology**, the **Grand Master's Palace** and the **Armoury** ensure that an enduring stream of visitors tramp the city's streets.

By night, however, it wears a sombre mask. Venture into Valletta after the sunset *passeggiata*, when all the shops are shut and the businessmen have returned home and you wonder if it's the same place. Everywhere is closed save for a few bars and the littered streets have a menacing atmosphere (this is deceptive, the streets are safe). Life does go on in the residential *quartiers* past **Palace Square**. Here the Maltese gossip on doorsteps, shout across the narrow streets, or tinker with their cars, but this is not a tourist town by night; there is nothing to do, nothing to see, and with two exceptions no good restaurants.

St John's Co-Cathedral

Moreover, until recently Valletta was a city without much civic self-respect. People, especially tourists, would arrive, see or do what they had to and leave, mildly shocked at the unkempt state of the place. Now it's once again becoming somewhere to linger—try any of the outdoor cafés surrounding Queen Victoria's statue in **Republic Square**—and to explore.

The Planned City: the Building and Architecture of Valletta

One month after the Great Siege was raised in September 1565, Grand Master de la Valette was confronted with vociferous disquiet in his ranks. To the older knights, 'the Turk always returns' was axiomatic, and in reality they hadn't won, the Turk had lost. Fort St Elmo was devastated, as were parts of St Angelo; the knights had neither the manpower nor the fortifications to withstand another onslaught, expected the following spring.

The Order simply had to remain somehow: they were the cork which kept the infidel Turk in his eastern Mediterranean bottle. Malta was as far west as the European monarchies and powers were prepared to let him venture. Before the end of 1565, and at the grand master's request, Pope Pius V sent Francesco Laparelli to Malta; 44 years of age, an ex-pupil of Michelangelo and a leading proponent of military engineering, his brief was to advise on the wisdom of creating a wholly fortified virgin city. A planned city.

The chosen site, **Mount Sceberras**, was an undulating peninsula of limestone rock. It jabbed out into the Mediterranean like an aggressive finger in between the Grand and the Marsamxett Harbours and was, save for Fort St Elmo, undefended and uninhabited. Within just six days of his arrival Laparelli proposed his plan: a girdle of fortifications built around Mount Sceberras. The fortifications would stretch up to the highest landward point on the peninsula, some 500 Sicilian *cannes* (1 *canne* = 2.065 m) inland from the pile of rubble that was Fort St Elmo's gate. Inside this massive fortress *enceinte* a grid-pattern city would be hewn mostly out of the living rock, the details of which could be improvised as they progressed. One of the most persuasive arguments Laparelli used to sway the vacillating septuagenarian de la Valette and his council was that it would be cheaper to erect a whole new city than to demolish the old fortifications and evacuate Malta. Like most architects he was wildly optimistic, but the Order's council believed him. The foundation stone of the new city was laid on 28 March 1566 amid much pomp, just three months after Laparelli's arrival.

Work was initially slow due to a shortage of slaves, labourers and masons; up to 4,000 were needed. By 1568, the year the magistracy had passed to the Italian del Monte, the streets had been laid and Laparelli felt able to return to Italy leaving his Maltese assistant, the parochial Gerolamo Cassar, temporarily in charge. (The quixotic Laparelli was to return only briefly the following year before succumbing to the plague in Crete while serving in the papal fleet.) Earlier, Cassar was dispatched to Italy to absorb as many aesthetic influences as possible. Architecturally at this time, mannerism and the beautiful Renaissance marriage of the straight line and the circle, were ready to give way and accept a new discipline, the curve of baroque. Cassar must have returned home in a quandary, for his paymasters were nigh on bankrupt after the enormous expense of the fortifications, and were after all monastic warriors of Christ with tastes to match. But Valletta was to be a truly joint effort between Laparelli, the Italian motivator with a grasp for the grand scheme, and Cassar, the skilled Maltese architect and details man. That said, with Laparelli's final departure Cassar's achievement was one stop short of totalitarian architecture. Before he died in 1581 he was responsible in Valletta alone for: the Grand Master's Palace, St John's Co-Cathedral, the seven original *auberges*, and many private houses and churches.

The complex project was executed following practices remarkably similar to those of the late 20th century. The Council of the Order set about purchasing all the required land and issuing stringent planning guidelines. There were approximately 1,125 private plots, none of which could be bought for speculative purposes, and to avoid undesirables nominee purchases were outlawed. A successful purchaser had to commence construction within six months, and complete the building by the end of the following year. No structure was allowed to be set back from, or impede onto the street, and courtyards had to be contained within the plot.

There was to be adequate provision for the storage of water, and connection to a central sewage system was mandatory. Laparelli's street plan was wide and designed to take advantage of the cleansing sea breezes. Anyone buying a corner property had to embellish the corners for the benefit of all. Unlike their accommodation in Rhodes, where the knights were ghettoed in a *collacchio*, there was no intention of segregating the Maltese; Valletta was 3½ times larger than Birgu (Vittoriosa) and could accommodate everyone.

Grand Master del Monte formally moved the Order to the unfinished city on 18 March 1571 and by 1610 all the plots were sold. Valletta was a resounding success, and the population rose to approximately 4,000 (today it is approximately 9,000). Later on in the 17th and 18th centuries, with the Turkish threat diminishing and the evolution of baroque, the Order grew to revel in the symbiosis of art, architecture and wealth. Its additions and embellishments subtly changed Valletta from principally a Renaissance to a baroque city—and despite even the gimlet-eyed attentions of the Axis bombers, it is still Laparelli's and Cassar's city.

Getting There

Just outside City Gate and revolving around the Triton Fountain like horses on a carousel is the island's fleet of **buses**. Hop on any bus from anywhere, heading away from the sea and you will end up here eventually. If you are in the Sliema/St Julian's area the least aggravating and quickest way into Valletta is on the **Marsamxett Ferry** which leaves approximately every 40 minutes from the Ferries in Sliema; the 5-minute crossing disembarks by the water-polo pitch.

Arriving **by car** is trickier than it appears on the map, not due to the roads or signposting—Valletta is flagged from most places— or to the city's convoluted one-way system, but on account of the near-impossible task of finding a safe and legitimate place to **park**. Gamblers can try to find a hole outside the Auberge de Castile et Leon, in Pope Pius V Street, by the bombed-out shell of the Opera House or in the car park in front of the Grand Master's Palace. The best spot is outside Giannini's Restaurant in Windmill Street by St Michael's Bastion; not only will the helpful attendant look after the hub caps, but for a decent tip, he'll wash your car as well. If all other gambits fail, try Floriana. **Taxis** and *karrozin* are near the Auberge de Castile et Leon, in Great Siege Square and by City Gate. For most of the day Republic Street is pedestrianized from City Gate to Palace Square.

The **NTOM** has an office at 1 Freedom Square, just inside City Gate. Its **free city map** is short on cartographic information but the staff are helpful. **Bank of Valletta's** main branch is on the corner of Republic Street and St John's Square. **Mid Med** has a **foreign exchange** office at 15 Republic Street and a main office at 32 Merchants Street. **Coppini Foreign Exchange Bureau** is at 58 Merchants Street. The **police station** is situated in the Law Courts [15], the **post office** is at the top of Merchants Street and **Telemalta** has an office for international calls in South Street. **Air Malta** has offices in Freedom Square and 285 Republic Street.

There are four **national museums**: Archaeology, Fine Arts, War, and the Palace Armoury. If you plan to visit all four buy a day pass (**Lm3**) at the first one, it will save you Lm1. Ignore the signs for the Lascaris War Rooms, they are closed indefinitely.

Disabled visitors should note that many of Valletta's pavements are cracked and none of the principal sights such as St John's Co-Cathedral, the Museum of Archaeology and the Grand Master's Palace have facilities which provide access *above* ground floor level. The Malta Experience (and the Maritime Museum in Vittoriosa) have disabled access.

Valletta City Tour

Adieu, ye cursed streets of stairs! (How surely he who mounts you swears!)
Lord Byron, *'Farewell to Malta,'* 16 May 1811

Orientation

Republic Street [3] is the main thoroughfare, the island's principal shopping street and the axis for a walking tour. Before it became Republic Street in 1974, its different monikers flagged the city's history—as Strada San Giorgio, Rue de la Republique, Strada Reale and Kingsway.

The city is on a neat grid approximately 1 km long by 650 m wide. The diminutive dimensions belie its roller-coaster topography. Apart from Republic Street there are two other main arteries: Merchants Street and Old Bakery Street, and both spine down the Sceberras peninsula from City Gate towards Fort St Elmo on the point. The cross streets fall off these streets in steps and/or alleys to the Grand and Marsamxett Harbours and a road rings the entire city.

Valletta is a **walking** city, but it is not well ordered for sightseeing and involves doubling back. This tour starts from City Gate, and follows a very approximate anti-clockwise route back to it. Principal sights are marked ★—if you only have a short time the sights marked ★★ are *musts*—and should take no more than one full day including a break for lunch. Note: Casa Rocca Piccola [22] closes at 1300, as does the Grand Master's Palace [19] in summer, and if World War II holds little interest, don't bother to venture beyond Casa Rocca Piccola other than to see the Malta Experience [24].

City Gate [1]. Known originally as the Gate of St George, this was the main entrance through the bastions into the city. It later became Porta Reale, and then King's Gate. The present dull City Gate was erected to provide a wider passage in 1964. Outside, the **Triton Fountain** is another contemporary Maltese work from the 1950s.

Palazzo Ferreria and the Old Opera House [2] give an untidy first impression of Valletta. The Palazzo Ferreria, on the left opposite the remains of the Opera House, was built in the late 19th century on the site of the Order's arsenal or *ferreria*, as the private residence for a wealthy wheat importer.

The Opera House was designed by E.M. Barry, architect of the Royal Opera House in Covent Garden, London, and completed in 1866. Its unpopular design was intended to reflect the imperial bearing of the British Empire. It was gutted by fire in 1873 and reopened four years later. The contentious structure was finally destroyed by the *Luftwaffe* in 1942 and has languished as an eyesore ever since. The 50-year polemic over its future design and use continues.

Our Lady of Victory [4]. This rather sorry-looking church was the first the knights built in their new city to commemorate their victory in the Great Siege of 1565. De la Valette laid the foundation stone and was initially buried here before being interred in St John's Co-Cathedral. Grand Master Perellos altered the façade in 1690 and placed the bust of Pope Innocent XI above the door.

Church of St Catherine of Italy [5]. Designed by Cassar for the Italian knights and abutting their auberge, St Catherine's church is also looking weary. The façade and porch were added in 1713 and the octagonal church is still used today by the Italian community. The main altarpiece of the Martyrdom of St Catherine is one of **Mattia Preti's** favourite subjects.

Auberge de Castile et Leon [6]★. The *auberge* of the knights of Spain and Portugal is the capital's finest example of 18th-century mature Maltese baroque and has a rare and grand symmetry. Situated at the highest point of the peninsula,

Valletta

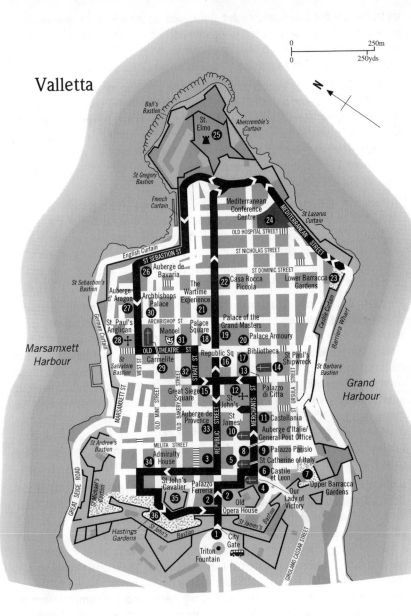

0   250m
0   250yds

N

Ball's Bastion

St. Elmo 25

Abercrombie's Curtain

St Gregory Bastion

French Curtain

Mediterranean Conference Centre 24

OLD HOSPITAL STREET

MEDITERRANEAN STREET

St Lazarus Curtain

English Curtain

ST SEBASTION ST

ST NICHOLAS STREET

St Sebastion's Bastion

Auberge de Bavaria 26

ST DOMINIC STREET

Auberge d' Aragon 27

Archbishops Palace 30

The Wartime Experience 21

Casa Rocca Piccola 22

Lower Barracca Gardens

23

German Curtain

St. Paul's Anglican 28

ARCHBISHOP ST

Manoel 31

Palace Square 18

Palace of the Grand Masters

19

Palace Armoury 20

Castile Curtain

OLD THEATRE ST

WEST ST

Carmelite 29

STRAIT ST

Republic Sq 16

Bibliotheca 17

St Paul's Shipwreck

St Barbara Bastion

St Salvatore Bastion

13

14

Barriera Wharf

Grand Harbour

Marsamxett Harbour

MARSAMXETT ST

OLD MINT STREET

OLD BAKERY STREET

Great Siege Square 15

STRAIT STREET

12

St John's

Palazzo di Citta

MERCHANTS ST

ST URSULA STREET

St Andrew's Bastion

Auberge de Provence 33

32

St James' 10

11 Castellania

MELITA STREET

Admiralty House 34

3

St John's Cavalier 35

Palazzo Ferreria

REPUBLIC STREET

8

5

9 Palazzo Patisio

St Catherine of Italy

6 Castile et Leon

7

Auberge d'Italie/ General Post Office

GREAT SIEGE ROAD

St Michael's Bastion

36

St John's Bastion

2

Old Opera House

4

Our Lady of Victory

Upper Barracca Gardens

Hastings Gardens

1

City Gate

Triton Fountain

St James's Bastion

GIROLAMO CASSAR STREET

on a site originally designated for the Grand Master's Palace and partially shadowed by St James Cavalier, it was remodelled in 1741 around Cassar's far more austere original of 1574. The effervescent façade with its precise detail was handled by either Domenico Cachia or Andrea Belli.

Grand Master Pinto, who commissioned the building for his Iberian countrymen was a showy, luxurious man, who revelled in the competitiveness of European monarchies. There is a wonderful portrait of him by **de Favray** in the Sacristy of St John's. Here, above the portal and set amidst flags, weapons and accoutrements, is a bust of Pinto, and over the central window is his escutcheon. The crowning decoration on top of the cornice is the arms of Castile et Leon. The two cannon date from 1756.

Historically, the grand chancellor of the Order was a knight of Castile et Leon, and the knights were to defend St Barbara's bastion facing the Grand Harbour. The *auberge* was once the British forces' headquarters and now houses the office of the prime minister. With a touch of irony, the statue facing the *auberge* from the roundabout is of Manwel Dimech, one of the founders of Malta's socialist movement.

Upper Barracca Gardens [7]. The colonnaded public garden, *Il Belvedere d'Italia*, on top of St Peter and St Paul's demi-bastion was once a covered play area for the boisterous Italian knights. A plot to overthrow Grand Master Ximenes, known as the **Priest's Revolt**, was hatched in the building in 1775, and the roof was removed after the plot had been rumbled. Overlooking the Three Cities and the harbour, the public gardens offer the best **panorama** in Valletta; this has long been a favourite spot for many, not just pigeon-chasing children. Among the statues are Sir Thomas Maitland (governor 1813–24 and known as 'King Tom') in a rare contemplative pose, *Les Gavroches* by Maltese sculptor Antonio Sciortino, and a powerful bust of Winston Churchill.

Auberge d'Italie/General Post Office [8]. The duty of the knights of the Italian *langue* was to defend the immediate bastions of St Peter and St Paul, the post of admiral of the fleet was traditionally the sinecure of their *pilier*. The ubiquitous Cassar designed this *auberge* as a single-storey edifice and it displays a typical example of his one major architectural hallmark, the use of massive and rusticated quoins—the external corners of walls. The Italian Grand Master Carafa added the top floor in 1683 at the same time as his deliciously theatrical, very Italian, piece of baroque nonsense above the main door; trumpets, Roman armour, flags, escutcheons, weapons, ornamental drapes, are all thrown together around his nonchalant-looking bust. The building once housed the law courts, and a museum.

Palazzo Parisio [9]. Opposite the post office is the Palazzo Parisio, another government building. This gloomy late 18th-century structure is notable only because Napoleon made it his headquarters for five days during his brief plundering stay en route to the Egyptian campaign in June 1798.

St James's church [10]. Built in 1612 to serve the knights of Castile et Leon, the church was to all intents and purposes rebuilt by Giovanni Barbara in 1710. The oval plan, rich detail on its narrow façade and ornate carvings above the central window are redolent of Roman baroque. In 1663 it was the focus of a religious scandal involving dark implications of satanic rituals (*see* p. 247).

Castellania [11]. On the corner of Merchants and St John's Street, the Castellania housed the law courts. It was completed in 1760 during Grand Master Pinto's reign (hence the florid stonework and his ever-present crescent emblem). The figures either side of the first-floor balcony represent Justice and Truth. After the **Priest's Revolt** of 1775, three of the conspirators were tried, strangled to death in the cells, decapitated and their heads placed on spikes by St James' Cavalier. At the apex of the building's corner is a pillory stone for lesser miscreants. For the hook above it, there are two explanations: one says it was used to hoist up the bells of St John's, the other more plausibly states it was used to suspend convicts sentenced to imprisonment in a cage.

The building has been put to somewhat less gruesome uses since then, it has even been a girls' school. In 1896 it became the office of the Health Department, and it was here that the physician and prominent archaeologist Sir Themistocles Zammit discovered the Mediterranean strain of brucellosis in 1905.

St John's Co-Cathedral and Museum [12]★★

> '*Magnificent church, the most striking interior I have ever seen.*'
>
> Sir Walter Scott, 1831

St John's houses Malta's finest art treasures and its splendour tests the limits of the lexicon, words like lavish and opulent fall short of the mark.

Hours. St John's: Mon–Fri 0930–1300 and 1330–1730; Sat 0930–1300 and 1530–1700; adm. free. **Oratory and Museum**: Mon–Fri 0930–1300 and 1330–1630; Sat 0930–1300; adm. 60c. Closed Sundays and public holidays.

History and Exterior

After the knights left Birgu (Vittoriosa) in 1571, the need to replace St Lawrence's church with a new conventual church—one for the brotherhood of the entire Order—was of paramount concern. But the new building, dedicated to their patron saint St John the Baptist, had to be more than a place of collective worship: it had in time to be a place which could embody the wealth, glory, and power of the Order itself. With tact, Cassar designed a clean but heavy façade in homage to the then austere military attitudes of his paymasters. For the next 80 years the interior remained as stark as the exterior.

Work commenced in the autumn of 1573 on a simple but somewhat heavy Renaissance-influenced plan: a wide screen façade, an entrance between two Doric columns with twin bell-towers either side (the spires of which were removed during World War II). The interior plan was also to be conventional—a single rectangular nave underneath a great barrel vault with an apse at the northeast end and eight side chapels, one for each of the *langues*, between the massive reinforcing buttresses.

The church was consecrated on 20 February 1578 and was built and paid for by the French Grand Master de la Cassiere. Other parts of this calmly severe building were added later; the sacristy in 1598, the oratory in 1603, and the loggia annexes in 1736. The two cannons date from 1600 and 1726; the former with lion handles bears the Battenburg coat of arms, and the latter the arms of Grand Master de Vilhena.

The Interior

'Inside there is no single spot where the eye can rest for one moment that is not ablaze with decoration.'

Evelyn Waugh, 1930

As your eyes adjust from the harsh sunlight to the muted, even gloomy interior they head straight down the 57.6 m length of the nave to the altar trying, and failing, to take in the opulence and the fields of frescoes en route. Nothing quite prepares you for the engulfing effect of such affluence; not even Napoleon's wholesale depradations have dimmed it. With every election to the magistracy, or even a promotion, a knight had, by statute, to provide a *gioia* (gift) to the Order's church. St John's and the neighbouring chapels of each *langue* were lavished with gifts in expensive rounds of knightly one-up-manship. As the threat of Infidel wars diminished, the Order grew wealthier (and softer) and its tastes became more and more flamboyant.

The nave [1]. The Order's inherent ostentation was given further rein upon the death of a knight, for only a knight, and then only one of distinction, could be interred in St John's. The entire pavement of the nave is made up of more than 400 tessellated tombs; the earliest, in the Chapel of Aragon dates from 1602. Some of the symbols are garish and some simple, but each is individual. One of the memorial slabs by the Republic Street entrance belongs to a French knight, Anselmo de Caijs. His inscription translates: 'You who tread on me, you will be trodden upon, reflect on that and pray for me'. Annoyed at not being promoted, he apparently took his grievance to the grave.

The bronze and marble baroque **mausoleum [2]** remembers Italian Grand Master Zondadari, nephew of Pope Alexander VII who was once an inquisitor in Malta.

St John's Co-Cathedral

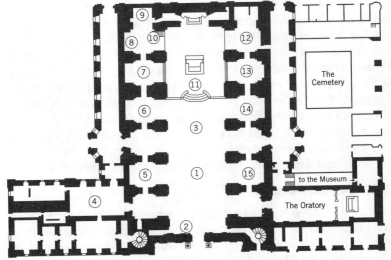

St John's Square

1. The Nave
2. Zondadari Mausoleum
3. The Vault
4. The Sacristy
5. Chapel of Germany
6. Chapel of Italy
7. Chapel of France
8. Chapel of Provence
9. Chapel of Anglo-Bavarian Langue
10. To the Grand Masters' Crypt
11. The Sanctuary
12. Chapel of Our Lady of Philermos
13. Chapel of Auvergne
14. Chapel of Aragon
15. Chapel of Castile

The vault [3]. Nikolaus Pevsner, the art historian, states that **Mattia Preti's** work depicting the life of St John the Baptist in the vault of St John's is 'the first realized example of high Baroque art anywhere'. The work was commissioned in 1661 by the Cotoner brothers, Rafael and Nicolas, grand masters from 1660 to 1680. The vault is illuminated by six oval windows and divided into six bays, which in turn are subdivided into three, thereby creating one stone canvas for 18 episodes in the Baptist's life. Not strictly frescoes—Preti painted in oils directly onto the barely primed and porous stone—they took five years to complete. The cycle commences on the left of the first bay by the main door and ends with the beheading, on the right above the altar. The figures on either side of the windows are of individual knights, and saints revered by the Order.

In the **sacristy [4]**, **Antoine de Favray's** terrific portrait of Grand Master Pinto, one of the island's best paintings, is poorly served by the lighting. Painted in 1747 it tells chromatically and stylistically how far the Order and its magistracy had departed from its crusading hospitaller origins. Dressed in flowing ermine robes Pinto almost sweats vanity and decadence as he points at the jewelled crown symbolically placed in front of his redundant steel helmet. Other works include the late 16th-century *Baptism of Christ* by **Matteo Perez d'Aleccio** (once St John's titular painting), the old Aragonese altarpiece of St George by Frederico Potenzano from 1585, a portrait of Grand Master Nicholas Cotoner by **Mattia Preti** and a portrait of Preti himself. In what is now the entrance to the sacristy there was once a chapel for the remainder of the English *langue*, which ceased to exist after 1540, following Henry VIII's break with Rome. Note Preti's *lunette* of the *Birth of the Virgin*. At the foot of the pillar is his tombstone; a grateful Order had made him a Knight of Grace.

The Chapels and Sanctuary

Walk clockwise beginning to the left of the main door. In Cassar's original layout each of the chapels was gated and compartmentalized; the narrow ambulatory that now exists was cut through the walls on Preti's instigation in the 17th century. The **Chapel of Germany [5]** is dedicated to the Epiphany. Towards the end of the 17th century Stefano Erardi painted the altarpiece, the *Adoration of the Magi* and the two *lunettes*. The white marble altar is the only remaining 17th-century baroque altar in St John's. The **Chapel of Italy [6]** houses the painting of *St Jerome,* the second of Caravaggio's works in Malta. It was stolen from St John's Museum in December 1984 and recovered in August 1987 after which it was restored and returned to its original setting.

Caravaggio's startling, almost photographicly precise style, manages to convey both the physical and metaphysical compassion in St Jerome even though the study shows only his face and torso (somehow even St Jerome's ever-present talisman, the skull, appears benign). By comparison, Preti's refined altarpiece of the Italian knights' patron saint, St Catherine, and the black marble mausoleum of Grand Master Carafa, pale into undeserved insignificance.

The **Chapel of France [7]**, dedicated to St Paul, was 'restored' in the 1840s by those who wished to purify Christian art and eradicate the baroque legacies. The walls and altar were changed and the only principal work to survive is Preti's altarpiece. The **mausolea** are a languidly reclining Vicomte de Beaujolais, brother of the future King Louis Phillipe, Grand Masters de Rohan and Adrien de Wignacourt, and his brother Marquis Giochim de Wignacourt. All except for the Vicomte's (and possibly the Marquis's) were badly 'altered' during the anti-baroque purges. The **Chapel of Provence [8]**: Provence was the most senior of the *langues*, and the chapel is dedicated to St Michael. The imperial eagle from Grand Master Lascaris's arms are on the wall and he and his successor, Grand Master de Paule, are both interred here. Their inlaid mausolea are typically ornate. Stairs down to the **crypt** are to the right as you face the **Anglo-Bavarian Chapel [9]**, also known as the Chapel of the Relics. Essentially a large niche, it was given to the *langue* in 1784 and held the principal collection of the knights' reliquaries until **Napoleon** stole them. The bronze gates are from the next chapel, to Philermos. The old wooden figurehead of St John is said to have come from *Grand Carrack* in which the knights sailed from Rhodes, and evidently had no cash value to Napoleon.

The **Grand Master's Crypt [10]** is not always open and houses the mausolea of the grand masters who reigned from 1522 to 1623, including de la Valette and L'Isle Adam. The only memorial here to a knight below the rank of grand master is dedicated to Sir Oliver Starkey, de la Valette's loyal English secretary— a great honour. At the east end of the south aisle is the **Chapel of the Blessed Sacrament [12]**, also known as Our Lady of Philermos and a much-venerated chapel. The most important remaining work is the **Renaissance Cross** dating from 1532. Tradition says the silver gates—a gift in 1752 from two knights— were painted black to resemble coarse iron when Napoleon was looting St John's for his war chest. If true, the ruse worked. In the **Chapel of Auvergne [13]** the only mausoleum belongs to Grand Master Chattes Gessan whose distinction comes from having had the briefest reign of any grand master, less than four months in 1660. The altarpiece between exaggerated barley-twist columns is of *The Martyrdom of St Sebastian*, to whom the chapel is dedicated.

The **Chapel of Aragon [14]** is the finest of the chapels and dedicated to St George. **Preti's** altarpiece of St George was the artist's calling card (from Naples) to Grand Master de Redin in 1658, which won him the coveted commission of decorating the vault of St John's (*see* p. 98). All the paintings in the chapel, including the *lunette* of poor St Lawrence about to be griddled to death, are by Preti and encapsulate a decade of his work. The four grand masters' **mausolea** are ranged in chronological order: de Redin, Nicolas Cotoner, his brother Rafael, and Perellos. Note the exuberant Florentine sculpture on Nicolas Cotoner's, where the whole mass of military paraphernalia is supported by two buckling slaves—predictably North African and Levantine. A sombre bust of Perellos sits above Mazzuoli's figures of Charity and Justice on his monument. The **Chapel of Castile et Leon [15]** is dedicated to St James, and the altarpiece is one of Preti's last works. De Vilhena's splendid bronze **mausoleum** (note him inspecting plans of Fort Manoel in relief on the front) is in contrast to the surprisingly classical and restrained monument to Grand Master Pinto. The oval mosaic of Pinto was taken from one of **de Favray**'s works. **The sanctuary [11]**. Following liturgical changes in the mid-17th century the sanctuary was balustraded off and the layout altered. The **high altar** is made of lapis lazuli and other semiprecious stones. The fine 16th-century Flemish bronze **lecterns** were a gift from the Duke of Lorraine, and Grand Master Garzes contributed the walnut **choir stalls**. The huge baroque sculpture of the *Baptism of Christ* dates from the very end of the 17th century. Above, in the apse, Preti painted *St John in Heaven*.

St John's Oratory and Museum

The oratory was built at the request of Grand Master Alof de Wignacourt in 1603, as a place of worship and for adult novices waiting to be admitted to the Order. Until Preti took charge of the decoration in the 1680s it remained, like St John's itself, clinically functional; the gilding, the painted soffits, Grand Master Carafa's marble altar were all added at Preti's instigation. His baroque updating was designed around **Caravaggio's** huge canvas *The Beheading of St John the Baptist*, which until then had been illuminated by a window on the eastern flank. Caravaggio's masterpiece—it has often been referred to as '*the* painting of the 17th century'—should not be missed, but sadly the lighting is poor.

The Beheading of St John the Baptist

As a painter, **Carravaggio** was defined by his unique ability to transform religious subjects into almost three-dimensional life—something the prevailing mannerist artists had been unable to do. For many of his contemporaries he had an altogether *too* realistic style. His inspired use of

Numbers in square brackets refer to the plan on p. 97.

shadow, halftones and subtle light gives powerful physical presence to his subjects—and nowhere more effectively than in this composition. *The Beheading* is a magnificent picture that captures the tortured emotions of each individual present at the chilling scene, set in the deep shadows of a prison. The old lady gripping her head knows the wrong that has been done, and the jug-eared gaoler with outsize keys points to Salome's salver which she clutches with trepidation. The most haunting image to emerge out of the chiaroscuro is not the pitifully trussed-up St John, but the executioner: from behind his back he stealthily removes a knife from its sheath, to finish the work his sword started; his brow is deeply furrowed and his body taut—this is one execution he would rather not have had to perform. He alone tips the painting from being violent into a vilification of violence. The expressions of the two curious onlookers serve to dramatize the pornographic nature of public brutality.

Caravaggio

Michelangelo Merisi da Caravaggio (1571–1610) was born in the town of Caravaggio in the north of Italy. He trained in Milan and is regarded as the greatest of Italy's 17th-century painters. By the time he journeyed to Malta from Naples in July 1607, he was already a celebrated artist in Rome, having attracted both public acclaim and personal notoriety. Soon after his arrival he commenced *The Beheading* for the oratory of St John's. During the ensuing year he painted prodigiously and trained as a novice in the Order; in July 1608, after a papal dispensation, Grand Master Alof de Wignacourt admitted him into the Order with the rank of Knight of Grace. His Maltese *oeuvre* includes paintings of de Wignacourt in different poses (the only one known to survive hangs in the Louvre), *St Jerome* which hangs in the Chapel of Italy, and at least two other works that are either 'lost' or destroyed.

As a master of realism, and light and shade, his skills were a revelation to Maltese artists and their patrons in the Order. But despite his success Caravaggio's fiery character was destined to cause trouble. Fourteen months after his arrival and just two months after he had received his Insignia of St John and Belt of Knighthood (and gifts of two slaves and gold from a grateful de Wignacourt) he was arrested for an unknown crime. The undocumented story states that he was imprisoned in the dungeons of Fort St Angelo from which he somehow contrived to escape and flee to Sicily. It has been cynically, but probably accurately suggested that his escape was orchestrated with de Wignacourt's blessing. Either way, he was tried *in absentia*, defrocked and expelled from the Order on 1 December 1608 as a 'putrid and fetid limb'. From Sicily he travelled back to Naples. Following a near-fatal fight, he sailed north to Porto Ercole, then a simple Spanish outpost, to await a papal pardon. After another violent altercation and a few days imprisonment, he died of malaria, alone and on the beach of Porto Ercole, in 1610, only days before his pardon arrived. He was just 38.

Cathedral Museum

From outside the oratory, and from some of the museum's upstairs windows, you can see the **cemetery** where many of the knights killed during the siege of 1565 are buried. The highlight of the museum is 29 finely crafted tableaux of **Flemish tapestries** found in its three principal rooms. The three cycles of tapestries were commissioned by Grand Master Perellos, upon his election to the magisracy in 1697, from Jodicos de Vos in Belgium for the incredible sum of 40,000 *scudi* (approximately double the cost of a major fort). The 14 square panels (6 m x 6 m) are divided into two seven-piece cycles and all are modelled on drawings by **Rubens**, with the exception of the *Last Supper* which was from a **Poussin**. One cycle tells the *Story of Christ* from the Annunciation, through his entry into Jerusalem to the Resurrection; the other portrays different allegories including the *Triumph of Charity*, the *Destruction of Idolatry* and the *Four Evangelists*. An additional 14 oblong panels (1.8 m x 6.6 m) are hung as fillers in between the principal square panels and majestically depict the disciples, the Virgin Mary, Christ and, rather immodestly, the gracious donor. The tapestries used to be hung in St John's each year on 24 June, the feast of St John the Baptist, but now are used only for special occasions; the last was Pope John Paul II's visit in 1990.

Among the other exhibits and vestments is a collection of **antiphonaries** (illuminated choral books) donated by the Order's first ruler in Malta, Grand Master L'Isle Adam. There is also a sparse collection of church **silverware**. The blame for the sorry state of what must have been one of the most valuable collections of silver in Europe can again be laid at **Napoleon's** door. He stole almost all of it in 1798, together with the silver plates from the Sacra Infermeria (*see below*), and melted his plunder into bullion. Ironically, it went down with his flagship *L'Orient* in Aboukir Bay during the Egyptian campaign. One surviving piece of interest is a 17th-century silver gilt monstrance (it looks like a very ornate mantlepiece clock with an oblong face), which held the Order's most treasured possession—part of the forearm, ostensibly, of St John the Baptist.

Grand Master von Hompesch took the forearm when he fled Malta in 1798 and it ended up in the Imperial Russian collections. Somehow, the monstrance slipped through Napoleon's greedy fingers.

Palazzo di Citta [13]. The Municipal Palace or Banca Giuratale (1720) are grand names for what was and is still the Public Records Office. The building gave many style hints for the splendid Auberge de Castile et Leon put up 10 years later. Built during the brief reign of strait-laced Grand Master Zondadari, it is somewhat out of character with its paymaster. It is a handsome squared-off building of accessible proportions, but with a leaden cornice lightened only by the baroque centrepiece which overflows like a fountain.

St Paul's Shipwreck [14]★. Cassar originally built this church but it has been remodelled and redecorated twice since. As befits a building dedicated to one of Malta's patron saints, it is lavish (though not always tastefully so), and it houses some venerated possessions. The plan is a Latin cross, the dome eliptical and the floor tessellated. The wooden gilded statue of St Paul is by **Melchiorre Gafa** and is solemnly carried through the streets on 10 February each year, the day St Paul's shipwreck is commemorated. Gafa's brother Lorenzo designed the chapel of the Blessed Sacrament in 1680 (left aisle), and **de Favray** painted the altarpiece. The ceiling frescoes depict St Paul's brief sojourn in Malta and were painted at the turn of the century, while the main altarpiece of St Paul and St Luke is from the late 16th century and by the Florentine, Filippo Paladini. Donated to the church by Pope Pius VII in 1818 and most treasured of all, is part of the block upon which St Paul was said to have been beheaded, as well as what is believed to be a part of his right wristbone. *Adm. free, but leave a donation. Multilingual leaflets and/or a sacristan are on hand. Hours tend to be 1100–1245 and 1600–1800 Mon–Fri and Sat 1100–1200 and 1600–1800.*

Great Siege Square and the Law Courts [15]. The Law Courts were built after World War II on the site of the Auberge de Auvergne, which suffered extensive bomb damage. The bronze Great Siege monument facing it is by the Maltese artist Antonio Sciortino.

Republic Square [16]★. Cafés have expanded into the square and it's an excellent place to pause for **refreshments**. During the Order's reign the square was known as Piazza Tesoreria after its treasury building, and in 1891 the British cleared its orange grove and renamed it Queen's Square. In the same year, Valenti's statue of diminutive **Queen Victoria** enveloped in Malta lace replaced the statue of Grand Master de Vilhena on the occasion of her Diamond Jubilee (de Velhena, having originally stood at Fort Manoel, now stands in Floriana).

Bibliotheca (1786–96) [17]★. Behind Queen Victoria is the Bibliotheca or National Library. The library, designed by the Italian Stefano Ittar, was a gift from the French knight de Tencin during Grand Master de Rohan's reign and the last major civil building project the Order was to undertake. The Order first established a library in 1555, soon after its arrival. In 1612 a law was enacted which forbade a knight's own volumes from being disposed of after his death and the library steadily grew from these and other bequests. Today the Bibliotheca houses all the written records of the Order from 1107 to 1798 including the *Processi Nobilari*, a knight's proof of his maternal and paternal lines of nobility, which was required to ensure his acceptance into the Order. Also stored here are the documents of Baldwin I of Jerusalem, the papal bull of Paschal II sanctioning the Order in 1113 and Charles V's 1530 donation of the islands to the Order. Records and minutes of the *Università* augment a collection of over 60,000 volumes and thousands of manuscripts. **Napoleon** ordered all the records be destroyed but fortunately knightly shuffling of feet saved the priceless collection.

There is a constantly changing display of documents and books, and the statue on the main stairs is of Dun Karm, the national poet. *Winter Mon–Fri 0800–1800, Sat 0800–1330. Summer 0800–1330 Mon–Sat. Adm. free.*

Palace Square [18]. This historic square is now a car park, mainly for the use of the Maltese parliament which sits in the Grand Master's Palace. The two most notable events to have taken place here are the execution of Father Michael Xerri and 33 others by the French after a failed plot to help overthrow the besieged French garrison in 1799, and the presentation of the **George Cross** to the Maltese people by King George VI during World War II.

The Grand Master's Palace (1571) [19]★★

The Grand Master's Palace is an almost square building occupying an entire block and housing Malta's House of Representatives, the Palace Armoury, the president's office and notable state rooms (the Armoury and the state rooms are open to the public). In days past it was the official residence of the grand master, and until 1928 the British governor's residence. The main entrance is from Palace Square but there's another and more pleasant entrance, off Republic Square into Prince Alfred's Courtyard, in the corner of which are stairs to the state rooms. On the Palace Square façade are tablet citations from King George VI and President Roosevelt.

The first site chosen for the Grand Master's Palace was the highest point of the new city, where the Auberge de Castile et Leon stands, but Grand Master del Monte preferred life in the more level centre of Valletta. Incorporating one of the very first of the new city's houses—which conveniently belonged to the grand master's nephew—Cassar began work on the Palace in 1571. The design is rather unsatisfyingly grand when taken as whole. It has suffered the usual tinkering (at the the second entrance, for example), and the squat elevation framed by heavy quoins needs to breathe within an empty square as Cassar had intended. By contrast, the two inner courtyards lend it grace.

The Grand Master's Palace

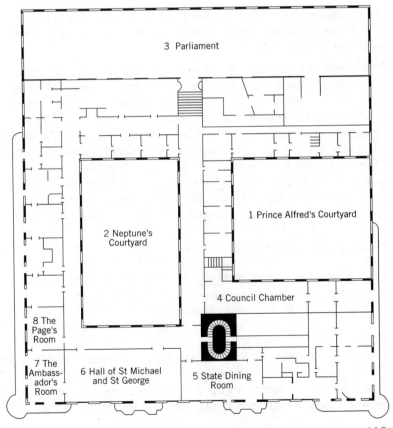

The Courtyards

Originally planted with aromatic orange trees, **Prince Alfred's Courtyard [1]** was rearranged by Governor le Marchand in 1858 and named after Queen Victoria's second son, who visited Malta that year as a humble midshipman. Recently restored, the palace clock was a gift from Grand Master Pinto in 1745 (needless to say the menial figures who strike the bells are Moors). In 1861 the statue of Neptune was moved to **Neptune's Courtyard [2]** from the fish market in the south of the city by Governor le Marchand. (Grand Master Alof de Wignacourt had placed the statue in the market to celebrate the completion of his Rabat–Valletta aquaduct, in 1615.) The large wall fountain behind Neptune bears the Perellos escutcheon.

The Interior

On the piano nobile, *the first-floor living quarters, are security men-cum-guides who will escort you through the state rooms. Their services are free but it is customary to leave a tip.*

The corridors (Armoury, Entrance and Prince of Wales) were undertaken by the Siennese Nicolo Nasini in the 1720s and paved by Governor le Marchand in the 1860s. Nearly all the *lunettes* tell of victorious seafaring engagements against the Turk and the pictures are of grand masters and European aristocrats. The Armoury Corridor leads to the House of Representatives, or **Parliament [3]** (closed to the public). Off it to the left is the **Council Chamber of the Order [4]** or the Tapestry Chamber, where the old legislative assembly sat. Grand Master Perellos, who donated the magnificent tapestries in St John's Museum, also made a gift of the exquisite Gobelin Tapestries, *'Les Tentures des Indes'*, upon his election to the magistracy in 1697, and like those at St John's they all bear Perellos's arms. The 10 panels are of Edenic scenes from the Caribbean and South America. Among the most colourful are 'The Animal Fight' and 'The Fisherman', but all overflow with fine description of what must have been for many contemporary viewers, alien creatures from an unrecognizably verdant land. They were woven in France based on paintings given to Louis XIV in 1679 by the German explorer Prince Johan Moritz of Nassau. It's said that during the sea voyage from Marseilles to Malta in 1702 they were seized by a privateer who forced the captain to ransom them back for their original price. Below the chamber's richly decorated ceiling are frieze panels depicting the victories and voyages of the Order's navy. In between are 10 figures symbolizing human virtues and a painted crucifix to which grand masters and council members would raise their hand when swearing oaths.

The State Dining Room [5] was badly damaged during World War II. It holds some unflattering and self-important portraits of British royalty from George III (Malta became part of the British Empire during his reign) to a youthful Queen Elizabeth II. The Chapter Hall of the Order became the **Hall of St Michael and St George [6]** after the inception of the British chivalric Order of the same name in 1818. The frieze is a contemporary and vivid account of 12 salient events from the Great Siege of 1565, painted by **Matteo Perez d'Aleccio** not long after the siege was raised; it commences to the left of the throne with the arrival of the Turkish fleet in May of that year. The minstrels' gallery opposite depicts six scenes from the Book of Genesis. It was once part of the grand master's private chapel and is said also to have come from the poop deck of the *Grand Carrack* in which the knights sailed from Rhodes. The Ambassador's Room (or Red Room) and the Pages' Room (or Yellow Room) are the only other state rooms open to the public. The grand master would receive foreign dignitaries and hold private audiences in the **Red Room [7]**. The frieze, also by **d'Aleccio**, illustrates episodes from the 200 years of the Order's history before its arrival in Malta. Of the many paintings in the Red Room, the most striking is of the dandified German knight, Frederik Langreve von Hessen. This femine and languid young man with long hair, lace and velvet clothing, and outrageous shoe buckles, was the gallant captain general of the Order's galleys in the mid-17th century. He died a cardinal and is buried in the cathedral at Breslau in Poland. The **de Favray** painting is of Grand Master de L'Isle Adam receiving the keys to Mdina after the Order was given the islands in 1530. The luckless and vain Louis XVI gave the portrait of himself to his compatriot and friend Grand Master de Rohan in 1784, seven years before his luck finally ran out on the guillotine. The suit of armour worn by Grand Master Alof de Wignacourt in his portrait is on display in the Palace Armoury. The **Pages' Room [8]** was the waiting room for the 16 boys who were enrolled in the Order as pages by their noble European parents before they were 12 years of age. When they were 18 they could apply to become a knight. The frieze, more of **d'Aleccio's** handiwork, depicts various noteworthy events of the Order's 13th-century history prior to its departure from the Holy Land. Note the four 16th-century Urbino majolica vases, and **de Favray's** stirring portrait of de la Valette. *Adm. free. Winter 0830–1545 Mon–Fri and summer 0830–1300. Closed Sat, Sun and public holidays.*

Palace Armoury [20]★

The original armoury on the first floor has been the House of Representatives since 1976; the present armoury is housed in the stables off the courtyards.

A knight's armour became the property of the Order after his death; only swords and daggers could be disposed of as part of his *quint* (see p. 56). The British jettisoned a large part of the collection to clear space, but the armoury still contains 5,000 pieces in its comprehensive collection of 16th–18th-century military hardware. Just about every piece of armour (pauldrons, rerebraces, vambraces, coudres, gorgets) of the 15-piece jigsaw that was needed to envelop a crusading knight is displayed. So too are many of the instruments (swords, arquebuses, forks, halberts) designed to penetrate it. Notable pieces include a full damascended suit, said to weigh 50 kg, made in Milan around 1610 for Grand Master Alof de Wignacourt (in Caravaggio's portrait of 1608 hanging in the Louvre, de Wignacourt wears this suit); a complete and wonderful Italian suit of armour made for the French Grand Commander de Verdelin; the Italian half-suit worn by **de la Valette** and, close by, a photograph of the ceremonial sword and dagger given to him by King Phillip II of Spain after the Great Siege. Needless to say, **Napoleon's** magpie-tendancies account for their absence: having stolen the dagger he always carried it in his luggage for good luck, and both weapons are in the Louvre today. Other items include a devilishly clever Italian combined sword and pistol, uncomfortable-looking helmets, cannon, mortar, pistols, arquebuses, and a grand master's carriage from the late 18th century. The standards are those of the different *langues*. The vanquished are also represented, with cases of Turkish weapons and what is claimed to be part of **Dragut Rais's** clothing. *Adm. Lm1 (Sun free). Winter 0830–1630 Mon–Sat, Sun 0830–1545. Summer 0745–1400 Mon–Sun.*

The Wartime Experience [21]★. Crumbling and tired, the Hostel de Verdelin (1662) is nevertheless a welcome ornate intrusion in bleak Palace Square. It was designed by Francesco Buonamici, the Order's resident engineer, who established the baroque style in Malta. Note the bird motifs on the façade: they were a part of the arms of Grand Commander de Verdelin; he once owned the house. Upstairs is a small theatre showing a lump-in-the-throat 45-minute archive film composition of the second siege of Malta during World War II. It's worth seeing. There is also a small static exhibition. *Adm. Lm1.30. Six shows a day Mon–Fri 1000–1600 on the hour. Sat and public holidays 1000–1200.*

Casa Rocca Piccola [22]★. Situated past Palace Square at 74 Republic Street is an elegant private *palazzo* open to the public. The Marquis Nicholas de Piro gives an erudite tour through the eight principal rooms of his home providing, together with the numerous heirlooms, a socio-historical record hitherto not found in Malta. Artefacts arranged on the *enfilade* first floor include children's toys, a knight's sedan chair, a fine piece of 16th-century furniture, a fascinating 'portable' chapel, a mid-17th-century marquetry bureau, numerous portraits, a Venetian chandelier and a rare set of late 18th-century medical instruments from the Sacra Infermeria. *Adm. Lm1, children 50c. Mon–Sat 0900–1300, closed Sun, © 231796.*

Lower Barracca Gardens and the World War II Memorial [23]. The gardens are part of St Christopher's Bastion and have a view of the harbour mouth. At their centre is a small Greek-style folly built in memory of Governor Sir Alexander Ball, who led the siege against the French in 1800 and subsequently became Britain's first civil commissioner of Malta. These gardens, like many of Valletta's open spaces, were cultivated by the French during the 1798–1800 siege, when even a rat was regarded as a treat.

Below and next to St Lazarus's Curtain, on what was an old gun emplacement, are the World War II Memorial and Siege Bell Monument. They commemorate both the 50th anniversary of the presentation of the George Cross and those who died during the conflict. The monument was unveiled in May 1992 by Queen Elizabeth II.

Mediterranean Conference Centre/Sacra Infermeria and the Malta Experience [24]★. Surrounded as they were by the trappings of wealth and privilege it is easy to forget that first and foremost the knights belonged to an Order of hospitallers, formed to heal the sick who pilgrimaged to the Holy Land. Maintaining a hospital was one the very first of the treasury's priorities; each knight, from the grand master down, had to serve and nurse in the hospital. A knight from the French *langue* was the Grand Hospitaller, each *langue* was allocated a day in the hospital during the week and their duties rotated; the grand master attended every Friday. Patients were addressed as *seigneurs malades*, irrespective of rank, race, creed (although non-Catholics had to receive instruction after three days in the Great Ward), and were attended to in the same manner. The finest medicines were dispensed. Pastoral care was undertaken and a 12th-century prayer was said every evening. Food was the best available, all the plates and cups were made of solid silver (which Napoleon's avaricious hands turned into 1,600 kg of bullion, lost forever when his flagship sank in Aboukir Bay).

The **Sacra Infermeria** was one of the first buildings in the new city, commenced in 1574 during the reign of pious old Grand Master de la Cassiere, who also built St John's. The Great Ward, 153 m long, and one of the longest unsupported-roofed expanses in Europe, was designed to hold 300 iron cots (with canopies of wool in winter, cotton gauze in summer), and could accommodate up to 900. The British maintained it as a hospital but in World War II it was virtually destroyed by Axis bombs. In 1979 it reopened as the immense Mediterranean Conference Centre.

The Malta Experience, set in the centre in an air-conditioned purpose-built auditorium, is a 45-minute commercial for Malta—in eight languages, romanticized and telescoped history, sound-bite script and wholesome images—yet it entertains and informs. *Adm. Lm1.50, students 75c. Six shows daily on the hour. Mon–Fri 1100–1600. Sat and Sun 1100 and 1200. There are facilities for disabled visitors.*

Fort St Elmo and the War Museum [25]★

Historic and battle-scarred Fort St Elmo now houses the police academy and is closed to the public. The **War Museum** opened in 1975 and occupies a fraction of the fort's enlarged compound.

History

When the Order first sailed into the Grand Harbour in the autumn of 1530 all that stood on the barren promontory of the Sceberras peninsula was a 15th-century fortified watch tower. In 1552 the star-shaped Fort St Elmo was hastily built by the knights on solid rock to provide protection to both the Marsamxett and Grand Harbours. But there was a flaw in its siting: the fort was exposed from the heights of the peninsula (part way down Republic Street).

When on 18 May 1565 the **Turkish** armada hove into view, the first, and what proved to be catastrophic, decision made by the Turkish command was to lay siege to St Elmo. To that end they established a battery of cannons on the heights of Sceberras; the small fort was expected to fall within 10 days.

Dragut Rais arrived on 2 June and immediately recognised Admiral Piali's and Mustapha Pasha's gross error, but too many Turkish lives had already been lost to alter tactics. So, he swiftly established a further position on what is now Dragut Point and set about cutting off St Elmo's lines of reinforcement across the Grand Harbour to Fort St Angelo. On 18 June Dragut Rais was mortally wounded but by the 20th the fort was effectively surrounded. The survivors of the beleaguered garrison knew that defeat was imminent. A parley was sought, but Mustapha Pasha would give no quarter. The fort was finally stormed and taken on 23 June 1565, the eve of the feast of St John, the Order's patron saint.

It had taken 31 days of remorseless bombardment during which 1,500 Christian lives were lost, 9 knights were captured, 89 were killed and 27 wounded, while only 5 Maltese soldiers swam to Fort St Angelo and safety. For the Moslems it was a Pyrrhic victory; their losses totalled over 8,000 including the octogenarian warrior Dragut Rais, nearly 25 per cent of their entire army. And the battle was the turning point in the Turkish campaign. As Mustapha Pasha was ruefully to remark, 'If so small a son has cost us so dear, what price must we have to pay for so large a father [Fort St Angelo]?'

St Elmo was rebuilt, enlarged and improved during the Order's reign, and was briefly captured during the 'Priest's Revolt' in 1775. The British reinforced the bastions in the late 19th century and added further gun emplacements in the 20th century. The St Elmo breakwater, jutting out to sea in a contortion of rusted steel was destroyed in a daring **Italian** E-Boat raid on 25 July 1941, before St Elmo's guns picked them off.

The War Museum

The entrance is by the east end of the French Curtain. The museum houses a small and poignant collection with exhibits from 1798 to 1945. The principal display item is the **George Cross** awarded to the entire population on 15 April 1942. Other larger exhibits include: a wingless *Faith*, one of the three Gloucester Gladiator bi-planes—nicknamed *Faith*, *Hope* and *Charity*—which were the sum total of the Allies' air-preparedness in the first weeks of the war; an E-Boat or *Barchiono Esplosivo*, a tame-sounding Italian name for a speedboat full of explosives; and General Eisenhower's Willis Jeep used in 'Operation Husky', the invasion of Sicily in 1943. Do not miss the two **milestones** at the entrance, one defaced. The Allied command naïvely believed that such a ruse would induce an invading Axis force to wander the island, lost and confused. *Adm. Lm1, Sun free. Winter 0830–1630 Mon–Sat; Sun 0830–1530. Summer 0745–1330 Mon–Sun.*

Auberge de Bavaria (1629) [26]. This *auberge* was built as a private house, the Palazzo Carnerio, and subsequently purchased for the newly instituted

Anglo-Bavarian *langue* in 1784 (the commander of the cavalry was usually drawn from its ranks). It has been an army officers' mess, a school and is now the government housing ministry, but it is not worth a detour.

Auberge d'Aragon (1571) [27]. Cassar built this, the first and the smallest of the *auberges*. The 'fat' Melitan mouldings around each of the three windows are typical, as are Cassar's chunky quoins. Through the 19th-century portico the intercommunicating rooms encircle a peristyle courtyard. Further down West Street is the Aragonese church, Our Lady of Pillar, built in 1670.

The head of the *langue* was usually the grand conservator in charge of all supplies for both soldiers and hospitals. The building was the prime minister's office in the 1960s and is now the Ministry for Economic Services. Like many of the government organisations here, they don't mind visitors.

St Paul's Anglican Cathedral (1839) [28]. The Auberge d'Allemagne was demolished to provide space for this cathedral, the only major non-military edifice erected by the British during their occupation, paid for by Queen Adelaide—Queen Victoria's aunt and King William IV's widow, while she was convalescing in Malta. From out at sea, its 63 m-tall spire blends in with the Carmelite's dome, and together they are something to aim for in inclement weather. The monument in front is to Dun Michael Xerri who was executed along with 33 others by the French.

Carmelite Church [29]. The present church with its landmark dome that dominates Valletta's skyline bears no resemblance to Cassar's original 16th-century work, which suffered irreparable bomb damage during World War II. It is not by chance that the dome *just* eclipses its Anglican neighbour.

Archbishop's Palace (1622) [30]. Designed by Tommaso Dingli, this dark and forbidding building is still used by the church. The second storey was added in the 1950s.

Manoel Theatre (1731) [31]★

Inconspicuously located in Old Theatre Street, this fascinating little purpose-built baroque building is said to be the third-oldest European theatre still in use. It was built by the benign autocrat Grand Master de Vilhena 'for the honest recreation of the people', according to the Latin inscription above the doorway. Before its restoration it served as a doss house, a dance hall, and a cinema.

The 650-seat auditorium is quite unlike a conventional 20th-century theatre, oval in shape with a tiny stage and orchestra pit. The stalls seat only 272, but above them and beneath the gilded ceiling and chandelier are three full tiers of boxes, including one very discreet grand master's box. All the delicate frescoes are of Mediterranean scenes and in 22-carat gold leaf.

The first performance on 19 January 1732 was of the tragic opera *Merope* performed by the Italian *langue*. The novices took the female parts, and the set was designed by de Mondion in a style less forbidding than his Fort Manoel. Today there is a resident orchestra for what is now Malta's national theatre. Sir Yehudi Menuhin, Dame Kiri Te Kanawa and Vladimir Ashkenazy are among those who have performed here. The *palazzo* Bonici a few doors away serves as a foyer and as a venue for recitals and displays of memorabilia. *Tours: 50c. Mon–Fri 1045 and 1130. Call © 222618/246389 for performance listings of drama, dance and music.*

Strait Street [32]. There is nothing to see here, but the narrow and grubby street is notorious. During the Order's reign it was a venue for illegal duelling, a 'sport' which grew in popularity among the young knights as the prospects of earnest warfare diminished. (Often in order to facilitate a duel, two knights would 'accidentally' bump into one another in the narrow street.) The punishment, if they were caught, varied from expulsion to solitary confinement in St Angelo's *oubliette*. During the British occupation Strait Street acquired the unattractive sobriquet, 'the Gut'—brothels, tacky bars, music-hall dives and streetwalkers, all under crude flashing lights. It was end-to-end sleaze, the Mediterranean fleet's peacetime Saigon. Fortunately, not much of the inglorious history remains.

Auberge de Provence/Museum of Archaeology (1571–5) [33]★★

The **Auberge de Provence** in Republic Street was the third of the French *auberges* (the Auberge de France was totally destroyed in 1942), and was designed by Cassar. The size of the building is deceptive, subtly hidden in the decoration of the façade; it actually spans from the heavy rusticated quoins, through four shops on either side of the portico, beneath the alternating triangular and segmental pediments. The knights of Provence were the most senior of the *langues*, and their head was the grand commandeur, president of the treasury and governor of the arsenal. From the mid-1820s to 1954 the *auberge* housed the Union Club of the British armed forces.

The **museum** is fascinating and should be visited in conjunction with an excursion to any of the principal prehistoric sites in Malta and Gozo (the oldest free-standing monuments in the world). The headless 'Fat' statues of the supposed deities found amongst the ruins are on display here, and there are helpful three-dimensional models of the sites.

Displays begin on the ground floor with **Roman** anchors, the largest of which weighs over 3 tons and was discovered off Buġibba in 1963. As a starting point for a tour use the central and beautifully decorated limestone altar from Ħaġar Qim; to the right is the long **Prehistory Gallery**. The displays here come from different sites and run in chronological order beininning with the Ghar Dalam phase on the righthand wall. The display cases contain various pottery shards, artefacts and primitive jewellery; the central ones show pottery and finds from the Hypogeum (temporarily closed). The next room off the

gallery is the **Tarxien Room** and contains finds and figures from the site and the period (3000–2500 BC). In the **Bronze Age Room**, off the Tarxien Room, relics show how life had changed after the Temple culture inexplicably collapsed and Tarxien became a crematorium (*see* p. 51). To the left of the Ħaġar Qim altar is the **Tarxien Sculpture Room**, containing a model of the site, the original and impressive headless statue of what is presumed to be the **'Fat' goddess of fertility**, the altar from the South Temple and an immense frieze block carved with ocular spirals. The museum also has Punic and Roman relics—including the *cippus* from Marsaxlokk (*see p. 232*)—on the first floor (above the mezzanine) which is due to reopen in 1993; enquire at the ticket desk. *Adm. Lm1, free Sun. Winter Mon–Sat 0830–1630, Sun 0830–1530. Summer Mon–Sun 0745–1330.*

Admiralty House/Museum of Fine Arts [34]★

One of the first of Valletta's buildings, the house was remodelled in the early 1760s as a knight's *palazzo* in the attractive and open style you see today. From 1821 to 1961 it became Admiralty House, the home of the British naval commander in chief of the Mediterranean fleet. Naval luminaries like Admiral Codrington and Lord Mountbatten were based here. Since 1974 it has housed the Museum of Fine Arts.

Allow at least 45 minutes for a look around the 30 rooms of exhibits, predominantly paintings, from the14th century to the present day. The knowledgeable curator, Dominic Cutajar, has an office next to Room 24 on the ground floor and is more helpful than some of the lighting. Begin on the first floor, Rooms 1–13. **Room 1**. 14th-century religious icons. **Room 2**. 15th century. Note the direct and bright *Madonna with Saints* by Domenico di Michelino and the

Nativity scene by Maestro Alberto. **Room 3**. 16th-century north Italian paintings, including work by the Tuscan, Filippo Paladini. He arrived in Malta as a man condemned to life in the galleys but Grand Master de Verdalle had more purposeful employment in mind: Paladini was to decorate the chapel at the Grand Master's Palace, and rooms in Verdala Castle. Note the dark rendition of St Lawrence's martyrdom over hot coals and griddle. **Rooms 4 and 6** have paintings from the Venetian school, notably the *Raising of Lazarus* by Andrea Vicentino and *A Man in Armour* by Domenico Tintoretto. **Room 5**. Dutch school. The painting by the Renaissance artist Jan van Scorel, *Portrait of a Lady*, is one of the museum's most treasured works and has in the past been attributed to Hans Holbein; note how tautly she clasps her hands. **Rooms 7 and 7a**. Apart from the 17th-century paintings the terrace room contains sculptures by the Maltese Antonio Sciortino including the *Great Siege Monument* and *Les Gavroches*. **Rooms 8–10** contain mainly large canvases from the 17th century. Note *Christ the Redeemer* by Guido Reni which used to hang in the grand master's bedchamber, the truly horrific *Martyrdom of St Agatha* by Giovanni Baglione, the portrait of Grand Master Alof de Wignacourt in his armour (itself on display in the Palace Armoury), another interpretation of St John's Beheading (the young girl with the platter awaiting his head is almost too eager) by Mathias Stomer and a painting by the French Caravaggist, le Valentin, in which Judith dispassionately beheads a slumbering Holofernes. **Rooms 12 and 13** are dedicated to the 17th-century artist **Mattia Preti**, whose work adorns many of the island's churches but who is most famous for his vault frescoes at St John's. The forceful *Martyrdom of St Catherine*, a theme to which he liked to return, is matched with the temperate *Baptism of Christ* and the very human depiction of *The Incredulity of St Thomas*.

On the ground floor in **Room 14** the 18th-century French painter **Antoine de Favray** successfully captures the pomp of knights he portrayed: the femininity of de Chambrey belies his seafaring skills, the grandiose Grand Master Pinto is tempered only by the studiousness of the penultimate of Malta's grand masters, de Rohan. In **Room 15** note Claude Joseph Vernet's *Fire on the Tiber*, a searing image of the destructive forces of fire. **Rooms 16 and 17** contain 18th-century Italian works. **Room 19** displays Italian paintings from the 19th century that feature Malta, and **Rooms 20–23** have Maltese works from the 17th to the 20th century. Note the striking 1966 *Benedizione* by Willie Apap. **Room 24** and the basement courtyard and loggia are devoted to contemporary exhibitions.

In the **basement** are artefacts relating to the Order: paintings, armour, coins, religious objects and some of the Sacra Infermeria's silver which Napoleon

missed, as well as a crude but effective model of the Valletta fortifications. *Adm.
Lm1, free Sun. Winter Mon–Sun 0800–0430. Summer Mon–Sun 0800–1400.*

**St John's Cavalier, the Embassy of the Sovereign Order of St John
(1582) [35].** Built either side of what was St George's Gate (now City Gate),
St John's and St James's Cavaliers were vital landward defences for artillery
inside the main *enceinte* of the fortifications, set above the bastions and counterguards in order to fire deeper into the enemy lines.

The Sovereign Military Hospitaller Order of St John of Jerusalem of Rhodes and
of Malta has maintained its embassy in the splendidly restored Cavalier since
1968. The Order is today based in Rome, in effect a state within a state, and the
present grand master is a Scot, Andrew Bertie. The Order continues to do charitable works in developing countries around the world, while locally they help
to maintain services such as a blood bank and the Maltese Cross Corps, a body
similar to the St John's Ambulance.

Hastings Gardens [36]★. When General the Marquis of Hastings, governor of
Malta, died at sea in 1826 his family built a neo-classical monument in which to
inter him. The public space that slowly evolved around the monument became
the Hastings Gardens. The sheer magnitude of **Valletta's fortifications** are
very impressive from here. Walk carefully along the sloping glacis; the stone and
earthworks are over 6 m thick.

Where to Stay

In keeping with the city's somnolent nocturnal bearing Valletta has
only a few hotels. Built in a 1920s colonial style the Forte-owned
Hotel Phoenicia★★★★★ (luxury), The Mall, Floriana, ✆ 225241,
always was the grandest of the island's hotels. Situated just outside
City Gate it has been completely modernized over the past three
years. The new plan has provided 136 rooms and suites and two
rooms designed for the disabled, two restaurants, two bars, a business
centre and a pool set in private 7-acre gardens. The **Castile
Hotel★★★** (moderate) Castile Square, ✆ 243677–9, is centrally
located next to the Auberge de Castile et Leon. It's a welcoming hotel
converted 23 years ago from an imposing old *palazzo*. There are only
38 rooms; those on the first or second floors are more generous. The
second of its two restaurants, the simple Italian La Cave, is in the
cellars—the other is atop the roof—and is frequented by the
cognoscenti. The **Osborne★★★** (moderate), 50 South Street,

Numbers in square brackets refer to the map on p. 93.

© 243656, was spurned by Evelyn Waugh in 1930 but patronized by HSH Prince Louis of Battenburg and the Duke of Bronte. It provides 60 efficient rooms 150 m from Republic Street. The old **British Hotel★★** (inexpensive), 267 St Ursula Street, © 224730, is tricky to find, perched above the bastions, but has stunning views of the Grand Harbour and the Three Cities. Family run for over 60 years, it has 44 simple rooms (nos. 105–6 have huge balconies), the ubiquitous sun-trap roof and a restaurant. It's good-value accommodation, especially for long periods. Almost next door, the **Grand Harbour Hotel★★** (inexpensive), 47 Battery Street, © 242219, with 34 rooms is similar, but a little smaller and lacking the quirky charm of its neighbour. If you just want a B&B in the middle of town, the **Hotel Cumberland★★** (inexpensive), 111 St John Street, © 237732, has 16 rooms all with private bathrooms. At Lm5 per night per person, it's the best budget accommodation available.

Cafés

The Italian influence prevails in the city's cafés. The most famous is the **Café Cordina** facing Republic Square; a two-sip *espresso* chased by an *averna* is the medicament of the lawyers and businessmen who frequent the long chrome bar. Shaded by large umbrellas in the square itself are **Cordina's, Eddies** and the **Café Premier** serving snacks and beverages all day. They are places to meet up, write cards and break for lunch under the watchful eye of Queen Victoria and her pigeons. Opposite the remains of the Opera House in South Street is the popular indoor café **Prego**. It's not swanky but serves a good *capuchino* and has been in the same family for over 50 years. **Café Ranieri** half way down Republic Street is a narrow marble-and-mirror establishment bustling at lunchtime. For a little quiet and shade try **Café San Giovanni** in small St John's Square. The best on-the-hoof snacks come from **Aguis** opposite St Paul's Shipwreck in St Paul's Street; it's no more than a cupboard but the *pastizzi* and flakey *timpana* are the tastiest in Valletta. Queue with the Maltese and improve your grasp of the language.

Restaurants

Eating out in Valletta is mostly the province of business- and expense-account holders, and then only at lunchtime; except at weekends, hardly anyone comes into the city to eat in the evening. The city's finest establishment (possibly Malta's) is **The Carriage** (expensive), 22–5 Valletta Buildings, South Street, © 247828. Lunch only Tues–Fri, dinner Fri and Sat. Set in a penthouse with terrace, atop a unprepossessing building designed by Dom Mintoff, it has *élan* with crisp white New York walls, navy furniture and food that is an unusual convention of Italian, French, American and Oriental cuisines; begin with borlotti beans with tomato and basil followed by steamed bass with ginger, and finish with pecan pie with honey and vanilla ice cream. Don't fail to try the creamed potatoes with olive oil and chives. For spectacular views of Fort Manoel and hearty portions try **Giannini's** (expensive), 23 Windmill Street, by St Michael's demi-bastion, © 237121 (in summer dinner only, and in winter lunch only). This converted townhouse is a good business venue, with a cool bar downstairs and a restaurant upstairs. Plump for the tasty *osso buco* and homemade ratatouille, the fish is sometimes over-cooked. Nibble *Helwa tal-tork*, literally 'Turkish sweet', over a coffee and muse over the expansive view. Book in advance.

Other, less serious restaurants include the **Sicilia** (inexpensive), 1a St John's Street, © 240569 (lunch only), on a platform terrace above the Victoria Gate overlooking the Grand Harbour and Three Cities. Inside is minute but everyone congregates on the terrace in summer. From the small menu pick *Spaghetti al Cozze* and the *lampuki* when in season, or a simple omelette. For a good wholesome no-nonsense *trattoria* you will not do better than **Da Pippo** (inexpensive), 136 Melita Street, © 248029. You could be in a Roman side street—cool rough-hewn stone walls, green-and-white check tableclothes, and a typical Italian menu of pastas, risottos and meat specials, snappily served. **Laronde Pizzeria** (cheap), 5 Windmill Street, © 239012 (opposite Hastings Gardens) is open 0800–2300 and serves 20 different pizzas in a clean little restaurant. Next to St John's Square is **Luciano** (cheap), 21/22 Merchants Street, © 236212. Up two flights of stairs it's as stark as an empty hospital ward, but here they do serve a set lunch of pasta, a glass of local wine and ice cream for Lm1.40. Or you can choose a pizza. In winter go to **La Cave** (inexpensive), Castile Square, © 243677, in the basement cellars of the Castile Hotel. Large crusty pizzas, a salad and a bottle of heady Barolo from a superb wine list will ensure the afternoon is a write-off.

A big **market** is held every Sunday in St James's Ditch, beginning at the Triton Fountain from approximately 0630 to 1300. You can find everything: puppies, plants, Sunday papers, stereos, watches, impossibly long 9-m fishing rods and tackle, antiques, *brocante* (which here means anything with rust on it), lace, confectionery, clothes, Tiger Balm. If you are ochlophobic avoid it. Valletta has a **daily market**, a scaled-down version of the Sunday one, beginning at St John's Square in Merchants Street; its stalls are full of bolts of cloth, religious pictures, tapes and useless but riveting cheap imports from the Far East.

You will only find **food** in the newly refurbished covered market a little further on in Merchants Street. The **fish market** beneath Lower Barracca Gardens on the wharf deals *wholesale*. This is where to come if you don't mind getting up at 0400—it's shut by 0630—and want to buy a box of a fresh catch.

For anything other than food shopping, Valletta is usually a place of last resort. Republic Street, the main thoroughfare, is for the most part pedestrianized and stores are to be found off it in most of the side streets before Palace Square. **Jewellery and clothes** shops predominate. Beginning inside City Gate at the would-be bazaar, Freedom Square, is the Artisans Centre with a comprehensive choice of good Maltese souvenirs. South Street has a few good shops: on the corner is Wembley's, a decent little **food store**; further down is Edwards, the best in the city for **handbags and shoes**; ABC is a comprehensive **stationers**; **Galea's Art Gallery** has watercolours from Lm20. Around the corner in Strait Street is **La Valette Art Gallery**. Back in Republic Street is Charles Grech for **spirits and cigars**, the **Economic British Dispensary** which serves 'toilet preparations', and Sapienza's with the best selection of **English books** in Malta. Further along Republic Street, Square Deal sells **clothes** for the sartorially brave and Tip Top has **audio and electronic** goods. Before St John's Square in Melita Street is Lapin, a delightful **children's clothes shop** and not far away in Zachary Street is Micallef with antique and reproduction **furniture and prints**. In St John's Square is the **Crafts Centre** and the charming old **flower kiosk** of F. Zammit. For the unstructured look in **men's clothing** try Pop 84 at the Merchants Street corner of the square. **BHS** is in Merchants Street along with the other tailors. For

cakes go to C. Camilleri which has been established since 1843; nearby L. Psaila still sells **confectionery** by weight from glass jars. **Marks and Spencer** has a branch in Old Theatre Street next to the Café Cordina, and on the other side of Cordina's is Ascot House for **classical men's clothes**. Republic Street continues past Palace Square and there is a small **antiques** shop and a couple of small **silversmith** workshops: The Silversmiths Shop and Ardnael near to Casa Roca Piccola. Palace Antiques is halfway up Archbishop Street.

Floriana

Floriana, Valletta's immediate suburb a few hundred metres' walk from City Gate, offers an interesting short walk down to the Argotti Botanical Gardens and St Philip's Gardens, laid out in what was the most landward of Mount Sceberras's fortifications and the Floriana Lines.

The town itself was planned by the compulsive builder Grand Master de Vilhena soon after he assumed the magistracy in 1722. The land was to be sandwiched between the fortifications of the Floriana Lines (which span the girth of Mount Sceberras from Pieta Creek to the Grand Harbour) and Valletta's bastions in a grid pattern with wide open spaces. In spite of Axis bomb damage during World War II much of the original scheme remains.

Festa

Floriana remembers **St Publius** on the 3rd Sunday after Easter.

The Floriana Lines: Defences for Fortress Valletta

Canny Grand Master de Paule feared a major Ottoman offensive in 1634 and, as often in times of crisis, turned to Rome for help. Pope Urban VIII heeded his request and sent the engineer Pietro Paolo Floriani, a celebrated military engineer and sometime critic of Laparelli, the engineer of Valletta.

Due to the longer ranges and increased destructive powers of 17th-century weaponry, Floriani proposed enclosing the high ground beyond Valletta itself with a massive rectangular *enceinte*. He planned further to add a complex of bastions, ravelins, counterguards, deep ditches and a neck-like hornwork protruding down the Grand Harbour. The stupendous cost of the proposals— they were larger than the entire fortifications of Valletta—met with loud criticism, but commenced in 1636. Two years later, and exasperated with the constant sniping, Floriani returned to Italy where he died later in the year. His replacement, Vincenzo da Firenazuola, began work on the Margherita Lines around the Three Cities instead and it wasn't until 1640 that work recommenced on the late Floriani's designs. The work on the massive defence system continued falteringly for many years.

A Tour

The easiest way to see Floriana is to take a short walking tour beginning and ending at the Phoenicia Hotel (see map, p. 122).

The Mall and Maglio Gardens [1]

'Here perish sloth, here perish Cupid's arts,
  Knights, where on you this strip I now bestow,
  Here play your games and steel your warlike hearts,
  Not let wine, women, dicing bring you low.'

The French knight Jean Lascaris was an ugly and stern authoritarian who succeeded the opulent de Paule. He was a killjoy and became grand master in his 75th year and died in 1657 a wizened 97; today he is remembered in a Maltese slang insult, *wiċċ Laskari*, meaning 'a really sour face'. Lascaris was convinced that his youthful knights needed physical exercise to keep at bay the eternal damnation that wine, women, and gambling would bring about. So in the first years of his long reign (1636–57) he built a narrow enclosure (since demolished) in what is now the Maglio Gardens, for the ball game *palla a maglio*, or pall-mall, and placed the stanza *above* in Latin on its wall.

Today the Mall and Maglio Gardens begin behind the impressive **Independence Monument** which replaced the grand and much-moved statue of Grand Master de Vilhena. (It has finally found a home in Pope John XXIII Square by St Anne Street, and previously stood on Manoel Island, and in Republic Square.) The 400-m long, narrow gardens are punctuated with statues of Maltese luminaries. The football pitch to the right of them was the old British military parade ground. To the left of the gardens are the **Granaries**, which look like rows of immense piggy-bank corks but are in fact the lids of the wood-lined underground grain stores in which the Order preserved two years' supply. With a banker's eye, the knights maintained a highly profitable monopoly on the sale of grain.

The Church of St Publius [2]. St Publius was the Roman governor at the time of St Paul's shipwreck in AD 60 and after his conversion to Christianity became the first bishop of Malta.

Originally designed by Guiseppe Bonnici in 1733, this is the last important parish church built by the Order. The entire structure was rebuilt after near destruction by the Axis bombing. The portico and its two tall bell towers were

Floriana

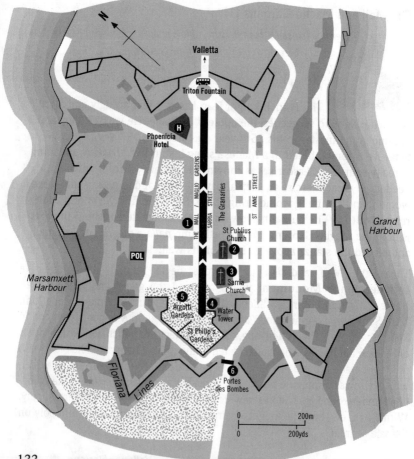

added in 1882 to a design by Dr Nicola Zammit, who was also responsible for the new façade at St Nicholas Siġġiewi.

Sarria Church (1676) [3]. This bizarre-looking small cylindrical church has a disputed but undoubtedly elegant provenance, being designed by either the artist Mattia Preti or Lorenzo Gafa. The first church on this site was built in 1585 by the knight de Sarria Navarro and dedicated to sailors. Grand Master Nicolas Cotoner commissioned the present building, hence his cotton-flower motif, following the virulent nine-month plague of 1675 when over 8,000 died. The lunettes and the paintings are by Preti. The church is maintained by the Jesuits.

Wignacourt Water Tower [4]. The rocket-like tower opposite was a staging post and fountain from fresh water that flowed along the Mdina–Valletta aquaduct built by Grand Master Alof de Wignacourt in 1615; it is his escutcheon above the door.

Argotti Botanical Gardens and St Philip's Gardens [5]. In 1805 a Carmelite friar with the deliciously implausible name of Carolus Hyacinthus was appointed Malta's first professor of natural history by the British governor, Sir Alexander Ball. Hyacinthus assembled the plants in Floriana's Mall and 50 years later they were moved to the site of the present **Argotti Gardens**, then the preserve of a deceased knight with the equally improbable name of Ignatius de Argote De Gusman.

The gardens are divided into two, the public and the private, and both are open to the public. There are many hundreds of cactii, succulents and plants, indigenous and foreign. (*Adm. free. Private gardens 0800–1130 and 1300–1545 winter, and 0730–1230 summer.*)

St Philip's Gardens are below the Argotti Gardens on the saint's eponymous bastion. This point is almost the very end of Valletta's landward fortifications; beyond lie the counterguards and the Portes des Bombes.

Porte des Bombes [6]. On any trip into Valletta you will pass through or by the Portes des Bombes, one of two gates built between 1697 and 1720 that once pierced the curtain-wall defences of the Floriana Lines (the northern gate, the Gate of Our Lady has been destroyed). Originally a simple single-arched structure with a drawbridge, the archway was doubled in 1868 when the curtain wall either side of it was dismantled to allow traffic to flow. Its escutcheon and emblems are those of Grand Master Perellos in whose reign it was constructed.

The Three Cities

Today tourism is Malta's single-largest money-earner and yet it remains a maritime nation. From the 7th century BC when Phoenician traders first anchored their vessels laden with precious eastern cargoes, the harbour has been the island's most valuable asset. Almost every seafaring power throughout history has at one time coveted the protection that the Grand Harbour could afford a fleet. The towns of **Senglea**, **Vittoriosa** and **Cospicua**, and their sheltered creeks, continue to be defined by their proximity to it.

The Three Cities (christened by Napoleon in the over-optimistic belief that a shared identity would impose civic order on the Maltese who lived there) are still also confusingly referred to by different monikers: collectively as 'the Cottonera' after the surrounding fortification lines and individually by their pre-Great Siege names of **L'Isla**, **Birgu** and **Bormla**. Together though, they cohere into one large industrious, not industrial town, strongly aligned to the Malta Labour Party; almost the entire workforce is dependent on the dockyards and its ancillary businesses for a living. Despite the island's common heritage, the inhabitants of the Three Cities have distanced themselves from the other towns and villages. Yet, perversely, they maintain a fierce pride and competitive spirit between each other. Even the people of Valletta used to refer to them as '*min naha l'ohrx* (those from the other side).

Anyone whose appetite has been whetted by the history of the knights should walk around the narrow little streets of **Vittoriosa**, where the Order first established itself and where the new Maritime Museum is located. **Senglea** and **Cospicua** have very little of conventional interest, due for the most part to catastrophic bomb damage during World War II. (In April 1942 alone, 3,156 tons of bombs fell in the dockyard area.) Don't expect genteel cafés or tranquility—they are for the most part unaffordable and unwanted commodities; the street life here is different and noisier. The housewives' high-pitched scream, '*aeya!*' used to attract the attention of children, friends, husbands or dogs and is an ear-denting and constant refrain. Idleness is not a common pastime and even on hot afternoons and Sundays you catch people fabricating furniture or rebuilding a wall. And the first time you hear a frightening screech rent through the hot mid-afternoon calm don't duck, it's just the old air-raid sirens signalling the end of the day's labours in the dockyards.

History

Phoenicians, Romans, Arabs and Normans all found shelter here, settled and fortified, however modestly, the site of Fort St Angelo. In addition (save for the 9th-century Arabs), they supposedly built temples to their gods—the Phoenicians to Astarte, their goddess of fertility, and the Romans to Juno, wife of Jupiter. Count Roger the Norman erected a church where the church of St Lawrence now stands. Alas, none of their heritage remains.

There were only two principal towns in Malta when the Order, weary and despondent from wandering the Mediterranean for seven years, first decamped under the leadership of Grand Master L'Isle Adam in the autumn of 1530: the capital, *Citta Notabile* (Mdina) and **Birgu**. As a hardened body of seafaring knights, the Order chose not to move in with a soft Maltese aristocracy in Mdina. So they moored their fleet between the two peninsulas of the Grand Harbour in *Porto delle Galere* or Galley Creek (now **Dockyard Creek**) and half-heartedly began to change the cramped settlement of ramshackle houses at the water's edge that was Birgu into a congenial convent of *auberges*, a church and a hospital.

L'Isle Adam found a ruinously poor fort at the tip of Birgu called **St Angelo**, where armaments consisted of 'two guns, two falcons, and a few old mortars'. He immediately set about reinforcing it, but it was not until 11 years later under Grand Master de Homedes that real works commenced. Initially, the Emperor of Spain's Italian military engineer, Ferramolino, advised abandoning Birgu altogether and starting afresh on Mount Sceberras; advice de Homedes rejected and the Order was to regret. The preliminary works in 1541 entailed the fortification of the northern flank of Birgu, the reinforcement of St Angelo and its separation from Birgu itself by a wide ditch. After Ferramolino was killed in 1550, his replacement Pietro Pardo advised on further defensive works to **L'Isla**, the parallel and uninhabited peninsula. Despite the unwelcome attentions of the Turks and Dragut in 1551, **Fort St Michael** on L'Isla was completed within three years. Nevertheless, the clever and quickly-built defences were improvised and anything but comprehensive.

Twelve years later during the **Great Siege of 1565** the towns of Birgu and L'Isla and their forts of St Angelo and St Michael were bombarded constantly for nearly four months. As a single fighting and defensive unit the two peninsulas were able to withstand the Turkish might: Vittoriosa (Birgu) was fortified to the east and south, Senglea (L'Isla) to the west and south, and to the north the **Great Chain** stretched across the mouth of Galley Creek (Dockyard Creek) protecting the fleet. After the Turks' defeat, the knights, instead of immediately repairing the damage, husbanded their resources and concentrated on their new project—the fortified city of Valletta.

During the middle of the 17th century, when the **Floriana Lines** immediately outside Valletta were under construction, focus returned to the Three Cities with construction of the **Margherita Lines** (1638) to protect Cospicua (and to a lesser degree Vittoriosa and Senglea) from the vulnerable east and south. In a similar, but far more grandiose vein, the Margherita Lines were themselves to be incorporated in a new defensive scheme. Work began on Grand Master Nicolas Cotoner's **Cottonera Lines** in 1670 to a design by the Duke of Savoy's engineer, Marizio Valperga. The defences were to provide fortified shelter for 40,000 people, with eight formidable bastions, two semi-bastions and connected curtains that would stretch in a vast semi-circle for 4,572 m from French Creek to Kalkara Creek. Grand Master Nicolas Cotoner nearly bankrupted himself with the project, and work came to an abrupt halt upon his death in 1680. (Much still stands, most impressively, the **Zabbar Gate**.)

In the early 19th century after Malta became a Crown Colony, the **British** continued to exploit the Order's established naval tradition. The Three Cities and the Grand Harbour became the home of the **Mediterranean fleet**; even Fort St Angelo was renamed HMS *St Angelo*. This era was to be the heyday of the Three Cities, when the magnificent warships of the 19th and 20th centuries provided employment and prosperity in a time of comparative peace in the central Mediterranean. Then the outbreak of hostilities in 1939 and the hitherto unknown (in Malta's terms) dimension of aerial warfare brought about in 27 months what the Turks had failed to do in 268 years—the near total destruction of the area. The skill of the *Luftwaffe* and the *Regia Aeronautica* meant a sizeable proportion of the £30 million postwar grant from a grateful Britain was spent on the reparation of the level rubble the Three Cities had in effect become. Unfortunately, the rebuilding was hasty and lacked a plan; but the communities returned and the dockyards began to function once again.

In the 1970s and early 1980s the drydocks expanded and diverse commercial concerns were courted by the entrenched socialist prime minister, **Dom Mintoff**; the Chinese built a massive drydock, and part of Fort St Rocco was converted into The Mediterranean Film Studios where, among many other epics,

'**Raise the Titanic**' was filmed, almost entirely in its huge water tank. The producer, Lord Lew Grade wryly commented on the financial black-hole that was his movie: 'Raise the Titanic, it would have been cheaper to drain the Atlantic'.

Getting Around

The Three Cities are the most confusing and frustrating places to find and negotiate by **car**. Don't be fooled by new road signs with the legend 'Three Cities'—they dissolve into thin air just when you need them. From Valletta follow signs for Marsa where, at the roundabout, all the helpful signs expire, then follow the sign marked 'Airport'. Pertinent signs should reappear but this time but will be marked 'Bormla' and 'Maritime Museum'; like a bloodhound stick to the trail of the **Maritime Museum** and keep the mosque's minaret on your right. At the next T-junction Senglea is to the left, and Vittoriosa (unhelpfully flagged Birgu) and Kalkara are to the right.

Upon arriving at **Vittoriosa**, go straight on if you intend to visit the new Maritime Museum. If you wish to explore Vittoriosa, enter via the main gate at the Poste de Provence. Just before the 'No Entry' sign at the beginning of Main Gate Street turn right into St John's Tower Street where you should be able to park; this is also the starting point of the Historical Tour (*see below*).

Vittoriosa **bus terminus** is opposite the Poste de Provence and for Senglea and Cospicua, buses stop adjacent to the main square.

The **Vintage Omnibus Co.**, © 331961/310435, has two regular tours lasting approximately 2 hours, which depart from the Ferries in Sliema every day (except Sunday) and take in the sights and remaining fortifications of the Three Cities. (*1000 and 1400. Lm3.25 adults, Lm2. children.*)

Tourist Information

The **NTOM** in Valletta give away a useful walking map of Senglea and Vittoriosa, but many of the street names have changed since its publication.

Don't be alarmed by stares or sideways glances. The people who live in these tight-knit communities are merely curious; they are amongst the friendliest and most open in Malta.

Senglea remembers the Birth of the Virgin Mary on 8 September, **Vittoriosa** has St Lawrence's feast on 10 August and in **Cospicua** the Immaculate Conception is celebrated on 10 December.

Senglea

This barren and stubby finger of land pointing into the Grand Harbour separates two strategic waterways, Dockyard Creek and French Creek. The town, along with its immediate neighbour Cospicua was almost totally destroyed during World War II, and there is little to see here except some early fortifications on the west and the photogenic *vedette*.

The peninsula was totally uninhabited until Grand Master de Homedes (1536–53) turned it into his lush private park. His successor Grand Master de la Sengle had more altruistic ideas; in 1554 he settled the land and distributed free plots to anyone prepared to build a house. After Fort St Elmo fell on 23 June 1565 during the **Great Siege** the Turkish commanders turned their fire onto Fort St Michael at the landward end of the peninsula. On the morning of 7 August 1565, the Turk simultaneously stormed both peninsulas (8,000 Moslem soldiers attacked Fort St Michael alone), but this proved to be another disaster for the Turks who lost 2,000 men, with a similar number of wounded; the knights escaped with comparatively light casualities. The historic old fort survived only to be dismantled by the British early this century to make way for two graving docks for the Royal Navy.

The postwar plan has one principal street, Victory Street, that runs from the rebuilt church of Our Lady of Victory at the landward end to diminutive **Safe Haven Gardens** at the harbour end. The view of Valletta, Vittoriosa and the whole of the Grand Harbour from the gardens provides a stirring panorama. Located here is Senglea's totem—an hexagonal *vedette*, or lookout post with an intricately carved relief of two eyes and two ears representing constant vigilance for an enemy fleet. Under the *vedette* and just below the surface of the water, the **Great Chain**, forged in Venice, spanned the mouth of Galley Creek (Dockyard Creek) to Fort St Angelo

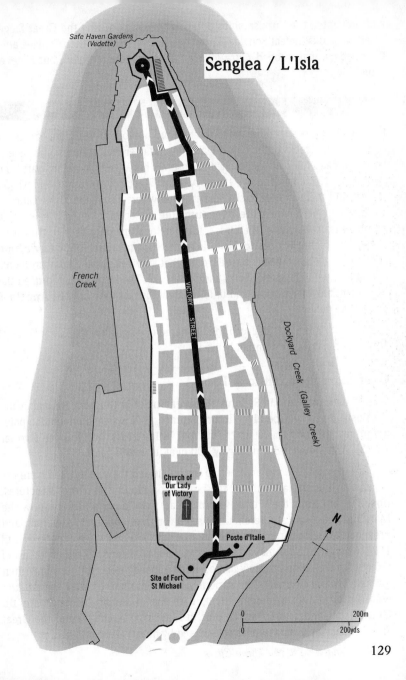

Senglea / L'Isla

Safe Haven Gardens
(Vedette)

French
Creek

VICTORY STREET

Dockyard Creek (Galley Creek)

Church of
Our Lady
of Victory

Poste d'Italie

Site of Fort
St Michael

N

0   200m
0   200yds

and prevented the Turkish ships entering the creek during the Great Siege. After the Turks' defeat Senglea (known originally as L'Isla, then Senglea after its founder), was dubbed *Citta Invitta*, 'the unconquered city', but it never caught on.

Vittoriosa

Historically, whoever commanded the thin promontory of Vittoriosa effectively controlled the creeks of the Grand Harbour, and over the centuries all invaders, hostile or peaceful, have established themselves here. Sadly, nothing apart from two Siculo-Norman windows (*see opposite* [9]) survives from the pre-1530 settlers. But there is more to see here than anywhere else in the Three Cities— an excellent new **Maritime Museum**, the unceremonious and seemingly humble first *auberges* of the Order, fortifications that date back to the Great Siege, the sombre **Inquisitor's Palace**, the stirring church of **St Lawrence** and amazingly many ancient little streets that survived horrific bombardments during both Great Sieges of 1565 and of 1940–3. The knights only fortified the northeast flank of Vittoriosa and unfortunately their historic **Fort St Angelo** is shut to the public.

Vittoriosa ('Victorious') replaced the old name of *Birgu* after the Great Siege of 1565. Both names are commonly used.

Orientation and an Historic Tour

Begin the walking tour in **St John's Tower Street** just in from the main gate, the **Poste de Provence [1]**. **Victory Square [14]** is a good orientation point if you get temporarily lost in the narrow little streets, but you can't go far wrong—Vittoriosa is 850 m long by 400 m at its widest point.

None of the old *auberges* are open to the public and the sites marked • are not worth a detour and are only for the history-conscious. The row of structures, **nos. 19–26**, along the Vittoriosa Wharf past the old Naval Bakery (now the Maritime Museum) are derelict. All seven original *auberges* (Auvergne and Provence shared quarters) were built around 1535 and were occupied until 1571 when the Order moved to Valletta. Four still stand, to the northeast of Victory Square in the bizarrely named Hilda Tabone Street (formerly and often marked Britannic Street). The various *postes* were named after the *langues* whose duty it was to defend them, with the exception of the **Poste de Genoa**—a Genoese ship was in port in May 1565 at the start of the Great Siege, and its luckless crew was conscripted by de la Valette into battle.

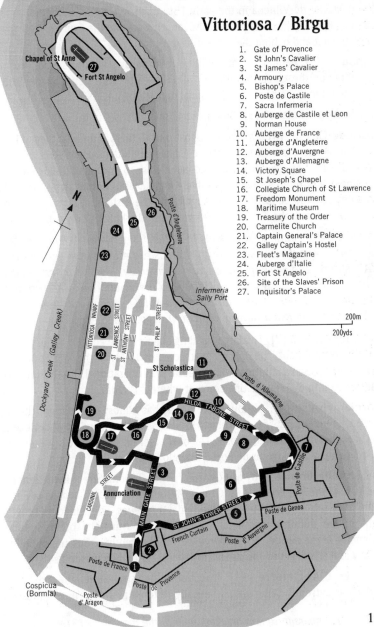

Vittoriosa / Birgu

1. Gate of Provence
2. St John's Cavalier
3. St James' Cavalier
4. Armoury
5. Bishop's Palace
6. Poste de Castile
7. Sacra Infermeria
8. Auberge de Castile et Leon
9. Norman House
10. Auberge de France
11. Auberge d'Angleterre
12. Auberge d'Auvergne
13. Auberge d'Allemagne
14. Victory Square
15. St Joseph's Chapel
16. Collegiate Church of St Lawrence
17. Freedom Monument
18. Maritime Museum
19. Treasury of the Order
20. Carmelite Church
21. Captain General's Palace
22. Galley Captain's Hostel
23. Fleet's Magazine
24. Auberge d'Italie
25. Fort St Angelo
26. Site of the Slaves' Prison
27. Inquisitor's Palace

The Gate of Provence [1]. The simple main gate into town was restored by Grand Master de Vilhena in the early 18th century. The two other entrances into the city, the elaborately carved Advanced Gate and the Couvre Porte Gate, are to the left and behind the Poste d'Aragon.

Armoury• [4]. Behind St James Bastion (now partly a training school) was the old store for the Order's ordnance. In the early 18th century the British converted it into their first naval hospital on Malta.

The Bishop's Palace• [5]. Built in 1542 and enlarged in the 17th century.

Poste de Castile [6]. On the 7 August during the 1565 Great Siege, 4,000 Turkish soldiers attacked the Poste de Castile (simultaneously a force of 8,000 stormed Fort St Michael in L'Isla) and came close to breaching the defences, at the time one of Birgu's most formidable. Grand Master de la Valette sucessfully led a tiny relief force from Fort St Angelo and the casualties, for such a bloody battle, were small: the Turks lost 200 men, and the knights only 60.

It is possible to continue to walk along all the old northeast defences as far as the Fort St Angelo ditch, taking in the Poste d'Allegmagne and the Poste d'Angleterre and leaving the Sacra Infermeria [7] on your left. Midway between the two postes *is a gap down to the water's edge known as the Infermeria Sally Port; here the wounded soldiers from the besieged Fort St Elmo were brought ashore at night during the Great Siege.*

Sacra Infermeria [7]. The large building almost at the edge of Victory Square was one of the first L'Isle Adam constructed in 1531. In the mid-1600s, and after the new Sacra Infermeria in Valletta was operational, the hospital was transferred into the Benedictine convent where it is today.

Norman House [9]. Although the house has almost fallen down through neglect, the first-floor 15th-century twin Siculo-Norman window and frieze are still in reasonable (restored) repair. The only other pre-1530 relic in Vittoriosa is a 14th-century window inside Fort St Angelo [25].

Auberge de France [10] at nos. 24–7 Hilda Tabone Street is the grandest and first of the *auberges*. Both Grand Masters L'Isle Adam and de la Sengle came from this, the wealthiest of the Order's *langues*. The window to the top right of the building was a later addition and ruins the otherwise calm symmetry of the façade. The *auberge* was until recently a museum of political history and it is believed the site of the Auberge d'Aragon was to its right.

Auberge d'Angleterre [11]. In cobbled Majjistral Street the old English *auberge* is currently being sympathetically restored as a government museum.

The house next door was the private residence of Sir Oliver Starkey, Grand Master de la Valette's loyal secretary (who has the singular honour of being interred next to his master in St John's Co-Cathedral, Valletta (*see* p. 99). The *langue* d'Angleterre, and therefore the *auberge* did not transfer to Valletta due to Henry VIII's break with Rome during the Reformation.

Auberge d'Auvergne et Provence [12]. Near to no. 17 Hilda Tabone Street was the shared home of the knights of these two *langues*. After the 1571 move to Valletta each built their own *auberge*. **Auberge d'Allemagne [13]**. Ironically the Lawrence Ironmongery store facing onto Victory Square is a part of the new façade given to the German *auberge* after it was bombed by the Axis in World War II. The large squat bollard in front marks the beginning of the *collachio*, the knights' living *quartier*.

Victory Square [14]. The centre of Vittoriosa's life for literally hundreds of years. During the worst of the Great Siege, Grand Master de la Valette marshalled his troops here and bolstered the morale of the hungry and cannon-weary civilians. But it suffered much damage in the last war when its old clock tower-cum-vedette was destroyed. Starting at the northwest corner of the square in St Anthony Street was the old Jewish ghetto before 1530. The Victory Monument (commemorating the Turks' defeat) was erected in 1705 and the white statue of Vittoriosa's patron, St Lawrence, in 1880. Note the iron railing on the former— the sword and cross pin down the Turkish crescent.

St Joseph's Chapel [15]. The 18th-century chapel is now a fascinating and comprehensive little museum full of social, ecclesiastical and military paraphernalia. Its most treasured possessions are the hat and sword of Grand Master de la Valette. Among the other exhibits are the last white ensign from HMS *St Angelo*, eight pennant flags from each of the different *langues*, a well-thumbed pack of cards from 1609, an 18th-century sedan chair, a Latin *Vulgatae* bible printed in 1598 in Venice, and a 16th-century Venetian atlas. Note the very long scissors with flat ends; they were devised by a crafty and cautious priesthood to administer the Host during outbreaks of the plague. (*Adm. free but leave a donation. Mon–Sun 0930–1200 and 1500–1600. The friendly curator is invariably on hand.*)

Collegiate Church of St Lawrence [16]. St Lawrence's church is one of, if not the most historically venerated churches in Malta. A church is said to have been built on this site in 1090 by Count Roger the Norman when Birgu was the island's second parish. At the beginning of the 16th century Roger's church was enlarged and on their arrival in 1530 the Order adopted it as their first conventual church. Two years later it was severely damaged by fire, destroying many of the treasures the Order had brought from Rhodes. The church was restored and it was here that Grand Master de la Valette assembled his knights and townsfolk on the eve of the Great Siege to say mass. He and the other survivors returned to give thanks after the Turks' ignominious defeat in the September of 1565. After the Order moved to Valletta it became the inquisitors' church for more than 200 years. In 1820 it was elevated to a collegiate church. During World War II much of it was damaged but has since been faithfully restored. To celebrate its 900th anniversary Pope John Paul II visited it in 1990.

There is nothing twee about this powerful baroque church **Lorenzo Gafa** designed in this his birthplace. The west-facing setting is almost too ideal: 25 m away from the water's edge on a high plinth it accentuates the Order's brand of militant seafaring Catholicism. Work began in 1681 and it took 16 years to complete. Gafa's plan provided for a wide three-bay façade with a two-storey centrepiece, not unlike his later cathedral in Victoria, Gozo. Only the left-hand tower was added in the early 18th century and the church remained very lopsided for over 200 years; the right-hand one was built around the outbreak of World War I (neither tower was to Gafa's design). The explosive depredations of World War II destroyed much of the outer church and, sadly, Gafa's original dome. The two statues in the niches either side of the main west door are of St Paul and St Lawrence.

Much of the rich marble Latin-cross interior is being totally refurbished and many of the paintings are swathed in protective dust sheets. Also, due to works on the dome, it is very gloomy, but the altarpiece of poor St Lawrence being griddled to death still shines out.

Freedom Monument [17]. In front of the church the monument poignantly, if naïvely, shows the end of a not always happy 179-year Anglo-Maltese relationship. Unveiled on 31 March 1979, the day HMS *London* and the Royal Navy weighed anchor in the Grand Harbour for the last time, it depicts a naval rating bidding *adieu* to a Maltese citizen.

Maritime Museum/The Naval Bakery [18]. The Admiralty architect William Scamp designed and built in 1841 the Naval Bakery on the site of the Order's principal arsenal and slipway. It remained in service providing bread and biscuits for the entire Mediterranean fleet for over a hundred years. In July 1992 the first phase of its conversion into the Maritime Museum was inaugurated.

Planned to expand over all three floors, the exhibits (mainly on the first floor) encompass diverse aspects of maritime history from marine archaeology to the instruments used by Customs. The lighting is superb and the paintings, models, instruments and ephemera are shown to good effect. Among the exhibits of note are: a fine painting of the Order's galley squadron engaging Muslim ships off Alexandria in 1644, two rare French cannons, and a massive reconstructed Roman anchor. The many models of note include Grand Master Adrien de Wignacourt's sumptious ceremonial barge, an oared 17th-century galley, a huge 2.5-m training model of one of the Order's 18th-century ships of the line and a model of the first lateenrigged Gozo ferry boats.

Auberge d'Italie• [24] is a site only. The Emperor Charles V's Act of Donation settling the islands on the Order stipulated that the Admiral of the Fleet was to be the *pilier* or head of the *langue* of Italy. To be near to their fleet and Fort St Angelo, the Italian knights built their *auberge* away from their brothers-in-arms.

Fort St Angelo• [25]. 'If so small a son [Fort St Elmo] has cost us so dear, what price must we have to pay for so large a father [St Angelo]', remarked Mustapha Pasha, the Turkish general, while gazing out to Fort St Angelo from the ruins of Fort St Elmo which he had just taken at a cost of over 8,000 of his men during the Great Siege of 1565.

The Order of St John has recently reassumed responsibility for Fort St Angelo after 190 years, but unfortunately it is not open to the public. Restoration works are in hand and they intend to use it for their own purposes. Permission to visit can be easily obtained by writing to the Order's embassy (St John's Cavalier, Valletta), and it is hoped it will be opened on commemorative days such as 8 September, Victory Day. Closed or open Fort St Angelo remains a monument to Malta's strategic role in the conflicts—military and religious—which have bedevilled the central Mediterranean for the last 1,000 years.

Primitive fortifications on the site are believed to have predated the 9th-century Arab occupation. After Count Roger the Norman sacked the Arabs in 1090 he strengthened what existed on this important position at the head of the Grand Harbour. A keep within a fortified *enceinte* subsequently served the feudal overlords until the arrival of the Order in 1530. Grand Master L'Isle Adam found a crumbling fort unable to withstand modern artillery and immediately began a programme of modifications which took 30 years to complete: the Italian engineer Antonio Ferramolino built a landward cavalier and excavated a deep wet ditch to separate St Angelo from Birgu (which also served as a harbour for the Order's flagship); the seat of the ousted governing de Nava family was converted into the magisterial palace, and the 15th-century Chapel of St Anne was restored. (It was here that Grand Master de la Valette prayed during the Great Siege and here, ironically, that he died of heat exhaustion aged 75 in August 1568 while praying after a good day's hunting in Buskett.)

As the Great Siege wore on in the hot summer of 1565, St Angelo was the vital keystone in Grand Master de la Valette's brilliantly-run campaign. From within the fort he kept St Elmo reinforced and victualled, provided supporting fire, and sent out relief troops to the *postes* in Birgu. Ultimately, it was here that he planned that the Order would make its final stand with a handful of brave knights in the event Birgu fell to the Turks. After the Order's victory and with the knights comfortably ensconced in Valletta, repairs were undertaken and it became the Order's dreaded prison.

The Only Coup

Grand Master de la Cassiere (1572–81) was the only grand master ever to be deposed by a *coup d'état* and imprisoned.

A monastic, tough-talking soldier with an unforgiving streak of Christian zeal burning through him, he was already in his 70s when elected in 1572. The liberalism of the Reformation and his somewhat debauched, lawless young knights were a cause of great anxiety to his orthodoxy: what had happened to the Order's crusading morals? In vain, he tried to stop the womanizing, gambling and duelling, and having failed he summoned papal intervention in a fit of pique—the Order was henceforth saddled with an inquisitor (*see opposite* [27]). The knights' patience was by now exhausted, and they staged a bloodless coup to remove the now deaf octogenarian on 5 July 1581. He was escorted to St Angelo, where his imprisonment caused little hardship: he was allowed four knights, four priests and more than 20 other domestics. But Pope Gregory XIII again intervened and summoned both him and his detractors to Rome. De la Cassiere was found innocent of all the 46 charges brought against him, but he died before he could return to Malta. He was given a triumphal funeral in December 1581 and his body was returned to St John's Co-Cathedral (which he had built and paid for), but his heart was removed and buried under a black marble slab in San Luigi dei Francesi in Rome.

Fort St Angelo remained largely unaltered until the end of the 17th century when Carlos de Grunenberg, the Emperor of Spain's engineer, advised that works to the northeast flank at the entrance to the harbours were necessary.

The then financially embarrassed Order subtly and successfully suggested he might like to pay for the four batteries himself. The works can be seen facing Kalkara Creek and were the last to be undertaken in the Order's reign. When **Napoleon** sailed into the Grand Harbour in 1798 the fort's 80 guns remained embarrassingly silent.

The *Oubliette*

In 1906 the British War Department turned Fort St Angelo over to the Royal Navy, and it became Malta's naval barracks. But just before the hand-over to the Navy a loose stone slab was uncovered, under which 4 m down in the living rock was a hollowed-out pit, the feared *oubliette*.

It was here in pitch darkness—freezing in winter, sweltering in summer—that miscreant knights were imprisoned indefinitely; sentences were arbitary and without a time limit but usually knights were kept there until they were either expelled from the Order, as 'putrid and fetid limbs', or executed. Those awaiting execution—by indelicate methods that only blue-blooded aristocrats could dream up: being strangled to death and left in the gutter to be eaten by stray dogs, or trussed up like chickens in weighted sacks and tossed into the Grand Harbour—were said to regard death as merciful release from the dank living hell of the *oubliette*.

The navy renamed the fort HMS *St Angelo*: the fort's governor became the flag captain, the different storeys became 'decks' and the rooms 'cabins'. HMS *St Angelo* took 69 direct hits from the Axis bombers in World War II and until the British forces' withdrawal in 1979 it remained the headquarters of the commander in chief of the Mediterranean fleet.

In the 1970s, an amusing, if surely apocryphal, story was told of a **NATO** Joint Command gathering in St Angelo. The Turkish representative, upon entering the reception remarked, 'Good evening, I believe I am the first Turk to have penetrated thus far.'

Inquisitor's Palace [27]. In Malta the Inquisition did not spend its time painfully extracting heretic confessions, and the palace (open to the public) is a dull building where the Pope's envoy resided; the courtroom and cells are almost disappointingly tame.

The palace is built around three small courtyards, and rooms sprout from them and the main staircase like a maze. Note the ceiling above the main stair on which the inquisitor's emblem—four linked black and white crosses chillingly resembling a swastika in reverse—is painted. The principal room at the top of the stairs gloomily displays the coat of arms of each inquisitor (the black hats denote the rank of inquisitor whilst the red denotes that of cardinal). The only fun to be had (some of the cells are used as broom cupboards!) is in the court-room, two rooms to the left. Sit in the inquisitor's chair and try to imagine the poor wretches forced through the low door (designed to make even the most heathen bow) to await their trial.

The history of the Inquisition in Malta began during the reign of Grand Master de la Cassiere (1572–81, *see above*). At his behest the Pope sent an inquisitor to try to ensure that only unsullied Catholic souls wore the cross of the Order. In reality this important post just caused political strife—the inquisitor answered to Rome and held certain authority over the sovereign grand master, while the appointment of the bishop of Malta was the responsibility of the Emperor of Spain. Of the 63 inquisitors who served in Malta, 25 became cardinals and two became Popes. The post was abolished by Napoleon in 1798. (*Adm. Lm1. Winter Mon–Sat 0815–1630, Sun 0815–1600. Summer Mon–Sun 0745–1400.*)

Cospicua

Dom Mintoff may have been born here, but there is still nothing to see in the narrow and stepped streets of the largest and last of the Three Cities to be founded except a forest of TV aerials, and parts of the Margherita Lines. The city's original name of Bormla was replaced by *Cospicua*, meaning 'conspicuous' on account of its valour during the Great Siege.

Eating Out

There are a handful of cafés where you will find a reviving cold drink. In **Senglea** the Equinox Café is by the church. In **Vittoriosa** try the Old City Pub by the wharf next to the Freedom Monument, and Tommy's in Victory Square. Also in the square is a fruit vendor, while 50 m away in St Anthony Street is a good baker; you can take a snack and sit by the water's edge and muse on the vicissitudes of the Grand Harbour.

The Northeast Coast

139

The industry of the Maltese in cultivating their little island is inconceivable. There is not an inch of ground lost in any part of it; and where there was not soil enough, they have brought over ships and boats loaded with it from Sicily, where there is plenty and to spare.

Patrick Brydone, *A Tour through Sicily and Malta*, 1773

This stretch of coast is the island's most intensely built-up and touristy area, and construction continues at a steady pace. The two biggest

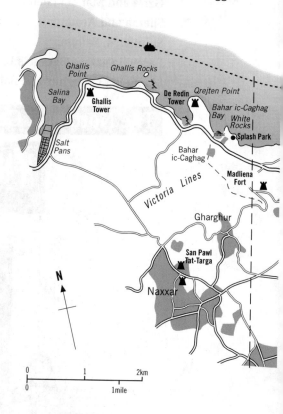

towns, Sliema and neighbouring St Julian's, have the highest population on the archipelago (albeit with just 24,000 inhabitants), and together they constitute Malta's most popular destination—each year 950,000 visit this area at some time during their stay. There are more than a hundred places to stay—hotels, guest houses and holiday complexes—and that figure does not include rental apartments. In addition you will find excellent shopping and nightlife; restaurants, bars and cafés; beaches and all the waterborne antics that money and human inventiveness can come up with.

The Northeast Coast

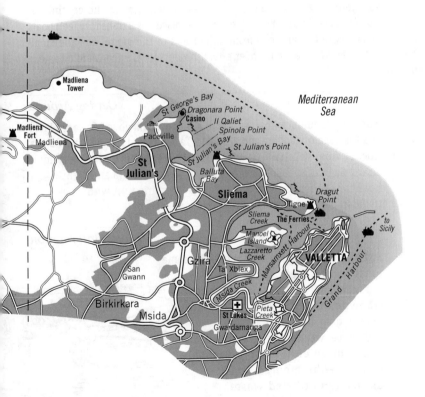

Yet, inexplicably, buzz and tranquility co-exist in the summer-parched streets: in the lunacy of Paceville after dark, the eerie splendour of Valletta bastions at night, or the spectacular fireworks of the *festa* reflected in the inky waters of St Julian's Bay. But the overbuilding has resulted in a straining infrastructure. There were no Ozymandian visions here, and instead of a harmonious skyline parts of the area simply resemble the gap-toothed grin of a none-too-successful prize fighter. The northeast coast has many good points, but aestheticism isn't one of them.

From Gwardamanġa to Ta'Xbiex

Apart from the **yacht marinas** at Ta'Xbiex and Msida there isn't much to detain you here. The yachts themselves are the star turn in the continuous suburb that encircles Marsamxett Harbour. The place has a transitory feel; boats and their crews sail in and out from all corners of the globe, and the small hotels of Pieta and Msida are lay-over establishments for US and Middle Eastern oil-workers.

Getting Around

Buses with numbers that start with a **4** or a **5** will go to Mosta via Pieta and Msida; a **6** via Pieta and Msida to Ta'Xbiex and Sliema. The **75** is a 'special' from Valletta to St Luke's Hospital. **Ta'Xbiex Marina** is not clearly flagged, so follow the one-way system for Gzira and then head for the masts. Msida can get badly snarled up with traffic in the early morning and evening rush hours.

Tourist Information

St Luke's Hospital in Gwardamanġa (sometimes abbreviated to G'manġa), is signposted off the roundabout. The **Għawdex ferry** sails from the Sa Maison quay in Pieta, daily for Gozo and twice weekly for Syracuse. **Do not swim in either of the yacht marinas—the moored boats discharge untreated waste.**

Msida's *festa* to St Joseph is on the 1st Sunday after 16 (Gwardamanġa and Ta'Xbiex celebrate Our Lady of Fatima, 4 June, and St John of the Cross on the 33rd Sunday of the year.

Yachting Information

The Malta Maritime Authority has divided up the two principal marinas, the **Msida Marina,** and **Lazzaretto and Ta'Xbiex Quays**. Msida can now accomodate 700 yachts up to 18 m on 15 fully serviced pontoons. The smaller quays at Lazzaretto and Ta'Xbiex are reserved for yachts longer than 18 m. The harbour master, John Farrugia, has an office at the **Yacht Centre** just over the bridge on Manoel Island by the Lazzaretto Quay. The centre has public conveniences and showers, international telephone facilities and offers a *poste restante* facility. The helpful staff of **Malta Customs and Immigration** are in a separate office 200 m beyond the centre. A secondary Yacht Centre office with the same facilities is in Marina Street, Msida, behind the newly laid out gardens and Malta's only set of traffic lights. For more comprehensive information, arrival procedures, berthing fees, forecasts, and other anchorages in the Maltese waters *see* pp. 45–8 and the inside cover maps.

Msida and Ta'Xbiex

Msida is known for its new yacht-marina and sometimes treacherous roundabout with attendant traffic jams. The warren of streets nearby is full of panel-beaters, an industry that will always enjoy full employment in Malta.

Msida Marina 143

Msida Creek is the most sheltered part of Marsamxett Harbour and was once a natural fishing settlement. It takes its name from *mysada*, the arabic word for a fisherman's hut, a further corruption of which is *sajd*, meaning fish. Until World War II the creek extended 80 m back to the old 18th-century wash house in the Birkirkara Road, built by a German knight and fed by an underground spring, the *Għajn tal-Ħasselin*. During the war, rock and rubble was purposely dumped in the creek's shallows and much land was reclaimed. The new, **huge yacht-marina** was developed by the present government in 1989 and has been a tremendous success for yachtsmen and tourists alike. The **parish church of St Joseph** (1893) has two altarpieces painted by Guiseppe Cali. **Ta'Xbiex** is a quieter, more genteel area of villas and embassies. A stroll along the quays of the second and **smaller yacht-marina** is—apart from the chandleries and a good little park—the main reason for lingering here.

The second marina is in **Lazzaretto Creek** and got its peculiar name from the sealed locker, or *lazaretto*, on a ship. The bed of the creek was the safest place for the submarines of the Royal Navy 10th Flotilla during the air raids of World War II (the Ministry of Defence and the War Ministry had foolishly decided against cutting submarine pens into the rock) and it remains the best of the many refuges in the archipelago. Malta imported most commodities including plagues (*see below*) and facing the creek is the old Lazzaretto quarantine hospital with its nearby scaffold from which transgressors of the quarantine were hanged. The scaffold was dismantled in 1839, but a vestige of the old precautions remains; these days a yacht arriving in Malta with a pet on board is required to lie at anchor in the creek.

Pieta and Gwardamanġa

There isn't much to see or do here. Gwardamanġa is mainly residential and Pieta is one of the main arteries leading to the west of the island.

Gwardamanġa used to be one of the more pleasant areas around Marsamxett Harbour. However, since the war it has become heavily urbanized and is now known for housing Malta's principal hospital, **St Luke's** (1938), which occupies almost the entire peninsula that divides the Pieta and Msida Creeks. On Gwardamanġa's higher ground Lord and Lady Mountbatten resided at Villa Gwardamanġa, and Queen Elizabeth II stayed at her uncle's villa during her numerous visits, first as princess and later as queen.

Before the outbreak of World War II, HMS *Terror*, a rusting survivor of World War I, awaited her scrapyard fate in **Pieta Creek**. Her feeble guns and the four

Gladiator bi-planes were the sum total of the Allied defence on Malta when Italy declared war on 10 June 1940. The first air-raid victims of **the war**, two children and their mother, were killed here at 0650 the following morning.

Where to Stay in Ta'Xbiex

On the Ta'Xbiex side of Msida Creek is the **Grand Hotel Les Lapins★★★★** (expensive), Ta'Xbiex Seafront, ✆ 342551–8, literally 'Big Hotel, the Rabbits' (the owner's name is Fenech, like the Maltese *fenek* meaning rabbit). It has a cool uncluttered marble lobby right behind the yacht marina, and the rooms are pleasant enough, the sea-view ones worth the extra. Amenities include two pools, a tennis court (at the balcony's edge of some of the rear rooms) and conference facilities. The large roof overlooking the yacht marina enables slothful yachties to check on their boats without moving.

Msida, Pieta, and Gwardamanga

This area offers a motley selection of hotels. The notable exception is the **Hotel Continental★★** (inexpensive), St Louis Street, Msida, ✆ 339620, on the higher ground between D'Argens Road and the Msida roundabout. A modernish place of 35 simple and comfortable rooms, a pool and family atmosphere, it is often booked well in advance. Two short-stay hotels are **Sa Maison★★★** (moderate), Marina Street, Pieta, ✆ 240714, a place of soulless corridors and barren rooms but with a passable Chinese restaurant; and closer to the marina, with a minute pool, is the **Hotel Helena★★** (inexpensive), Marina Street, Pieta, ✆ 336417, with 12 rooms in a narrow building.

Eating Out

Choice is limited. Try the **Manhattan** (inexpensive), Msida Yacht Marina, ✆ 344877, in a spectacularly ugly modern building with a terrace facing the Msida Marina. The kitchen specialises in hamburgers, fried chicken and ribs. Children love it. For tea or a quick snack of local pastries the **Busy Bee** is only 70 m away. Impossible to miss on the Ta'Xbiex and Msida headland is the schooner ***Black Pearl*** (moderate), Ta'Xbiex Marina, ✆ 343970, which lies like a whale on the quay after a chequered life which began in Sweden in 1909, and ended ignominiously at the bottom of the sea during the filming of *Popeye*. The food and service is equally chequered but the old-ship decor and position lend an authentic note.

Gzira seafront is not an ideal holiday destination but nor is it as grim as *Which Magazine* implied in 1992, when they singled out nine of the world's holiday black spots that 'should be avoided like the plague'; Gzira ranked sixth on the list. Some of its easily avoided offerings include sleazy prostitutes, uncollected garbage and fetid water. Yet life in the quiet streets off Gzira Circus behind the seafront is totally different: immaculate terraced houses, clean pavements, excellent local shops and pharmacies—all the hallmarks of community pride—are in evidence.

Manoel Island is joined to the mainland by a short 40-m bridge. Steeped in history, the island is currently the subject of a much-needed major redevelopment proposal; but the current condition of **Fort Manoel**, the **Lazzaretto** buildings and the rest of the island remains disgraceful. All that currently stands are **The Manoel Island Shipyard**, undoubtedly the best yacht slipping facilities in the central Mediterranean, the **Phoenician Glass Factory** (open to visitors) and **The Royal Malta Yacht Club** at Couvre Porte, the old baroque entrance to Fort Manoel.

Getting Around and Tourist Information

By car, follow the signs for Ta'Xbiex and Sliema. There is a **taxi** stand adjacent to the Valletta-bound bus stop, and Joe in the **petrol station** next door has a **telephone** for local calls. On the 2nd Sunday in July, Gzira celebrates its *festa*, Our Lady of Mount Carmel.

History: Plagues, Wars and a Fort

> '*Adieu, thou damned'st quarantine, that gave me fever, and the spleen.*'
>
> Lord Byron, 1811

In 1643, more than a hundred years and two serious plagues after the Order came to Malta, Grand Master Lascaris constructed the *lazzaretto*, or quarantine station, on the south shore of what was then called Bishop Island, now Manoel Island. The Order had already instituted a quarantine system in Rinella Creek and Corradino in the 17th century. By the mid-18th century Lascaris's new station handled a thousand visitors and their cargoes at any one time.

With their usual determination the Order managed to keep the worst bubonic plagues out of Malta; even letters were slit open, soaked in vinegar and fumigated, sleeping on the job by the yellow-uniformed health guards (today the internationally recognized quarantine flag flown by all arriving ships is yellow) was punishable with a three-year term as a galley slave, and the noose awaited those who broke the quarantine. Irrespective of rank, all visitors were incarcerated for a period of 18 to 80 days, depending on their point of embarkation. Lord Byron, already not over-enamoured with Malta, which he referred to as 'this infernal oven', spent 18 days in the *lazzaretto* on his homeward journey from Greece in 1811. In Greece he had carnally overindulged on women and boys, and gorged himself on food and wine. According to his companion John Galt, he had acquired an interesting concoction of ailments: 'an ague, and a clap, and the piles all at once'. Somewhere in the remains of the *lazzaretto* is a stone upon which he carved his name like a petulant schoolboy locked in the sanitarium. Unfortunately history does not reveal any secret ailments of some of the better known *lazzaretto* alumni—Disraeli, Coleridge, Thackeray and Sir Walter Scott. Scott remarked on his own incarceration in 1831, 'It is unpleasant to be thought so very unclean and capable of poisoning a whole city'.

Outbreaks of the plague vanished from Europe in 1841 but the *lazzaretto* remained in use for many years. It was converted into a quasi-hospital during **World War I**, when at Churchill's instigation Malta reverted to its hospitaller origins and became 'the nurse of the Mediterranean'. At the begining of hostilities in **World War II** all the buildings were requisitioned by Allied Command for the 10th Submarine Flotilla; the isolation units were converted into dormitories and stores. To supplement their starvation rations the submarine crews established a private pig farm. The Axis bombed the base incessantly, and no one knows who got to the 30 or so pigs first.

Fort Manoel

Fort Manoel represents the zenith of fort design and construction. It was once described as 'the classic example of a baroque fortress, bold yet precise, elegant yet a hard functional machine'. The complex challenge for military engineers was to protect the besieged as well as to satisfy their paymasters aesthetically.

Grand Master Manoel de Vilhena commissioned the French military engineer de Tigne to protect the Marsamxett Harbour. His initial plans, modelled on the technical mastery of Vaubon, were altered by the Order's resident engineer, de Mondion. In 1723, a year into de Vilhena's reign, ground was first broken on the fort he personally was to pay for and which was to bear his name. The huge building took three years to complete and is low, almost squat, with four fierce corner bastions; the imposing curtain walls are protected by ravelins under which lurked a cobweb of mines. The raised centre parade ground housed a fine little baroque chapel to St Anthony of Padua, de Vilhena's patron saint, a governor's house and barrack blocks. The fort was designed to accommodate a 500-strong garrison and even what remains of it shows off a powerful mathematical and geometric form. The Couvre Porte, the southern gateway and now **the Royal Malta Yacht Club**, is a grand baroque gesture to the exuberant tastes of the paymaster.

When the **French** invaded in 1798 Fort Manoel fell after just a couple of hours. Ironically, after their own defeat in 1800, many French soldiers were imprisoned here before being shipped back home. **World War II** saw terrible punishment inflicted on the fort from Axis bombs meant for the neighbouring submarine pens. Fifty years decay and the indifference of both the British and Maltese governments have taken an almost equal toll. Yet Fort Manoel's massive but elegant outline can still be appreciated from Valletta's higher bastions or, better still, from the balcony of Gianini's Restaurant in Valletta.

Manoel Island has itself been the subject of countless development proposals over the years. In 1992 interested development consortia were invited to submit proposals for the island and Tigne Point. The government's Lm200 million proposal includes the comprehensive restoration of Fort Manoel. The winning consortium is to be announced in 1993/4. Until then most of the land on Manoel Island will continue to be a place to burn mattresses and flytip. Beware of the packs of aggressive mutant dogs that roam about the island.

Where to Stay

Along the Strand towards Sliema, 30 m apart, are two modern and good hotels of a similar size. **The Milano Due★★★** (moderate), 113 The Strand, ✆ 345040, is the newer and plusher of the two with generous rooms, a sun terrace and the better restaurant. The more expensive **Kennedy Court★★★** (moderate), 116 The Strand, ✆ 314668, has the big advantage of a rooftop pool and bar but neither the bedrooms nor the public rooms are as good. The **Adelphi★★★** (moderate), Victoria Street, ✆ 335110, has a tired face and window boxes of flowers long since dead. For overnighting, the small 23-room **Taormina★** (inexpensive), 6–7 Ponsonby Street, ✆ 316473, is perfectly adequate.

The **restaurants** in Gzira do not amount to much, the culinary high-point being the **Wimpy** by the bus stop. Next door is **La Nocciola**, excellent for girth-increasing confections. The *pastizzi* at **Maxim's** are also good. Near Maxim's you can get a sandwich at the **Britannia Bar**, an ex-pat's haunt. Further down The Strand and past the two hotels is a group of bars like the **Wells Fargo** that appeal to serious drinkers who like to begin not long after breakfast and end not long before breakfast. On Manoel island is **The Royal Malta Yacht Club** (inexpensive), Couvre Porte, *©* 333109, at which it is very pleasant to eat outside in summer. The oleander trees and the glamour of the fort's archway almost make the food immaterial, but when *lampuki* is on, order it. Membership is required and temporary passes are available for a modest fee.

Sliema, St Julian's, Paceville and Around

The suburbs of Sliema and St Julian's have grown in limestone leaps and concrete bounds. The majority of tourists and Maltese gravitate towards this area. An oil and water mix of staunchly middle-class Maltese and a youth intent on heading into the social stratosphere (via an apartment on Tower Road) co-exist with many good hotels, restaurants and bars, busy nightlife and shops. Twenty-four thousand Maltese—that's seven per cent of the island's population—are spread amongst seven parishes, and from April to October the continuous coastal development of Sliema to St Julian's is wall-to-wall holiday town. Be prepared to leave with a smouldering wallet and molten credit cards; like everywhere in the Mediterranean, Malta can be expensive.

Sliema

Sliem, meaning 'hail', is the first word of a fisherman's prayer to the Virgin Mary. Beginning as a fishing settlement, by the end of the 19th century Sliema had grown into a summer retreat from the claustrophobic heat of Valletta. Wandering in the quiet backstreets you will see a handful of the graceful turn-of-the-century villas that once made up the town. Those which remain are destined to be replaced by rivetingly dull blocks of flats; even the last elegant and detached villa in Balluta Bay has been sold for redevelopment.

Today, a Sliema address is the aspiration of many Maltese, and the town is a place for **shoppers**. If you cannot find what you require within the approximate

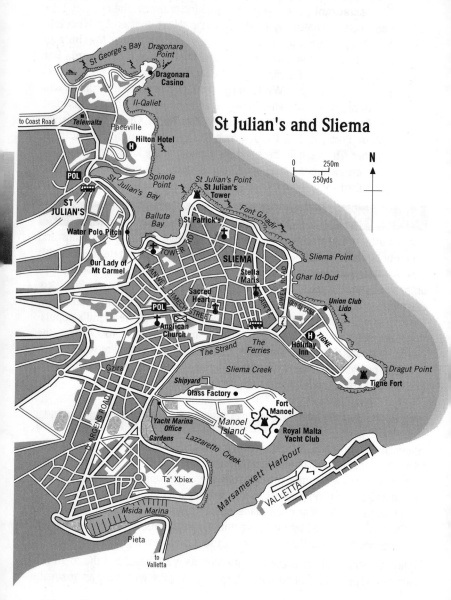

St Julian's and Sliema

St George's Bay

Dragonara Point

Dragonara Casino

Il-Qaliet

to Coast Road

Telemalta

Paceville

Hilton Hotel

POL

ST JULIAN'S

St Julian's Bay

Spinola Point

St Julian's Point

St Julian's Tower

St Patrick's

Balluta Bay

Water Polo Pitch

Our Lady of Mt Carmel

TOWER RD

Font Ghadir

SLIEMA

Sliema Point

Stella Maris

Ghar Id-Dud

MANUEL DIMECH STREET

Sacred Heart

ST JOHN

TOWER ROAD

QUI SI SANA

Union Club Lido

POL

Anglican Church

Gzira

The Strand

The Ferries

Sliema Creek

Holiday Inn

TIGNE

Dragut Point

Tigne Fort

0   250m
0   250yds

N

Shipyard

Glass Factory

Yacht Marina Office

Gardens

Manoel Island

Fort Manoel

Royal Malta Yacht Club

Lazzaretto Creek

Ta' Xbiex

Marsamxett Harbour

VALLETTA

Msida Marina

Pieta

to Valletta

boundaries of Mrabat Street, the head of Balluta Bay, Tower Road and Dragut Point you probably don't need it anyway; there are all manner of shops in the main streets and tucked up blind alleys. Amid this modern affluence, one of Italy's more gratifying pleasures has long been adopted, the *passeggiata*. Before dusk closes in, circuses of Maltese families with their sleeping babies, and marauding children who twist in and out between the adults' ankles, gravitate slowly along the coastal promenade between the Għar id-Dud and St Julian's, making frequent pit-stops for nuts, seeds, nougat and ice cream.

Getting Around and Tourist Information

The **Marsamxuetto Ferry** is the quickest and least aggravating way of exploring Valletta. The journey is only 5 minutes, every 35–40 minutes from the area known as the **Ferries** at the bottom of Tower Road on the front. By car the capital is only 5.5 km away, but the traffic is usually tiresome. The bus terminus, the day **cruise boats** and the **Marsamxuetto Ferry** also leave from the Ferries; the **Gozo–Sliema Hovermarine** docks here as well. **Car parking** can be a problem here and transgressors of the hard-to-spot 'no parking' signs end up with a Lm5 ticket. When you do find a space in the free central island car parks by the Ferries, tip the attendant 10c as you leave. **Taxis** are plentiful and there is a seemingly inert rank by the Magic Kiosk café.

The **NTOM** has a not-very-visible bureau at the top of Tower Hill and Bisazza Street, ✆ 313409. Next door is **Telemalta**. There is a large **post office** in Manwel Dimech Street (also known as Prince of Wales Drive). Impossible to miss near the front is Sliema's one remaining 'fleapit', the **Alhambra Cinema**, and just up the hill is the **Air Malta** office at 28 Tower Road, ✆ 330646. **Thomas Cook** has a foreign exchange bureau in the Piazzetta on Tower Road.

Festas

 Sliema's four parishes celebrate **Our Lady of the Sea**, or Stella Maris, on the Sunday after 18 August; **Our Lady of the Sacred Heart** or Sacro Cuor on the 1st Sunday in July; **St Gregory the Great** on the 1st Sunday in September; and **St Dominic** on the 3rd Sunday in July.

The awesome bastions and curtain walls of Valletta, one of the most spectacular sights in Malta, can only really be appreciated from the **Sliema Creek**

promenade at night. The powerful orange glow of the illuminations casts spectral shadows and dazzling highlights, and conjures up dreamy images of the knights and their armies of sturdy workmen toiling night and day to erect the Christian fortress city. At night, and from a distance across the water, the city is a somnolent yet dazzling feat of architecture.

There is not much to see on the headland region around Dragut and Tigne Points as they are zoned for redevelopment, but they are rich in history. The Turks established an artillery battery on the Tigne headland and pounded away at Fort St Elmo during the **Great Siege** of 1565. It was on this tip of land, at the mouth of Marsamxett Harbour and Sliema Creek known as **Dragut Point**, that the besieging corsair and mercenary Dragut Rais was mortally wounded by a splinter of rock from a cannon ball, three days before Fort St Elmo fell (*see* Topics, p. 82).

Long after the Christian victory, the knights' military engineers inexplicably continued to ignore the strategically important promontory. **Tigne Fort** (1792) was the last of the Valletta defences to be commissioned, and was paid for by Grand Master de Rohan and Chevalier Tigne who intended it to be a secondary foil to the might of Fort St Elmo. The 15 cannons of the diamond-shaped fort, when fired in concert with those of Fort St Elmo, would slam the door on an enemy attempt to occupy Marsamxett Harbour. Tigne's cannons gave spirited covering fire in support of the brave knight de Soubiras who put to sea in his lone galley to defend what was left of the Order's honour during the **French** invasion of 1798. He attacked and sank a French warship after it had landed men in St Julian's but two hours later his own guns were silenced by Napoleon's General Vaubois. A year later, while the Royal Navy blockaded the French in Valletta, the cannons of Forts Tigne and Manoel bombarded the city. The British steadily enlarged the fort until it bore little resemblance to the original and by **World War II** it positively bristled with guns and searchlights.

On the Ghar id-Dud is yet another coastal defence converted into a pizzeria, **Il-Fortizza**, which was the old Sliema Point Battery, built by the British in 1872. The drastic change of use has been well executed: the gothic-style doors and vaulting remain, and it is easy to appreciate the vantage point it enjoyed. The tower was added in 1905 when the battery became an observation station.

The architecturally unadventurous **church of the Sacred Heart** houses an evocative altarpiece of the emaciated St Jerome in his cave, with only death's head, a bible and a cross for company. Generally acknowledged to be **Guiseppe Cali's** masterpiece, it is a powerful and indoctrinating image.

Beaches

The word beach liberally translates in Malta to 'seaward entry point' and can therefore be anything from sand to rock; precious little of the former exists in this area but there is an abundance of the latter. All the public beaches are free and don't become uncomfortably crowded, even in the height of summer, but getting in and out can be tricky for very young children and the elderly. There are also many private lidos along the coast which incorporate other facilities, such as restaurants and sports equipment hire.

Heading east from the Balluta side of St Julian's Tower to the end of Tigne beach is more than 3 km of mostly smooth rock beach all invisibly named and divided up. From inside Balluta Bay to the Tower is the **Torri and Exiles beach** named after the waterpolo team who have their pitch, café and public gardens there. Next is a long stretch extending past the Surfside Lido known as **Font Għadir**, meaning 'deep pool', for the cobalt blue water falls away deeply off the rocks here. Along this stretch are uniform squares hewn out of the rock which used to be the private summer 'pools' for the ladies of Sliema. Not only were the rock pools lined with canvas, but a three-sided screen was erected to ensure that the bashful ladies were safe from inquisitive eyes. On very rare occasions you still see this practice in Malta or Gozo when nuns go swimming. The next port of call for the beachcomber is the **Għar id-Dud**, literally translated as 'cave of worms'. The rocks are not so smooth here and if there has been a swell the waves can crash around viciously. Left towards Tigne on the northeast peninsula is **Qui-Si-Sana** meaning 'here you become well' and the final stretch of beach is called **Tigne Beach**. At the far end is the **Union Club Lido** where young boys are initiated into the ethos of Latin *machismo* by diving from the tops of the rocks into the sea. Occasionally a complete hash is made of a dive and you are left wondering what irreversible harm has been done.

Private lidos have anything from parasols and sun beds to three-course lunches. Beginning at St Julian's Tower, the best are the **Surfside**, the **Preluna**, the Jumbo, the Plevna, the Tigne Court and the Union Club. *Entrance is usually Lm1–1.50, depending on facilities.*

Sports and Activities

Dive Systems, © 319123 or 317137, is a reputable diving school situated just before Tigne Point. Five-day internationally recognized P.A.D.I. courses cost approximately Lm95. It has the full range of equipment for hire. The **Merkanti Reef**, off the point of St Julian's, is suitable for divers of all abilities. Somewhere in the murky seabed by Dragut Point is what is left of the destroyer HMS *Maori.*

The **Captain Morgan cruise fleet** operates from Sliema Creek. Other companies operate, but none come near to matching the Captain's standards of food or service. The longest cruise goes around all the islands from 0845–1830 (Lm12.95 and children Lm7.95); day trips to Comino and into the creeks of the Grand Harbour are popular. New excursions include an **historical bus tour** of the Three Cities, and a trip in a **submarine**, © 331961 or 343373 to enquire or to book.

The **Oki-KO-Ki Boat Hire Co.**, © 339831, near the Cavalieri Hotel in St Julian's give **skiing** lessons and hire out small put-put boats and more powerful speedboats from Lm20–Lm55 per day, as well as rowing boats for those of a more nervous disposition. In rough weather you could venture into the **Alhambra Cinema** where they change the programme twice daily. **Water polo** is played at the Sliema pitch beneath the *Il Fortizza* on the Ghar id-Dud. But the neighbouring Neptunes team in Balluta Bay are the team to watch.

Shopping

Retail activity is centred around Tower Road and Bisazza Street up from the Ferries and nearby in the long uphill slog of Manwel Dimech Street (also known as Prince of Wales Drive). The new **Plaza Shopping Complex** *will undoubtedly provide a balanced mix of trades, as well as further parking problems.*

Clothes. Most international brand names and chain stores are represented, but prices are often higher than in the UK. Standa, a general Italian chain, has a better value store in the Preluna Towers.

Food. There is a good local **baker** 200 m up St Vincent Street behind the Ferries, and **Jesper's** the excellent Danish bakery has an outlet in 28 Creche Street—they bake European breads and other gooey things. Three **vegetable and fruit** vans operate the lucrative pitch by the Ferries; the very freshest is sold early in the morning when the Maltese housewives do their shopping. At the beginning of Tower Road is a local **confectioner**, the Chocolate Box, cool and full of Italian cakes and sweetmeats. At the top of Tower Road and Bisazza Street is a **supermarket**, Tower Stores, and next door is Bon Vivant, a **wine and spirits** merchant;

between them they will have everything you need. For cranky eaters there is Casa Natura, a well-stocked **health food** shop at 30 Main Street.

Miscellaneous. A few metres further along towards the Ġħar id-Dud Promenade **Kodak** have a one-hour-developing shop, nearly double the price of the UK. At the entrance to Tower Arcade is a good **shoe shop**, where espadrilles are just 90c a pair. In the Piazzetta Centre, at the beginning of the Ġħar id-Dud Promenade, is a large **chemist**, Chemimart, which stocks European brands.

Gifts. Tacky resort apparel, baseball caps, T-shirts, rucksacks and lighters all fluorescently emblazoned 'Malta', are available everywhere. On the other hand, there is always a silver filigree cross of the Order of St John (**a Maltese cross**) from Victor's Jewellery in Tower Road which should cost no more than Lm5, or one of the expanding collection of excellent **miniature Heritage Homes**, which can be bought for approximately Lm10 from Jomar at 4 Main Street, or Lada in Tower Road. Malta produces a prolific and well-printed selection of **books** that make perfect souvenirs. Morris, at 45 Tower Road, is the best—they will also keep back daily **newspapers**—if they don't have what you want ask Pierre or try the Audio Visual Centre in neighbouring Bisazza Street. Tucked up Tigne Street, off Tower Road and opposite the Union Club, is Charles Palmier's tiny **art gallery**, with reasonably priced souvenir prints. For **antiques,** Thru the Ages at 16 St Paul Street has smaller gift type antiques and *objets d'art* and the Antique Centre at 322 Manwel Dimech Street is more bric-a-brac and maps, but with the odd worthwhile find. Tucked up behind Ballutta Bay in Bay Street is Serendipity, with a changing and very good stock. For the bigger spender, Antiques and Fine Art at 197 Tower Road have a mixed stock of furniture and paintings at toppy prices. For the 30- or 40-something man welded to the memories of a happy childhood **The Collectors Shop** in Tower Arcade (next door to the shoe shop), is mecca. A pristine collection of 50s and 60s Dinky toys, models, stamps and cigarette cards. It would be hard to find a more impressive collection.

Where to Stay in Sliema

Luxury/Expensive

At the top of the pile, the **Holiday Inn Crowne Plaza★★★★★**, Tigne Street, ℃ 341173 is a well-run hotel with good service that deserves its rating (despite its cheap white plastic outdoor furniture). The rooms are generous, with uninterrupted sea views; the nearly 15% cheaper 'cityview' rooms on the top two floors have good views of the Valletta bastions. Facilities include a huge pool, squash and tennis courts and a bar with a *belle epoque* mood and for those who hate leaving home, a British-style pub. By far the best of the four-star establishments is the **Fortina★★★★**, Tigne Seafront, © 342976. Professionally run and brimming with facilities, including an extensively equipped gym, two pools and a private lido. The rooms have been recently modernised and have multi-channel satellite TV; sea-view rooms have terrific views over Sliema Creek to the bastions. The **Preluna★★★★**, Tower Road, © 334001, faces Ghar id-Dud Promenade and the sea but can be a little noisy. The lobby is a bit gloomy but the rooms brighten up; it too has a lido and pool at the water's edge. The **Diplomat★★★★**, Tower Road, © 345361, opened in 1992 and is a walk from the centre, midway between Sliema and Balluta Bay, facing the sea. The pleasantly decorated rooms are small but comfortable; only the side rooms have balconies. The rooftop pool is a sun trap.

Moderate

The majority of hotels in Sliema carry three stars. The most notable are listed below. The **Imperial★★★**, Rudolphe Street, © 344093, was once an old hunting lodge; the sweeping staircase, high ceilings and old-world charm remain; there is a secluded pool. The **Tigne Court★★★**, Quis-Si-Sana, © 332001, not far from the Holiday Inn, has modern rooms and overlooks the sea at Tigne; it has a private lido and pool. Sandwiched in between the Holiday Inn and the Fortina is the very friendly **Midas★★★**, 45 Tigne Street, © 337822, with an 'honour bar' and a full roster of loyal clients. The sun deck has the smallest hotel pool anywhere, 2 m in diameter. Just past the Preluna is the **Europa★★★**, 138 Tower Road, © 330080, with basic amenities but a central position—a place for those who want to drop their kit and get amongst it. The other side of the Preluna is the **Hotel Roma★★★**, Ghar il-Lenbi Street, © 318587, small and modern with useful café-cum-meeting place on the ground floor, no pool but a sun deck. Not for those with limited mobility: reception is on the first floor up a long, steep flight of steps. In the centre of town, the **Hotel Regina★★★**, 107 Tower Road, © 310633, has a quaint, slightly run-down charm, a pool at the rear and a good coffee shop. The **Tower Palace★★★**, Tower Road, © 337271, faces the sea, and has access to rock beaches. Each room has a generous balcony and there is a sun deck on the 7th-floor terrace. Next door is the Lungomare Gelateria, selling the wickedest ice creams around. The **Metropole★★★**, 71 Sir Adrian Dingli Street, ℂ 330188, towards Balluta is the largest of the three-star establishments, with 160 none-too-sharp-looking rooms. But Tony, the delightful barman, compensates as he ping-pongs between his ground floor and the rooftop bar with its brand new 'poolette'. If you don't mind being in between the Rawhide Saloon and Sharon's Pub the grandly named **Carlton★★★**, Tower Road, ℂ 315764, close to Balluta Bay is a safe choice. The rooms are a little dated but comfortable; the bus stop and petrol station are opposite so from the sea-view rooms you hear the traffic grumbling below. A sun deck and restaurant are on the top floors. The **Galaxy Hotel** (Class I), Depiro Street, ℂ 344205, **aparthotel** is a modern mixture of 190 hotel rooms and 50 apartments in differing configurations bristling with facilities: two outdoor pools with children's pools, the ubiquitous gym, two restaurants and bars.

Inexpensive

Of the two-star hotels the best is **Howard House★★**, 102 Howard Street, ℂ 313764. Only 250 m away from the seafront, it can be monopolized by Scandinavians, whose exacting standards the hotel matches. The **Hotel Elba★★**, 52 Sir Arturo Mercieca Street, ℂ 336418, is equally close to the sea, and while it lacks a Scandinavian gleam, it is a comfortable and reasonable place to stay. Both have lifts. Basic accommodation can be found at the **Kent★**, 24 St Margaret Street, ℂ 330928, a short walk from Balluta Bay and the Exiles Beach.

Eating Out

There are countless **cafés** behind the Ferries and along the Għar Id-Dud, offering a *cappucino*, a beer, or simple freshly prepared snacks. Anni Venti, the Magic Kiosk, Giorgio, Café Roma and La Columba are all reliable. **The Army and Navy** (cheap) on The Strand (no telephone) is the old Forces stalwart; they fry up anything and everything better than anyone else. Fifty metres away is **Il Lanca** (inexpensive), ℂ 338743, but known locally as the Village Gossip or Manuels. Excellent chicken salads, *ftira* sandwiches, mean Long Island iced teas but so-so pasta dishes. In summer people watch outside and in winter the menu and mood changes; it becomes all very cosy with warm terracotta walls, wooden-beamed ceilings and Van Morrison music. The small **Il Galeone** (expensive), 35 Tigne Seafront, ℭ 316420, is a long-time favourite for lunch and dinner, serving mainly Italian dishes with a few home-spun inventions; it rarely disappoints. Further up, and next to the Fortina Hotel is a Turkish restaurant, **The Mangal** (moderate), Tigne Seafront, ℭ 341046, with a view of the bastions. The menu is resolutely Turkish and good: *meze*, a selection of cold starters, spicy kebabs and fish, followed by treacly Levantine desserts. Service can be erratic. Along the Għar id-Dud Promenade and next door to the Café Roma is **Blondino's** (inexpensive), Għar il-Lenbi Street, ℭ 344605. It is easy to miss, but do not be put off by the position or the unimaginative decor. This small restaurant serves wholesome and good value local food and is open for lunch on Sunday. Continue up the same road and tucked behind the corner is a welcome sight for British taste buds. The long-established **Hole in the Wall** (moderate), 32 Main Street, ℭ 336110, has old favourites like scampi and mixed grills, all cooked well. In summer there is a cool garden and in winter, despite the dated decor, it's snug. Thirty metres away, behind the forbidding entrance to an apartment block is another institution, **The Haven** (inexpensive), Main Street, ℭ 313915, more frequently and accurately known as **'Sally's'**. Mr Sally cooks obediently in the corner while Sally serves the handful of gingham-covered tables from a short and ever-changing menu of rustic Italian and Maltese dishes. Midway along the promenade that stretches from the Għar id-Dud to St Julian's are two other noteworthy restaurants. The **Surfside** (moderate), Tower Road, ℭ 335686 is on the Font Għadir beach, 10 m away from the sea, opposite the Tower Palace Hotel. The position, set above the beach, offers panoramic views of sea and yet more sea. It specializes in fresh fish but the meat doesn't disappoint, and whatever you eat will be spiced with drama and maybe a little salt if the sea is rough. An excellent rendezvous for a business lunch. The **Ponte Vecchio** (moderate), Stella Maris Street, ℭ 341591, is another safe bet. It can be a little formal but what is on the plate is studied Italian food and the helpful staff will customize most dishes. In summer there is a pleasant but fumy terrace. Afterwards, have an ice-cream from the **Lungomare** next door. *Pizzerias* are abundant. **Il Fortizza** (cheap) Tower Road, ℭ 336908, was one of the first, and it enjoys the best position, overlooking the sea in the old

British watchtower. The pizzas are good, too. Almost opposite is the **Bella Italia** (inexpensive), 132 Tower Road, © 318943, which is sometimes too crowded in the evening but saner at lunchtime; there is a plentiful *tavola calda*. **The Pizza Place** (cheap), Holiday Inn, Tigne Street, © 341173, also gets busy and serves only crusty, tasty pizzas. For **ice cream** two places count: the **Offshore** by the Ferries, and, next door to the Tower Palace Hotel, the **Gelateria Lungomare** with more than 30 different homemade flavours.

St Julian's, Balluta, Paceville and St George's Bay

St Julian's Bay takes its name from a chapel dedicated to St Julian, where during the Order's reign the fishermen would congregate; now it's the island's year-round mecca for eating, drinking and nightlife. The curving bay (sometimes referred to as Spinola Bay) is trying to return to its fishing origins, and many of the buildings at the water's edge have benefited from skilled and sympathetic restoration.

When Sliema gently nods off after the evening *passeggiata*, St Julian's and the sometimes raucous and younger neighbouring *quartier* of **Paceville** begin to stir for what will be playtime well into the early hours. Here, culture is something you find on last week's hamburgers.

History

After the **Great Siege** had begun in May 1565 the scourge of Malta, Dragut Rais, landed in St Julian's Bay with a small armada of 15 ships and 1,500 men. At the age of 80 this old warrior was again enlisted by his old paymaster, Suleyman the Magnificent, to join in what the forces of Islam hoped would be the final annihilation of their old foe, the Order of St John. It was to prove one campaign too many for the man known as 'The Drawn Sword of Islam'. He was killed by a stone splinter on what is now called Dragut Point, in Sliema.

By June 1798, when **Napoleon** invaded Malta, enough time had passed for the knights to acquire dissolute and high-handed habits. His arrival literally and metaphorically obliterated their horizons with a forest of masts; 472 French ships were anchored along this coast. General Vaubois, Napoleon's governor of Malta designate, had an almost unopposed landing with his troops in St Julian's Bay before marching to Mdina to dine with the bishop. The fact that it took as long as 48 hours for Napoleon to extract Grand Master Hompesch's ignominious capitulation was the only surprise. The tide turned when **Nelson** arrived to blockade the island and St Julian's became a victualling and repair base for his fleet.

Tourist Information

Mid Med in St George's Road, midway between St Julian's and Paceville, has a 24-hour multi-currency exchange machine. St Julian's *festa* is on the last Sunday in August. Our Lady of Mount Carmel has a feast day on the last Sunday in July.

Getting Around

St Julian's is 8 km from Valletta via the regional road and more than 4.5 km from Sliema on the coastal road; both are signposted. Be careful at the turning for St Julian's when coming from Valletta; conflicting notions as to who has right of way often leads to conflicting metal. **Parking** can be a major problem, especially in Paceville. If there has been a 'disturbance', the weekend before, roads into and out of Paceville are sealed off. The Maltese exchequer receives a healthy boost from parking fines every weekend, so do not think you are safe because the sun has set. Try to park on the slip road down from the regional road. **Bus 62** terminates at the head of the bay, the **67** and **68** carry on to St Andrew's. **Bus 70** runs between Sliema and Buġibba along the coast road in summer. If you get stranded, Wembley's, © 332074/345454, between St Julian's Bay and Paceville, operates a reliable 24-hour **taxi service**.

On arrival in Malta a knight was not automatically entitled to a residence in an *auberge* of his *langue* and some preferred to 'live out'. In 1688 the Italian knight, Admiral Raffael Spinola built the **Palazzo Spinola** on the then deserted hill sloping down to the bay. His grand-nephew, Giovanni Spinola, a bailiff of the Order, reconstructed the Palazzo Spinola in 1733 in its present form—an imposing confection with a confused but elegant façade. Sandwiched between two contemporary neighbours, a dodgeem-car ring and the Hilton Hotel,

Mass among the fishermen - Spinola Bay

it is now the offices of the Malta International Business Association. The small **church of the Immaculate Conception**, 250 m away (next door to Peppino's restaurant), was built in 1688 by Raffael Spinola to ease the burden of his pastoral care (Valletta was then a tiresomely long horse ride away).

Another and much later confection is the **Dragonara Palace**, now the **casino**, on the very tip of Dragonara Point. Folklore tells that a dragon lived in the caves and hollows hereabouts, but the noises were no more than howling wind traps and the scurrilous tales of the dragon were spread by canny smugglers.

The palace was built as a summer residence for Emanuele Scicluna, a shrewd banker who was made a Marquis in 1875 on the strength of a loan to Pope Pius IX. The new Marquis, not a shy retiring man, lived up to the motto engraved over the large stone entrance gate of his carriageway: *Deus Nobis Haec Otia Fecit* ('God made these leisures for us'). The central courtyard, now the gaming rooms, contained lush gardens, around which the interconnecting rooms of the colonnaded villa were built. A humanitarian and a hedonist, he would surely have approved of the subsequent uses of his villa as a hospital in World War I, a home for bomb refugees in World War II and a casino from 1964. He would undoubtedly have disapproved of its grim ochre paintwork, the neon signs and a bizarre bottle-green statue of himself in the forecourt.

Beaches

All along the coast from Balluta Bay to St George's Bay are **lidos**, most with concessions such as water-skiing, windsurfing, etcetera. The new Neptunes water polo team pool in Balluta Bay is open for matches and swimming.

Between Spinola Point and Il-Qalie are the private lidos of the **Hotel Cavalieri** and the **Hilton**. If you don't mind sharing the scrubland with prides of cats, there are tricky, but uncrowded, rocks to swim off.

The **Reef Club** lido on Dragonara Point is owned by the Dragonara Palace Hotel (being redeveloped and due to reopen in 1994). At the time of writing the new operators vowed that a much-improved lido would open by May 1993. The old one was good, with a bamboo-shaded restaurant, a popular bar, and the **Divewise** diving school. It was and will be frequented by the thirtysomethings.

Around the headland in **St George's Bay** the age groups are at both ends of the scale: those who come to prey and those who come to play; all with swimwear in inverse proportion to their ages (the older, the briefer). The energetic atmosphere is a cocktail of aromatic sun lotion, snack foods and cold drinks. There is a useful 80-m stretch of sand at the head of the bay that is perfect for children. Flanking it are two lidos, **the Cresta Quay Beach Club** and the **San Gorg Lido**. Both have all types of aquatic concessions and the San Gorg has a children's pool. Except for the shallows of the sandy beach the bay is a firm favourite with the posing and often careless speedboat fraternity; on shore the crank-up-the-volume set rule the roost.

Sports and Activities

The most popular non-water **activities** are in St George's Bay and are owned by the Eden Leisure Group. A sophisticated 20-lane air-conditioned **bowling** alley has a **roller-skating** rink on its roof as well as a brand new air-conditioned 6-screen multiplex **cinema** for new releases. The bowling alley can get booked up; telephone © 319888/341196 to reserve a lane. For people who don't want to risk twisting an ankle or dislocating an arm, the bowling alley has a bar.

Where to Stay

*More than 20 hotels are dotted about this area, excluding the massive St George's Park complex with 685 apartments. For other **apartments** and houses to rent (or buy) recommended agencies are **Dahlia**, © 318974, **Frank Salt**, © 337373 and **Godwin Lowell Estates**, © 311766. All in front of the Hilton Hotel on St George's Road.*

St Julian's

The Hilton Hotel★★★★★ (luxury), © 336201, is a longtime favourite with business people or those who want some peace within a frenetic environment. The low-built hotel enjoys the best of secluded seaward positions within its own landscaped gardens. The rooms and the public halls are looking dated; ask for a balconied sea-view room, it will be worth any extra. Amenities include two good tennis courts and pools, a water's-edge private lido, a huge private car park and a mini golf course. Edwin Galea, a well-known local painter, has a small shop inside. The **Hotel Cavalieri★★★★** (expensive), Spinola Road, © 336255, on the spit where the bay opens to the sea, can be seen from anywhere along Tower Road. The hotel has 117 air-conditioned rooms, let down only by a less than commodious entrance and bar; the layout and furnishings are uncomfortable and in dubious taste. But it is a popular hotel with the sense of humour to make the dedicated children's duck pond in the shape of a huge duck! The top-floor sea-view rooms are real sun traps and the lido is private. The **Hotel Alphonso★★★** (moderate), Il-Qaliet Street, ✆ 330053, is a friendly, family-run hotel. The central location, off the main road, has made it a favourite, especially with the Italians. No views at all, but it does have a sun deck and its own pasta restaurant.

Paceville

You either love it or hate it here, but wherever you stay the parking will be a nightmare. If you are a light sleeper pack ear-plugs, pills and a bottle of Scotch; you will probably need all three. **The St George's Bay Complex** (Class I), ✆ 311782 is huge and comprises four prin-cipal buildings designed in a post-modern pastiche of cream and pastel colours. They house over 800 beds in different configurations; studios to penthouses; two pools, a games room, a mini-market, a hall-sized restaurant and a pub within its soulless confines. If you want tranquility you shouldn't come to Paceville, but the **Hotel Rokna★★★** (moderate), Church Street, ✆ 330595, is a compromise with 21 rooms and a pizzeria, facing the Hilton's gardens and an eye-poppingly hideous modern church. The English love the **Hotel Ascot★★★** (moderate), Elia Zammit Street, ✆ 338550. The Mill Reef Bar is a long-time favourite and it has more facilities than a lot of other neighbouring three-star hotels: pool, children's pool and play area, games room and a small health club. The Hotel St Julien★★★ (moderate), Dragonara Road, ✆ 336272, is short on facilities but does have larger than average rooms, and a popular bar and coffee shop. The **Tropicana Hotel★★** (inexpensive), 32 Ball Street, ✆ 341188, with 60 smallish, light rooms, is right in the middle of noisy Paceville. Its name conjures up alluring images of 1950s Cuba and attracts a clientele of young Latins. The same owners have the Ghall Kafe (open 24-hours) on the ground floor and the San Gorg Lido.

St George's Bay

The Eden Beach★★★★ (expensive) seems to control most of the activ-ities in St George's Bay, from Styx II disco to the roller-skating rink. The hotel has 126 modern air-conditioned rooms, a pool, tennis and squash courts and is only 250 m from the beach. **The Villa Rosa★★★** (moderate), St George's Bay, ✆ 342708, has welcoming service and countless facilities that place it well above most other three-star establishments. The old Villa Rosa (30 m above the hotel and used for weddings and summer schools) was built at the end of the last century as a nobleman's token of love for his Italian opera-singer mistress, Rosa. She died mysteriously one night and, heartbroken, he abandoned the villa. The charming hotel of only 105 rooms is set at the bottom of the old villa's tiered grounds right behind the beach. A pleasant garden of roses, palms, and oleanders separates the large pool club from the hotel.

Eating Out

No one eats around here much before 2100; the bars (see below) are the first port of call. Some restaurants here charge big-city bills for food which is inconsistently prepared by volatile chefs, but a smorgasbord of kitchens prove that there is life beyond pasta.

St Julian's

St Julian's hosts the current crop of fashionable restaurants. The proprietors of **San Guiliano** (expensive), St Julian's Bay, ✆ 332000, were responsible for the revival of the old fishing area, and consequently the restaurant has an enviable position overlooking the bay. The standard of the Italian dishes varies according to chef's moods and the service can be dilatory. Fish, veal and home-made *tiramisu* are good choices. Dining here during the St Julian's *festa* firework display is worth twice the bill even if the chef *is* crabby; you need to book at weekends and access is via a spiral staircase only. Underneath the San Guiliano is its sister restaurant, the **Caffe Raffael** (inexpensive), ✆ 319988. Closer to the water's edge, and also enjoying a superb position, this serves pastas and pizzas outside under large canvas umbrellas. The service can lag here too, even when it's not busy but the atmosphere in the evenings is as buzzy as the pizza Diavola is hot. Next door is a busy ground-floor pizzeria **La Papparazzi** (inexpensive), ✆ 374965/6, while upstairs is its sister restaurant **La Dolce Vita** (expensive), ✆ 337806. It has been serving reliable Italian food for years, but stay with the fresh fish and pasta in summer, and soups and meat in winter. The bamboo-covered terrace is very popular in summer, so book in advance. Opposite and next to the old church is **Peppino's** (moderate), ✆ 373200, one of the current 'in' places for a rendezvous. On the ground floor is a wine bar with a good selection of foreign wines and a small selection of invariably overcooked pasta dishes; the main restaurant is upstairs. The quality of the cooking depends on how busy it is but the atmosphere never flags and it can get pleasantly hectic later on. Around the corner in Spinola Road is the **Sumatra** (moderate), ✆ 310991, a hybrid of Far-Eastern kitchens with bamboo furniture, oriental prints and a smiling service; book at the weekends. **Il Parapett** (inexpensive), ✆ 333394, is a long-established pizzeria and restaurant just before Paceville on St George's Road. The Maltese swear by their extensive pizza menu and a good local stuffed beef dish, *bragioli*. If you just want a good snack, and the fruit van at the head of the bay is too healthy an idea, nearby is **La Nocciola** (cheap), 9 St George' s Road, ✆ 335962, for salads, pastas, cakes and coffee in a spotless café. Not far away above Lines Bar is the current best of the Italian crop of restaurants, the **Bella Romagna** (moderate), ✆ 317961. The Sardinian chef puts together a traditional meal; excellent *pasta fagioli*, veal Marsala that actually has wine in it and if roast suckling pig is on don't even think of ordering anything else. Toasted local herb-bread, attentive service and a complimentary sip of an after-dinner liqueur are welcome extra touches. Ask for a table near the window when you book.

Paceville

Almost top of the curiosity league is **Kandles** (moderate), ✆ 333640, a wholly successful off-beat mix of Italian, Indian and oriental food. The stone floors, wooden tables and helpful service all contribute. Try the Javanese chicken. Not far away is the **Bouzouki** (moderate), Gort Street, ✆ 317127, a serious Greek restaurant in a quietish street with sensible prices. The decor is spartan and the service efficient. Begin with mixed starters, *meze*, and then have properly cooked kebabs or garlicky grilled prawns. During the week they have a good value set menu. You can't smash plates to the hackneyed strains of Zorba the Greek in this establishment. The new Russian restaurant, the **Cossack** (moderate), Elia Zammit Street, ✆ 374595, is worth a try for those who miss chilled vodka, *borscht* and *shashlick*. Oriental plate-grazing at the **Marco Polo** (expensive), Dragonara Road, ✆ 331995, is not a bargain, but it serves a patois of Chinese and Malay food in elegant, if characterless, surroundings. This is the best oriental restaurant in Malta but for some reason it doesn't keep *sake*. Further down the road, towards the casino, is a cheap-and-cheerful hamburger, pizza, and pasta restaurant, **The Upper Crust** (cheap), Dragonara Street, ✆ 373861. Better than many clones, the food is freshly prepared and the tablecloths are gingham, not plastic. **Big Al's Fish Bar** (cheap), Paceville Avenue,

© 319628, takes some beating. The British and Europeans alike happily munch on fish and chips—sadly not wrapped in the *Daily Mirror*—prepared as only the British know how. Not far away—nothing is in Paceville—is the **Ir-Rokna** (cheap), Church Street, © 311556, offering good thin crusty pizzas with quickfire service in uninspiring surroundings. If you eat there at night the hideous church is tastefully unlit. Side by side in Ball Street, the **Baruffa** (moderate), © 373840, **Il Siciliano** (inexpensive), © 373852, and **The Bombay** (inexpensive), © 376134, make odd neighbours. The Baruffa serves, albeit a little slowly and in cramped surroundings, some of the best local fish to be found in the area. The meat dishes are more adventurous and less successful. Il Siciliano is not what you would expect, more Italian than Sicilian, which is a pity, but still a safe bet. The Bombay holds no surprises, but like most Indian restaurants, it rarely disappoints; if you crave a curry with basmati rice, the Bombay is the island's best choice.

Nightlife

Saturday night is lemming night and Paceville is the cliff's edge off which the young population, tourists and locals throw themselves; it's traditional in Malta to let your hair down at weekends. Bars, discos and a shoulder-rubbing vibrancy are all squeezed into this small steaming area. The social order of the island is changing and Paceville can and does explode, but on the whole the police are able to manage Latin tempers when 'boys get upset over girls'. If age is a sensitive issue, it's easy to feel like a pensioner from another planet; you don't have to be young to enjoy the activity, but it does help.

Malta has just one **casino**, on Dragonara Point. The gaming rooms open at 2030 and stay open until 0200 and sometimes later. Entrance is Lm2 and free if you are dining in the restaurant, the Marquis Room. In July and August the dress code is 'smart-casual' and for the rest of the year a tie is required. The 'slots', where no dress code applies, are at the rear and the casino has a *salon privé* for the high-rolling Italians. Even for non-gamblers, the casino can seem a million miles from Paceville as it catches what little evening summer breeze the Mediterranean has.

Bars

Bars are the evening's first course, where people congregate in the balmy nights of summer to spill out onto the pavements. In **St Julian's**

Bay, **Saddles** is long-established and attracts the teenage crowd, while **Peppino's** wine bar is the new boy for the next generation up. Above the bus terminus is **Lines**, another meeting place. The **St Julian's Band Club** is well located, with a sleepytime porch from which an older generation look on with bemused expressions.

As the hours wind on the pastel and neon decor of **Paceville** comes alive. A ghetto of graphically designed and evocatively named bars offer fuel for the night. The names sometimes change but the places remain the same. By the entrance to Dragonara Point is the popular **Bamboo Bar**, actually half a dozen open-air and indoor bars. **BJ's** in Ball Street is for an older crowd and has weekly jazz bands in summer. **Straws**, next door to the Marco Polo, has all manner of multicoloured cocktails with umbrellas. Adjacent to the St George's Complex is the real thing: both **Stings** and the **Footloose Bar** have karaoke mikes. The **Għall Kafe** next door to the Napoleon Pub is open 24 hours for snacks. The **Turkish Delight** is a kebab pit-stop. **The Easy Rider, Crossroads, Clouds, Hiccups, The Alley;** the names and bars go on like their patrons into the night until it's time to head for the discos.

Discos

AXIS and Styx II are thundering discos from a Hollywood set-maker's dream. Sophisticated lasers, banks of TVs and ear-bending sound systems are manipulated by a changing roster of foreign DJs.

They open their doors in daylight for 'the first sitting' of young teenagers from the outlying villages who have to beat the parental curfew and catch the last bus home. But the large floors don't begin to move until past midnight, and they heave well into the next day. In a predictable act of discrimination ladies on their own are invariably allowed in free while men are charged Lm1.50.

Madliena, Għargħur and Baħar iċ-Ċagħaq

On the Coast Road going towards St Paul's Bay, **Madliena** occupies the hills and valleys that form the wild sprawl of high ground in between the sea and the start of the Great Fault and the Victoria Lines. Primarily a residential community of villas for the well-heeled, neither Sliema nor Valletta are far away.

Hidden behind it is **Għargħur**, the old village of the Madliena area. The medieval village would always have been safe; the **Great Fault** is at its most impressive and impenetrable nestled between the Falka Gap and the valley, *Wied id-Dis*. It is another place to walk or cycle. The village of 2,400 people keeps very much to itself, aloof in its ancestry and sealed off from outside influences. Bubbling under the seeming tranquillity is a spooky air of trespassing into the unknown. Even the name Gharghur offers a little hint: għar means cave and għur means ogre.

Getting Around and Tourist Information

Madliena can be reached off the main Sliema–Mosta Road but the easiest route is either through St Andrew's or off the Coast Road. The main signposted turning before White Rocks is best for both Madliena and Gharghur. The signpost to the Madliena Cottage restaurant leads to a road—the absurdly named Caf Caf Lane—of suspension-destroying quality. No bus would make it up Madliena Hill so the Baħar iċ-Ċagħaq **buses 68** and **70** stop at the bottom. **No. 67** terminates beforehand in St Andrew's. Gharghur's only bus service, **No. 55**, plies a tortuous route via Naxxar infrequently. The Great Fault, the scenery and relatively few cars has meant that fit **cyclists** and **walkers** are commonplace. There is a striking short walk along the Great Fault from the Naxxar Gap to Gharghur. Gharghur's *festa* to St Bartholomew is on 24 August or the 1st Sunday thereafter.

Madliena and Gharghur

Fort Madliena, at 132 m above sea level, is an inconspicuous fort constructed by the British in 1878 to beef up the northeast flank of the Victoria Lines. Radar played a vital role in Malta's survival during **World War II** and the fort housed the main radar station. After the war NATO operated it until the British Forces left in 1979. St John's Medical Corps—the last recognizable vestige of the Order—now uses the fort as its training school.

Coming from Madliena Hill the road to **Gharghur** snakes over a defunct viaduct and up through the village's back door past an old 17th-century church. The road winds around the old flytipping favourites of fridges and car wrecks (most of which seem to have done a high mileage on their roofs) towards the Great Fault. From this belvedere the whole of the north of Malta stretches out below and it's easy to see how the landmass formed; it simply shattered in two and the hard coralline limestone falls away vertiginously beneath.

The church is at the centre of this anachronistic and picturesque village, where despite numerous access roads there is a pervading sense of being cut off in time. Horse-drawn carts plod slowly through the square, trapped finches hop dementedly in miniscule cages hung from the doors of the *kaċċatur* or hunters. Old women swelter in black clothes while they scrub the stone steps of their houses a few metres away from the Playboy Bar. Behind the church, in perennial shade, is the King George VI Bar with its classical and proud sign contrasting with the crumbling stone. The parish **church of St Bartholomew** has been credited to Tommaso Dingli. Work commenced in 1638 and from stylistic evidence it took 20 or more years to complete. Parish churches, apart from being the centre of their villages, are symbols of ostentation and wealth, but this church with its gloomy interior and more contemporary façade, is like the village, subdued.

By the small bay of **Baħar iċ-Ċagħaq** and clearly visible from the road, is the **Splash Park**, ✆ 375021, a spaghetti-junction of chutes that empty hordes of shrieking children—and adults—into a deep pool. At a safe distance is a large circular swimming pool for those more interested in doing nothing. Next to the pool is a children's play area of weird fibreglass prehistoric animals. The bellies of scarlet dinosaurs house slides, and swings dangle under the wings of mauve pterodactyls. Most disturbing. *Entrance is from 1000 and use of all the facilities and unlimited rides costs Lm3.25 and Lm2.25 for children. Lost or damaged swimwear can be replaced at the small kiosk, and there is a **café** and changing rooms.* In the summer months an Italian **funfair** sets up shop adjacent to the Splash Park.

The **beach** at Baħar iċ-Ċagħaq is not ideal, due to its proximity to the road. The rock bathing is safe and the refreshment caravans attest to its popularity with the Maltese. During World War II, to be posted here as a lookout was considered a plum job: outside of the main target areas and by the cool waters. On Qrejten Point is another of the 13 coastal towers Grand Master de Redin constructed in 1658–9.

Where to Stay

In St Andrew's is the **Atlas Hotel**★★★★ (expensive), St Andrew's Road, ✆ 370493, painted an unflattering pale brown. Inside it has all the requirements of its rating including a small health club and two pools. The rooms are uninteresting but it's perfect for people who like to be away from the main tourist drag. **The White Rocks Holiday**

Complex (Class III), Baħar iċ-Ċagħaq, © 342520, was once part of the British Forces accommodation, but don't be put off. On the unspoiled sloping ground above the sea, 90 different-sized apartments and 12 houses have one of the best positions along this coast. Facilities include two pools, a mini-market, tennis and basketball courts and a restaurant.

Eating Out

Up Caf Caf Lane towards Madliena, and completely isolated, is the **Madliena Cottage** (expensive), © 375589. For a quiet romantic summer's evening this long-established restaurant has still views down to the Mediterranean from the terrace, competently cooked food (excellent duck) from a cosmopolitan menu and reliable service. The added bonus of its own car park is not to be taken lightly at the weekends. Further along the Coast Road next to Baħar iċ-Ċagħaq Bay is **Ronnies**, where you can get snacks and cold drinks. Over the road in Baħar iċ-Ċagħaq proper, on a dust track immodestly called 'Palm Beach', is the small **Marron Glacé** restaurant (inexpensive), © 374975. Apart from its *à la carte* menu they have a pasta evening every Friday: the chef cooks six different pastas, you get a little of each and the whole set menu is Lm2.75. Excellent value.

The Northern Coast

The Northern Coast

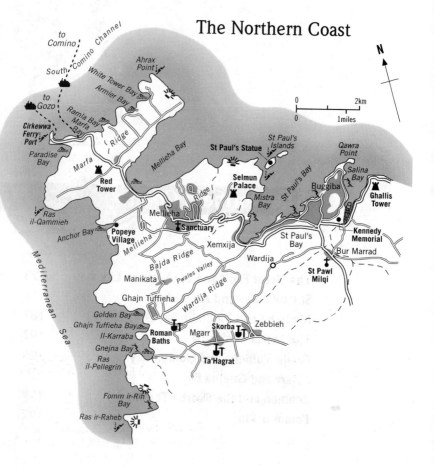

N

to
Comino

South Comino Channel

to
Gozo

Cirkewwa
Ferry
Port

Paradise
Bay

Ras
il-Qammieh

Anchor Bay

Ahrax
Point

White Tower Bay

Armier Bay

Ramla Bay

Marfa Bay

Marfa
Ridge

Mellieħa Bay

Red
Tower

Ridge

Mellieħa

Popeye
Village

Mellieħa

Bajda Ridge

Pwales Valley

Manikata

Għajn Tuffieħa

Golden Bay

Għajn Tuffieħa Bay

Il-Karraba

Gnejna Bay

Ras
il-Pellegrin

Fomm ir-Riħ
Bay

Ras ir-Raħeb

Sanctuary

Xemxija

Wardija Ridge

Wardija

Roman
Baths

Mgarr

Ta'Ħagrat

Skorba

Zebbieħ

St Paul's Statue

St Paul's
Islands

Selmun
Palace

Mistra
Bay

St Paul's Bay

St Paul's
Bay

St Pawl
Milqi

Qawra
Point

Salina
Bay

Buġibba

Kennedy
Memorial

Bur Marrad

Għallis
Tower

Mediterranean Sea

0   2km

0   1miles

Then cried the soul of the stout Apostle Paul to God:
'Once we frapped a ship, and she laboured woundily.
There were fourteen score of these,
And they blessed Thee on their knees,
When they learned Thy Grace and Glory under Malta by the sea!'

Rudyard Kipling

For many thousands of visitors each year the northern coasts are much more than just another holiday destination—it is one of the Christian world's great tenets that the Apostles St Paul and St Luke were shipwrecked here, at St Paul's Bay, during a *gregale* in AD 60. There is no proof, but for the visitors and Maltese the belief remains unshakeable.

This region of inland ridges and fertile valleys was until the 18th century the island's poorest. Cut off from three-quarters of Malta by bad communications across the Great Fault, nobody really called it home until 150 years ago. The rugged open bays lay prey to any invader, from opportunistic Barbary corsairs to Napoleon. Now the shores have become Malta's *costa* and the armada continues, but in Boeings rather than galleys.

There are few surprises or illusions along this coastline today. The *sine qua non* of the package holiday has conquered: big hotels, unedifying blocks of flats and half-built sites muscle-in amid the ever-so-plausible patter of the time-share touts. To obliterate the worst horrors you will need dark glasses and a sense of nostalgia (after all, the northern coasts always were difficult to defend).

The Great Fault and the Victoria Lines

Millions of years ago the Maltese islands split from Europe so that they no longer formed the final brick in the marshy land mass south of Sicily. The landmass shattered producing a series of faults and rift valleys which tilted downhill in an easterly direction and formed the landscape much as it is today. The most serious of these is the **Great Fault** which almost bisects the island and runs from Fomm ir-Riħ in the west until it peters out in Baħar iċ-Ċagħaq, 15 km away on the east coast. Its near-vertical face— 239 m at its highest—means the valleys and settlements below and to the north of it have always been indefensible and expendable. Smaller faults such as Wardija, Bajda, Mellieħa and Marfa Ridges bump along less dramatically northward towards Comino.

With the arrival of the Order in 1530, warfare left the era of 'rape, pillage and enslave' and entered a more sophisticated period. The natural defence afforded by the Great Fault to the harbours, Malta's prize asset, became apparent. In the 17th century the knights began to construct entrenchments in the gaps at Binġemma, Falka and Naxxar, and a fort at Nadur ('look out'), the highest point along the fault.

During the 1870s, when Malta was under British colonial rule and the rumbles between the British, French and Russian Empires continued, the defences along the Great fault were reinforced even further. A late 19th-century engagement would involve an enemy out of sight of land armed with massive guns capable of firing shells 7 km or more. In 1875 the construction of the three great gun-enplaced forts began at Binġemma, Madliena and Mosta. Further defences and batteries were built at Għargħur and Tarġa and a continuous line of coralline limestone entrenchments linked them, along practically the entire fault line. None of these defences were meant to defeat a northern invasion, simply to delay a naval assault on the harbours. In 1897 the then complete and impressive defences were officially called the **Victoria Lines**, in honour of the monarch's Diamond Jubilee.

What remains of the Victoria Lines, can best be appreciated on foot, especially at the western end by Binġemma Gap. For the more slothful, any of the corkscrew hairpins that twist down the four main gaps of Binġemma, Falka, Tarġa and Naxxar indicate what the escarpment must have been like to an invader.

Salina Bay

A cake-shaped sliver of that rarest of sights, an undeveloped section of the northern coast, separates Salina from the *costa* that begins in Qawra and ends in Xemxija. The Suncrest Hotel, Malta's largest, is built on the northwestern shore of the bay.

The salt-making industry that had survived intermittently since Roman times switched to Salina, meaning 'salt pan', after Mellieħa was depopulated in the 16th century. Malta has always had very little exportable local produce and in order to make such a precious commodity in quantity Grand Master de la Valette had the original salt pans dug at the head of the bay. After the Order was sacked by Napoleon in 1798 the pans fell into disuse; in the middle of the 19th century the British reworked them.

Getting Around and Tourist Information

There is no direct bus service; the nearest terminus is Buġibba/Qawra, and the **no. 70** runs between Sliema and Buġibba only in summer. If you are driving east towards Valletta, treat the Salina Bay corner by the Għallis Tower with extreme caution. There's a dangerous reverse camber, and many motorists have come to grief at the crash barrier and on the rocks below. Salina Bay relies upon the services of its neighbours.

Don't bother to stop at the remains of the **Għallis Tower** on the eastern headland, another of the 13 towers built by Grand Master de Redin between 1658 and 1659. Its opposite number on Qawra point, the **Fra Ben Tower**, now a restaurant, was built by Grand Master Lascaris some 20 years earlier; both were designed to be defended rather than being simple signalling relay stations. The knights further improved their fortifications in the bay with the *fougasse*, a wickedly clever early mortar-cum-landmine which the British kept loaded and primed during World War II. It consisted of a 2-m hole dug in the living rock, at the bottom of which was a fused keg of dynamite. On top of this were packed sufficient rocks, bits of metal and hurtful debris to maim if not slaughter an entire enemy platoon. The gaping hole is still in the rocks by the entrance to what was the Salina Bay Hotel.

The inauspicious **Kennedy Grove Memorial**, an understated and simple structure, is at the head of the bay behind the salt pans. The shady grove of trees was planted in 1966 as a living memorial to JFK. The three principal species reflected the prevailing view of the man at the time: the olive represented peace, the oak strength, and the flowering oleander his love of beauty and life.

Where to Stay and Eating Out

The Salina Bay Hotel is currently undergoing a needed re-fit but 500 m away is the **Lancer Hotel★★** (inexpensive), Naxxar Road, Salina, © 573891, with 13 tired rooms, a perfect place to dump a suitcase and sleep for a few hours. Do not expect much else. Annexed to the Lancer is yet another TV-inspired bar, and the only one around, **Charlie's Angels**. The **fruit van** on the Salina Road sells watermelon in summer.

St Paul's Bay and Around

At the turn of the century St Paul's Bay was a listless, peaceful fishing village with 180 inhabitants. In the last 20 years it has grown like a giant, unhindered on a diet of foreign currency, to become unashamedly Malta's *costa*. It's Marbella without the crooks and Blackpool without the illuminations, where the Bognor Regis Restaurant exists happily with bumper cars, saucy postcards, pale ale and timeshares; it's basically a mass-market destination (trying ever-so-hard to be something else). But it does provide what is required to work off 50 weeks tension in two—there's sun, sea, and sex. Break out the sunscreen, shut your eyes and slab out like a seal on the rocks—the wonderful waters have escaped almost unscathed.

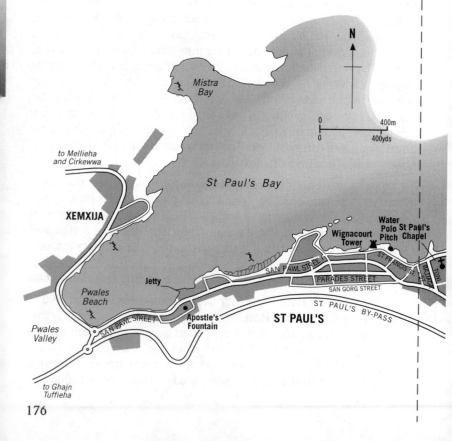

History

> 'Then Festus, when he had conferred with the council, answered, "Hast thou appealed unto Caesar ? Unto Caesar shalt thou go".'

Acts of the Apostles 25:12

In AD 60 the governor of Palestine, Porcius Festus, allowed **Paul of Tarsus** passage from Ceasarea to Rome to stand trial for heresy before the Emperor Nero, and in so doing set Malta's religious destiny in motion.

In the autumn, under armed guard, the Apostles St Paul and St Luke sailed from Palestine for Crete, their intended refuge for the winter months. Rome, wise in the vicious winter habits of the Mediterranean forbade all voyages

St Paul's Bay and Buġibba

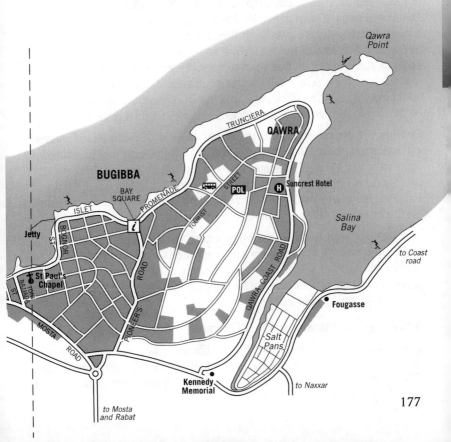

between 11 November and 5 March. But Julius, St Paul's centurion guard, wanted to press on as far eastward as possible. He was ill-advised: the *gregale*, an infamous and violent northeast winter wind, struck soon after they left Crete. The storm overtook their ship and after 14 days and nights of lashing seas and tempestuous winds, all 276 passengers and crew were shipwrecked on the northern coast of Malta.

St Luke wrote: 'And when they were escaped, then they knew that the island was called Melita. And the barbarous people shewed us no little kindness: for they kindled a fire, and received us every one, because of the present rain and because of the cold'. (*Acts of the Apostles*, 28:1–2). The local inhabitants—St Luke uncharitably referred to them as 'barbarians' as they spoke neither Greek nor Latin—were a little bemused by their unexpected visitors. But in the chilly winter dawn they hospitably gathered wood for a large fire near the head of the bay. While building the fire, on what is today the site of the church of St Paul's Shipwreck, a deadly snake bit St Paul's hand. He shook it off into the flames as if swiping at an insect. Within moments this bedraggled Jew (St Paul was a short bow-legged man with thinning hair, an incongruously straggly beard and a beaked nose that lunged out from under wide bushy eyebrows) had not only survived certain death but secured himself a place in Malta's history and folk-lore. Local people believe that it is thanks to St Paul that there are no poisonous snakes in the archipelago, and that the poison he took from the viper he threw into the tongues of the women, notorious for their gossiping.

Publius, the Roman governor of the islands, heard of St Paul's bizarre survival and welcomed him at his country villa, where today the remains of the church of San Pawl Milqi ('St Paul Welcomed') stand. St Paul then cured Publius's sick father at the governor's main residence, said to be the site of Mdina Cathedral, and converted the grateful Publius to Christianity. (Publius was subsequently to become the first bishop of Malta and then Athens; he was later martyred and canonized.)

Although they were Rome's valuable prisoners, Publius allowed St Paul and St Luke three months at liberty preaching on the island. When the seas had calmed and another vessel was found, crowds of newly converted Maltese gathered to witness their departure for Syracuse and Rome, and whatever grisly fate Emperor Nero had in mind.

A Catalogue of Invasions: AD 61 Onwards

Thanks to its inviting topography, St Paul's Bay was always going to be near the top of any prospective invader's list. In 1090 the Norman, **Count Roger I**, used St Paul's Bay to end 220 years of Arab occupation. A tiny Norman force landed at the head of the bay and duped the entire Arab army into rushing down from Mdina onto the plain while Roger's main army landed further westward.

The Moors plagued the island with invasions in the early 15th century, but it was not until the mid-1400s that they arrived in earnest. Eighteen thousand of the King of Tunis's mercenaries landed along the north coasts, laying siege to Mdina. St Paul is celebrated as intervening from the heavens on a ferocious white charger. He and his horse repelled the Moslem arrows and saved the day. There is a Preti painting of this scene in Mdina Cathedral.

In 1565 the **Turkish** General Mustapha Pasha attempted a final and desperate re-invasion, after the initial evacuation of his troops following the Turks' defeat in the **Great Siege**. He must have pondered the grim end to an otherwise illustrious career that awaited him in Constantinople. With a demoralized force of 9,000 he marched towards Naxxar and Mdina while Admiral Piali's ships headed for St Paul's Bay. Their plan was as badly executed as the earlier siege. Mustapha Pasha's men were stopped in their tracks and retreated to St Paul's Bay. On the summer-parched Pwales Valley and the beach at St Paul's, a bloody hand-to-hand battle took place. While trying to board their ships, and survive a rearguard action in the Bay's shallows, the Turks were mercilessly slaughtered by the Christian knights. Mustapha Pasha and Admiral Piali sailed off for the Levant at sunset, leaving more than 3,000 bodies to putrefy in the blood-red waters of St Paul's Bay.

The invasions paused during the Order's reign, but **Napoleon** disembarked troops here and at Mellieħa in the dead of night in June 1798. During the ensuing and ultimately successful British naval blockade of 1798–1800 the bay's wide mouth was, with Marsaxlokk, one of **Nelson's** victualling ports.

During **World War II**, when St Paul's was still no more than a fishing village, the RAF built a much-used rest camp for pilots and mechanics. A few bombs from Axis bombers landed on the village, one of which obliterated the original church of St Paul's Shipwreck. After the Italian surrender in September 1943, St Paul's Bay (again with Marsaxlokk Bay) was home to the 76 warships of the defeated Italian Navy.

Tourist Information

In Bay Square, Buġibba there is a **NTOM** open only in summer, next to a **Mid Med** bank with a multi-currency 24-hour foreign exchange machine. **Telemalta** has two offices, in St Paul's Bay and in Qawra.

The nearest 24-hour **poly-clinic** is in Mosta above the police station. Local doctors have open surgeries for minor complaints; your hotel will advise you which is the nearest.

Festa

The parish church is to **Our Lady of Sorrows**, and her *festa* is celebrated on the last Sunday in July. The **Shipwreck of St Paul** is celebrated on the Sunday closest to 10 February with an evening procession to the church of St Paul's Shipwreck, where a bonfire is lit. On 29 June an open-air mass is said at 1800 underneath the statue of St Paul on Selmunett, the largest of St Paul's islets.

Getting Around

A **car** is vital. Valletta is about 16 km away.

St Paul's Bay is the hub for what little cross-routing can be achieved. *See* route map p. 172. **Taxis** are in Bay Square, Buġibba; and in Qawra along the Coast Road fronting on to Salina Bay.

Qawra, Buġibba, St Paul's Bay, Xemxija and Mistra Bay

Grand Master Alof de Wignacourt (1601–22) was a prolific builder, aided by the engineering skills of Gerolamo Cassar's son Vittorio. **The Wignacourt Tower** (1609) overlooks the northern approaches to the bay and was a prototype for the subsequent and much larger forts of St Lucien, St Thomas and St Mary's on Comino. The tower has been restored and houses a tiny local museum. (*Adm. free. Check locally for times.*)

Five hundred metres away, in the fisherman's cove of **La Scaletta**, opposite the Il-Gillieru Restaurant at the end of Toni Bajada Street is the chapel-like **church of St Paul's Shipwreck**. According to tradition it was on this site that St Paul and St Luke first kindled the physical and spiritual fire of 'the barbarous [Maltese] people'. A place of worship has been known to exist here since the early 14th century. Grand Master Alof de Wignacourt enlarged the church with a portico arcade on a podium. His addition of the three arches on either side and a tiny bellcote together give the building more gravitas without detracting from its intimacy. A stray bomb almost levelled it during the last war but it has been sympathetically restored.

What can look like just another of the many roadside shrines on the St Paul's Road near the head of the bay is in fact **Għajn Razul** (the Apostle's Fountain). Two stories are told about this shrine to St Paul: one is that he and his fellow survivors were thirsty after the shipwreck, so he struck a stone and water miraculously gushed out; the other says that he baptized the first Christians from the spring. Either way, the water is *not* drinkable.

Heading north out of St Paul's Bay through Xemxija is an easily missed turning for **Mistra Bay**, a secluded inlet in St Paul's Bay. Just before the turning is a weathered archway that was once the sumptuous mid-18th-century entrance to the Monte di Redenzione estates of Selmun fame. The little narrow beach of coarse sand and seaweed is approached through a corridor of rampant bamboo. This is not speedboat territory, and the **bathing** and **snorkelling** are good. In 1658 Grand Master de Redin built the **Pinto Redoubt** and Grand Master Pinto added a stable block in the 18th century for the cavalry stationed in Mdina. Today it is the home of a Monagasque-owned fish farm. Since its arrival in 1991 the number of hopeful fishermen sitting peacefully on their miniscule stools with their 7-m long bamboo rods has increased dramatically.

Sports and Activities

The obvious aquatic variations proliferate along this coastline. A patch of smooth rocks, a bit of shade, a few cold drinks and a ladder into the water constitutes a **lido**; add somewhere to eat and a wallet-full of motorized toys and you are on the way to an empire. The Luzzu and the Club in **Qawra**, the New Dolmen in **Buġibba** and the Fekruna and Beachaven in **Xemxija** have many facilities to choose from, and are among the more popular.

The best **diving** is off Qawra Point and around the islets of St Paul's. Many Roman anchors have been discovered in the sands off Qawra Point, the largest being over 4 m long and weighing 3½ tonnes. Three licensed establishments for beginners and experts are **Strand Diving** underneath the Il-Gillieru restaurant and **Maltaqua** in Mosta Road (both in St Paul's Bay) and **Subway** in Xemxija. **Fishermen** can cheat in Mistra Bay—escapees from the fish farm are easy prey.

Water polo, the summer's football, is played at the Sirens' team pitch, 100 m from the Wignacourt Tower in St Gerald Street, St Paul's Bay.

The Captain Morgan *Sea Below* goes for a one-hour cruise (*Lm3.95*), five times a day from the quay in Buġibba next to Bognor Beach. Its glass-panelled keel shows off what marine life there is, as well as the statue of the 'Seafarers' Christ', plonked on the seabed after Pope John Paul II's visit in 1990.

Where to Stay

Without exception the accommodation in this area is block-booked by major tour operators, making hotel rack rates essentially meaningless.

Qawra

Driving along the Qawra Coast Road fronting onto Salina Bay, the immense hotels and apartment blocks are reminiscent of old Hollywood sets; impressive façades that have you wondering what really goes on behind them. **The Suncrest★★★★** (expensive), Qawra Coast Road, ✆ 577101, is the biggest hotel in Malta and the best in the St Paul's area, with 424 rooms. It is marble-clad and swanky, but the staff have a professional and genuinely caring manner. Amenities include 6 restaurants, squash courts and small gym, three pools and two lidos with their own diving school. A little further down from the Suncrest, the **Qawra Palace★★★** (moderate), Qawra Coast Road, ✆ 580131, is not as big but has the same views, pleasant rooms, two pools and a lido onto Salina Bay. The drawback is a massive restaurant which can get like feeding time at the zoo. Nearly lost in the no-man's-land that divides Qawra and Buġibba is the **Hotel San Mark★★★★**(expensive), Il-Konz Street, ✆ 572027, a well-run place with 75 cosy refurbished rooms. The pool is also on the small side but is secluded behind dry-stone walls and a couple of hardy trees. Also in the no-man's-land between Qawra and Buġibba is the impressive-looking but unpretentious **Cape Inch★** (inexpensive), Merlux Street, ✆ 572025, with 30 simple well-presented rooms and an air-conditioned restaurant. As it has no lift to the three upper floors, or direct-dial telephones it warrants only one star. Excellent value for the independent traveller.

Buġibba

Block after block of self-catering apartments, guest houses and hotels are to be found here. The **New Dolmen Hotel★★★★** (expensive), Trunciera, ✆ 581510, the second biggest of the island's hotels, is all sub-Dallas flash with mirrored glass curves. The impressive facilities include four pools, a private lido and a huge conference hall. Nearly all of the 389 air-conditioned bedrooms enjoy excellent views and unlike the Suncrest there is an antiseptic and self-important air to the place. Looking very out of place in the garden by the pool are the remains of a prehistoric fisherman's temple. Having inadvertently damaged it (one of the blocks with a fish motif made it to the Museum of Archaeology), the hotel then took its name and logo from the trilithon entrance. The **Mediterranea★★★** (moderate), Buġibba Road, ✆ 571118, is on the high road between St Paul's and Buġibba. From this terrific vantage point the view spans the bay and the islets, and the hotel offers some respite from the crowded centre. The **Hotel Hyperion★★★** (moderate), Tourist Street, ✆ 572481, is good unpretentious holiday accommodation. A large pool makes up for the spartan rooms. The **Buġibba Holiday Complex** (Class I), Tourist Street, ✆ 580861, is the biggest local complex, but away from the seafront. The rooms are comfortable, the pools adequate and the shelves of the mini-market well stocked. At the centre of the action, Bay Square, and 50 m from the enticingly named 'Bonkers Bar' is **Villa Mare★★** (inexpensive), Bay Square, ✆ 573824, with only 12 rooms. For those who loathe missing out on anything, including noise, this is the place. In a similar but quieter vein the **Buccaneers** (Class

II), St Anthony's Street, ✆ 571671, is a very friendly guest house with simple, cool and comfortable rooms. The bar and restaurant are popular, especially with the jingoistic British, and have excellent coffee.

St Paul's Bay, Xemxija and Mistra Bay

The accommodation is mostly **holiday apartments**. Walk around and look for landlords' signs in windows or ask at a newsagent or super-market: someone's brother-in-law will have a second cousin who knows of a cheap, clean apartment to rent. Over the brow of the hill is the jewel in Malta's tourist-complex crown: **Mistra Village** (Class I), Xemxija Hill, ✆ 580481. The village was built of local stone in the

1970s and sits in 9 acres of landscaped gardens with amusing touches like a restored British red pillar box and phone box and a labyrinthine layout. The accommodation falls somewhere between an hotel suite and a self-catering apartment; and into two categories, standard and superior, both thoughtfully designed and furnished. It has excellent sports facilities, a market, three restaurants and even a small Greek-style open-air theatre. This well-run complex is marred only by the white outdoor furniture which glares whiter than magnesium under the noonday sun. **Xemxija**, meaning sunny place, is on the north side of the bay and has limited hotel accommodation. The **Ambassador★★★** (moderate), Shipwreck Promenade, ℭ 573870, on the waterfront is a peaceful hotel with soporific views, which is contracted out exclusively to Thomsons Holidays. At the head of the bay and on the busy road is the dated but friendly **Xemxija Bay Hotel★★** (inexpensive), Xemxija Hill, ℭ 573454. The rooms at the front and the first-floor terrace restaurant have an uninterrupted view of the bay, the quieter rooms at the back look down on the uninteresting Pwales Valley. There are two guest houses in St Paul's Bay (both Class II): **Il Gifen**, St Paul's Street, ℭ 573291, and **Green Arches**, St George's Street, ℭ 573417, with 10 and 8 rooms respectively.

Eating Out in Qawra

Qawra has a couple of noteworthy restaurants. The tiny **Gran Laguna** (moderate), Qala Street, ℭ 571146, above the briny saltpans of Salina looks as if it has been created out of the Sicilian owner's sitting room. Far more attention has been paid to the predominantly Sicilian menu than the decor, and the fish is invariably well cooked. Overlooking the Kennedy Grove is **Savini** (expensive), Qawra Road, ℭ 576927. The decor is Laura Ashley twee, and the food is good but can be fussy—their specialty, a surf 'n' turf of steak covered in a lobster sauce. Food is always prepared to order. Be patient.

Buġibba

One of the few restaurant foods that has more profit in it than pizza is ice cream, and **Buġibba** is overflowing with both. The British palate is also well catered for: all the 'with chips' favourites are easy to locate.

Buġibba's first superior-class restaurant, **Da Michele Restaurant** (expensive) in Tourist Street was just about to open at the time of writing. At the moment the best table in terms of cooking, service and position is the **New Portobello** (moderate), St Luke Road, ✆ 571661, on the high road between St Paul's and Buġibba. Try to reserve a table near the front for the dusk view over the bay and islets. The food is traditional Italian with a lightish touch and the decor is pleasant but uninspired. Book at weekends. Next door is **Portobello Pizzeria**. Decorated in an outrageously pseudo-Cantonese style, the **Peking** (inexpensive), Tourist Street, ✆ 580696, offers a welcome gastronomic break. It's large and buzzy, and the food can be erratic, but worth a visit. For the carnivore the **Monte Carlo** (inexpensive), San Xmun Street, ✆ 576581, serves variations on steak. The cooking and service can be like an 'amateur night at the opera' accompanied by embarrassed grins, yet it is an intimate and friendly place. In the middle of town is the **Hotel Villa Mare** (cheap), ✆ 573824; small, lively and best on a Friday pasta evening, when you can eat as much as you like for Lm1.75. **Jespers**, Sajjied Street, ✆ 580031, is a sensational Danish bakery, open from dawn to dusk, and everything from the scrummy pastries to the wholemeal bread is homemade.

St Paul's Bay

Hard to miss on the Mosta Road coming into St Paul's Bay is one of the much-lauded restaurants of Malta, **Le Pilier** (expensive), 14 Mosta Road, ✆ 576887. Unless you are fan of pretentious cooking, slow service, and an overbearing management that leaves you wondering who is doing who the honour, it's well worth missing. Pity, because the dining room is comfortable and moodily lit. Down by the sea and clumped around the church of St Paul's Shipwreck are three good and different restaurants but parking can be a problem here. The oldest is **Il-Gillieru** (expensive), ✆ 573480, built over the water and with its own jetty to which boats can be tied in summer. (From the water, head for the new Harbour Hotel.) Not surprisingly, this restaurant specializes in fish; it's huge, and takes itself a little too seriously. Do not expect culinary fireworks or the throb of a continental atmosphere, but the lapping sea and the views are hard to beat; come here on business, or a special occasion. Opposite is **da Rosi** (moderate), ✆ 571411, a small narrow restaurant that attracts a younger set who crowd it out in summer. The pasta is good and the plain grilled meats are well prepared. This is a place for a date. In the basement next door is the **Macedonia** (cheap), ✆ 573391, very popular with the locals for its good crusty pizza but the pasta is invariably overcooked. It can hop late in the evenings and at weekends, and there is a bar where you can wait for your table. Upstairs they have a restaurant proper. Locked in the one-way system heading towards Xemxija, you definitely can't miss the **Palazzo Pescatore** (moderate), St Paul's Road, ✆ 573182. This imposing 1774 building was, like the casino, another residence of the Marquis Scicluna family, and it has been a restaurant for more than 20 years. The walls could do with a coat of paint but the kitchen is up to scratch. Fresh fish is displayed, and cooked well, and some of the Mediterranean-influenced local dishes are sound. The restaurant extends into the semi-covered garden in summer. For those in a hurry or with less to spend, the owner—Ben—also has **Macbenny's** next door; if it's the real McCoy you crave, avoid it. For something a little more eccentric the **Ipanema** (inexpensive), Mosta Road, ✆ 572260, is hard to beat and has the only Brazilian kitchen in Malta. The **Porto del Sol** (moderate), Xemxija Road, ✆ 573970, is another well-run family restaurant frequented by locals which for some reason forbids young children. The decor is eclectic but the bay views are pleasant. The wine list is thin, and stay with the locally caught fish. Open for lunch and dinner. Further up the hill in Xemxija in Mistra Village is **Ir Razzett** (inexpensive), ✆ 580481, renowned for expansive Sunday buffet lunches; and children are welcome. The hot and cold spread comprises whatever the chefs have prepared fresh that day. The decor is rustic, the staff are helpful, and it's excellent value for money.

Bur Marrad and the Wardija Ridge

Bur Marrad is an amorphous sprawl of truck garages and houses either side of the main road that runs from St Paul's Bay to Mosta. With a couple more filling stations it would resemble a continental rest-stop.

Wardija, with no distinct village, is the limestone ridge nearest to the Great Fault and rises to 143 m, lower by 2 m than the highest ridge, Mellieha. The Wardija ridge spans from Għajn Tuffieħa to St Paul's Bay and is the residential preserve of very well-to-do Maltese. It is sparsely populated and a good place to amble or ramble, for more than anywhere else in Malta the air has a wild aroma all year round. The scenery is panoramic, especially from the old

British gun enplacements overlooking St Paul's Bay (even Buġibba looks pleasant). Standing here it is easy to understand how the area got its name: Wardija means 'guard'.

Getting Around

Six **buses** stop in **Bur Marrad**, but you will need a car to get up to Wardija; no bus would ever make it up the hill.

On the slopes of the Ġebel Għawżara hill is the partially restored **church of San Pawl Milqi**, *milqi* meaning received or welcomed. It is badly sign-posted, and then only from the Mosta direction. Tradition states—and some scanty evidence supports it—that in AD 60 Publius, the island's Roman governor, had a sprawling country villa here, where he fed the two Apostles and fellow survivors. A community has been known to exist here since 2 BC until destroyed by fire early in AD 1, a date that conflicts with the tradition. The site was resettled again midway through the 4th century and the first record of a church dates back to 1488. The present structure was built around 1620.

During World War I British troops discovered evidence of a large stone wall but the site was not properly excavated until the 1960s. The Italian Archaeological Mission unearthed a substantial Roman settlement primarily involved in producing olive oil: de-pipper stones and basins still exist. One set of engraved symbols translated to PAULUS, another was of a man and two ships. Even so, it remains unclear whether the two saints spent their first three days here or near Tal-Ħereb in Wardija, where other scant traces were found.

The church was a vandal's playground and is now walled in; the key is available from the Museum of Archaeology or the sprightly can clamber over the eastern wall. Evidence of Roman ingenuity is clearly visible but expect to be a little disappointed at the poor maintenance of this important site.

Mellieħa and Mellieħa Bay (Il-Għadira)

> *'Qisu mill-aħrax tal-Mellieħa.'*
> *He comes from the wilds of Mellieħa.*
>
> Maltese insult said of an uncouth man.

Mellieħa is a craggy and picturesque hilltop town with bewitching cave dwellings and houses that cling like limpets to the rock face. Like Mġarr it has a comparatively modern street plan, with none of the haphazard charm of the southwest. But Mellieħa has its own different and more affluent appeal.

The village was built on top of the Mellieħa ridge as one of the 10 original parishes of 1436, and was entirely depopulated within a hundred years, because of the indefensibility of the northern shores against the itinerant corsair slave-traders. The mainstay salt industry collapsed—Mellieħa roughly translates to someone who makes or deals in salt—and was not finally re-settled until the 1840s under the safety of the British umbrella. Today, with 4,750 people, the population is equal to that of St Paul's Bay.

Mellieħa Bay is the largest **sandy beach** in the Maltese islands, 1.5 km down the ridge and out of town. The gently shelving approach to the water makes it ideal for children, and unlike some of the northwestern beaches there are no dangerous undercurrents. Unfortunately there are the inevitable crowds in peak season and at weekends, and a busy road which runs parallel to the beach. In all weathers the bay is popular with windsurfers.

It is also known as **Il-Għadira** meaning 'the swamp', as it once was. The marshy land behind the road is now a much-needed **wildlife preserve**.

History

Mellieħa Bay, with its wide mouth and shallow sea has always been a natural place to land, and not just for invading corsairs. A theory put forward in 1952 by the precise-minded Professor Burridge, states convincingly that **St Paul** fetched up here, and not on the rocks of St Paul's Bay. The many Roman wrecks discovered in Mellieħa Bay seem to add weight to his contention.

On 7 September 1565, in the very last hours of the **Great Siege**, Don Garcia of Toledo, the Spanish viceroy of Sicily, disembarked his long overdue 8000-strong relief force. After a bloody battle in the shallows of neighbouring St Paul's Bay, the battered remains of the Turkish army fled back to Constantinople to face the Sultan's wrath.

Napoleon chose Mellieħa Bay as one of his seven points of invasion in June 1798, when General d'Hilliers and his troops marched up the beach. Over a century later, and almost as an afterthought, the British built 45 m of slit trenches below the western ridge of the town overlooking the bay. During **World War II** the limestone caves in the ridge's face were used as bomb shelters.

Since the bypass around Mellieħa to Ċirkewwa (signposted at the main roundabout) was opened in the 1980s, much less traffic has ploughed up and down Mellieħa's snaking roads. The road to Mellieħa itself is well signposted from St Paul's Bay, 4.5 km away; allow 25–30 minutes if travelling from Valletta by car and much longer by bus. In this split-level village none of the public services are grouped together. The **bus terminus** is in the shady 26th May 1990 Square next to the Sanctuary of Our Lady of Mellieħa and a snoozing **taxi-driver** is never far away. **Buses 43, 45,** and **48** serve both Mellieħa and the beach.

Festas

On 8 September there is a national holiday to celebrate the end of both Great Sieges. Mellieħa's *festa* is the **Birth of the Blessed Virgin**.

Selmun Palace is an eye-catching castle perched at the top of Mellieħa ridge, and clearly visible along most of the northeast coastline. The land upon which it was built was given to Monte di Redenzione degli Schiavi, a charitable organization established in 1607 under the patronage of Grand Master Alof de Wignacourt to ransom enslaved Christians. The palace itself was constructed in the mid-18th century by Domenico Cachia to imitate, but not mock, the Verdala Castle; despite its baroque features, such as the elaborate balcony, it still has a castle's robustness. The escutcheon above the entrance is that of the Redenzione and nearby is the aptly named chapel of **Our Lady of Ransom** (*both are usually open at weekends*).

In Mellieħa the parish church of **Our Lady of Victory** is a cumbersome turn-of-the-century edifice with a beacon-like position in a benchless corridor of a square. Inside is a stirring painting by Guiseppe Cali of *The Shipwreck of St Paul*, which is not flattered by the gloomy interior.

Of much more interest is the chapel of the **Shrine of Our Lady of Mellieħa**, situated near the parish church off the main street in 26th May 1990 Square (renamed after the day Pope John Paul II visited the sanctuary). This domed little building, the oldest Marian shrine in Malta, was once the original parish church. Legend says it was built on the site of a cave-church visited by St Paul and St Luke and that the faded icon of the Madonna above the altar was painted by St Luke, an unlikely supposition. Everything about it is friendly and uplifting. Inside is a tiny museum with hundreds of votive offerings. These range from the frankly absurd—a signed picture from Norwich Town Football Club thanking the church for its Second Division championship in 1972—to heart-rending prayers of thanks. A display of memorabilia from Pope John Paul II's visit is behind a screen; you can even buy souvenirs with his Holiness stamped on them. *Adm. free. Open every day.*

For an example of the simple power of faith, visit the **Grotto**, a cave-shrine dedicated to the Madonna. The entrance is on the road opposite the steps that lead down from the square. Descend about 70 steps to reach an underground spring at the heart of the cave. The waters are said to have miraculous powers to heal the diseases of children, and the rock walls are covered with votive gifts.

Where to Stay in Mellieha

At the main roundabout before Mellieha is The **Maritim Selmun Palace★★★★** (expensive), ℂ 521040. Discreet and well-run under German management, it is a favourite with those who like a more hushed poolside environment. Set in the palace grounds, the hotel's 150 rooms are big on modern comforts and short on soul; a sign that forbids the early-morning reservation of sun loungers will bring a smile to the faces of the more laconic British. In Mellieha itself it would be hard to miss the modern **La Salita★★★★** (expensive), ℂ 520923/9, halfway down Borg Olivier Street. This hotel, where you are a patron not a guest, is a garish toothpaste blue; its 75 well-equipped rooms are decorated in unflattering pastel hues. Decor aside, there is a tinkling piano at weekends and the rooftop pool has a good view. The small **Panorama★★★** (moderate), off Valley Road, ℂ 573511, is a quiet place on the edge of town, popular with the British, and is balanced almost on the ridge itself with an uninterrupted view of the bay. The **Splendid** (Class II), Magri Street, ℂ 573769, is the only guest house in the Mellieha area; it has 10 clean and reasonable rooms that book up early.

Mellieha Bay

On the north side is the **Mellieha Bay Hotel★★★★** (expensive), ℂ 573844, an uninspired piece of architecture, but all 302 rooms have uninterrupted sea views. Don't be put off by the pokey lobby and coffee shop, this is one of the better holiday hotels around. The garden runs almost to the water's edge and there are good facilities for watersports and children. On the south side of the bay, and offering facilities for the disabled, is the brand new **Seabank Hotel★★★★** (expensive), Marfa Road, ℃ 521460/9. The 97 generous and calmly decorated rooms are air-conditioned, and have decent balconies. There is a pool and it's one minute from the beach and, unfortunately, the road. Just behind the Mellieħa Bay road is the excellent Danish-owned **Mellieħa Holiday Centre** (Class III), ℃ 573900, offering 150 two-bedroom bungalows set in manicured gardens thick with butterflies. There is a big, children's adventure playground, good restaurant, decent pool and private tunnel access to the beach. Be grateful there aren't any private telephones, that's the main reason for its lowly rating.

Eating Out

Two of the island's better restaurants, **The Arches** and **Guiseppi's**, are in Mellieħa. Coming into town by the main roundabout is the **Belleview**, a long-established and massive bakery with excellent substitutes for overpriced and indifferent beach food; it is also a good pit-stop if you are returning from Gozo in the small hours. Further along on the left is the restored **Il Mulino** (moderate), 34 Borg Olivier Street, ℃ 520404, in an old windmill of dark weathered stone. The cooking invariably involves sauces but the service is sound. At the top of steep Borg Olivier Street is the **Rovers Return** (inexpensive), 4 St Anne Street, ℃ 520921, in a far more imposing building than its UK counterpart. No prizes for guessing the house style, but the kitchen produces reliable fare. For the more cosmopolitan palate **La Rampa** (inexpensive), ℃ 520610, is 50 m away. Omelettes, salads, pizzas and Italian coffee are competently cooked and served, both inside and out. Almost opposite is **Guiseppi's** (moderate), 8 St Helen Street, ℃ 574882, Mellieħa's best, run by Malta-TV's 'Galloping Gourmet', Michael Diacono. His kitchen can be relied upon to create imaginative food from a menu that varies according to his mood and available produce. It is a small place with a wine bar feel downstairs, and a more intimate atmosphere upstairs. (*Dinner only and closed Sundays; booking essential.*) **The Arches** (expensive), 113 Borg Olivier Street, ℃ 573436, is an altogether different affair. Smartly dressed staff lead you up a curving staircase to a large and sometimes noisy restaurant. It's a little starchy but a worthwhile treat. Stay with the pasta or the fresh fish.

None of the many restaurants and snack bars on **Mellieħa Bay** beach are noteworthy. Two nearby alternatives are the **Great Dane** (moderate), Mellieħa Holiday Centre, ✆ 573980, where the food is reliable and will appeal to children. The service is attentive, and you can eat inside or out. **The Pizzeria** (inexpensive), ✆ 573116, at the new **Seabank Hotel** serves crusty pizzas and especially fine seafood ones. Both are open for lunch and dinner every day.

The Marfa Peninsula: Paradise Bay, Ċirkewwa, Ramla, Armier

This is an isolated part of the island, and unless you are staying at one of the two hotels the main reason for coming here is to catch the Gozo ferry. It gets very crowded at weekends, but there is excellent diving and the mini-cliffs at Aħmar are peaceful.

Marfa, meaning 'landing place', is a 7-km stretch of hard coralline limestone and *maquis*. Permanently uninhabited, it has mainly been used as a signalling outpost. Some of the redoubts, entrenchments and towers that deterred a catalogue of prospective invaders still exist.

Getting Around

By car the journey time to Ċirkewwa should be 35 minutes from the Sliema area, and 45 from Valletta; follow the signs for Mellieħa and then Ċirkewwa. On a hot August day the bus journey can be a sweltering hour-long trip. **Taxis** are always at the landing, but be prepared to be held to ransom; here there really are two different prices. It is a tourist rip-off at Lm10–Lm12 from the Valletta area. At the **Marfa** landing, 'Gozo Charlie' operates a regular and reliable service to **Comino's Blue Lagoon** on the unregal *Royal 1*. A placard next to the fruit vans in Xemxija will alert you to any delays on the **Gozo ferry**. Arrive at **Ċirkewwa** 30 minutes before the scheduled departure time in summer, the system is first-come first-on.

St Agatha's Tower or the **Red Tower** commands the high ground on Marfa ridge. The huge, forbidding and faded terracotta-coloured fort was built by Grand Master Lascaris and became operational in 1649. The tower's size and position gave it a dual role: not only a defence but also a signalling link between the towers on Gozo and St Mary's on Comino which ultimately led to Valletta. A brief but spirited defence was put up by the 49-strong garrison when the French landed in 1798 and the British used it as a signalling station during the last war. Today two men monitor local shipping from it, and visits are at their discretion.

Beaches and Activities

The beaches are sandy coves, and sometimes seaweed traps. The best two are **Little Armier**—signposted Ray's—and **Paradise Bay**, accessed via a steep flight of steps. **White Tower** beach is crowded and unclean while the tower itself is private and guarded by a pack of savage dogs. **Ramla** is reasonable, although it does seem to catch a swell, and **Armier Bay** is simply untidy. In mid-week the current through the Comino Channel keeps the sea clean and makes the coast ideal for snorkelling, diving and rock fishing. Avoid all the beaches here at weekends and public holidays, when the Maltese invade.

The shape of the promontory means that whichever way the wind and sea are going, you can **dive** here. Ċirkewwa has a cliff-dive down to 30 m off the point and is popular with photographers. The caves beneath the cliff are home to groupers and other fish. A good beginner's dive is **Aħrax Point**, the northern tip of Malta. The water goes down to 10 m, below which is a reef full of marine life and a cave. Not-so-ace speedboat-drivers like to cut this point very fine, so take a marker buoy. The boulder-strewn shoreline of **Ras il-Qammieħ** round the Ċirkewwa headland is accessible only by boat and has an exposed cave dive.

The *Lampuka* is a brand new 24-seat **submarine**, the 1992 addition to the Captain Morgan fleet. It departs from its purpose-built jetty at Ċirkewwa approximately 12 times daily and twice a night. The sub goes down deep, about 100 m, and snoops around a shipwreck and marine life. (*The trip lasts approximately 45 minutes and costs Lm16.95, children Lm13.95. It provoked a big outcry when it first arrived, with dramatic gestures like a hunger strike from some members of the diving fraternity.*)

Where to Stay

The **Ramla Bay Hotel★★★★** (expensive), Marfa, ℂ 573521, is a small hotel with more amenities than the rating would indicate, but rather worn out. Try and arrive at night or the ghastly approach road (no fault of the hotel) might make you turn and flee. The pleasant beach lido and pool are open to non-residents. The **Paradise Bay★★★★** (expensive), Ċirkewwa, ✆ 573981, is constructed in a curved sweep to give every room a view of the snug bay and its fish-shaped pool. Through a short tunnel it has a private beach which is ideal for watching the ferries come and go but not much else. The hotel is self-contained with squash and tennis courts and recreational facilities for children, much needed in this cut-off end of the island.

Eating Out

The Beachcomber (cheap), at Armier is a conventional beach establishment, but the fish and the salads are always fresh and the beer ice-cold. You need dark glasses at **Ray's** (cheap), in Little Armier. Painted snow white, not even the big square canvas umbrellas dull the glare of the Mediterranean sun. Eat inside or out. The excellent, homemade, grilled, Maltese sausages are not for the health-conscious.

Anchor Bay or Popeye Village

This was the prettiest and the smallest bay in Malta until 1979 when the director Robert Altman re-created **Sweethaven** here and scarred it indelibly with Hollywood's leaden boot. Neither Robin Williams as **Popeye** nor the world's cinema-going public liked *Popeye the Movie*; the film sank quicker and deeper than the Roman anchors from which the bay takes its name. Sadly, it will be known as Popeye Village until Hollywood makes a sequel in which Bluto wins the hand of Olive Oyl and destroys Sweethaven in a genuinely heroic act of revenge.

Getting There

You are not allowed to miss this, so the signposting is good from both Mellieħa and Għajn Tuffieħa. The nearest bus stop is at Mellieħa Bay from which it is a 1.5-km walk west.

The whole place is too ghastly for words. Faceless amusement-arcade bodies of Popeye, the Oyl Family (Olive, Castor et al) and the rest of the cast accompany a shed full of tacky souvenirs, but sadly no spinach stall.

In the old cartoons, Sweethaven looked like a gaggle of clapboard houses built in a topsy-turvy and lean-to manner by a team of shortsighted, drunk or incompetent carpenters. It does in reality too. The village was built in 7 months and was designed to stand for a further 8 months. That was 14 years ago.

Fortunately, the tissue-sized coarse-sandy beach has been left alone. Lie there and try to imagine what the Romans would say if they travelled back in time to collect their lost anchors. *Adm. Lm1.50. © 472430. There is a* **café**.

On the northwest coast, undercurrents can become strong after bad weather.

Għajn Tuffieħa and Golden Bay

A headland separates the two popular sandy beaches of **Għajn Tuffieħa** ('the spring of the apples', so named after an underground spring) and **Ramla tal-Mixquqa** (unimaginatively called 'Military Bay' under the British and now referred to as Golden Bay). Both beaches lie at the north-western end of the Pwales Valley, 6 km from St Paul's Bay and in between the Wardija and Bajda ridges. Thousands of years ago the greater part of the valley was under water, but today it is the most fertile valley in Malta and is cropped all year round.

On the eve of the **Great Siege** in May 1565, the Turkish fleet anchored and watered its ships in Għajn Tuffieħa prior to their invasion at Marsaxlokk. Grand Marshall Copier, in command of the Order's cavalry squadron, must have wondered how long it was for this world as he helplessly watched the armada of 181 vessels, packed with Moslem soldiers, approaching.

During **World War II** Għajn Tuffieħa Bay was used to train the naval canoeists who would eventually provide vital information for the Allied invasion of Sicily. In Golden Bay the British built an unattractive military camp (which is now the greatly improved **Ħal Ferħ Holiday Village**) and a naval rifle range.

Getting Around

The easiest route is along the valley floor from St Paul's Bay. For Golden Bay turn right after about 5 km and for Għajn Tuffieħa continue straight on for another 500 m. **Golden Bay** has a large **car park** with a **taxi rank** and easy access to the beach. The buses run frequently in summer, less so in winter and the service ends before dusk. **Għajn Tuffieħa** has a much smaller rough patch of rock that doubles as a car park in front of the shell of the Lascaris watch tower (1637). The Għajn Tuffieħa **bus terminus** is in the Golden Bay car park. You can reach the beach by boat or a long swim round the headland. From the land, it is only accessible via a couple of hundred steps cut into the rock.

Tourist Information

When the weather is rough, or has been rough there can be a very dangerous undertow on both of these beaches, that has been known to exhaust the strongest of swimmers. In the high summer of 1992, bouts of sea pollution occured here for the first time.

The bays along this coast are sheltered from the prevailing northeast summer wind so at weekends and public holidays the commonest sight is flesh in shades varying from lobster pink to coconut brown. All **watersports** from a sedate *pedalo* to the irksome jet-ski are available on both beaches, but Golden Bay beach offers more variety. Fed up with sand castles? There is horse riding at the **Ħal Ferħ Stables** behind the car park, ℂ 573360.

Off-road walking is a popular recreation and to the north the tracks will ultimately feed you into Mellieħa via the hamlet of **Manikata**. The modern church was designed by Richard England after the style of 1930s architecture as an imaginative complement to the low-built local farmsteads. The red and white fairy lights that adorn its edges are the villagers' experiment. The southern and rougher cliff track leads on to the Ġnejna Bay area (*see* below).

On the road to Mġarr 1.5 km away are the **Roman Baths**. Discovered in 1929 by farmers and excavated in the same year, the baths were restored again in 1961 by UNESCO. The setting with its tangled prickly pears and vegetation is striking but marred by yet another burnt-out car at the entrance. Bathing was an integral part of Roman culture and the 'spring of the apples' would have been the nearest plentiful water supply to Mdina/Rabat. The sparse remains demonstrate how sophisticated they and their engineering were; with changing rooms, U-shaped communal lavatories, a small swimming pool, a *caldarium* built above a small furnace, a *tepidarium*, and the final and inevitable *frigidarium*. The best-preserved of the colourless mosaics are in the changing rooms and the *tepidarium* and the whole compact complex is flash with ingenious design. *Adm. free. Karmen can show you around Mon–Sat 1030–1600, 1200–1400 on Sundays. Times-ish*

Where to Stay and Eating Out

The **Golden Sands**★★★ (moderate), Golden Bay, ℂ 573961–3, is a sprawling 1960s affair built on the cliff, a typical holiday hotel and none the worse for it. The majority of the 300-plus rooms have good sea views, and amenities include a private area on the beach, two pools, tennis court and conference facilities. Ideal if you don't want to be part of the *costa* scene. The **Ħal Ferħ Holiday Village** (Class II), Golden Bay, © 573882/3, is a well-converted series of hotel rooms and self-catering bungalows screened on all fronts by trees and therefore without any view. All the usual recreations and amenities are on site. The 'Great British Breakfast' as interpreted by **The Apple's Eye** (cheap) in the Golden Bay car park is cooked until 1300 every day. Lunch is in a similar vein.

Mġarr and Ġnejna Bay

The village of **Mġarr** at the top of the Ġnejna Valley, in between the Victoria Lines and the Wardija Ridge, is not to be confused with the harbour of the same name in Gozo. Settled only in the 1850s, it is an undecided little place of 2,400 people, known for its agriculture and for being the Land Rover capital of Malta. The villagers are to be seen either dismantling trashed gearboxes and engines or lugging crates of tomatoes to market (Mġarr can also mean 'market place').

Mġarr and the sandy beach at **Ġnejna Bay** were loved by Admiral Sir William Wordsworth Fisher (the poet's grandson) and Sir Harry Luke (lieutenant governor of Malta 1930–38). Their affection was reciprocated: both had a street named after them but Fisher's has since been renamed.

Getting Around and Tourist Information

From St Paul's Bay the road is signposted to Għajn Tuffieħa and forks left for Mġarr; alternatively the route is west from Mosta and Rabat. Neither **bus no. 46** nor **47** goes onto Ġnejna Bay.

To demonstrate their frustration at the perennially unattended police station the villagers bricked it up in 1992. The **bus stop** is next door. Mġarr's *festa* is The Assumption on 15 August.

You cannot miss the **Egg Church**, as has always and will always be known. The nickname for the church of the Assumption was earned in a true tale that illustrates the devoutness of Maltese Christian faith.

In the 1930s Father Salmone, Mġarr's charismatic parish priest whipped up support from the impoverished villagers for a new church to be built out of the produce of the land. Every week each villager delivered eggs or vegetables for him to sell, the proceeds going into the building-fund. The church took many years to build and the large dome and the tiny cupola, resembling an egg in a cup, serve as a permanent reminder of its origins. The last detail, made when both funds and farmers were exhausted, was the painted second clock, its hands steadfastly fixed at two minutes before the devil's hour of midnight; in such a devout village, surely an unnecessary superstition.

The **Ta'Hagrat Temples**, 100 m from the police station, are historically significant but not much to look at, and are probably only of interest to keener students of archaeology. The site, which is fenced-in, was first excavated in 1925. The remains hint at two temples, one large and one small on either side of a small courtyard, dating bach to the Ġgantija and Saflieni phases respectively. (*Keys are at the Museum of Archaeology in Valletta.*)

Castello Zammitello on the Ġnejna road was built in the early 19th century as the delightful honeymoon lodge of the noble Sant Cassia family. After the unsolved and mysterious murder of the Count Sant Cassia on the Castello's doorstep in 1989, the family not surprisingly sold up. Ironically, the Castello has been converted into a wedding hall.

Eating Out

Charles Restaurant (inexpensive), Sir Harry Luke Street, ℰ 573235, opposite the church, is one of *the* places for *fenkata* in Malta. Ignore the scarlet carpet hung on the wall, depicting matador and bull locked in mortal combat, and concentrate on the pasta with rabbit sauce, the rabbit stew with garlic and white wine, or other local dishes. On Saturdays be prepared for noise, bustle and the all-permeating aromas of a Maltese kitchen. Not to be missed. **Victor's Bakery** by the Ġnejna road will provide the basics for a picnic.

Ġnejna Bay

Ġnejna Bay is known as Mġarr's beach and is signposted 3 km west out of Mġarr past Castello Zammitello. The road plunges into a 20% gradient, which is murder on foot, especially on the way back up. There is a car park of sorts at beach level but no bus service. The **sandy beach** is ideal for children, and the arc of multi-coloured boathouses hollowed into the soft limestone cliff face add to the charm of this naturally pretty but sometimes crowded bay. Above are the remains of the **Lippia Tower**, one of four similar watchtowers built by Grand Master Lascaris in 1637.

Beyond the **Western Kiosk** refreshment caravan and around the rocks to the right towards the bulbous headland of **Il-Karraba** is a secluded area of smooth rocks, the nearest you will get to 'adventure' bathing in Malta.

Żebbieħ and the Skorba Temples

Żebbieħ is a nondescript place whose couple of hundred inhabitants would surely have slunk into Mġarr, less than 1 km away, were it not for tradition and the important **Skorba Temples**.

Getting Around

The Skorba Temples are down a path on the left on the Għajn Tuffieħa road, and are poorly signposted.

The fabric of the ancient **Skorba Temples** has fragmented badly, but their history remains intact. Skorba's importance lies in filling in hitherto well-kept secrets in the calendar of Malta's prehistory, specifically the pre-Copper Age. Together with Ġgantija they are believed to be the oldest free-standing structures in the world.

The complex was uncovered by the archaeologist David Trump during his excavations 30 years ago. Evidence in the shape of a wall told of a prehistoric village on the site. Further evidence of human habitation, livestock and crops were found and carbon-dated back to the earliest prehistoric phase, the Għar Dalam.

In the middle of the site are the flattened stones of a three-apse temple from the Ġgantija phase. The floors made of *torba*—a crushed compound of limestone and water and still in use today—can be seen, so too can one eroded megalith approximately 3.5 m tall.

Red Skorba and Grey Skorba are the names given to neolithic periods and corresponding pottery, fragments of which are on display in the Museum of Archaeology, where the keys to the site are available.

Fomm ir-Riħ

Fomm ir-Riħ is basically an inaccessible bay, one of the most beautiful and the last remaining undeveloped bay in Malta. Clear azure waters, good snorkelling (and a dive for skilled divers off the point of Ras ir-Raħeb), deserted rocks and stunning sunsets are all on offer. The cliffs and the headland of Ras Il-Pellegrin are praised by walkers, picnickers and doe-eyed lovers.

The only approach to the gravelly foreshore, other than by boat, is by a very tricky footpath cut into the rock face by the ex-prime minister, Dom Mintoff. He obviously liked to flirt with his own mortality, for he rode his horses on this narrow path at the weekends. He survived—his equestrian skills must have equalled his political nous. By car the terrible road to the footpath goes through Baħrija and is about 7.5 km from Rabat. For those who suffer from minor bouts of vertigo and don't fancy the footpath, the clifftop of Fomm ir-Riħ can only be approached by an even worse track that branches left off the Mosta–Mġarr road 1 km before Żebbieħ. There are no facilities, yet, but the land has recently been acquired by the Dolmen Hotel Group, which sadly will not be deterred by the bay's name—Fomm ir-Riħ, or 'mouth of the wind'.

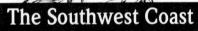

The Southwest Coast

'Cedant Curae Loco: 'Here cares end.'
Grand Master de Verdalle's motto, Verdala Castle.

The southwest is a friendly area with a slow tempo. The landscape is too wild and too lunar for concerted tourism and that's its charm, being disconnected from the air-conditioned hullabaloo of the northern shores; one small 'apart-hotel' is the sum total of the accommodation available.

Yet the area has more than its share of interesting places to visit and things to do, including **Dingli Cliffs**, the **Verdala Castle**, two **prehistoric sites**, a forcefully extravagant baroque church and a seductively charming medieval one. You can take a *luzzu* ride to the **Blue Grotto** or a stroll around the mysterious pattern of limestone ruts known as '**Clapham Junction**'. The southwest is somewhere to flee the amazons of Buġibba, to picnic, walk, or simply daydream.

Of all the sights, the cliffs at Dingli are the most impressive: at 260 m the highest point in Malta. From here the Mediterranean

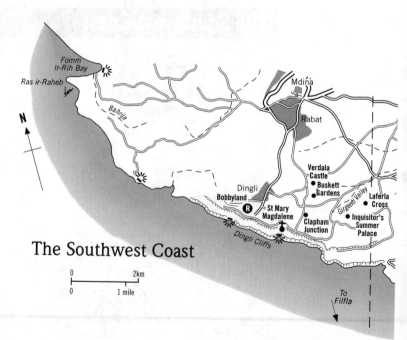

The Southwest Coast

appears benign, even when the white foam angrily whips the indigo water below. The horizon brims full of mirages; it is easy to believe you can actually see North Africa.

Further south, on the barren coralline rocky outcrops, are the prehistoric temples of **Haġar Qim** and **Mnajdra**, where scholarly history tells of an ancient people who worshipped pagan gods and symbols of fertility. Inland, the landscape becomes more fertile and terraces are cut into the low hills, like a giant's staircase. From the hilltops the horizon is dominated by the domes of parish churches or Verdala Castle, the erstwhile opulent summer residence of Grand Master de Verdalle.

Ras ir-Raħeb and Baħrija

The point of Ras ir-Raħeb marks the southeastern tip of the beautiful, if exposed, bay of Fomm ir-Riħ. There are very few inhabitants in the triangle of land north of Dingli and south of Rabat. This is languid rural Malta. Old ladies sit under the sparse shade of a tree while their precious goats chomp away on grass and wild red flowers. The men work the fields' thin brown topsoil with hoes as their lazy *tal-feneks* (rabbit or pharaoh hounds) snooze nearby. The crops and tiny vineyards are ambushed by the sinister shadows of prickly pears, thoughtless flytipping and encroaching wild bamboo before the harder coralline limestone and *maquis* nearer to Dingli take over.

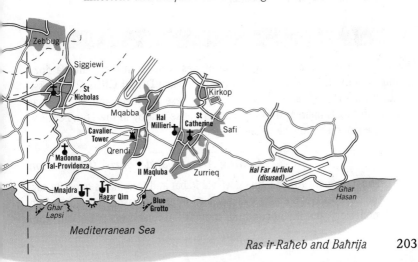

Mediterranean Sea

Rabat or Mġarr are the nearest **bus termini**; the Rabat **buses 80–84** are the best bet. **Taxis** will only be ranked up in Rabat.

The empty quiet spaces and peaceful walks are the main reason for coming here, but it is also the only way down to the bay of **Fomm ir-Riħ**. Off the point of Ras ir-Raħeb—only accessible by boat—is a tricky **dive** site for the experienced. The road to the point and the small car park for Fomm ir-Riħ runs through the village of **Baħrija**, once the site of a fortified village in 800 BC. Out from underneath the southern walls of Rabat, the road runs past a sign for the distinctly unimpressive **Chadwick Lakes** and on into the village, where you would think you were south of the Mexican border as the poor road surrenders to a wide dust bowl.

The North Country Bar and Restaurant (inexpensive), Baħrija, ℂ 456687/8, is situated on the north side of the village. Joe is-Slais (Joe the Butcher) prefers reservations, 24 hours in advance—cash only, please—should you want horse meat. If you don't, there's a choice of rabbit, steak or fish, and the fried rabbit is excellent. A set three-course lunch is Lm3.75 and a bottle of Baħrija wine, non-vintage, will cost you 60c (the nearby vineyards are a great comfort after the first few glasses). Open Wed–Sat for dinner and Sunday for lunch. For a cold drink, the **New Life Saloon** is opposite.

Dingli

The village of Dingli, at 240 m, is the highest village on the island; a dozy farming community you will drive through to reach **Dingli Cliffs**. Tommasso Dingli, a noted 16th- and 17th-century Maltese architect and Sir Thomas Dingley, an Englishman said to have had a house nearby in the 16th century, are given equal credit for the village's name.

The infrequent **no. 81 bus** goes via Rabat and terminates here. By car, the road out of Rabat forks right to Dingli opposite the Dominican monastery, but if you continue straight the road leads to Buskett from where you can still reach Dingli and the cliffs. It can be a nice **walk** from Rabat—4 km to the village and the cliffs are 1 km further on. The *festa* of Holy Mary is held on 20 August.

A Spy Story

During **World War II** a consistent irritant to the Axis high command was its inability to infiltrate Malta with so much as one spy. At 0200 on the night of 18 May 1942 Caio Borghi, also known as Carmelo Borg Pisani of Senglea, rowed ashore from an Italian torpedo boat to the cave at Ras id-Dawwara, 2.5 km north of Dingli Cliffs. Pisani was a Maltese fascist symapathiser educated on a scholarship in Rome. To feed his ideology and repay his moral debt he volunteered to recce the defences and supplies prior to the planned Axis invasion of Malta, Operation Herkules. But the sheer cliffs above him were impossible to scale, and within 48 hours all his rations had been washed away by the sea. Following his frantic waves to the British patrol boats he was arrested, and subsequently confessed. The British hanged him as a spy, aged 28, on 28 November 1942.

Dingli Cliffs

The cliffs fall 260 m to the sea and are a paradise for daydreamers and walkers. But here, most of all, it is the Mediterranean itself that impresses—wine-dark, like a great ocean, it just doesn't look like an inland sea.

The cliff road stops alarmingly at the precipitous edge. The track to the left eventually links back to Buskett. One and a half kilometres along, with only Filfla as neighbour, is the chapel dedicated to the patron saint of prostitutes, **St Mary Magdalene** (1646). For 364 days a year it stands alone and silent, but at 1930 on 22 July each year a delightful mass is said on its steps at the cliffs' edge as the sun dips into the sea behind. To the right the road is smoother, and with the sunset and the onset of dusk it becomes 'steamy window alley'. Cars park along the cliffs' edge and lovers gulp in romance. (Malta is a small and Catholic country where privacy can be hard to find.) Further along is the **Bobbyland** restaurant. Only the cautious should proceed beyond Rdum de Piro; the low anonymous building is a gunpowder factory.

The village **church of the Assumption** with its tall silver-coloured cupola and twin bell-towers is as visible as a lighthouse. The church, of no particular merit, is only approximately a hundred years old.

Eating Out

In Dingli itself there is the new **Café Plaza**, opposite the church, for a coffee or light snack. By the bus terminus is the Nationalist Party bar, the **Aldo Moro**, oddly named after the murdered Italian President.

On a sunny day a picnic by the cliffs is the best idea. Fresh bread, tomatoes, goat's cheese and fruit can be gathered from the **Up-to-date Confectionery**, and Carmenu at **Charles's Grocery**, 70 m before the bus terminus. For more substantial fodder turn right on the cliff road for **Bobbyland** (inexpensive), Panoramic Road, ✆ 452895. There is, as with most things Maltese, a tale behind the seemingly absurd name, and it's best revealed by Reno the owner. The huge restaurant is very popular, especially at weekends, with every stratum of Maltese society—from burly stevedores to politicians. The food is like the atmosphere, bustling, generous and frank, but service can lag. Rabbit and lamb are specialities and you can eat inside or out. Open for lunch and dinner all week except Monday. Book at the weekends; it has become an institution.

Clapham Junction

Clapham Junction is the nickname given to the largest convergence of Bronze Age (approximately 1500 BC) cart ruts yet discovered in Malta: parallel concave grooves 1.5 m apart and 40cms–60cms deep, cut or worn into the coralline stone. Cart ruts occur in Malta and Gozo—and in parts of Sicily and Greece—especially where outcrops of hard stone are found. Mystery and speculation surround their origin and use.

Getting Around

As a much-vaunted 'sight', Clapham Junction has yet to receive the accolade of good signposting. The road by the Buskett Forest Aparthotel forks into a 'Y'. The right fork will take you to Dingli and 300 m down the left fork is Clapham Junction.

L-Imnarja, the feast of St Peter and St Paul, celebrates the summer harvest. Its name is a corruption of the Latin *luminaria*, which referred to the bonfires of Mdina and Rabat that illuminated the feast. (*See* p. 255)

The *festa* begins on the evening of 28 June and runs through the night. At the Mnarja races the next day donkeys, mules, and horses are all ridden bareback, with much hilarity, down Racecourse Street. The tradition dates back to the days of the knights and today the winners receive an elaborate cloth, the *paliu*, from Malta's president, which the winners' church will use as an altar cloth. The Maltese eat and drink more rabbit and local wine than seems feasible at this feast.

One of the saner theories attached to the site states that the ruts were a complex series of tracks for people to drag their goods around on stone-shod carts. Unfortunately this theory does not explain the absence of scarred wearing, or why some of them disappear off the cliffs' edge, or why, as is the case here, they converge like a railway siding. The BBC carried out tests for a documentary many years ago, but all they came up with was that a wheeled structure kept jamming. A different and plausible notion suggests they were used for irrigation channels, but far less credible is the theory proposed by Erik von Daniken, author of *Chariot of the Gods*, who declared them to be skid-marks left by visiting aliens.

Two hundred metres further along the outcrop is the shrubbed crater **Għar il-Kbir**, and the last troglodyte cave in Malta, inhabited until the 1830s. The British, publicly incensed at the insanitary conditions, but privately no doubt unsettled by the thought of cavemen living happily in a corner of their Empire, moved them against their will to Siġġiewi— where presumably their descendants still live.

Buskett

Boshetto (little wood), as it was called by the knights, is the only woodland area in Malta and is overlooked by the Verdala Castle.

Getting Around

Buskett is 4 km out of Rabat on the road to Dingli and is signposted. For the woods, turn left at Verdala Castle and twist your way down to the bottom where there is a small car park. The Dingli **bus, no. 81**, will drop you on the road, leaving you a brief, pleasant downhill walk.

No more than 2 km away from Dingli cliffs and sitting under the watchful eye of Cardinal Grand Master de Verdalle's summer retreat, are **Buskett Gardens**. Panoplies of foliage spread their shade over the valley floor, providing a welcome respite against the heat of summer; don't expect anything Amazonian but the greenery can be very welcome. Orange trees, tall sad cypress trees, irregular cactuses, leguminous carobs, aromatic firs and the Judas tree (destined to foretell Easter with its pink blossom, and the tree from which he is said to have hung himself) are some of the randomly planted flora. A sign warns that the picking of fruit will lead to prosecution—it's a pity there is not a similar legend about littering. *The gardens are open all year and picnicking is permitted.*

Verdala Castle

Grand Master de la Valette was a humble man of granite Christian morals who was content with a tiny hunting lodge in the Boshetto from which he would hunt with his crossbow. Cardinal Grand Master de Verdalle, who reigned only 14 years later, was less the warrior and more the sybarite. The Verdala Castle was his specially commissioned *palazzo*, disguised as a castle; somewhere he could escape the oppressive summer heat of Valletta and feed

his voracious appetite for the trappings of state. The site he chose was on top of the hard rock overlooking the *Boshetto*, from which he could see nearly all his archipelago.

The design of the three-storey castle is credited to Gerolamo Cassar and construction began the year he died, 1586. Initially, all the castle's stone was quarried from the site and the excavations formed the existing dry moat. In each of the four corners—the plan is basically symmetrical—is a bastioned tower which rises above the top floor. At the garden entrance Grand Master de Vilhena, another later epicurean, added both the elaborate balustrade and his gigantic escutcheon.

Inside the main door is a further signpost to its egocentric creator. A marble bust shows off his Byzantine collection of facial features: a tall slender forehead over hard eyes and flared nostrils set in a tight face that ends in a goatee on a virile chin. This is the face of a man who did not find his penchant for piracy incompatible with holding the office of cardinal to the Pope (the only grand master to receive this honour). On his deathbed de Verdalle bequeathed to the Order all his vast wealth—even his *quint*—which he had accumulated with the Order's laws, thereby silencing from the grave his many detractors.

The ceiling above the ground floor is by Paladini, whose frescoes show the high points of de Verdalle's illustrious life. Note the broad shallow steps of the beautiful oval staircase (the knee joints in a 35-kg suit of armour were not very flexible). In the adjoining hall two chessboards carved into the stone floor are by French officers imprisoned here by the British during the Royal Navy blockade of 1800 (there is another in the top garret). The bastioned towers are divided into passages, grim little cells and torture chambers for anyone who fell foul of the grand master. From the roof you can see most of Malta through 360° as well as the southern Ta'Ċenċ cliffs of Gozo.

In the gardens and abutting the castle, is the **chapel of St Anthony the Hermit**, built at the end of the 16th century. The work by Preti, *The Madonna and Child*, is in need of restoration and is therefore overshadowed by a garish sculpture of the Madonna holding the dead body of Christ. Note the granite **milestone** at the entrance to the castle drive: it's one of the many on which the distances were chiselled off by the Allies during World War II in the daft hope that invading Axis forces would get hopelessly lost. *Adm. free: Tuesday and Friday* **only**, 0900–1200 and 1400–1700, as it is used as a state residence for visiting dignitaries.

Buskett Forest Aparthotel (Class III) Buskett, ℗ 454266/454328, is the only hotel in this area. A kilometre beyond Verdala Castle on the Buskett road, it is a small family-run and modern complex of hotel rooms and self-catering apartments. Facilities include a rooftop pool, restaurant and glittery bar. Pity about the crane park next door.

Eating Out

The shade of a tree for a picnic is the favoured venue. Failing that, the **Buskett Roadhouse** (inexpensive), ℗ 454233, halfway down the road which threads past the castle to Buskett Gardens, is for those with fond memories of Butlins-style holiday camps. They serve lunch and dinner every day, with live music of sorts in the peak summer months.

Siġġiewi

One of the ten original parishes created in 1436, Siġġiewi lies midway between Rabat and Żurrieq in the fertile Girgenti Valley, which begins near the cliffs of Dingli. It is from the fruits of this valley that the sleepy village has grown. Today about 6,000 people live hereabouts. There is a southern Italian air about the oversized square with its green benches upon which the villagers rotate like the hands of a clock, keeping one step ahead of the sun. At high noon in summer not even a cat will cross the square, and the 'Friend to all Bar' is eerily quiet. St Nicholas stands aloof on a roundabout in the centre of the L-shaped sloping square, in front of his baroque extravaganza of a church.

Getting Around and Tourist Information

The road from Rabat is the easiest, even though it doesn't look it on the map. To reach Siġġiewi by way of Qormi and Żebbuġ is a study in frustration brought about by bad signposting. Only **Bus no. 94** goes on to **Għar Lapsi** on a Thursday and Saturday in summer. St Nicholas of Myra (and later Bari), sometimes known as Santa Claus, is also the patron saint of sailors and pawnbrokers; Siġġiewi celebrates his *festa* on the last Sunday in June.

The parish **church of St Nicholas**, one of Malta's most august baroque churches, dominates the centre of Siġġiewi. Lorenzu Gafa finished it, his first baroque church, in 1693. Perhaps because it was also his first major commission, he adopted certain elaborate Italian and Sicilian idioms, but its classical baroque features retain a feeling of light and space.

The west-facing façade and the huge dome were not Gafa's design but were added in 1864 by a resident of Siġġiewi, Dr Nicola Zammit. To ensure his dome was visible from the bottom of the sloping square, he extended the height of the drum so it would not be lost between the two bell-towers. Quentin Hughes' the noted historian of architecture, wrote: 'The treatment of the façade is truly dynamic. Like a ship in full sail, thrusting its bow forward, it is set trailing its two campaniles in the wash.' Most of the lavish decorations—including the eight segments of the dome—were added long after Gafa had completed his brief. The altarpiece is **Preti's** last and unfinished work, a painting of St Nicholas.

Behind the bus terminus is the **chapel of St John the Baptist**, built by Fra Salvatore Cutaja in 1730, who is buried underneath the centre marble. The chapel is small and unremarkable except for a truly gruesome picture of St John's beheading. The Madonna looks on unperturbed from the left-hand wall. The chapel is seldom open but the usual viewing window enables you to see most of the gore. Opposite and next to the petrol station is the crumbling, box-like **chapel of Our Lady**, which only opens during the *festa.*

A couple of kilometres south of town, on the road to Għar Lapsi, is a very beautiful chapel, **Madonna Tal-Providenza**, set in the middle of a field. This tiny octagonal chapel was built in 1750 and looks no more than a dome and a bellcote. Fable has it that the church grew weak after being struck by lightning and the dainty portico was added to lend support in 1815. The whole is a study in the main elements of pantheon design; note the small statues against the roof line. Mass is said here just once a year, on the first Sunday in September. At all other times the portico and the bellcote are used exclusively by the birds. A viewing window will provide you with a glimpse of the nave; the cannon ball on right of the altar is, according to hearsay, from the Great Siege of 1565. (Nissen huts and other deleterious buildings have been built with mind-numbing insensitivity next door.)

About 4.5 km west from Siġġiewi, on the secondary road that just about links Dingli to the head of the Girgenti Valley, are the **Inquisitor's Summer Palace** and the **Laferla Cross** or **Tas-Salib**. The inquisitor's Summer Palace was built in 1625 by Inquisitor Visconti, who perched this narrow building on a ledge overlooking a wild valley of bamboo and pomegranate trees. The little chapel was added in 1760. It suffered years of disuse (in World War II it housed records from the Grand Master's Palace) but is now the official summer residence of the prime minister and cannot be visited. **Laferla Cross** or **Tas-Salib**, at an elevation of 218 m, is clearly visible from most of the roads leading to Siġġiewi. As neither the cross nor the chapel are impressive, it is only worth climbing up for the views—the Verdala Castle stands to the northwest like an bold sentinel, to the east is Marsascala, and to the south the islet of Filfla.

From this vantage point the church domes spread out below and, like signatures, tell instantly which town is which. The hill has been a romantic rendezvous for years, the earliest of the neatly carved names on the steps of the cross dates back to 1907.

Eating Out

The Friend to All Bar serves all manner of drinks, and *pastizzi* are available 100 m past the church at **King's Confectionery**. The nearest restaurant is in Għar Lapsi.

Għar Lapsi

Għar Lapsi, 'the cave of Ascension', was a fishermen's secret hidey-hole until a direct road replaced the path, and is often referred to as Siġġiewi's beach; it's a good spot for **diving**. Traditionally the local people swim here on Ascension Day, 15 August.

Getting There

Bus 94 leaves Siġġiewi on a Thursday and Saturday, but only in July–September. Otherwise it's about a 4-km hike.

For half of the year Għar Lapsi looks like a deserted frontier town, a windswept area with one low-built restaurant, a car park, some half-finished buildings, a children's play area and a few hardy divers. In the summer it's awash with three generations of Maltese families picnicking and enjoying themselves.

At the bottom of the steep steps and slipway at the water's edge are fishermen's *luzzus*. The caves and easy access from the little jetties and rocks into the water make it a favourite with swimmers and cave divers; this part of the coast is octopus territory. For those that don't want to swim there are paths that lead in the direction of Wied iż-Żurrieq (Blue Grotto) or benches to sit on and gaze out to Filfla and the sea.

The Lapsi Seaview Bar and Restaurant (inexpensive), Għar Lapsi, known locally as 'Maria's', is the only place. The ugly duck-egg blue building and its decor are lifted straight from the pages of a 20-year-old copy of *Canteen Catering Weekly* but don't be put off, this is a popular restaurant. The menu is small and lists tried and tested favourites like rabbit stew, swordfish steaks and chicken; everything comes with chips.

Żurrieq, Qrendi, Mqabba, Kirkop and Safi

Some people say the real heart and soul of Malta lies in this backwater. In the countryside that surrounds these villages and along the Wardija ridge in the north, the air feels drier and the wild herbs and flowers so pungent they almost claw your nose. The dry-stone walls are built higher to protect the crops from the wind and a few hardy trees remain undefeated and bow just a little bit. A canopy of tall palms lends a North African air to the open spaces and village squares; invariably this was where the *sirocco* and the Barbary corsairs struck first.

The villagers in this corner of Malta are a devout people; religion is the foundation stone upon which their lives are built. Historically, their lot in life has been to serve the more influential citizens of Mdina and Valletta, to man the watchtowers, to farm and grind corn or to quarry stone in Mqabba. Each village developed its own character or industry and there exists a fierce but friendly rivalry over the *festa*: who can out-firework who, and which band club can make the more euphonious din.

Żurrieq

The name Żurrieq is apparently derived from the Arabic *Israq*, which means azure or blue, associated with the clear blue waters of Wied iż-Żurrieq (Blue Grotto), some 3 km away. It also accounts for the delightful idea that if you come from Żurrieq you will have blue eyes (in the late 11th century Aryan Normans founded a settlement here).

Żurrieq is one of the original 10 parishes of Malta, and the largest land-locked village of the area, with approximately 8,500 inhabitants. It has little of the charm found in its neighbours, but is close to the lovely medieval church at **Ħal Millieri**, and is en route to the Blue Grotto or to the temples of **Ħaġar Qim** and **Mnajdra**.

Take a good map. The quickest but least scenic route is to follow the signs to Luqa and the airport, and then pray there is one to Żurrieq—there normally is, but things have a habit of changing. There is a more scenic and longer route via Rabat. **Buses 32** and **34** serve Żurrieq and **do not** go to the Blue Grotto. There is a **taxi** rank by the bus terminus, and a **market** on Thursdays in Mattia Preti Square. The *festa* of St Catherine of Alexandria falls on the first Sunday of September.

Ħal Millieri

This site is the highlight of the area and well worth traipsing to, even if you are all 'churched out'. To get there, turn right on the main road that runs from Żurrieq to Wied iż-Żurrieq just past the petrol station. There is no signpost and it lies 1 km down this narrow track on the right.

Ħal Millieri was originally a medieval settlement until it became depopulated and ultimately deserted. Sandwiched between stone walls and surrounded by fields, all that remains are two 15th-century low-built churches—no bigger than chapels—and a cross.

Like a huge doll's house at the end of a garden brimming with flowers is the **church of the Annunciation**, probably built after 1430. A farmer used it as a stable for his donkey, paying the church Lm1 per annum in rent until 1968, when a fund was established to restore it. A simple door and three steps down into the dim interior almost gives the impression of entering a cave; the walls are illuminated with naïve angular frescoes of saints, now partly restored but still showing the effects of humidity and salinity. The whole pretty structure epitomizes the simplicity of medieval Christian worship.

The Annunciation, Ħal Millieri

Outside the bigger later church of **St John the Evangelist** is an old Roman olive crusher that was once used as a baptismal font. The cross in front marked the centre of the settlement. The gates to the garden and both churches themselves are locked, but either the parish priest of Żurrieq, Father Aguis, or Tony Mangion of the conservation society, ℂ 333903–5, will open it up by **prior** appointment.

Back in Żurrieq, the **church of St Catherine** (1632), designed by Don Matteolo Saliba, the local parish priest, took over 25 years to build. Somewhat dull and overworked, it was built in a period before Maltese baroque had evolved, a good example of what can happen when successive generations tinker with buildings in the vain hope of improving them. To be fair, Saliba's initial design was caught in that period when the influences on ecclesiastic architecture were evolving into what became Maltese baroque. Furthermore, St Catherine's is not helped by being hemmed in by the police station and the large red banners of the Malta Labour Party, but the lights of the *festa* lend it a certain gravity.

The square format of the interior has been lifted by the work of **Mattia Preti**, who fled to the village to escape the plague of 1675 and ended up executing some magnificent paintings: behind the altar is St Catherine being freed by angels and in the nave St Andrew is depicted labouring magnificently under the weight of his cross. A triptych panel in the vestry dates back to 1604; it came from a cave chapel on the islet of **Filfla**, where the parish priest used to say mass for the fishermen up to the outbreak of World War II.

In the parish priest's garden, is part of a **Punic** tower, the only example on the island. The cornice has the tell-tale Egyptian lip. What is remarkable about it, is the condition of the soft limestone structure, bearing in mind it must have been built between 5 BC and 600 BC. The massive bricks were laid without mortar, each having—like the pyramids—a concave and convex face to ensure a perfect fit. (*Adm. to Father Aguis's private garden by permission.*)

In **Mattia Preti Square** (which doubles as the bus terminus) are a couple of delightful, typically Maltese village sights: an immaculate 30-year-old white Ford Zodiac taxi, whose driver seems rooted to the square until the next person wants a ride to the Blue Grotto; and the terminus snack bar, a stone café entirely faced in aluminium, and looking like an industrial kettle. At the end of Mattia Preti Square is the **Armeria**, built as an armoury at the end of the 1600s and used by Grand Masters Pinto, Ximenes and de Rohan. It is a plain and classical structure that echoes a nobleman's town *palazzo*. The eight worn semicircular steps and the balcony hint that it may once have been something special and the twin dolphin door-knockers are traditional Maltese door-furniture. The building was sold in 1784 to the Crispo family, a branch of which still own it today. There is no admission.

Eating Out

Hole-in-the-wall bakery **Prima** in Main Street sells large squares of doughy pizza for 12c, or Timpana for 25c. Open from 0530–1930, except on Sunday when it closes at 0930. **Guy Bocci Clabb** (bocci is a local game similar to boules), is a cheap café adjacent to a children's recreation park on the Nigret Road, and serves uninspiring hot food in the hamburger mould.

Wied iż-Żurrieq (The Blue Grotto)

From the cliffs above Wied iż-Żurrieq Grand Marshall Copier and a cavalry squadron shadowed the Turkish Armada of over 181 galleys on the eve of the Great Siege of 1565.

Legend has it that the Blue Grotto was home to the sirens—sea nymphs—who serenaded sailors to their destruction with soft verse. Brightly painted boats and *luzzus* leave every 15 minutes, providing the sea is calm, for the natural caves and grottoes along this stretch of coast. The Blue Grotto is one of six caves on the 25-minute trip. Try and go early in the morning when the queues are shorter and the sun is bright and reflects off the white sand of the sea bed. The cost of the excursion is Lm1.75 (Lm1 for children) and each boat carries a maximum of eight people. If the weather looks dodgy your hotel will ascertain the sea conditions in advance.

For those who turn queasy at the mere sight of a boat, there are benches, a shell collection and a filigree-jewellery shop. This is easy to spot: displayed outside is a life-size cardboard troglodyte wearing a Maltese cross.

Getting Around

By car follow the signs for Luqa if you are coming from Valletta. Take the Mosta road and then the Żebbuġ or Rabat roads if you are staying on the northern coasts. Buses terminate in Żurrieq, so take a taxi (the white Zodiac) from the rank opposite the terminus. The walk from Żurrieq is a dull 3 km.

Tour companies offer narrated visits to the grotto, which might be coupled with a trip to the nearby prehistoric sites of **Ħaġar Qim and Mnajdra**, *see* below.

Eating Out

Half-dozen restaurants and bars, all inexpensive, none inspiring, offer pasta, hamburgers or grilled fish. The best are the **Kingfisher** and the **Dolphin** (featuring a fearsome shark's mouth and photos of the largest Great White caught in the Mediterranean).

Qrendi

Qrendi has a distinctive quasi-Moorish and Maltese feel to its twisty streets; you might only stop here on your way to the prehistoric sites of Ħaġar Qim and Mnajdra.

Getting Around and Tourist Information

The road routes are either via Luqa or Siġġiewi. The tension mounts with the summer heat, for both Qrendi and Mqabba share the same *festa*, The Assumption on 15 August. Expect their respective band clubs to compete for volume, not tune.

On the road in from Valletta is a little chapel dedicated to **St Mathew**. Right next door, in the shade, is a green and white sign pointing down some steps to **Il Maqluba**, meaning 'overturned or upside down'. It's an overgrown geological fault—a large cave must have collapsed during an earth tremor—some 45 m deep (90 m from the top) and 65 m across, with a green floor of tangled bamboo, fruit trees and shrubs. It's worth seeing simply for the dotty legend that accompanies it, *see* pp. 223–4.

It's suggested that Lorenzu Gafa was partly responsible for the **church of St Mary**, for he inherited an incomplete structure when he began work in 1685. What gives the church presence are the steps up to the *zuntier* (forecourt) and the huge carved wooden doors.

Altogether more fun is the octagonal **Cavalier Tower**, 200 m off the west side of the square and surrounded by 16th-century dwellings. This is the only such tower in Malta, three storeys high with octagonal floor plans and roof terrace. From here the gallant inhabitants of Qrendi would pour boiling pitch, hoops of fire, and any other handy projectiles down on to the heads of those intent on slaughtering or enslaving them.

Eating Out

There is a choice of three bars: the **Elvis Presley** bar in St Matthew Square, the **Hunter's** bar opposite St Mary's church and the **Nationalist Party Club** where a sign in three languages welcomes visitors.

Mqabba

The word Mqabba is derived from the Arabic and may have referred to a domed building in the village which no longer exists. It's the largest of the four villages, with a population of 2,390, about 40 more than Qrendi.

Getting Around and Tourist Information

Mqabba is situated almost on the threshold of runway ⁙ of MIA, so follow the airport signs or go via Siġġiewi.

Like Qrendi, the *festa* of the Assumption is on 15 August.

Mqabba is the centre of the quarry area, there to fuel Malta's voracious appetite for building. As you approach the village the vast creamy pits appear on either side of the road, from which lozenge-shaped blocks are extracted, swarming with workers and antediluvian machinery.

Once in the village the narrow streets almost lean inwards and echo the North African feel of Qrendi. The **George V Band Club**, built in 1910, is a rather pompous building, unlike its neighbour the parish **church of the Assumption**. Tucked away behind it is the 16th-century church of **St Basil**.

The **New Life Bar** is behind the church. **Anton's Bakery** has fresh bread and sweet rolls.

Kirkop

Getting There and Tourist Information

All the buses for Żurrieq and Qrendi stop here. Alternatively head for the airport and just after the tunnel which takes you under the runway is the village. St Leonard of Noblat was a French abbot who lived in the 5th century; his *festa* is held on the 3rd Sunday in September.

If it were not for the proximity of the runways, the triangular little square with its half-dozen evergreen trees and knackered benches would be a very pleasant place to while away an hour or two.

The **church of St Leonard** was rebuilt in the 18th century and is a narrow gutted little building with two bell-towers which squeeze all but the cupola on the dome out of view. The remains of St Benedict were donated to the church by Pope Pius in 1790 and are held inside.

Safi

Safi, the smallest of the four villages, is almost a suburb of its bigger neighbour Żurrieq. Its name means clear or pure. Here more than anywhere in this area the North African stamp is evident: the palm trees are tall and their fronds generous, and a few of the buildings have fore-courts with aromatic plants and herbs. With the exception of the new band club, all the buildings have hints—in their window or door designs—of Moorish influence.

Getting Around

Bus 34 stops in Safi *en route* to Żurrieq. Once in Kirkop follow the signs for Żurrieq.

Festa

Safi's *festa*, celebrates the Conversion of St Paul on the last Sunday in August.

In the main square, **centru pastorali**, the green of the palms takes the hard glare off the stone and polarizes the sunlight. Between it and Żurrieq is the only interesting sight in the area, the **Xarolla windmill**. The now tumble-down windmill was introduced to the island during the reign of Grand Master de Homedes (1536–53); the Order maintained a monopoly on this revolutionary way of grinding corn. Other windmills were erected in the area by Grand Master de Vilhena two hundred years later. Up until approximately 15 years ago this particular windmill was fully operational, but during a terrible *gregale* the sails and mill were damaged beyond repair. Further into town on top of another cylindrical hulk of a windmill—now inhabited—are the horns of a cow: an old Maltese superstition holds that this guards against the evil eye.

Ħaġar Qim and Mnajdra

The structures of Ħaġar Qim and Mnajdra date from the **Ġgantija and Tarxien phases** (3600 BC–2500 BC, the Copper Age). They are believed to be temples where prehistoric man worshipped goddesses of fertility, although there has been some controversy over the true purpose of Mnadjra, *see* below.

At the Museum of Archaeology in Valletta many of the original finds are displayed, as well as helpful three-dimensional models of the structures.

Tourist Information

For the disabled, Ħaġar Qim is accessible, and Mnajdra less so, but just about feasible with the help of a companion—the smooth and straight 480-m path that leads to it falls away steeply in a 1:13 gradient.

The **Ħaġar Qim Bar and Restaurant**, 50 m from the car park, is open with the temples every day except Monday.

Getting There

Take the road to Żurrieq and then towards the Wied iż-Żurrieq (Blue Grotto). The road is signposted 'Ħaġar Qim' on your right, 1 km before the Blue Grotto. Alternatively you can take a short detour through Qrendi, again following the Blue Grotto sign; this route goes right past Il Maqluba, *see* above.

Buses go via Qrendi to Żurrieq where they terminate. **Taxis** park near the terminus.

Ħaġar Qim

Ħaġar Qim (meaning 'sacred stones' or literally 'stones of worship'), is a megalithic structure in a commanding position on a barren rock plateau overlooking the sea and Filfla. The site remained buried under mounds of earth until its discovery in 1839, when clumsy attempts were made at excavation; the site was not properly revealed until 1910. The orthostats here are the only ones in Malta to be made of the soft globigerina limestone, and have been weathered by sun, wind and sea air.

There appears to be no specific reason, solar or otherwise, for siting the main five-apse temple with a southeastern aspect. The restored trilithon façade (two upright stones supporting one stone lintel) with its striking entrance belies the confused layout within. Unlike any other temple site the prehistoric builders of Ħaġar Qim did not adhere to a trefoil arrangement (symmetrical layout of three chambers); the chambers and apses connect with one another but not in a uniform plan. Each was built almost as an individual place of worship and it is supposed the whole later evolved into one temple, when it is believed to have been entirely roofed.

Points of note are: the seven 25-cm tall headless **'Fat' deities**, believed to represent symbols of fertility [1], the so-called headless and nude *Venus of Malta*, and the exquisite pitted **altar** with its growing plant motifs [2] (found here and now on display in the Archaeological Museum). Also note two pedestalled altars [3], a betyl or tall cylindrical stone [4], and the largest megalith, more than 7 m long and approximately 20 tons [5]. The little boulders the size of bowling balls strewn about the site were used rather like castors on which the orthostats were painstakingly inched into place.

True knowledge of prehistoric man's beliefs, habits and culture is hard to ascertain; much is scholarly guesswork. The evidence unearthed here and at Tarxien strongly suggests a highly sophisticated culture; just look at the intricacy of the designs and the engineering of the robust structures themselves.

Ħaġar Qim

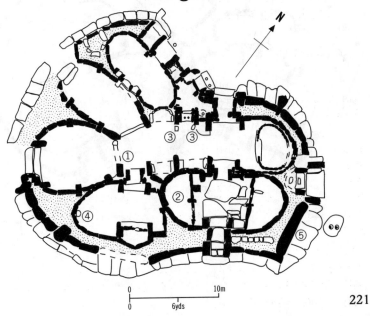

0   10m

0   6yds

Mnajdra has the most dramatic setting of all the prehistoric monuments in Malta: 480 m due west from Ħaġar Qim towards sheer cliffs along a steep and paved straight path. As you descend along this path you will notice a dozen or more small **ramshackle redoubts** in which, during a much abused season, *kaċċatur* or 'hunters' trap and shoot migrating birds. Sadly, they show how little man has progressed in the 5,000 or so years since he built Mnajdra. To the left of the path by the cliffs' edge is a **memorial to Sir Walter Congreve**, a governor of Malta, who died in 1927 while in office and was buried at sea between Malta and the island of Filfla.

The Site

The site, with its common southeast aspect, was first excavated in 1840 and reveals smaller and better-preserved temple structures than Ħaġar Qim. The

Mnajdra

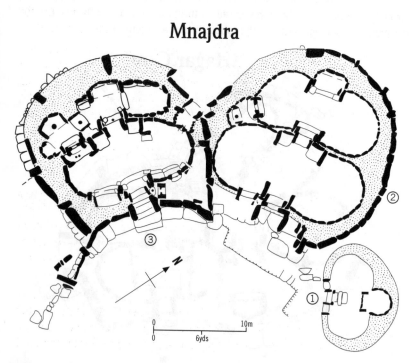

outer walls are made from the harder coralline limestone which has survived the worst of the weather.

The Mnajdra complex which spans the Ġgantija and Tarxien phases (3000 BC–2500 BC) comprises three temples set around a semi-circular fore-court: the oldest and hardly recognizable **Trefoil Temple** [1], Middle Temple, the last to be built [2], and the now controversial Lower Temple [3], *see below*. The concave walls surrounding all three suggest this was a roofed complex. The **Middle Temple** gives a further indication that the deities worshipped were ones of fertility and rebirth. The plan, with its two elliptical apses, suggest a primeval female form with the worshippers entering through the womb-like entrance in a rite of fertility. Decoration, such as scarring and pitting on the trilithon inner entrance of the Lower Temple, is more elaborate than at Ħaġar Qim. Apart from minor artefacts there have been no other finds here.

The **Lower Temple** was until as recently as the 1980s assumed to be an adjunct to the Middle Temple. It is now suggested that it is a highly sophisti-cated **solar observatory**, capable of predicting the four annual solstices using the sunrise and sunset. Prehistoric man would undoubtedly have needed the information that such a 'calendar' might offer for agricultural and religious rites.

Mathematics supports the calendar theory. The main trilithon entrance runs, with the exit, almost exactly along the same east–west axis as the sun's rays at the time of an equinox. On summer and winter solstices the rays of the sun clip exactly at the very edges of the stones. Most impressively, the odds against this happening have been calculated at 26,000 x 26,000 x 26,000 to 1. In addition, while attempting to prove the theory that man developed an accurate and prac-tical calendar, those involved in the recent study have applied their own date to Mnajdra: 3700 BC.

Filfla

Filfla is an uninhabited and somewhat foreboding rocky islet, 8 km offshore and clearly visible from the southwestern cliffs. It has always been treated as the archipelago's unwanted orphan, until in 1970 it was finally declared a nature reserve.

Filfla is the unhappy victim of the nasty (and absurd) legend of **Il Maqluba** (*see* Qrendi): the evil inhabitants of Il Maqluba so displeased God that he tore the ground from beneath them and sent them crashing through to hell. So base were they that not even hell could hold them, and in desperation the devil threw the depraved sinners (and the earth, trees etcetera) out of hell and back into the night sky. The tangled mass of rock, vegetation and godless souls landed in the sea and thus created Filfla. From such an egregious birth as that, its fate was set.

The next, and more tangible, calamity to befall Filfla came at the hands of the Royal Navy and Royal Air Force, which used Filfla for target practice. For more than 25 years they bombed it in the full knowledge that it was home to the only known colony in the world of a large dark green and red spotted lizard (*Lacerta muralis var. filfolensis*). Miraculously, the lizard and a rare species of Mediterranean stormy petrel which breed on the islet have survived, albeit in greatly reduced surroundings.

The waters run very deep around Filfla which was used as a refuge by local fishermen until World War II. The parish priest of Żurrieq would journey out once a week to say mass in the small medieval cave chapel. Thankfully some of the delicate icons have been saved and can be seen in St Catherine's in Żurrieq. Today it is forbidden to land, moor a boat, or dive near its peaceful, rocky shore as not all the British ordnance detonated upon impact.

The South

The south is often forgotten; the landscape has an isolated
mood and the greedy god of tourism has shown little interest—
he's too busy on the northern coasts. Yet the region has some
of the oldest archaeological sites to be found anywhere in
Europe—the **Tarxien Temples** and the **Hypogeum**—as well
as some interesting prehistoric bone deposits in the cave of
Ghar Dalam. The rock bathing along the coast from Marsascala
to Delimara Point is good, and if you hire a boat you will find

The South

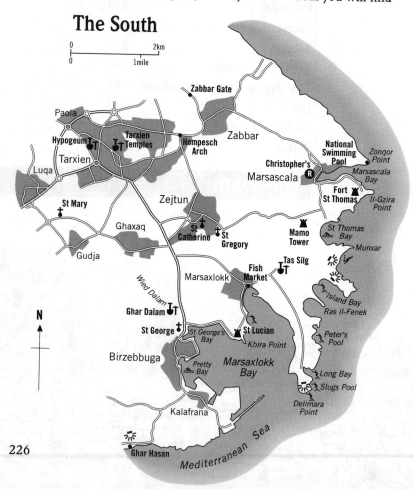

bays that are uncrowded. The fishing village of Marsaxlokk is picture-postcard pretty; **Marsascala** has a superb restaurant, and **Żejtun** has two fine churches.

For centuries the area was outside the protective embrace of the Three Cities, and therefore out of the mainstream of Maltese life; fish and agriculture were all that kept it spiritually attached. Nowadays, fishing—not an industry but a way of life—coexists uneasily with a massive new generating plant and freeport, situated in once-picturesque Marsaxlokk Bay. In the struggle between technology and ecology parts of the area seem to have lost out.

The people of 'the forgotten south' have a surly rebellious side that is especially evident at election time, and in the night-marish slaughter of birds, the *kaċċa* or 'the hunt' in and out of a much-abused 'season'. This has resulted in blighted and 'no-go' areas for Maltese and tourists alike. A walk along Delimara Point can be intimidating, as men stroll about with arsenals of firepower. The authorities choose to turn a blind eye and, apart from a short spell during the 1989 Bush-Gorbachev summit, the *kaċċatur* have had it their own way.

The Marsaxlokk Bay Area

Marsa means harbour and *Xlokk* is the Maltese name given to the *sirocco*, the hot southern wind that blows in from North Africa. Until this century it was known as Marsasirocco Bay. Today, sadly, this historic bay is unkempt.

The single largest bay in Malta and geographically orphaned in the south, Marsaxlokk has proved ideal for two massive government development projects: a new electricity generating plant and a freeport. Damage to the environment, the bay's natural beauty and marine life has been immense. More positively, the freeport generates valuable foreign exchange, and the power cuts and surges which bedevilled the island are now events of the past.

The coves on the Delimara peninsula have escaped development, and the fishing village of Marsaxlokk is a genuine 'photo opportunity'. Here at any one time more than a hundred *luzzus* of all sizes swing at anchor in the shallows of the bay, their primary colours splashing an air of tranquility as they have always done.

History

Throughout Malta's history the almost circular shelter of Marsaxlokk Bay has provided hospitable waters (safe in summer and winter except during the very worst *gregales* and *siroccos*), and an ideal landing point for invaders. At noon on Saturday 19 May 1565, the day the **Great Siege** began, the Turkish Admiral Piali anchored his 181-strong fleet and disembarked Mustapha Pasha's army of 35,000 from here. The *gregale* is a fierce winter wind, its lungs exhausted by the end of March, but Piali believed it could blow any time. So, fearing for his Sultan's precious fleet, he overruled Mustapha Pasha's well-formulated plan to wage a land war from Marsaxlokk and to blockade the Grand Harbours from the south. Instead he insisted on the safer anchorage of Marsamxett Harbour, which meant Fort St Elmo had to be taken first. His decision was the first of many catastrophic errors that led to the Turkish defeat.

The Turks tried their luck again in 1614 with a much smaller force of 60 galleys but were repulsed by the mighty defences of **Fort St Lucian**; they then headed round Delimara Point for Marsascala, managing to reach Żejtun before being driven back by a squadron of the knights' cavalry.

On 10 June 1798 **Napoleon** disembarked the bulk of the French army in the Bay under General Dessaix. Of the seven landing sites he had chosen, Fort St Lucian was one of the very few of the Order's defences to offer any resistance. During **Nelson's** ensuing blockade of the French, Marsaxlokk Bay was used as one of three victualling and repair stations for his warships.

Between the two **World Wars** the relatively calm waters of the bay at Kalafrana provided the perfect landing site for the magnificent flying seaplane hotels of **Imperial Airways** as they plied their pioneering routes to the ends of the then predominantly pink globe. At the outbreak of **World War II**, Kalafrana (now home to the very unglamorous but profitable freeport), became the Fleet Air Arm's base. It was on this jetty, crated for dispatch, that the four Gloucester bi-planes that defended Malta in the summer of 1940 were found.

Swordfish seaplanes and the mighty four-engine Sunderlands roared in and out of the bay in all weathers during World War II. In the middle of an horrific *sirocco*, on the night of 13 October 1940, one such Sunderland flight carried Anthony Eden, then the British Secretary of State for War, who came within centimetres of being embedded into the limestone of Delimara Point; only the pilot's skill saved all on board. Meanwhile, the Axis was planning the invasion of Malta at Marsaxlokk Bay, **Operation Herkules**, but by the end of 1942 the plan was abandoned so that Hitler could pursue his fatal obsession with Russia.

The Allied forces in the bay and at Kalafrana suffered terribly at the hands of the Axis bombers right up to 8 September 1943, when the armistice with Italy was signed. By the end of that month 76 ships of the surrendered Italian Navy were anchored around the island, predominantly in the bays of Marsaxlokk and St Paul's. With sang-froid, Admiral Cunningham cabled the Admiralty in London: 'Be pleased to inform their Lordships that the Italian battle fleet now lies at anchor under the guns of the fortress of Malta.'

Birżebbuġa

This region once had hardy olive trees in abundance (*bir* means 'meadow' and *żebbuġ* is both Malti and Arabic for 'olives'). Once a simple fishing village and a quiet summer resort, over 6,000 people now live on the headland and coastal sprawl that seeps from Kalafrana to Fort St Lucian on Kbira Point. Maltese women still love to sit in the shade on upturned beer crates and play *tombla* or cards, or gossip in small groups under the shade of the Southend Apartments. Their disinterested men, meanwhile, swim with their children in the sometimes polluted waters off the sandy beach of **Pretty Bay**—a sad misnomer.

Getting Around and Tourist Information

A **car** is imperative. Due to the condition of the roads, borrow or hire one: don't use your own. The bus services can be tardy and erratic, and the journey from Valletta can take as long as an hour.

In many instances Birżebbuġa is abbreviated to B'buga or B'bugia. The grim-sounding St Peter in Chains is Birżebbuġa's patron saint, whose *festa* takes place on the 1st Sunday in August.

There is much more to see than do here; the waters are sometimes polluted, but the surrounding area is rich in prehistory.

The cliff cave of **Għar Ħasan**, admittedly a secondary sight, is imbued with Saracenic legends and has fine views of the sea. (*It's well-signposted about 3 km from Birżebbuġa. Adm. free.*) An old man sitting in the shade of the desolate car park will rent you a dim torch for 20c. Access is via steps (a rusty railing is all that separates you from the sea 130 m below) until you reach the cave itself, where Hasan, the last of the 11th-century Saracens, is supposed to have lived. The view of the deep-blue sea from the natural 'window' in the cliff face on the right as you go in is as spectacular as the legends about Hasan are unreliable.

Many stories are told of the heathen and his harem of young Maltese women, and how he sold his harem into slavery by lowering them on a rope into ships below. The best tells of how he fell in love with a member of his harem—they lived a blissful existence until, hearing Count Roger's Christian soldiers coming, they leapt hand-in-hand to their deaths into the sea below. (The Catholic version of this story says the lady in question was kidnapped and held unwilling hostage.)

Għar Dalam

Of more interest and significance is Għar Dalam, 'the Cave of Darkness', an extraordinary prehistorical *cul de sac* containing the bone remains of animals stranded on Malta at the end of the ice age. (*Signposted 600 m from the St George's Bay end of Birżebbuġa on the Żejtun road.*)

The cave was first scientifically investigated in 1865 but was not opened until 1933—during World War II it was used as an air-raid shelter. Unfortunately, the most important and irreplaceable relics (such as four tusks of a dwarf elephant and the skull of a Neolithic child) were stolen from the museum in a commissioned theft on the night of 7 April 1980, presumably at the behest of a mysterious private collector.

What is unique about Għar Dalam are the bone deposits of long-extinct fauna, such as dwarf-elephants, bears and hippopotamuses which date back approximately 180,000 years. Together with the even earlier deposits of bone-free material they offer a window of understanding into the Pleistocene era.

The history and story of Għar Dalam spans the entire Quaternary period (1 million–2 million years ago), from the early Pleistocene epoch to the late Pleistocene era (the ice age). The ice age was punctuated by climatic fluctuations of rain, thaw and freeze. During a part of the ice age there were thousands of years of rain—the pluvial age—when Malta's valleys were formed. A torrent of water coursed through what is now the *Wied Dalam,* and its river slowly ate into the limestone rock fissures of the riverbed causing a subterranean tunnel imperceptibly to erode over the centuries, creating the cave that exists today.

During the interglacial periods of thaw the climates normalized, and European fauna, like modern man, migrated south to warmer climes. Malta was at the time joined to Sicily and the continental European landmass—but not Africa—via a swampy land bridge and was as far south as the fauna could go. Gradually, as the ice melted and the rivers drained into the inland

(Mediterranean) sea its level rose, trapping hippopotamuses, elephants, brown bears, giant swans, deer, wolves, voles and mice on the newly created islands; at this stage Marsaxlokk Bay was a fresh-water lake. Imprisoned and unable to swim north or south, the animals underwent remarkable adaptive changes, becoming smaller and smaller, requiring less food and so increasing their chances of survival.

When the stunted animals eventually became extinct, starting with the hippopotamuses 180,000 years ago, their bones were sucked down through the holes and fissures in the river bed and solidified into bone breccia in the clay. Layer upon layer was built up over the years as each species died. The mystery (and there always is one), occurs after the deer became extinct 18,000 years ago. In 1981 the curator, Dr Zammit-Maempel, recorded a thick layer of volcanic ash on a similar Pleistocene deposit in central Malta which would indicate an unexplained cataclysmic occurrence such as untold years of constant volcanic eruption and earthquakes; whatever caused it will never be known for sure.

The illuminated cave is 145 m long (80 m of it is open and not in any way claustrophobic) with one entrance where you can see across the valley to what was the other end of the cave. The single-most fascinating part is the free-standing layered sandwich section that, like a 180,000-year-long egg-timer, clearly shows part of evolutionary history.

Għar Dalam is undoubtedly the best maintained site in Malta. The flowers leading down to the cave are flagged and watered, the paths swept, and the cactuses and carob that normally wear summer clothes of opaque dust, glisten. *Open 0800–1345 in summer and 0815–1700 in winter. Adm. Lm1. Attendants will help the disabled as far as the small museum or the terrace overlooking Wied Dalam and the gardens.*

Between Pretty Bay and St George's Bay, the old **Pinto Battery** of 1752 has long been an oil depot and opposite is the bizarre monument erected in December 1989 to the **Bush-Gorbachev summit**. Its sympathies must be with the old Soviet Union: it is neglected, rusting and falling apart.

Further on, just before the Żejtun road, is interesting **St George's Chapel**, the impact of which is somewhat diminished by the public convenience next door. Built by the knights in 1683 on the site of a medieval chapel, it is the only forti-fied church on the coastline. Access was via a drawbridge and portcullis at the back of the small church. The knights often wintered their galleys in the bay and mass was said here before a voyage. The path behind the church leads to the historically significant **Borġ in-Nadur**; the hilly area all around here and *Wied Dalam* was a late Bronze Age settlement. A 4D-imagination is needed today, however, for all that exists is an overgrown wasteland of boulders, shotgun cartridges and bird traps.

Where to Stay and Eating Out

There is little choice. The **Sea Breeze Hotel★★★** (moderate), ✆ 871256, overlooking Pretty Bay is by far the best. It's clean, the restaurant is air-conditioned, the rooms comfortably furnished and the staff attentive. If you don't mind the extra noise, the rooms at the front have large triangular balconies. Of the two guesthouses (both circling the bus terminus in Pretty Bay) **Reno's** (Class II), ✆ 871165 and the **Southend** (Class I), ✆ 828441, Reno's is smaller and better, and has a reliable restaurant. The **Al Fresco Restaurant** (inexpensive), St George's Bay, ✆ 681422 has a large terrace with generous umbrellas and a welcoming interior. The food is pizza and its ilk, and fresh fish when available, and it has an imaginative children's menu.

Marsaxlokk

Marsaxlokk is the fishing capital of the island. Strong traditions and a tightly knit community have allowed it to remain a village of cosy charm. Around the harbour a ribbon of houses is protected by oleander bushes in different shades of rose and white. Nothing, except of course the church, rises more than three storeys. The colours of the *luzzus* flicker off the still waters, their eyes of Osiris staring balefully back at onlookers. Men sit on the quay with their legs apart making sense of the tangles of spaghetti-like nylon that are miraculously transformed into nets every night. Sometimes their tired faces in the early morning light tell the true size of a catch long before even the wily urban wholesaler has noticed. This is an easy place in which to lose a day or a week.

Two *cippi*, low marble sepulchral pillars, were discovered in 1697 near the village of Marsaxlokk. Their carved inscriptions in Phoenician and Greek of vows to Melkert, Lord of Tyre, were the key pieces in the linguistic jigsaw that unlocked the Phoenician dialect—just as the Rosetta stone deciphered the secrets of Egyptian hieroglyphics. One *cippus* was given to doomed Louis XVI by Grand Master de Rohan and is still in the Louvre—the other is in the Museum of Archaeology.

Only **Bus 27** goes to Marsaxlokk. Our Lady of Pompeii is celebrated noisily in the square by the waterfront on the 2nd Sunday in July; the fireworks light up the *luzzus*. Maltese women traditionally stipulated in their marriage contracts that they were to be taken to two *festas*, L-Imnarja and the Pilgrimage to the church of St Gregory in Żejtun on the 1st Wednesday after Easter (*see* p. 248). At the heart of their insistence were the non-secular activities that followed, and still do, in Marsaxlokk.

At the **fish market** the best of what can be fished in Maltese waters (and probably some sea bass poached from the government fish farm) can be purchased every Sunday till late in the afternoon. Try to arrive early, if only to see the swordfish.

The **swimming** is cleaner off the rocks between Fort St Lucian and Marsaxlokk village than at Birżebbuġa. Finding a **fisherman** to take you fishing is not too hard if you ask around the quay or the bars. Haggle playfully. A **tourist market** on the waterfront sells mostly machine-made lace tablecloths and, even in 35°C, thick locally knitted Aran sweaters.

Fort St Lucian was built by Grand Master Alof de Wignacourt in 1610 and designed by Vittorio Cassar to dominate and protect the bay. That's a hard brief for 7 sq km of water and 9 km of coast, but one they fulfilled with equanimity. The massive fort, sitting broad-shouldered on the high ground of Kbira Point and encircled by a deep trench, successfully saw off a Turkish invasion of 60 galleys in 1614. With uncanny foresight Grand Master de Rohan (whose escutcheon is above the main gates) strengthened the fort and the seaward battery in 1795. Three years later the garrison of 160 men kept the French at bay for 36 hours, and were eventually defeated only by lack of rations. Today, somewhat ironically, the fort accommodates the government-owned **fish farm**.

On the secondary road north to Delimara and Żejtun is **Tas-Silg**, a pair of sites steeped in history and not much else. Limestone walls encircle the barely discernible ruins of four different periods: a temple from the Tarxien period (3000 BC–2500 BC), a Bronze Age settlement, a Graeco-Punic temple to the goddess Astarte (Juno to the Romans) and an early Christian (AD 4–6) place of worship. The Italian Archaeological Mission unearthed the remains of the Graeco-Punic temple during its 1960s excavations. Pottery, ivory and stoneware were uncovered to suggest it might have been the **Temple of Juno** which was looted lock, stock and chalice by **Verres**, the kleptomaniacal Roman governor of Sicily and Malta between 73 BC and 70 BC. During Verres's subsequent impeachment in Rome, Cicero stated in his charges, 'I do not know where you obtained those 400 jars of honey or such quantities of Maltese cloth or 50 cushions for sofas or so many candelabra, but what could you want with so many garments as if you were going to dress all your friends' wives?' As the evidence mounted against him, Verres, evidently not wishing to end his days as a lion's snack, fled to the Levant, presumably to plunder the Mosques. *You can climb over the walls, but otherwise the keys are available from the Museum of Archaeology in Valletta.*

Where to Stay and Eating Out

Accommodation is limited to the **Golden Sun Aparthotel** (Class III), Kajjik Street, ✆ 871762, in a dusty side street. It jollies up inside, with a bar that harks back to an English pub. The stone-floored rooms are cool in summer, and there are swimming pools as well as a restaurant. Fresh fish—which can sometimes be surprisingly expensive—is always on the menu around here. **Pisces** (moderate), ✆ 684956, is popular with the locals in spite of being next to the police station. The cooking is excellent with generous portions, all of which unfortunately come with packet French fries. They plain-grill fish to perfection but lose their touch with sauces. Ask for a table by the window on the first floor for lunch or dinner. **The Harbour Lights** (moderate), ✆ 871202, is on the corner by the seafront and is easily mistaken for the Skuna. Inside, it is all fishing paraphernalia and check tablecloths. The trouble with fresh fish displays is you can never be sure whether you get the one you choose, but here you seem to. There are other dishes for non-fish eaters. There is a separate (and cheaper) open-air salad and snackbar, if you want to enjoy the activity of the little harbour. **The Hunters Tower** (expensive), ✆ 871356, is a long-established place at the end of the quay next to a decaying old villa; an expensive and reliable (if uninspired) restaurant serving mainly fish, and famed for its romantic views. A favourite haunt for a tryst.

Delimara

Delimara offers excellent uncrowded rock swimming, sunbathing, walks and an education in the barbarous activities of the *kaċċatur*, or hunters. This desolate limestone peninsula of wild green *maquis*, inhabited solely by geckoes, juts southwards, forming one of the first and last landfalls for exhausted migratory birds. Unfortunately, primeval traps and redoubts have mushroomed unchallenged, marring the beauty of the landscape, frightening innocent walkers, and corrupting the heady natural aromas even more than the new generating plant. In the four summer months, when the hunting season closes, sit on the rocks that edge into the sea, watch the incandescent apricot sun sink into Africa, and listen to the gentle *wop-wop-wop* as the fishermen chug slowly out to sea in their small *luzzus*.

Getting Around

One road goes out to Delimara Point from Marsaxlokk; towards the end it peters out into a rough track. By the signposted turning is one of the few remaining British milestones defaced by the Allied commanders during World War II (*see* p. 209).

Beaches on Delimara Point

The inlets for bathing on the eastern coast are Peter's Pool, Long Bay and Slugs Pool. Access is tricky for the elderly and very young; take care if there is a swell. North of Peter's Pool are twin bays separated by Ras il-Fenek (Rabbit Point), the larger being **Island Bay**. You need to charter a boat to reach them but it's well worth it: they're free of day-trippers and the clear waters offer some of the best swimming and snorkelling on this coast. Turn a blind eye to the radio masts. The **dive** off the tip of Delimara Point is for the experienced only. **Peter's Pool** has been signposted by an enterprising youth who sits in the rubble-strewn field of a car park, and collects 20c for the privilege. Rudimentary steps lead down to a flat rock which looks like a through-section of an industrial-sized layer cake; the wind has kindly formed it so that it provides a little shade. A few crude steps have been cut into the water, providing easier access than the other pools. Young summer love has been here for generations, and countless hearts and promises are tattooed into the golden limestone. **Long Bay** had a restaurant which closed many moons ago but left a good, free, car park. Steps go down to the pencil-shaped inlet, smaller and shadier than Peter's Pool. If the sea has been rough, seaborne rubbish can collect here. **Slug's Pool** is invariably deserted on account of its name and position. The swimming is excellent, but the rocks are jagged and shade is scarce.

Marsascala and St Thomas Bay

Defenceless **Marsascala** was the scene of the last Turkish invasion of Maltese soil in the late spring of 1614, a revenge attack on the knights for plundering grain. The 5,000-strong force, repelled at Fort St Lucian, came ashore here but was driven back to its galleys once it reached Żejtun.

The long thin creek of Marsascala was the favoured fishing port of the Sicilian community from the north of Żejtun. It became known as Marsa Ta'sicali, 'The Sicilians' Harbour', and was frequented by the well-to-do from Żabbar. Now 2,200 people live on the slopes that rise up from the sea, but numbers sometimes quadruple at the very peak of summer. It is the most developed village of the area but has managed to maintain its identity as a fishing community. The buildings that snake from Zonqor Point to Fort St Thomas are mostly low and small; the topography prevents high rises craning for a seaview. Families tend to vacation here and enjoy the evening *passeggiata* along the head of the bay while the action-seeking young prefer to be sardined along the northern coasts.

In winter, after the salty sea air has welded shut the shutters on the summer apartments and the tourists have returned to even chillier climes, Marsascala is another place where time, like a *luzzu's* anchor in a storm, can easily come adrift.

Getting Around and Tourist Information

Unless you are coming on the main road from Żabbar, bring a compass, distress flares and tranquillizers; you might need all three by nightfall. The signposts have either disappeared or been used as target practice by the *kaċċatur*, turning the secondary roads into a maze fit to confound Daedalus. From Valletta, 13 km away, the best route is Marsa–Paola–Fgura–Żabbar, after which the signposts (two of them) begin.

The headland of Il-Gżira separates the bays of St Thomas and Marsascala, and was the most suitable place on which to construct a fort. Just after the last Turkish invasion the prolific team of Grand Master Alof de Wignacourt and Vittorio Cassar hurriedly began **Fort St Thomas** at the enormous cost of 13,450 *scudi*. Cassar designed the tall bulky fort with its four corner towers and seaward battery to be garrisoned by 100 men in times of emergency, and to field eight cannon and a mortar. The seaward battery was eaten by the elements and finally demolished in the 1970s to make way for the Jerma Palace Hotel. Fort St Thomas, its imposing walls not yet completely covered in matted green clumps of wild shrubs, is now the **It-Torri Pizzeria**.

On the Żejtun to St Thomas Bay road is the 17th-century **Mamo Tower**, a miniature fort built in the shape of the cross of St Andrew, with one floor and a vaulted ceiling. St Thomas Bay, with its wide undefended coastline, was a favourite of the North African slavers, for the shallow waters made it easier to drag the Maltese peasants off to their new lives. Understandably, the Mamo family found it hard to attract labour for their nearby estates, and so they constructed the tower as an early example of an employee benefit. Later the family used it as a summer residence; the small chapel 50 m away was its place of worship. It is currently being restored by the Malta National Trust.

Zonqor Point, the northern tip of Marsascala Bay, houses the **National Swimming Pool**, where important water polo matches are played. The local team play on the north shore of the bay itself where the team and spectators are catered for by the 'ET, at your Service' café. The National Swimming Association has more information, ℗ 829369. **St Thomas Bay** takes its name from a long-since demolished church and is not very attractive, but has reasonable swimming and snorkelling. Very popular, it can congest with four generations of Maltese at the weekends. In May and June you'll find the old men sitting on crates next to the shingle beach lovingly painting their *luzzus*. From Delimara Point or Marsaxlokk it is a reasonably easy 3–4 km **walk** and the cliffs along the south coast are not unnervingly high. **Diving** off the Munxar reef is only for the skilled. Many ships have been caught unawares by the reef along this coast.

Where to Stay

Marsascala

The part-Libyan owned **Jerma Palace Hotel★★★★** (expensive), ℗ 823222, is situated on the very tip of Il-Gżira Point. Designed to take in the sea (literally, in very bad weather) on all sides, it has many amenities including indoor and outdoor pool, gym and recreation rooms. A good hotel of 350 rooms and suites, nearly all with sea glimpse, it is let down slightly by a journeyman kitchen and sombre public rooms. The only other hotel is the **Cerviola Hotel★★** (inexpensive), Qaliet Street, ℗ 823287, an unkempt affair of 32 rooms on the southern road. The entrance hall is reminiscent of a 1960s airport lounge and is not aided by the proximity of the kitchen. There is a very small pool and a sun deck. Perfect if you want a cheap base. Further along on the left is **At Alisons** (Class I), Vajrita Street, ℗ 823265, a guesthouse with 11 double rooms and mini-swimming pool. Good service has given it a justifiably high reputation. Near the Cerviola is the **Etvan** (Class II), Bahhara Street, ℗ 823265, a modern guesthouse; the rooms at the front all have uninterrupted views of the bay. On the other and quieter side of the bay is **Ta'Monita** (Class III), ℗ 827882, a small holiday complex with 36 apartments, a couple of minutes' walk up from the head of the bay. It attracts loyal visitors every year because of its homey feel, and has a pool and a restaurant. Two streets back from the head of the bay is the small **Fawlty Towers Guest House** (Class II), 'Ponderosa Lodge' (remember Bonanza?), Iskal Street, Marsascala, ✆ 823110; six rooms. **Apartments** are plentiful: enquire at Dahlia South, 31 Marina Promenade, ✆ 684491, or the Shik Complex 100 m away at the Piazza Mifsud Bonnici, ✆ 829949.

St Thomas Bay

The only guest house, **Ramla Lodge** (Class I), St Thomas Bay, Marsascala, ✆ 824933, caters predominantly to Germans. The 31 rooms and public rooms are clean and ordered and everything on sale is German. There is a pool, and the beach is less than 100 m away.

Eating Out

Marsascala boasts the finest restaurant of the three islands: **Christopher's** (expensive), Marina Promenade, ✆ 829142 (closed for three weeks in July). Everything about this 30-cover establishment is polished—imaginative continental food, crisp linen and faultless service—plus rustic decor, and a congenial atmosphere. The dishes on the changing menu are cooked to order and the consistent standards of excellence achieved would wrestle with any major capital city establishment. Book and go, but ask for a table away from the noisy coffee machine. Further along the promenade is **Al Kafe**, for pizzas, salads and ice creams, and a place where people congregate all day and well into the night. There are two other main cafes. **Grabiel**, ✆ 684194 (with a restaurant next door), is situated by the roundabout at the head of the bay and named after the old oil tanker that lay grounded on the reef for years. Eighty metres away is the **Shik Cafe**, underneath large umbrellas, trees and the apartment block of the same name. Both have all-day food and cold drinks. Possibly the smallest restaurant in Malta is **Tiberios** (moderate), Qaliet Street, ✆ 684166. The bare white walls are cold in winter and unkind in the Mediterranean summer sun, but in the evening the chrysalis cracks and tables spill colourfully onto the street. The short menu is earnestly cosmopolitan and wok-happy, with pasta, fish, chicken and other meats. Towards Zonqor Point is **La Spigola** (moderate), Zonqor Street, ✆ 684288, which has a minute terrace overlooking the picturesque bay and manages to retain a romantic air despite bizarre deep lilac decor. The food is 'mid-Med' with the emphasis on fish. Worth a visit. Marsascala has a penchant for small eateries; further along Marina Promenade and next door to the youthful, buzzy **La Playa**, is a **Chinese takeaway** the size of a broom cupboard, for those who want to sit by the water in the still evenings and see if the fish eat fried rice. In **St Thomas Bay** is **San Tomaso** (cheap), © 829394, out of the beach lido mould but none the worse for it, and also the **Fishermen's Rest** (inexpensive), St Thomas Bay, © 822049. This is a basic fish restaurant with no pretensions. Have the fish soup; as you chase the bits around the bowl with Maltese bread the rudimentary decor will fade.

Żabbar

The two *casals* of Żabbar and Żejtun (*see* pp. 248–50) are similar in many ways. They both grew out of agricultural communities—Żabbar means someone who prunes trees—and both enjoyed the dubious honour of Grand Master Hompesch's patronage. (Żabbar was elevated to city status in 1798 with the immodest new name of *Citta* Hompesch—it never caught on.) Today both are political hotbeds, left of centre. Tough and hard men come from these parts.

As Malta's economy became increasingly dependent on the harbours, the villages diverged. Żabbar, on the doorstep of the Three Cities, became urbanized and lost its old country feel. With 13,000 people, it has grown into the area's largest community. Rural features remain, but there are fumes and especially noise now in the centre of town by the church of Our Lady of Graces.

History

On 18 May, the dawn of the **Great Siege** of 1565 the Turkish invasion forces trampled the older Żejtun and set up their camp at the village of Żabbar; life outside the fortified protection of the Three Cities was uncertain. It was not until 1670, when Grand Master Nicolas Cotoner began construction, funded from his own purse, of the 5 km of defences known as the Cottonera Lines that the villagers felt more secure: at the first sign of an invasion, the principal entrance into the fortifications, the Żabbar Gate, was no more than a quick 1.5-km dash.

In 1800 Żabbar and Żejtun became one of the three British land force bases and the headquarters of the Maltese insurgents who blockaded the **French** within the walls of Valletta and the Three Cities. The guns of the French garrison did immense damage to the village and destroyed the dome to the parish church.

Further damage was done during **World War II**, when the area's proximity to the Grand Harbour meant that it fell prey to stray Axis bombs. The last civilian to be killed by enemy bombing, shortly after midnight on 26 July 1943 and 24 hours after Mussolini's fall, was Vincent Attard of Żabbar.

Getting Around and Tourist Information

It is easy to get lost in this area where one town moulds into the next, but Żabbar is flanked by the Hompesch Arch and the Żabbar Gate; anywhere between is bound to be Żabbar. By car take the Paola road from Valletta and then follow the signs for Żabbar or Fgura. The **bus terminus** is halfway down the wide main street, Santwarju Street. Our Lady of Graces has her *festa* on the 1st Sunday after 8 September.

The fussy, confused-looking parish church of **Our Lady of Graces** sits alone on an island site. Designed by 50-year-old Tommaso Dingli in 1641, it has since been added to by others less skilled, and detracted from by human and seismic violence. Dingli's design sensed the wind of architectural change blowing south from Italy and did not call for the bold bell-towers; these were added in 1738–42. The dome erroneously credited by some to Lorenzo Gafa was badly damaged over the years and finally replaced in 1928. The stunning barrel vault in the nave, the bays of which are decorated in a linear pattern, is one of the best surviving features of Dingli's original design. Currently, the church is undergoing restoration work. Congregations of elderly men gather outside twiddling their rosaries and speculating over the next modification to their beloved mongrel church, while the town elders still lament the 'new dome' erected in their now-distant childhood.

The church has a small museum (*open Sunday mornings only*) established in the 1950s, consisting of votive paintings from sailors miraculously or fatefully rescued from the seas by Our Lady of Graces.

The Last Grand Master to Reign in Malta

Guarded by the later and unnecessary addition of two rusty cannons on an isolated roundabout, is a triumphal arch erected in honour of **Grand Master Hompesch**, the last grand master to reign in Malta. The arch, like the man, is neither grand nor flamboyant, and was a gift from the people of Żabbar, and one which crowned his sad life.

The Bavarian Hompesch was elected in 1797 and was the only German grand master in the Order's history. He had a tremendous regard for the Maltese and was the only grand master to speak their language. History's chroniclers have not been kind, however, partly because of his almost eager surrender to Napoleon 11 months into his reign in June 1798. By the time he assumed the magistracy, the Order had become a faction-ridden and none-too-exclusive club of petty despots, fifth columnists and drunken aristocrats. As a weak but kindly leader he lacked the resolve and ability to reform the Order militarily or spiritually, being no more than a supplicant to those—especially the knights of French *langues*—he was meant to lead. The reason for the Order's existence, the 11th-century Holy Crusades, seemed to have been forgotten.

Where to Stay and Eating Out

There is nowhere to stay in Żabbar, nor are there any restaurants, so head for Valletta or Marsascala. The **Buona Pasticceria,** at the end of Romanesque Santwargu Street that leads to the church, provides tasty snacks. The **King Edward VIII** bar has hot and cold drinks.

Tarxien and Paola

There are two reasons to visit these towns: the **Tarxien Temples** and the **Hypogeum**. Unfortunately, the latter has been closed indefinitely since August 1991. Other less touristy sights include the prison, Addorlarata Cemetery, the Mosque, and Qaddafi Gardens where the great man planted a cypress in 1973.

There have been agricultural settlements at **Tarxien** since the time of the early temple-builders (3,000 BC). The street pattern follows the infuriatingly delightful plan of the old *casals* or villages and wind aimlessly around the 17th-century parish church of **Our Lady of the Annunciation**. Today Tarxien is the home of the former prime minister, Dom Mintoff and 7,000 others.

Paola is the 17th-century 'new town' sewn into the north edge of Tarxien. Called *Casal Nouva* when it was founded by Grand Master de Paule in 1626, it was designed for the higher ground above the harbour to catch the sea breezes of summer. It did not catch on immediately, partly because new towns never do, and partly because it was outside the harbour area fortifications and near the burial ground for plague victims. Today it has over 12,000 inhabitants.

Vittorio Cassar's church of 1626, **Santa Ubaldesca**, 350 m west of the prison, had been outgrown by the turn of the century. To accommodate the parishioners (and as a sign of the parish's growing importance) an imposing new church to **Christ the King** was begun in 1924. Designed by Guiseppe Damato (better known for 'The Rotunda' in the Xewkija, Gozo, *see* p. 319) it has a neo-classical style and was built using modern techniques and materials.

Getting Around and Tourist Information

More than 16 different buses go to Paola; 10 carry on to Tarxien. For both the **Hypogeum** and **Tarxien Temples**, alight at the main terminus in Piazza Paola. The temples are 450 m to the east of it, and the Hypogeum 300 m to the south in Burials Street; neither are well flagged. By car, head for Paola and park in the bustling square, which sometimes hosts a market. **Paola** has two *festas*: Our Lady of Lourdes on the 1st Sunday after 15 August, and Christ the King on the 4th Sunday in July. **Tarxien** celebrates The Annunciation on the 5th Sunday after Easter.

The Hypogeum at Hal Saflieni

The Hypogeum is Malta's finest archaeological monument and is closed pending the completion of major works; there is nothing to be seen on the surface.

Hypogeum is a word derived from Greek, meaning an underground burial vault. The vault comprises a complex of interlinking subterranean curvilinear chambers on three levels hewn by hand out of the limestone rock to a depth of 10.6 m, and dating back to approximately 3,200 BC.

Hal Saflieni is a part of Paola, and the Hypogeum was, like so many other archaeological sites, a chance discovery. In 1902 a builder crashed through the roof of the upper chamber of the burial site while excavating for a new housing development. Unfortunately, he kept his discovery quiet until he had finished his entire project, resulting in more avoidable damage. Detailed excavations were begun in 1905 under the direction of Dr (later Sir) Themistocles Zammit. By 1909 the bones of 6,000–7,000 people had been found in the side chambers along with pottery and personal artefacts. As the excavation progressed it became apparent that the complex was more than a burial site. Informed speculation suggests that the main chambers were used for initiation and training in rites associated with those enacted at the nearby Tarxien Temples.

Because it is underground it has survived (Maltese builders notwithstanding) the elements and the ravages of war for more than 5,000 years; its overall condition is remarkable. It also miraculously escaped the Axis bombing of the Grand Harbour area when it was used as an air-raid shelter. However, even restricted visits have unbalanced the internal microclimate: the CO_2 we exhale has already taken its toll and the structure of the whole is threatened. The site will eventually re-open, but UNESCO, the Maltese authorities and the other international bodies involved are wary of putting a date to it.

Those who are disappointed may like to console themselves with the thought that the site is incredibly claustrophobic, and that they can visit the National Museum which has a scale model and some of the genuine artefacts on display.

The Tarxien Temples

The temples are the most important megalithic structures on Malta and power-fully impressive, although hemmed in by 20th-century buildings. Historians agree that what remains in Tarxien today was part of a much greater settle-ment, but modern developments seem to have precluded the possibility of further exciting discoveries.

A visit to the **Museum of Archaeology** in Valletta is advisable, to help trans-late what can appear at first sight to be an impressive but random collection of large rocks. The museum has a helpful three-dimensional model of the site and an artist's impressions of what the structures originally looked like. It should be noted that many (easily discernible) preventative repairs have been made, and that the altars, statues and friezes are copies. The originals and other finds are housed in the museum.

Not long before World War I, and after the discovery of the Hypogeum, a farmer complained at the constant blunting by large stones of his plough. The antennae of Dr Themistocles Zammit twitched and in 1914 he began his five-year excavation of the site.

Three main temple structures and the remains of a small fourth were unearthed: The South **[1]**, the Central **[2]**, the East **[3]** and the Early **[4]**. All except the last structure to be built, the Central Temple, are sited in a southeast quadrant. With the exception of the Early Temple, which dates back to the older Ġgantija phase, the three principal temples date back to the eponymous Tarxien phase (3,000 BC–2,500 BC). These were the last of the temple structures to be constructed by prehistoric man in Malta.

In the four-apsed **South Temple** is the huge and sadly headless statue of an elephantine female, possibly the **'fat' goddess of fertility [5]** (she must have stood more than 2.5 m tall). Dr Trump, the former curator of the Museum

Tarxien

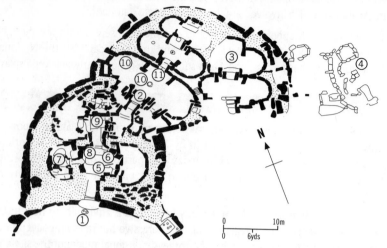

of Archaeology, has eloquently described her: 'she wears a very full pleated skirt. It would be ungentlemanly to quote her hip measurements, and her calves are in proportion. She is supported, however, on small, elegant, but seriously over-worked feet.' To her right is an **altar niche [6]** above delicately carved spiral stonework. The space behind the niche revealed a collection of animal bones and a flint knife presumably used for sacrifices. There is no indication of human sacrifice having taken place. To the left or in the west apse are more **animal friezes [7]**, although less recognizable, and in the centre a **pitted bowl [8]**. Through what was the temple's inner door is the decorated **central niche [9]**.

The Central Temple, more than 23 m high, is unique in Malta for having three pairs of apses rather than two and was built after the South and East Temples. The predominant feature is reddening of the stone, possibly caused by an inferno that marked the end of the temple-building period 4,500 years ago. The further you go inwards, due to the lie of the land, the more the structure's condition improves. The central court is striking, if only for the manner in which man was able to fit huge slabs of limestone together. There are two bowls in the **left apse [10]**, the larger of which was hewn from one piece of rock. Entry to the third pair of apses, and what may have been the priests' inner sanctum, is barred by the finest and most powerful carving here, the **oculus motif stone [11]**. Very little is left of the **East Temple** and even less of the oldest **Early Temple**. The large stones outside were part of the enclosing wall.

While it seems highly unlikely that the Tarxien Temples witnessed anything other than religious rites, bring an inquisitive mind. They might, after all, have been a cattle market. *Adm. Lm1 Mon–Sat. Sunday free.*

Where to Stay and Eating Out

Tarxien is able to offer the **Health Farm**, © 666477, which is classed as an hotel, but they keep mysterious hours. A strict hierarchy of benches appears to operate in the shady centre aisle of Paola's main piazza. If your tastebuds aren't assuaged in the café here, head back to Valletta or on to Marsaxlokk or Marsascala.

Luqa

> *1987: Money No Problems—1992: Problems No Money*
>
> Inscription outside the the Labour Party Club, Luqa

Luqa, although named after the white poplar tree, is synonymous with arriving and departing. The fate of this friendly village of 5,650 has been inextricably linked to that of the nearby airport. Brought into commission in June 1940, Luqa was the islands' main and only concreted airfield during **World War II**. Wellington bombers flew from here, and when inclement weather or Axis bombs shut down Hal Far or Ta'Qali it became Malta's only airfield. Without air strike capability the islands would have been doomed. Not surprisingly, Axis bombs almost levelled the village (an agricultural community since 1634), but the airfield's longest inoperational period was a remarkable 48 hours. The new airport, 3 km away from the old one and renamed Malta International, will always be known as Luqa.

Getting There and Tourist Information

By car, follow the signs for the airport, then turn right towards the old terminal, instead of left towards the new. The *festa* of St Andrew is celebrated on the 1st Sunday in July.

Much of the village has been sympathetically restored since the war, along the same old winding street. Buildings take a long time to complete in Malta but the unfinished one opposite the parish church must take first prize—it was begun in 1946.

There is some ambiguity as to who actually oversaw the design of the parish church of **St Andrew** but it is credited to Tommaso Dingli between 1646 and

1656. The faithful post-war restoration took more than 25 years. It's no masterpiece, but the benches underneath the trees outside are ideal for people-watching. To the west is the small **Chapel of the Assumption**, with a fine little bellcote. Peer in through the viewing window at the tessellated marble floor of those buried beneath. By some fluke it survived the war unscathed.

Where to Stay and Eating Out

There is nowhere to stay in Luqa, but there is an array of typically Maltese bars, from the splendidly named **GA GA Bar** to the colourful **Phoenicia Cafe**, adorned with racing pictures. To the left of the church as you face it is one of the friendliest **fruit vendors** in Malta, tucked into a small hole in the wall. Feel free to sample before choosing; he has only the sweetest produce. Buy a bag of *bambinelli*, uncooked nuts and watermelon, and find some shade. If that does not appeal, on your way down St Andrew Street you can buy *pastizzi* or a slice of pizza.

Gudja and Għaxaq

Gudja stands alone and Għaxaq almost forms part of Żejtun. Both villages, of 2,350 and 3,860 inhabitants respectively, date back to the 14th century when they were probably agricultural satellites of Żejtun. The medieval church of St Mary Ta'Bir Miftuħ (early 15th century) and the narrow twisty streets of Gudja attest to how long these villages have existed. Gudja was the birthplace of the remarkable Gerolamo Cassar, architect of many of Valletta's buildings.

Ever since the airport began to expand in the 1970s Gudja has found itself uncomfortably close to the runways. The new terminal roads encroach even further; Ta'Bir Miftuħ looks sadly out of place next to its new neighbours. People live behind closed doors here; the sense of community is underwhelming, due in part at least to the cramped village square where the church seems to gasp for air.

Getting Around and Tourist Information

Follow the road to Luqa and the airport, and from there Gudja is signposted. Għaxaq is tripped over easily after leaving Gudja on the Żejtun road. Gudja has a particularly good **public garden** near the bus stop, with swings, etcetera. The *festas* of Gudja and Għaxaq both celebrate the Assumption on 15 August.

The church of **St Mary Ta'Bir Miftuh** (St Mary of the Open Well), on the Luqa–Gudja road before the town itself, was mentioned in, and possibly predates, the 1436 report of the 10 original parishes. Double the size and a few years younger than the church at Ħal Millieri (*see* p. 214) it is constructed in the same box-like idiom and has been added to over the centuries. The most notable features are the cyclopean window above the Norman-influenced door, and the simple late 16th-century bellcote. The very high parapet conceals not only the pitched roof but five long waterspouts. Inside, some tantalizing pieces of original stone-painted frescoes of the Last Judgement have just about survived.

Mystery at St Mary's

In 1663 the silver pyx of consecrated Hosts was stolen from the church of St Mary, an act of religious vandalism so outrageous that Grand Master Cotoner and the inquisitor excommunicated the mysterious thief or thieves, and placed a death penalty on their head. Three days later, propelled perhaps by a dose of Catholic guilt, the empty pyx was found in St James, the church of the Knights of Castile et Leon in Valletta. The fate of the Hosts, and the reason why the thieves ran the enormous risk of entering the heavily guarded city has never been discovered. In *Il-Għafrid* (The Devil), a contemporary novel, the local author suggests a theory, which echoes the unsolved crimes of Jack the Ripper, that the thieves' rank may have placed them above suspicion—or, more scandalously, above prosecution.

In between Gudja and Għaxaq is the **Villa Bettina** or **Dorell Palace**, known to the villagers as *Il Palazz*. Built in 1770, it has survived as one of the finest private houses in Malta and is not open to the public.

Bettina Muscati married the French Marquis Dorell and became Lady-in-Waiting to Carolina, Marie Antoinette's sister and wife of the King of Naples and the Two Sicilies. After jealously upsetting the queen, she returned to Malta and assumed the role of grand hostess. Among others, she is said to have entertained Napoleon here (it's one of the more sympathetic and likely refuges the Corsican might have sought). But during the blockade of the French in Valletta she showed the élan of a capricious host, when the villa's keys were put at the disposal of General Thomas Graham, the British commander-in-chief. She reached the summit of her social mountain in May 1800, when Nelson accompanied by Sir William and Lady Hamilton dined at the villa. Little is known about her luckless French husband, who presumably footed the bill for his enemies' entertainment.

Żejtun

Żejt means oil and the village was famous for its olive oil, yet not one tree remains. Situated midway between the Grand Harbour and Marsaxlokk, it prospered as a market garden through Punic and Roman times to become the main parish hereabouts. Today it is a welcoming village of 12,000; the stares from the men outside the band clubs or on the church steps are not hostile just curious. One of the finest old parish churches in Malta, **St Gregory's**, falls within its boundaries while its present parish church is a monumental and powerful 17th-century edifice by Lorenzo Gafa.

Contrasting with the slow tempo of the village is the temperament of its people. The tight-knit population has evolved under a myriad of differing yokes a fierce sense of independence and pride. The villagers are outsiders, and while the inhabitants of Żabbar might disagree, the men here are probably harder.

Getting Around and Tourist Information

By car, follow the signposts via Marsa and Paola. Żejtun is about 7.5 km from Valletta.

The 1st Wednesday after Easter is the *festa* of St Gregory. Many tales are told about the reason for its inauguration: Count Roger the Norman's conquest of the Arabs in 1090, deliverance from the plague by St Gregory in 1519, as a supplication to God's wrath at mankind in Europe in 1543. It was once customary that a bride would have written into her marriage contract that her husband would take her to this feast; today the celebrations still continue in Marsaxlokk and St Thomas Bay after mass at St Gregory's. The procession now leaves from St Clements in Żejtun. Żejtun's conventional *festa* for St Catherine is on a floating date in June.

History

By the time the long-expected **Turkish** invasion got under way in May 1565, the village of Żejtun was prepared; emptied of people and livestock, on de la Valette's Orders. Grand Marshal Copier's cavalry, which had the unfortunate job of patrolling the Żejtun area and the cliffs up to Għajn Tuffieha, encountered the first detachment of Turks as they headed for Żejtun. The first blood of the **Great Siege** was spilled in an engagement that would prove to be crucial. Two young knights, French and Portuguese, were captured and the lies they uttered

248   *The South*

to Mustapha Pasha's skilled torturers before they were killed helped to seal the fate and failure of the Turkish invasion.

The Turks landed again in 1614 at Marsascala and the 5,000-strong army were forced to retreat by a cavalry detachment after ransacking the south of Żejtun. This was the last Christian-Moslem skirmish on Maltese soil.

The village has many noteworthy buildings. See them at their best when the bells for evening mass sound and the sun throws long shadows and a rich light onto the honey-coloured stone. A handful of the less devout sit resolutely on chairs spilled out from clubs and bars; the day's work is done.

The centre of the village is dominated by the fortress-like parish church of **St Catherine** (1692–1722), a fine example of Maltese baroque shaped by Roman and not Sicilian influences. It is possibly **Lorenzo Gafa's** finest parish church. The whole of the island site has been used to great effect and purpose. The wide façade with its seven bays retains a horizontal feel from the clever use of single Doric and Ionic pilasters; the two perfectly scaled bell towers are encircled with Corinthian pilasters. Side screens and arcades which lead-you-nowhere-but-everywhere maintain the coherence of the design.

Gafa became a master craftsman of domes as a result of his Roman training. The great octagonal dome here was structurally a less-successful forerunner to his masterpiece at the Cathedral in Mdina, its vault having to be replaced in 1907. Yet the style of the interior shows more restraint and is more satisfying than his earlier St Nicholas at Siġġiewi.

Opposite, in **St Catherine's Street**, are less meritorious buildings, but all are worth a quick look. On the right as you go down is the sensibly inconspicuous right-wing Nationalist Party Club which used to be the old law courts. Next door to it is another smaller church, the only one in Malta dedicated to the **Holy Ghost**, built at the same time as St Catherine's and credited to Gafa. At the bottom of the hill is **Casa Perellos**, once the country home of Grand Master Perellos. Today it is a sad victim of family inheritance squabbles and is falling apart. On the right-hand pilaster is his Aragonese symbol, the *Perellos* or pear. During the procession of the feast of St Gregory the nobility would watch the pageant from the balcony supported by four wonderful gargoyles, as it passed en route to the eponymous church.

The former parish church of St Catherine, now known as **St Gregory's**, is the best of Malta's older churches. It was built in 1436, the year Żejtun became one of the island's 10 parishes, in an amalgam of styles: military, puritanical and Italian. The only parts that remain from the original structure are the nave and the façade, with its perfectly proportioned bellcote. The west-facing Renaissance main door with its fluted pilasters—it was thought all churches should face west to Mdina, the then capital—was added in the mid-16th century just after the Order arrived in Malta. The knights' austere Rhodian style coupled with seven years in the Mediterranean wilderness turned their architectural clock back, so their additions were already dated. For example, notice the Gothic-style diagonal vault and the transepts, both added in 1606. At the eastern end is a further display of a military temperament with the wall sloping away like a battlement to the road. The reddish dome is thought to be the earliest in Malta and dates from 1495, its saucer shape belies its depth.

The serenity inside is amplified by the flagstones, the almost throne-like confessional, and the shaft of incandescent light that rotates with a sun dial's precision from the eye of the dome. If you stand at the main door you will notice it is left of centre. The reason, it is said, is to confound the devil, who always walks in a straight line and is therefore prevented from interfering with a liturgical service.

It would be very un-Maltese if a church such as this did not have a **secret** or two. In the vestry, a small spiral staircase leads up to two narrow passages first discovered in 1909 by two children who were too frightened to tell anyone. In 1969 the parish verger, Mr Debono, rediscovered the bones of 50 or so people, possibly those missing in Dragut Rais's raid of 1547. It is assumed they died from the smoke caused by the Moslem soldiers desecrating the church.

St Gregory's has had a chequered life: it has been a fishermen's store, a British hospital during the French occupation, a dormitory in World War II, and finally a store for the Royal Engineers who blithely whitewashed over the precious old wall-paintings. *The church is open at the weekends when mass is said. For a more detailed tour, including the secret passages, contact the very helpful Żejtun parish office, © 693704.*

Where to Stay and Eating Out

There are many **bars and clubs** near the imposing St Catherine's church. All serve pizza slices and *pastizzi*. The **Che Sara Sara** gets the vote. In addition to the two political clubs there are the **Rex** and the **Juno**. As an alternative have a **picnic** of local bread and tomatoes in the walled-in shade of the **Luqa Briffa Gardens,** 50 m from St Gregory's. The dedication plaque above the entrance is wrong; the village built it in the early 18th century as a fruit orchard.

An 18th-Century bronze gun
bearing the Royal Coat-of-arms of Charles Bourbon,
King of the Two Sicilies

Mdina, Rabat, the Inland Towns

> *'Citta Notabile della mia Corona'*
> (Notable City of my Crown)
>
> King Alfonso V of Aragon, 1428

Few sights in Malta are as impressive as **Mdina**. High on a plateau in the middle of the island, away from industry and the Grand Harbour, it still is Malta's patrician old capital; set back in time, another age caught within its mellow walls. For more than 2,000 years Mdina has played a key role in the island's history. On a wider stage, as one of the few remaining fortified medieval cities in the Mediterranean it has special status. Put it at the top of your 'sights to see' pile, above historic but sometimes wearisome Valletta.

Outside the walls are **Rabat**, with acres of catacombs, and a Roman Villa that was once a wealthy merchant's house *inside*

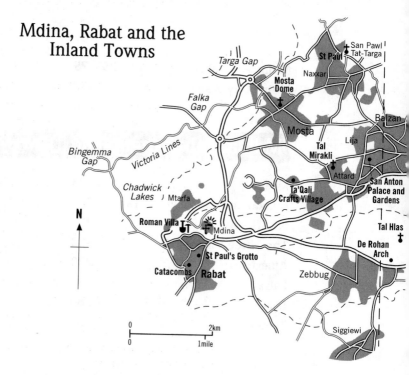

Mdina, Rabat and the Inland Towns

the citadel. Further afield in **Mosta** is the most contemporary of Malta's, as opposed to Gozo's, ecclesiastic extravaganzas, the parish church of St Mary, known as the Mosta Dome. The seamless suburbs of Birkirkara, and the **Three Villages** have a great wealth of Rennaissance and baroque architecture, including five churches worth going out of your way to see, and the public gardens in the **San Anton Palace**. The old parish of Żebbuġ, *Citta Rohan*, was once the adopted village of one of the Order's youngest and more enlightened grand masters. All are far from the busy coasts, and since the railway linking Mdina and Valletta closed in 1931, the towns and villages in the middle of the island have reverted to their quieter historical roots.

Mdina and Rabat

One of the smallest and most compact of historic cities, and entirely and wholly complete within the circle of its walls. No sooner has one set foot in Mdina, one has only to walk through this gateway, then time rolls back and one is in another age.

Sacheverell Sitwell, *Malta*, 1958

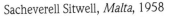

Mdina, in Arabic 'a walled-in city', was the old capital of Malta. Two hundred years after the Arab occupation ended in 1224 it was renamed *Citta Notabile*, and in 1571 when Valletta became the capital, *Citta Vecchia*, 'the old city'. Today, within its panoramic bastions and cool narrow alleys there is evidence of a civic self-respect not found anywhere else in Malta: it's clean, only residents' cars are allowed inside, and even the street signs are elegantly scripted on china plaques. There is charm and enchantment in its twisting streets where shadows, as in an old master, are thrown onto the honey-coloured stone walls. (Do not be deceived by such apparent confusion; the shadowy alleys were built to keep the town cool, and confuse invaders.)

This is the only true Maltese city; the knights' influence is restricted to a few, albeit fine, buildings including the magnificent **Palazzo Vilhena [4]** and the stunning baroque **Cathedral of St Paul's [10]**. Mdina's zenith was during the darker medieval times of the Normans and Spanish, and though all Arabic traces have long been eradicated, some of the existing architecture predates the Order by hundreds of years—from the medieval **Palazzo Falzon [14]**, where the grand master received the keys to the city in 1530, to the original Roman city walls.

Today Mdina has the smallest population in Malta of just 420 people. By contrast, over 13,000 live in neighbouring **Rabat's** sprawling suburbs, a grimy town with little to commend it. Its sites, however, are worth taking in: the **Roman Villa**, **St Paul's Chapel** and **Grotto**, and the **catacombs of St Agatha** and **St Paul**. Rabat was once no more than a suburb and necropolis to Mdina, created under an ancient Roman law which stated the dead had to be disposed of outside the city limits. However, before the Arabs reduced Mdina by four-fifths to its present, easily defendable size, the old city wall used to encompass Rabat's northern quarter, where the numerous catacombs still honeycomb the subterranean rock.

Getting Around

The road to Mdina and Rabat is signposted from Mosta, Msida and Valletta. Despite rotten signposting, the new **Ħamrun/St Vennera bypass** is the quickest route from both St Julian's and Valletta. But the less manic and easiest route is still via Birkirkara. Visitors' **cars are banned** in Mdina and the ticket-issuing police are like the *karrozin*, they lie in wait where tourists gather, so use the **car park** by Howard Gardens.

Taxis can be found lurking in the shade around the car park and streets outside the Main Gate, Saqqajja Square and occasionally Parish Square. Unlike its Gozitan twin, the Citadel, Mdina is reasonably level and **wheelchair access** to many places is good.

Tourist Information

Try to arrive as early or late as possible *before 0930 or after 1530* unless you enjoy being swamped by tour groups. Outside the Main Gate are **public conveniences** and a large **map**. Just inside the Main Gate at 1 St Publius Square, the souvenir shop hires out walkman equipment for a **self-guided tour**, *English only, Lm1.75*.

Numbers in brackets refer to the map on p. 258.

Mdina celebrates the conversion of **St Paul** on the last Sunday in January, and **Rabat** the feast of **St Paul** on the 1st Sunday in July. The traditional festivities during the national holiday of *L-Imnarja* (the Feast of St Peter and St Paul) on 29 June include horse and donkey races. They begin in the Siġġiewi Road (Racecourse Street) and end at the dotty winning post, the extravagantly baroque Casino Notabile or Loggia [6]. (*see* map p. 267)

History

Mdina's history is, for what was the capital city of one of the central Mediterranean hubs until the late 16th century, remarkably uneventful. The usual cast of aggressors—Romans, Arabs, Turks and French have all at one time besieged and or occupied this 190 m-high fortified city. The **Romans** were the first, excluding Neolithic man and the Phoenicians, to seriously colonize the plateau. Their settlement, named for simplicity the same as the island, 'Melita', was the seat of their *municipum*. The city walls spread into Rabat and afforded them in the northern and eastern quadrants good natural defences.

The wily **Arabs** adopted Melita as their capital in AD 870, renamed it Medina ('the walled city'), quickly reduced it to its present size, dug a moat and strengthened the southern walls. The defences proved strong enough for 220 years, until Christianity spread south and in 1090 it was taken by Count Roger the Norman. He found a crumbling city, built a new rectangular-plan cathedral and introduced a north European feudal system.

Between 1194 and 1530, under Swabian, Angevin, Aragonese and Castillian influence—known under the collective misnomer, the **'Spanish Period'**—Mdina not only prospered but became an aristocratic Maltese city. In the 14th century it accommodated the almost mute *Università*, or governing body, established by the Spanish viceroy in Sicily. Alphonso V of Aragon visited in 1428, rejuvenated flagging morale, vowed the city would forever remain Spanish, and renamed it *Citta Notabile*. (George VI awarded the island the George Cross in 1942 in a similar public relations coup.) In 1530 Charles V broke his ancestor's promise and ceded the islands to the wandering **Order of the Knights of St John** (*see* History p. 57). Grand Master L'Isle Adam received the silver keys to *Citta Notabile* in Palazzo Falzon from the *Hakem* of the *Università* soon after his arrival in the autumn of 1530. His promise to maintain all their privileges and rights, was promptly broken.

The Order was a seafaring body, the harbour was its base and, in all but name, its capital. *Citta Notabile*, therefore, became increasingly less important. During the ensuing **Great Siege** of 1565, *Citta Notabile* was a refuge from which the cavalry squadrons and local militia, under the command of the Portuguese knight Don Mesquita, harried the Turks' camps on the Marsa and Corradino. After the Turks finally withdrew, defeated in the September 1565, a limp second attack on *Citta Notabile* was made from the beach at St Paul's Bay. Like their first invasion it was a badly executed and mistimed disaster.

Mdina was eclipsed with the building of Valletta, and became known as *Citta Vecchia*, 'the old city'. For most of the 17th century it was in decline. People left, and with the exception of Grand Master de Redin's polygonal southern and eastern bastions, the defences were weakened. So the **earthquake** of 1693 came as a blessing here, an opportunity for a new start and a fitting end to the century. The first of the major reconstructions was the cathedral in 1702, and by Grand Master de Vilhena's reign (1722–36) the Order, wealthy now and used to silk not cold armour, was lavishing money on the city. As the century progressed the gracefully ageing stone palaces of *Citta Vecchia* silently witnessed the slow, inevitable crumbling of the Order that had built them.

By midday on 10 June 1798 the keys to the city were formally in the hands of **Napoleon's** governor designate, General Vaubois, and the Order's reign was over. Napoleon's war effort urgently needed funds, and within three months the French set about auctioning treasures looted from the city's Carmelite church. Incensed, the devout Maltese rioted, killed the French commander and set in train the rebellion that led to the French being besieged inside Valletta and eventually, with the aid of the British, overthrown.

The **British** abolished the powerless *Università* in 1819 and Mdina, no longer referred to as *Citta Vecchia*, retired like an old and weary campaigner behind its quiet walls for more than 130 years. **World War II** brought very little damage to the city, despite the proximity of the fighter airfield of Ta'Qali at the foot of the plateau, but a few stray bombs damaged Rabat.

Mdina City Walking Tour

Mdina is pedestrianized. The route suggested marks notable places to visit and historical landmarks; with a 0930 start you can see it all before lunch. If you would rather read or soak up the sun, head for the open-air **Café Fontanella [12]** on the northern bastions.

Main Gate (1724) [1]. Designed by de Mondion, the triumphal gate was built by Grand Master de Vilhena to replace the older gateway to the right. It's a splendid, if top heavy, example of restrained baroque by one of the Order's most prolific builders. The escutcheon bears his arms—the growling lions in front are a part of them—and the inscription records the restoration of parts of the city walls.

Following the election of a new grand master he and his procession left Valletta for Mdina, where he was met at this gate by the head of the *Università*, or the *Hakem*, Captain of the Rod. Having received the silver keys to the city the new grand master promised to 'observe the privileges, and franchises and usages of this city'—a promise all too often and readily broken.

On the inside façade are three statues of St Publius, St Paul and St Agatha, the island's and the city's patron saints, all of whom carry palm fronds to symbolise their martyrdom. The remaining escutcheon is that of the island's oldest nobles, the Inguanez [20], while the blank one was defaced by the French in 1798.

Mdina Dungeons [2]. Spookily set in the old cells below the Courts of Justice [6] the walk through more than 20 different waxwork set pieces offers a study in man's ingenuity in extracting information, until the British abolished torture in 1813. Children love it. *Adults Lm1, children 50c; open 7 days 1000–1830, winter 1000–1730.*

Torre dello Standardo [3]. The Signal Tower of the Standard was once a guardhouse and is now the police station. De Vilhena tinkered with the original 16th-century building which formed part of the island's chain of signalling stations.

Palazzo Vilhena/Museum of Natural History (1730) [4]. This is one of the most rewarding examples of Grand Master de Vilhena's benign and somewhat egocentric compulsion to erect impressive buildings. Inside on the main staircase is a white marble bust of de Vilhena which shows his well-composed and dainty features: a small feminine mouth and flowing bouffant locks, marred only by bloodhound eyes.

The building was designed as de Vilhena's summer residence, on the site of the *Università*, either by Maltese architect Giovanni Barbara or, more likely, the

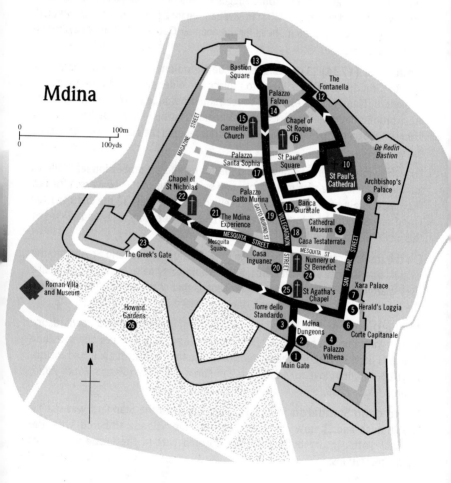

Mdina

resident French architect de Mondion. The fullsome three-sided *palazzo*, built on an irregular French plan around a central courtyard, imitates an auditorium and—with its arched balconies and boxes—the Manoel Theatre in Valletta, also built by de Vilhena (*see* pp. 112–13). The entrance screen is embellished by his fanciful and ubiquitous escutcheon and leads to a main door, gathered in by magnificent French banded columns with de Vilhena immortalized in a bust of bronze relief set above.

In 1908 the *palazzo* became the Connaught Tuberculosis Hospital, named after King Edward VII's brother, then naval commander-in-chief, and did not shut until 1956. In 1973 it was converted into the **Natural History Museum**. The entrance fee, Lm1, can only be justified by the *palazzo* itself and not the unspeakably dull collection of tired exhibits housed within, the most interesting of which is a chip of the moon given to Malta by President Nixon in 1979. A stroll around the courtyard is free.

Herald's Loggia [5]. From the security of the first floor, the herald or town crier would shout out the orders for the day to those gathered in the small square formed by the Xara Palace Hotel and the Corte Capitanale. The orders, known as *bandi*, were issued by the *Università* and are preserved in the **Cathedral Museum [9].**

Corte Capitanale/The Courts of Justice [6]. The Courts of Justice formed part of the Palazzo Vilhena and except for the **dungeons [2]** are closed to the public. The figures on the left and right of the balcony symbolize Justice and Mercy. A secret underground passage used to lead from the courts to the **Archbishop's Palace [8].**

Xara Palace [7]. A local nobleman's house, which once belonged to the Strickland family, it served as an RAF officers' mess during World War II and is now an hotel, *see below.*

Archbishop's Palace (1722) [8]. The present building was constructed in the wake of the 1693 earthquake. Mdina was the seat of the bishops of Malta until 1816 when St John's in Valletta became the Co-cathedral. The bishops, appointees of the kingdom of Spain and the grand inquisitor, himself a Papal appointee—were often vocal and powerful irritants to the Order's power. The French General Vaubois dined here in 1798 as the guest of his conquered enemy.

Cathedral Museum (1733) [9]. Commissioned as a seminary by Bishop de Bussan, the design is often and incorrectly attributed to Giovanni Barbara who died five years before. The unknown architect (possibly Andrea Belli) produced a crisp and impressive structure with effusive Sicilian decorations that complement the earlier cathedral. The concave window and balcony supported by two Atlantean figures on the first floor neatly separate the façade. Cicero stayed in a house on this site while preparing his case against the thieving Roman governor, Verres (*see* p. 233–4).

The museum sprawls over two floors around an airy central courtyard and, unlike the Natural History Museum, houses articles of importance, beauty and value including the cathedral's and **Inquisition's archives**. Many of the artefacts, including the **Dürer** collection, were bequeathed by Count Saverio Marchese in the early 19th century. Notable exhibits include a comprehensive collection of **coins** and **medals** from ancient Malta through to the present day, Dürer woodcuts from the early 1500s (no. 64 of St Jerome, with his ever-present skull, is worth the entrance fee alone), relics of the pre-1693 cathedral including the dramatic early 15th-century Spanish school polyptych altarpiece depicting the life of St Paul, and paintings by **de Favray** and **Preti**. *Adm. 60c. 0900–1300 and 1330–1700, winter 1630, and closed Sunday.*

St Paul's Cathedral (1697) [10]

Of all the churches on the islands, St Paul's Cathedral is the finest and most mature example of Maltese baroque; not fussy and ornamental but the work of an articulate pen imbued with all the influences—Roman, Sicilian, and Italian—from which the idiom evolved. From all perspectives this monumental church with its bold austere swathes takes charge: at the screen façade, from a distance, in silhouette and from inside.

Tradition states the cathedral is built on the site of the villa belonging to the Roman governor, Publius, where the shipwrecked St Paul healed Publius's father and converted the grateful governor himself to Christianity. (Publius later became the first bishop of Malta and was martyred in Greece.) The simple 12th-century Norman structure of Count Roger was enlarged in 1419, and the present cathedral was built following the earthquake of 1693 which destroyed much of southeast Sicily and Malta. A new cathedral had been talked about before the earthquake; Lorenzo Gafa had added a new choir in 1679 and after the earthquake he was commissioned to create the new building. The site on the northeast corner of Mdina must have flattered Gafa's inspiration—this domed cathedral would be seen from afar—and the structure went up rapidly: five years after the foundation stone was laid in 1697 it was consecrated.

St Paul's Cathedral sits on a low podium at the end of the eponymous rectangular square. The near-square façade with its three cleanly divided bays gives it a light but solid air. The Corinthian order of pilasters below the composite ones span the entire façade without interruption, leaving above the two side doors brave expanses of honey-coloured masonry. The bell towers—each with six bells—are squat, adding to the façade's heaviness, but with Gafa's deft touch they appear lighter, for the twin clocks nudge into the lower lip of the cornice. Note, in relief at the top of the bell towers, St Paul's viper twists out of the flames. Above the main door on the left is the escutcheon of Grand Master Perellos (during whose reign the cathedral was built) and on the right that of Bishop Palmieri, who consecrated it in 1702 two years before the dome was completed. In front are the obligatory cannons, part of the knights' ordnance: to the left a Dutch cannon from 1681 and to the right, bearing the coat of arms of the Duke of Savoy, the Duke's gift cannon to commemorate the knights' defence of Rhodes.

And finally, sneaking out from under cover of the towers and pediment, is Gafa's dynamic swansong, the light octagonal dome, with eight stone scrolls above a high drum leading up to a neat lantern. Similar in design to St Catherine's in Żejtun, it is best studied from inside or from a distance. *Hours Mon–Sat 0900–1300 and 1330–1645. Adm. free.*

The Interior

Gafa's plan for the church is a Latin cross with a vaulted nave, two aisles and two small side chapels. Space under the rich tessellated floor of extravagant and macabre tombstones is reserved for Maltese nobles and high-ranking clergy, unlike at St John's in Valletta, where only knights of the Order could be buried.

The Sicilian white marble **baptismal font (1)** was a gift from Bishop Valguarnero in 1495 and survived the earthquake. The **statue of St Publius** and the two **lecterns of St John and St Luke (2)** by the main altar are by Guiseppe Valenti, who also made the statue of Queen Victoria in Republic Square, Valletta. The **frescoes (3)** in the cross-vaulted ceiling were painted by two Sicilian brothers, Antonio and Vincenzo de Manno in 1794 and depict the life of St Paul. The beautiful carved **door to the sacristy (4)** is made of solid Irish oak and was the main door to the original cathedral which somehow survived the 1693 earth-quake. In the side **chapel of the Annunciation (5)** is Mattia **Preti's** unconvincing image of St Paul hysterically chasing the Saracens away from the city's bastions during a brief siege in the early 1400s. In the **chapel of the Blessed Sacrament (6)**, the icon of the Madonna bejewelled and shrouded in reverential grime, is alleged to have been painted by St Luke. (Sadly there is no

Numbers in brackets refer to the plan on p. 262. 261

St Paul's Cathedral

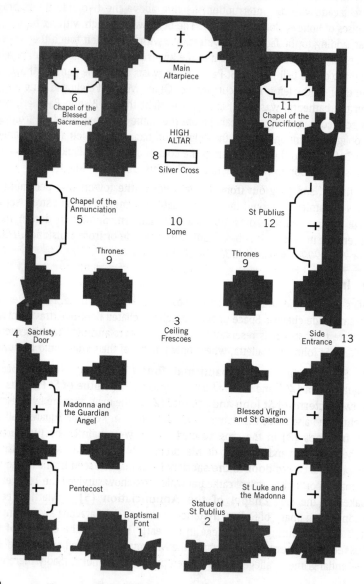

7 — Main Altarpiece

6 — Chapel of the Blessed Sacrament

11 — Chapel of the Crucifixion

HIGH ALTAR
8 — Silver Cross

Chapel of the Annunciation
5

St Publius
12

10 — Dome

Thrones
9

Thrones
9

3 — Ceiling Frescoes

4 — Sacristy Door

Side Entrance — 13

Madonna and the Guardian Angel

Blessed Virgin and St Gaetano

Pentecost

St Luke and the Madonna

Statue of St Publius
2

Baptismal Font
1

evidence to support this, or the notion that he painted a similar icon in the Sanctuary in Mellieha.) The silver tabernacle is Roman and dates from the early 18th century. The **main altarpiece**, the *Conversion of St Paul*, the side panels and the marvellously graphic rendition of St Paul's shipwreck in the **apse (7)** were all painted by Mattia Preti in the late 17th century; they too survived the earthquake intact. The **Royal Arms of Spain** hang at the apex of the arch in remembrance of the Emperor Charles V who gave the islands to the Order in 1530. The two Italian **oval portraits** by the front pillars are marble mosaic compositions of photographic clarity depicting St Peter and St Paul and date from 1873. Rarely on display is the **silver cross (8)** brought by the knights from Rhodes. A weak supposition states Godfrey de Bouillon carried it into Jerusalem in the First Crusade in 1099. The two **thrones (9)** are reserved for the bishop of Malta and the grand master. The original paintings in Gafa's splendid **dome** were ruined by inclement weather and the present images represent the *Divine Mission of the Church* **(10)** and were painted about 40 years ago. Like the other side chapel, the **chapel of the Crucifixion (11)** has delicately inlaid marble floors resembling a carpet and sombre black and gilt 18th-century gates. The crucifix was fashioned by a Franciscan monk in the 17th century. The **altarpiece (12)** of the martyrdom of St Publius and his baptism by St Paul has sometimes been attributed to Preti but is only his school. **Side entrance (13)**.

Returning to the tour mapped out on p. 258:

Banca Giuratale (1730) [11]. The Order referred pompously to prosaic civil records offices as Municipal Palaces or Banca Giuratale, and this is still a records office. It is also an exquisite example of de Mondion's baroque handiwork. Two storeys of crisp detail, florid carving and elaborate windows are set beneath two equally elaborate corners of what look like limestone flowerpots of dotty ornaments. It housed for a time the *Università*, which was politely ejected from its old site, on which Palazzo Vilhena [4] was being built.

Nearly opposite at no. 11 Ville Gaignon St, known as the **house of Notary Bezzina**, in 1798 the luckless French officer Captain Masson was pitched off the balcony to his death by the bloodthirsty Maltese mob, after his countrymen's attempt to auction off the plundered treasures of the Carmelite church [15].

The Fontanella [12]. A refuge for light refreshment at the very edge of the north bastion (*see* p. 271).

Bastion Square [13]. Bastion Square was the old parade ground and 40 m away in Magazine Street the munitions were stored. The old firing bastion, the

Bastione de Vaccari, has a superb **panorama** of Malta—from Valletta, the Mosta Dome (in the middle), to St Paul's Bay. Part of Camilla's gift shop is on the site of what was the Jewish Synagogue before the Jewish community was expelled from the island by King Ferdinand of Aragon in 1492. **Villegaignon Street**, the 350 m-long main street which runs from the Main Gate to Bastion Square, is named after Nicholas de Villegaignon who defended the city against Dragut's corsair raid of 1551. Its other names have been *Tal Muyeli* or the Street of the Gentry and Strada Reale.

Palazzo Falzon/The Norman House (1495) [14]. In 1530 the first of Malta's grand masters, the Frenchman L'Isle Adam, received the keys to the city here after the knights were given the islands by Charles V. (There is a painting of him receiving the keys in the Grand Master's Palace in Valletta.) The building is in fact medieval not Norman and, in keeping with medieval design, the living quarters were on the first floor—the ground floor was for kitchens, stables, etcetera—hence the more intricate arched windows with their colonettes above the twin cornice of triangular corbels. There is a small private **museum** on the ground floor. *Adm. 25c. 0900–1300 and 1400–1700.* Next door the **Palazzo Costanzo** is undergoing restoration at the hands of the Mdina Dungeon entrepreneurs and will obviously become a 'tourist attraction'.

Carmelite church (1660) [15]. The church and its associated monastery is also known as Our Lady of Mount Carmel; the Carmelites were a Sicilian Order who came to Malta in 1370. Designed by Francesco Sammut and 12 years in the construction, the interior with its seven altars and Palladian pilasters under an oval and well-lit nave-cum-dome is unexpectedly rich, despite the French army's looting of the church in 1798 to fund Napoleon's war effort.

Chapel of St Roque (1798) [16]. St Roque is the patron saint of diseases, often invoked during the plague-infested 14th–19th centuries when the sick would congregate and pray for their succour. Grand Master de Vilhena demolished the earlier chapel of St Roque which was uncomfortably close to his intended summer residence, the Palazzo Vilhena, and built this one much further away.

Palazzo Santa Sophia (1233?) [17]. The date plaque may be unreliable. The first floor was added in 1938 to what is still probably Mdina's oldest building.

Casa Testaferrata [18]. The Testaferrata family still live behind the red main door. The Marquisate was created by Grand Master Pinto in 1745. (The majority of Maltese titles were created during the reign of the knights.)

Palazzo Gatto Murina [19]. Tucked away in Gatto Murina Street, the early 15th-century *palazzo* has a fine example of restored arched windows above strident arcaded coursework. The eponymous *murina* or lamprey motif is set above the spindly colonettes. The building is off **Mesquita Street**, named after the Portuguese knight Don Mesquita who commanded the cavalry garrison and governed the city during the Great Siege of 1565. It is said that after the fall of St Elmo he hanged one Turkish prisoner every morning from the walls of the city until the siege ended.

Casa Inguanez [20]. Occupying an entire block, the house has been the Inguanez home since the 14th century. Cicco Gatto was created Baron in 1350 for quelling an uprising of the Gozitans against their Aragonese masters, and his direct descendants the Inguanez are the oldest of Malta's 29 noble families. In 1432 King Alfonso V of Aragon stayed here, as did Alfonso XIII of Spain in 1927.

The Mdina Experience [21]. Mesquita Square is a leafy gap under the evergreen ficus trees. The Mdina Experience is in an extremely well-converted old building with a cool ground-floor café and the inevitable souvenir shop. Audio-visually 'the experience' recounts in a modern auditorium the history of Mdina. *Lm1.20. Shows—25 minutes long and in five languages—1100–1600 Mon–Fri and 1100–1300 Sat.*

Chapel of St Nicholas (1550) [22]. This is one of the oldest and most tranquil *quartiers*, and many of the 16th- and 17th-century buildings have survived. The little chapel was remodelled in 1692.

Magazine Street and the Greek's Gate [23]. The gate, like so much of Mdina, owes its restoration to de Vilhena. It was named after a small Greek community that lived in the southwest of the city in the 16th and 17th centuries. The steep slope leads out to the defensive ditch surrounding this part of the city, and there is a separate entrance known as 'the hole in the wall' in Magazine Street. Easily visible from a few hundred metres away in the valley below is the old Valletta–Mdina railway station, now a restaurant. During World War II the tunnel was part fuel dump part shelter.

Nunnery of St Benedict and chapel of St Peter (St Benedict) [24]. The building dates from the 15th century, as does the Benedictine community. The Order is a very strict and devout one: no man is allowed into the convent without the bishop's permission, with the exception of a doctor and, traditionally, the whitewasher who in times of plague would disinfect the walls; nor are any of the 20 or so nuns allowed out. Until 1974, even after a nun had died she had to be buried within the grounds of the convent. The chapel was restored in 1625 and the altarpiece is another work by **Preti**.

Chapel of St Agatha (early 15th century) [25]. St Agatha is said to have fled to Malta from Sicily in AD 249, following persecution by the Emperor Decius, after refusing to marry Quintianus the governor of Catania. Upon returning to Catania in AD 251 she was imprisoned and on the orders of the spurned Quintianus and met with a grisly end. Her left breast was cut off— statues like the one on the city side of the Main Gate often depict her holding either her breast or the shears used to remove it—and then she was burnt to death over hot stones. The chapel was remodelled in 1694 by Lorenzo Gafa. Mass is said here on 5 February, the day St Agatha died.

Howard Gardens [26]. Named after Malta's first prime minister (1921–3), the gardens were made public in 1924 and ramble down towards the Roman villa. The old Cross is said to have been a gift from Count Roger the Norman, to celebrate the reinstatement of Christianity after he took the islands from the Arabs.

Rabat

The easiest way to see Rabat is on foot; leave Mdina by the Main Gate. The five principal places worth visiting are a short walk down St Paul's Street from the Roman villa. You can invariably park near Parish Square or outside the Roman villa.

Roman villa and Museum [1]. The villa probably belonged to a wealthy Roman merchant or a senior official; its position and size confirm this. The siting has an Italian flair, looking west over the valley towards what is now Mtarfa.

The villa and its grounds were first excavated in 1881. The clean neo-classical temple museum-building now camouflaged by a forecourt of citrus trees was built in 1921–4 during the second round of excavations. Not all the museum's exhibits were unearthed within the villa's grounds. Among the artefacts and architectural fragments is an olive-pipper found in Marsaxlokk, parts of flour mills made from Italian lava, and tombstones. The cabinets display terracotta ornaments, theatrical masks, glassware, amphorae, lamps from Imperial Rome, and a section of fine mosaic from the villa.

The corner stairs lead down to what remains of the villa itself. The main attraction is the (now roofed) square mosaic-covered *atrium*, or central court, enclosed by 16 columns, only one of which is original. The whole of this area would have been roofed except for the *impluvium* of two birds sitting on a water bowl, from which rainwater would drain to the cistern in the corner. The two rooms off the *atrium* were, on the left, the *triclinium* or dining room (which housed the mosaic in the museum) and a reception room. Some heavy handed restoration has left the remaining mosaics in poor order. In the small annex are relics from later Arabic graves found within the grounds.

Other items in the courtyard include the famous but disappointingly small motif of an astonished open-mouthed woman from a mosaic's border (*see* illustration, p. 268), a blurred scene of either a satyr being teased by maenads (orgiastic nymphs) or Delilah and Samson, and marble statues and busts including Octavia—the mother of the Emperor Claudius—who looks handsome only in profile.

Grotto and parish church of St Paul [2]. Tradition has stated that during his enforced three-month stay in Malta, and while a prisoner of the island's Roman governor, Publius, St Paul eschewed the comfortable surroundings offered to him and chose this subterranean **grotto** instead. It seems unlikely

Mdina and Rabat

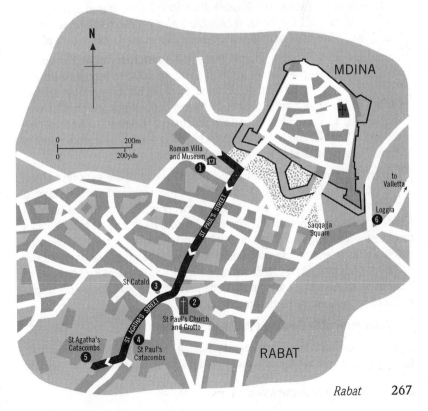

that one of Emperor Nero's more valuable prisoners would have been allowed to pass the winter in an exceedingly damp and cold cave; he probably just preached from here. Other widely held and even less tenable beliefs are that St Paul's presence imbued the stone walls with an antidote to poison, and that however much stone is chiselled away the grotto will remain exactly the same size. The statue of St Paul was donated by Grand Master Pinto in 1748 and the silver galley hanging from the ceiling was the gift of the Knights of St John in 1960 to mark the 1,900-year anniversary of St Paul's shipwreck. The eight coats of arms are of each of the *langues*. Pope John Paul II prayed in the grotto while on his visit in May 1990. *0930–1200 and 1400–1630. Adm. free. A guide is usually on hand to deliver a dead-pan explanation, if so leave a tip.*

Annexed to both the church and the grotto is the **sanctuary of St Publius**. A Spaniard, Juan Beneguas, came to Malta in about 1600 to become a knight. Upon seeing the grotto he changed his mind, swapped his shiny armour for grey sackcloth and became a hermit. By 1617 he had both money and papal favours to his credit, and was able to build a sanctuary. Lorenzo Gafa completely reworked it in 1692 and his brother Melchiorre executed the marble statue of St Paul. The altarpiece of St Publius is by Mattia Preti.

The **parish church of St Paul** (1656–81) was one of the very first of the island's churches to be built on a grand Latin-cross scale and has been altered many times. The author of the slightly overworked three-pediment baroque façade is probably Francesco Buonamici. Lorenzo Gafa is thought to have had a hand in the vaulting and dome in 1692 whilst working on the neighbouring sanctuary. In an enormous gilded frame, the famous painting *The Shipwreck of St Paul* (1683) by Stefano Erardi depicts a very dry St Paul shaking off the viper in front of an astonished gathering of 'barbarians' and Romans, as his ship is pounded to smithereens by the stormy seas.

The catacombs of St Catald, St Paul and St Agatha

The early Christians were forbidden by Roman law to bury their dead within the city limits, and as cremation was not an acceptable solution families and fraternities developed the intramural catacomb. Hewn out of living rock there are six variants which date in this area from the 1st to the 8th century AD. Catacombs are dotted all over the island and all have had diverse uses ever since as sources of plunder, as cattle pens and as air-raid shelters.

Terms

Loculus: a small rectangular recess cut into a wall, for infants and children.

Canopied table tomb: the most common normally consisting of two graves exposed by two or four arches above 1m from the ground. The graves were sealed by separate stone slabs to leave a flat surface under the arches.

Saddle-backed canopied tomb: similar in height and positioning to the table tombs, and with the same arched appearance, in this instance the body would be interred underneath the pitched roof via an opening in the lower wall.

Arcosolium tombs: also known as window graves, they resemble an arched window cut into the rock at a lower level.

Floor graves: cut into the ground with head rests or divots and sealed with a stone slab.

Agape table: unique to Malta, and made up of a circular table and a semicircular bench. A highly civilized ceremony, not unlike a wake, would take place at the burial. The family, friends and a priest would gather to pray, mourn and feast. The agape would also be used for religious rites and is usually found near the entrance to a catacomb.

St Catald [3]. Just outside the perimeter ditch of the Roman city and diagonally opposite the parish church is the tiny 18th-century church of St Catald, built on the site of one said to date back to AD 400. Hollowed out beneath it is a small group of catacombs dating from the late 2nd and early 3rd centuries in what was originally a Punic burial shaft. One of the best examples of an **agape table** is on the left at the bottom of the stairs, and the majority are fine **canopied tombs**. *Adm. free during daylight hours.*

St Paul [4]. Seventy metres from the square into St Agatha Street is the main entrance to a large labyrinth of catacombs dating from the 3rd century. In all it accommodated more than a thousand corpses throughout its 2,200 sq m. Not all are accessible, but apart from **arcoscolium tombs** all types can be seen

At the bottom of the steep steps, 7 m into the catacombs, are two striking rooms divided by a central pillar. The main crypt, just to the right, has a high ceiling, and at either end a raised plinth and **agape tables**. Down a couple of steps, the crypt to the left has been called a chapel and has a recess at the far end which may have been an altar. Stand with your back to the entrance steps (note the sad **loculi tombs**) and use the main crypt as a reference point; to the right is more extensive and two long corridors, each approximately 25 m long, lead to groups of **canopied** and **saddle-backed tombs**. To the left is even spookier, and apart from another small group of canopied tombs, there is a long twisty passage leading to a lower level. *Adm. Lm1. Bring a torch, the illumination is either just poor or done for effect. A useful little map is included in the back of a 60-c historical pamphlet on sale at the ticket office.*

Catacombs and Museum of St Agatha [5]. Flagged 100 m past St Paul's are the more exciting catacombs and **frescoes** of St Agatha. Entrance to the catacombs is down a few steps via the crypt, again hewn out of rock, where St Agatha is said to have spent her time in exile praying and teaching (*see* p. 266). On the walls are 31 detailed **frescoes** in varying states of restoration from the 12th to 15th centuries, many of which are of St Agatha in pious poses. The tour of the catacombs lasts 20 minutes and takes in only 10 per cent of the honeycomb necropolis which is said to cover nearly 4,000 sq m. The ceilings are disorientatingly low, but the tombs, including the **arcosolium**, are much better lit. People who suffer from twinges of claustrophobia should stay put in the crypt. The **museum**, one of the island's better kept secrets, contains a little of everything—related and unrelated. Among the exhibits are coins, vestments, ancient pottery, an eccentric mineral collection and a remarkable 1 m-high statue of St Agatha, carved from a solid piece of alabaster in 1666, which was originally the crypt's altarpiece. *The catacombs, crypt and museum are private and entrance to all, and the informative guided tour given by Father Camilleri or his assistant, are free. Leave a generous donation. Open Mon–Sat 0900–1145 and 1300–1600, except Sat when the pm hours are shorter. Closed Sun and public holidays.*

Where to Stay in Mdina

Mdina only has one hotel, the moderately priced **Xara Palace★★** (inexpensive), ℂ 454001–3, and it can only be described, albeit affectionately, as a little shabby. But its tranquil position makes it an ideal billet for fugitive writers, reclusive lovers or long-term visitors to hole up in. It has bags of charm, but don't expect hot and cold running service. Of the 18 rooms, no. 28 is the best: a loggia-enclosed mini-balcony overlooks the bastions and the northeast of the island. In between Mdina and Rabat in Saqqajja Square is the inexpensive **Point de Vue** (Class II), Saqqajja Square, Rabat, ℂ 454117, a base from which to explore this part of the island. Destroyed during World War II when it served as an RAF mess, it's now an adequate family-run guest house with 17 rooms (nos 1, 2 and 11 all have large balconies). There is no standing on ceremony in the hotel, or either of its two restaurants.

Rabat

The 1970s not-so-inspired **Grand Hotel Verdala**★★★★ (expensive), Inguanez Street, © 451700–9, is stuck on top of the hill and has long been a white elephant; a much needed upgrading of the 164 rooms is planned. On the positive side, the public rooms are imposing and cool, the pools and terraces large, and it catches any cool breeze there might be in summer. Tucked away and not easy to find on the southern outskirts of Rabat is the **Medina Hotel**★★★ (moderate), Labour Avenue, © 453230. A modernish little hotel with 40 recently-done-up rooms and comprehensive amenities: two pools, a restaurant and bar.

Eating Out and Nightlife in Mdina

There is one small **provisions shop** opposite Casa Testaferrata where the ingredients for a simple picnic by the bastion or Mesquita Square can be purchased. Situated above a small citrus courtyard on the edge of the north bastion with panoramic views is the **Fontanella** (cheap), 1 Bastion Street, © 454264. Even when it is deserted the service is diabolical, and the tea almost undrinkable, but it's redeemed by the best homemade apple and chocolate cake in Malta. Wash the cake down with bottled refreshment and if you are hungry, and patient, they will contrive to deliver a good toasted sandwich sometime the same day. Less than 100 m away and next to a charming house with a forecourt of oleander bushes and a tall cypress tree is the **Casa Mdina** (cheap), 6 Bastion Square, part souvenir shop and part snackerie serving what has to be *the* bargain lunch. Its 'ploughman's' consists of cheese, ham, bread, tomatoes, onions and a glass of local wine and costs only Lm1. Down a narrow street opposite the cathedral is **The Medina** (moderate), 7 Holy Cross Street, © 454004. The courtyard garden, with its large tree, hanging oleander and rough-hewn walls, is the most memorable feature of this established converted-townhouse restaurant. The food is reliable and less fussy than at the Bachus (below), but the smaller menu also has old-fashioned French pretensions. The puds are either homemade or come from the Fontanella. It is sometimes open for lunch, call to check. **Bachus** (moderate), Inguanez Street, ✆ 454981, used to be an ammunition magazine and is refreshingly cool in summer, yet snug in winter, and offers a reasonably priced set lunch and à la carte. The too-adventurous French cooking means everything is ladled with cream or a heavy sauce but the food is well prepared and slickly served. Also open for dinner, morning coffee and afternoon tea. Enquire first if a tour group is pre-booked, if so avoid it. Outside the city walls and as part of the guest house is the **Point de Vue** (inexpensive), 5 Saqqajja Square, ✆ 454117. It has a restaurant and a pizzeria, apart from serving snacks all day both inside and outside. Set menus start at a reasonable Lm2.55. **It-Trunciera**, Saqqajja Square, no telephone, had just closed down at the time of writing, but *did* provide good pizzas and average Italianish food served at a snail's pace. On a summer evening its open terrace at the edge of Mdina's bastions was hard to beat, and knowing Maltese entrepreneurial spirit it will soon re-open.

Eating out in Rabat

There isn't a commendable place to eat. A proliferation of snack vendors, fruit vans and cafés are grouped in and around Parish Square, which during the summer becomes a convention centre for bad-tempered coach drivers. Flee.

Follow the headlights snaking their way like fireflies to **Ta'Gianpula nightclub** situated nearly 3 km off the Rabat–Siġġiewi road. Open only in the summer months this smart open-air discotheque is in the grounds of an old farmhouse. The music, while not Barry Manilow, is less techno than in Paceville's two haunts and the crowd will never see their teens again. Under the stars and around the owner's swimming pool are three bars and a semi-sunken dancefloor. The solitary drawback is trying to remember the field in which you parked your car, at 0300. *Summer, Saturday only. Adm. Lm1.50. ✆ 450354/450238.*

Shopping

Mdina has a handful of shops all obviously geared to the tourist. **Mdina Souvenirs** in St Publius Square by the Main Gate has books, nick-nacks and hires out the 'Sound Alive' walkmans. Further on at 13 Villegaignon Street, **Casa Castelletti** sells little 50c-pots of honey and, for some reason, massive copper saucepans. **Greenhand Leathercraft** fashions wallets, belts, etcetera on the premises, and sells glassware.

The **Maltese Falcon** stocks silver filigree and films, and at the end in Bastion Square the discreet **Camilla's** sells books, paintings and the occasional interesting antique curio. Anyone determined to get rid of money will not have missed the signposts on the main Rabat road for the **Ta'Qali Crafts Village** in the nissen huts of the disused World War II airfield, *see* pp. 36–7.

Mosta

Situated near the very middle of the island, Mosta's name derives from the Arabic for 'centre'; 13,000 people live in this thriving and not particularly attractive hurly-burly town atop the safety of the Victoria Lines. Ever since World War II the spread of new building around its older centre has continued apace. From many places in Malta the dome of St Mary's stands out like a beacon. Relegated to fourth-largest in Europe by the upstart Xewkija parish church in Gozo, **Mosta Dome** can still claim third place on volumetric measurement; either way it's well worth seeing .

Getting Around

Mosta is as near to a cross-route hub as the **bus** system has. The easiest route by car from Valletta, 9 km away, is via Birkirkara and Balzan. From the north the road going through Bur Marrad is best. **Taxis** can be found near the bus terminus next to St Mary's.

Tourist Information

Almost a provincial capital, Mosta has many services grouped together to the left of the church facing Constitution Street: the **police station**, a **polyclinic** (medical centre), **post office** and **public conveniences**. The ticket-issuing police are white-hot around here; park in a side street if there isn't space in the meagre car park. Mosta is one of eight parishes to celebrate its *festa* on 15 August, the Assumption. St Mary's looks even more spectacular when dressed and illuminated.

Parish church of St Mary (Mosta Dome or the *Rotunda*)

As a symbol of a simple farming community's devotion the huge 19th-century church of St Mary's is remarkable. Unlike St John's at Xewkija (Gozo's great *rotunda*), St Mary's was begun in 1833, long before immigration had enriched its then tiny population; it must have appeared a daunting and possibly ludicrous concept. From day one the church was dogged by misfortune and controversy. First the collection of building funds was diverted to help with a cholera epidemic in the 1830s. Next the architect, George Grognet de Vasse, was embroiled in an infantile scandal with the Académie Française over the provenance of a piece of Mdina stone he alleged came from the lost city of Atlantis, of which he averred Malta was the northwest tip! Finally, even the bishop snubbed the project by refusing to lay the foundation stone in 1833; he sent a minion priest instead. The bishop, like many others, thought de Vasse's radical departure from cruiciform to a circular 'mosque'-style plan had pagan associations.

The church took 27 years to build and the entire dome was constructed without the use of scaffolding, around and partly supported by the old parish church which was then dismantled. De Vasse's design takes a lead from the massive twin rows of six pillars in the Pantheon façade. The whole has been likened to the Pantheon itself, but the likeness stops with the façade. The two intricately decorated belfries don't sit comfortably with the curves of the massive dome behind (inside it's 7 m wider than that of St Paul's in London). The local limestone has a warm apricot hue even in winter and has weathered to a deeper colour than other buildings on the islands. But the real mastery and fun is inside. Underneath the towering and mercifully simple dome with its 16 windows spiralling up to the lantern are six side chapels. The floor is an intricate geometry of two different marble inlays—no tombstones here—that weave an interplay of patterns with the ceiling. The murals were painted by **Guiseppe Cali** early this century. Before the main altar and to the left is the sacristy. Displayed among the usual souvenirs, is a replica of a large **Luftwaffe bomb** that pierced the dome at 1640 on 9 April 1942 as more than 300 people milled around awaiting early-evening mass. It was one of three to hit the dome—two bounced off—and like the others was designed to explode after a delay. The bomb rolled across the floor, startling the congregation; miraculously it never exploded. *Adm. free. 0500–1200 1500–2000. Wheelchair access. Wardens are on hand to answer questions. No shorts. Visits to the top of the dome by permission only.*

Despite the earnest signposts, give the **National Park** a wide berth. Hurriedly built in 1990 it has since fallen into a sorry state of neglect. The central pond is full of everything except water.

Where to Stay

The only place to stay, the **Central Hotel**★★ (inexpensive), Independence Avenue Street, ✆ 434178/9, is inconveniently located on the southern outskirts of Mosta. Run efficiently by a German company, it serves as another good and clean establishment to dump your belongings. The small rooftop pool and sun deck compensate for the stark rooms.

Eating Out

Mosta is not somewhere to seek out culinary gems. The too-well advertised **Ta'Marija** (moderate), Constitution Street, ℂ 434444, is not worth a special trip. It's aimed directly at the tourist as a Maltese specialty restaurant serving local dishes (which it does), but their 'Folk Evenings' in the old-farmhouse setting are all pretty tacky and part of the kitchen is in the dining area adding unwelcome 'authentic' aromas. Not many Maltese eat here. **Snacks** are the order of the day in Mosta. Obliquely across from the church look for the large red Coca-Cola vending machine, and squeezed into a cupboard is a **pastizzeria**. If *timpana* and *pastizzi* on the hoof are too unhealthy, usually there is a fruit van opposite. Other bars, such as **Joe's**, the **Olympic** or, towards the end of Main Street, the **City Café Bar**—note the Queen Victoria letter box in the wall—are all sound places to water at.

Naxxar and San Pawl Tat-Tarġa

Naxxar, one of the original 10 parishes of 1436, was once a sleepy farming village close to Mosta. Now over-building has linked the two communities in places and, with a population of just 7,000, it's half the size of its neighbour. Yet, beyond the radio mast towards Għarghur the urban sprawl gives way to fields and the old agricultural way of life.

For the casual visitor, the annual **International Trade Fair** held in July in the grounds of the Palazzo Parisio is Naxxar's principal attraction; but further north towards the lip of the Victoria Lines, **San Pawl Tat-Tarġa** has one of the earliest of the knights' defences. Both towns are linked to St Paul. Naxxar translates as 'to hang clothes to dry', and it is claimed that it was here that St Paul was first received and dried his robes over the fire after the shipwreck—a doubtful supposition as St Paul's Bay is a difficult 8-km hike even in summer, let alone in soggy clothes on a winter's dawn. Naxxar also relates phonetically to *Insara* meaning Christians, and San Pawl Tat-Tarġa, meaning St Paul of the Step, refers to the step from which he is supposed to have first preached.

San Pawl Tat-Tarġa is less than 1 km northwest from the terminus in Naxxar although it's not signposted from Valletta 11 km away (take the Birkirkara Road). From Sliema take the road through San Gwann. The Naxxar Gap corkscrews down the Victoria Lines towards the northern coasts. Despite its many associations with St Paul, Naxxar's *festa* is the Birth of the Virgin Mary and is held on 8 September which is also **Victory Day**, a national holiday.

Gathered around the little church, the suburb of **San Pawl Tat-Tarġa** has a genteel air of lace curtains and prying neighbours; in fact everything but a privet hedge. The neighbouring residence of the British high commissioner, with its fluttering Union Jack, is probably to blame.

On the *zuntier* or forecourt of the elegantly humble **church of St Paul** (1696) is a statue of St Paul partly sheltered by a cooling umbrella of pine trees. Tradition says he preached from here so forcefully that his voice was heard in Gozo. Behind the church, within the natural defence of the Victoria Lines, is the private **Gauci Tower** (1548). This is one of the first of the island's defences, built with Grand Master de Homedes's permission after a stealthy corsair raid when members of Cikko Gauci's family were carted off into slavery. The drop boxes on the roof, from which Mr Gauci hoped to pour hot oil and drop projectiles, echo the design of the older octagonal tower in Qrendi. On the other side of the road is the (private) **Torri tal-Kapitan**, the Captain's Tower (1558), built by the knights to keep a vigil on the northern plain and coasts.

Birkirkara

Birkirkara is the single-largest town in Malta; more than 21,000 people live within its confusing maze of streets. The town is bisected by the main road which links the Valletta suburbs with both Rabat and Mosta and has become somewhere you drive through. Stay awhile and ferret around some of its antique and *brocante* (bric-a-brac) shops or visit some of the area's numerous churches.

Birkirkara is often abbreviated to 'B'kara' and all roads lead to it; from Valletta go via Ħamrun (avoid rush hours) or take the slightly longer route via Msida and the Regional Road. From the south, go via Luqa then Valletta. It's signposted from Mosta and Rabat. Access to the Three Villages is more complicated (*see below*).

In **Birkirkara** there is a children's **play park** behind St Helen's church, but a much better one in the gardens of the old railway station next to the church of the Assumption. Birkirkara's *festas* are St Helen's on 18 August, and St Joseph the Worker on the 1st Sunday in July.

The **parish church of St Helen's** (*north of the main road heading west to Rabat*) is big, flashy and lively. Begun in 1727 and completed in 1745 towards the end of the rainbow of the Maltese baroque period, the pen of the designer has been obscured by time (it could have been that of the young Domenico Cachia or Salvu Borg, and was probably a joint effort). It doesn't matter, for whoever undertook it had a great command of the language. Sneaking into the sunlit square from narrow and dark St Helen Street is poor preparation: design details make this Sicilian-influenced façade one of the islands' finest, with tightly coupled pilasters and angels gesticulating wildly around the intricate bell-towers; there is a rhythm to the three ground-floor door- and window-pediments that even the strangely out-of-sync centre window can't disturb. Inside it's conventional Latin-plan, a little heavy but lightened by rich frescoes, and in direct contrast to the bubbly façade.

The old parish **church of the Assumption** (*south of the main road*) fell into terrible disrepair and almost collapsed. It is now undergoing a total, and deserved restoration. It will be some years before the works are finished but it's still worth a look. Designed by Vittorio Cassar at the beginning of the 1600s when Renaissance was merging with baroque, Tommasso Dingli's façade completed the older Cassar's work in 1617. Still evident is the painstakingly delicate detail on the twin superimposed Corinthian columns and the crisp motifs above, all set beneath the shallow, now broken, triangular pediment. In the shoe-box idiom, is the old **railway station** next door to the Assumption. The restored Birchircara (as it was spelt) station area has a third-class carriage and a good children's park. The railway line and trains—in Malti, *Xmundifer* (prounounced *shmun-di-ferr* and a phonetic play on the French *chemin de fer*)—began in 1883. British-manufactured steam trains puffed their way between Valletta and Mdina, stopping at Ħamrun, Birkirkara and Attard. Although they carried over 1,500,000 passengers a year in the 1920s, the enterprise was a financial disaster and ceased in 1931.

The Three Villages

Beyond Birkirkara's indefinable limits are the Siamese triplet villages of Attard, Balzan and Lija, known collectively as the Three Villages. During the last three to four hundred years these small settlements gathered around village churches and amongst fertile groves have grown into solid and wealthy towns, where even the stray cats are plump. Though comparatively young, they are not brassy like Madliena; the pace is slower and amateur watercolourists sit peacefully in the shade on tiny stools, picking out architectural details. **San Anton Palace** is one of the many fine houses in this area: the president of Malta, and the American, German and EC ambassadors call the Three Villages home, and the incumbent grand master, Andrew Bertie (a Scot), has an unofficial residence in Attard.

Getting Around and Tourist Information

The road out of **Birkirkara** forks left for **Attard** and right for **Balzan** just after St Theresa's, the nadir of contemporary church architecture, a grubby dollop of concrete resembling an upended mushroom. For **Lija** take the right fork signposted Naxxar, before St Theresa's. If you get lost, ask—local knowledge goes a long way in these narrow one-way streets. Attard has one of the eight *festas* to the Assumption on 15 August. Balzan: the Annunciation on the 2nd Sunday in July. Lija's is famous for having one of the more rumbustious and pyrotechnically accomplished *festas*—the firework displays are terrific. It's on 6 August and celebrates St Saviour.

Attard

A Lavish Grand Master's Court

The reign of Grand Master Antoine de Paule (1623–36) was for many the very beginning of the end for the Order. As a Frenchman he gave full vent to his self-indulgent and sybaritic ways; no expense was ever spared. For his celebratory dinner feast at the San Anton Palace he entertained an immodest 600 guests so bounteously that it sent Inquisitor Chigi—later Pope Alexander VII—into a pre-papal tirade. The lieutenant governor of Malta (1930–38), Sir Harry Luke, describes his outrageous—even by the standards of an eastern potentate—court thus: 'Besides the seneschal, the chaplains and the physicians, the game-keeper and the falconers, the drummers and the trumpeters, the valets and the pages, grooms and a host of other domestics in descending order of importance, there were the wig-maker and the winder of clocks, there were even a rat-catcher and a baker of black bread for the hunting dogs.' Conveniently, de Paule ignored his vows of poverty and chastity and despite his excesses soldiered on unabashed until he died a ripe 85 in June 1636.

In 1620 Antoine de Paule began to enlarge his country house near Attard. When he became grand master three years later he so disliked the long journey to the traditional summer palace at Verdala that he adopted **San Anton Palace** as his summer retreat. The palace has been tinkered with by successive grand masters. During the siege of the French in 1799, Sir Alexander Ball and the National Congress were based at San Anton and the formal surrender of the French was signed here. It later became the governor's summer residence, and replaced the palace in Valletta as the permanent residence in 1928. Since 1974 it has been the official quarters of the president of Malta.

The public section of the **gardens** were opened in 1882 by Governor Burton. The oldest part of the well-maintained and mature grounds is the **Eagle Pond** dating from 1623, at the opposite end of the palace. In addition, there is a small **aviary** and most of the trees, plants and flowers are flagged. Among the numerous species are Washington palms, Jacaranda, Norfolk Island pines, citrus, avocado, bamboo and the wonderfully twisted old roots of the fat-leafed *ficus benghatenis*. A limited part of the palace terrace is open to the public; de Vilhena's chapel of 1722 to **Our Lady of Pillar** is on the right at the start of the tunnel to the St Anthony Street entrance. *There are two entrances to the gardens, the main one with de Paule's and Sir Arthur Burton's escutcheons above, and a smaller entrance in St Anthony Street. There is meagre car parking by the main gate. Adm. free. Open every day until sunset.*

St Mary's parish church is the best, and probably the last of the handful of Renaissance-style churches built on Malta. Architectural design had passed over the cusp into the more effervescent baroque when work commenced in the early 17th century; the date inscribed on the wall is 1613, which possibly indicates the church was begun 10 or more years beforehand. Its design is attributed to an ageing Vittorio Cassar or a youthful Tommasso Dingli, who was born here. The façade is nearly identical to that of the Assumption in

Birkirkara (also credited to Dingli), and is a pleasing relief from the baroque style, with an elegant temple front and a neat triangular pediment above a circular window; the main door columns are finely detailed stone carvings and the six niches are occupied by saints. The campanile was added to the cruci-form plan in 1718. There is a small pastoral **museum** to the right of the church. *Open Sun. Adm. free.*

Balzan

The most interesting part of Balzan is in Three Churches Street (It-Tliet Knejjes) at the eastern corner of the square: 120 m from the square, in the oldest part of the village and grouped together around an old meeting or cemetery cross there are, not surprisingly, three old churches. Little **St Roque**, sophisticated in its simplicity, was built in 1593 during a terrible plague. (Roque is the patron saint of plague.) For what must have been a rapid building programme there is some fine, if naïve, detail. Note the cyclopean circular window above the door which uses a set of six ordinary intertwined semi-circles to form a striking pattern. Above its setting, a crude moulded square, is a charming tiny triangle pediment enclosing a delicate flower. *Open every Sunday, but mass is said only once a year.* The other two churches are the earlier **Annunciation** and **St Leonard's**, which is now a house (during World War II it was a refuge).

Lija

The **parish church of St Saviour** was designed by Giovanni Barbara in 1694 when he was just 24. It's an austere building in an equally cold square, but most of its detail is original and the lights of the *festa* lift its sombreness. To the right of the church, past a statue of St Peter, is the early 16th-century parish church to St Saviour, now shaded by ancient gnarled olive trees.

Further afield is **Tal-Mirakli**, Our Lady of Miracles, said to be built at the precise centre of the island. (*Follow the one-way system out of the square, turn right at the Three Villages Bar into Annibale Preca Street, and it's at the end, about 1,250 m from the square.*) Built by Grand Master Cotoner in 1664 on the site of an earlier church, it's a neat building with an unusually generous dome. The thoughtful main altarpiece, unkindly served by poor illumination, is of the *Virgin and Child* by **Mattia Preti**. To the right is the much-venerated 16th-century wooden triptych of the Madonna. According to legend, tears flowed from her eyes during the earthquake of 1743. Opposite the church is an old farmer's shed with a different kind of superstition attached: the horns of a bull to ward off the evil eye.

Shopping

Nearly all Malta's **antiques** and *brocante* (bric-a-brac) dealers are situated in this area. Don't be afraid to haggle, but be warned, the Maltese dealer has a very stubborn streak. The island's best **art gallery** is in Lija, **The Melitensia**; and for different souvenirs of a cheaper kind try the **pottery studio**, the Ceramica Saracina in Attard.

Birkirkara : Paul Borg Antiques, St Roque's Street; and in Naxxar Road, **Versailles Antiques**, **The Baptist Antiques** and **Sciberras Antiques**. **TouchWood**, 60 Mannarino Street (the main road), has a larger shop in St Venera. **Byblos Antiques**, 108 Mannarino Road, deals mainly in *brocante*. Around the corner, **The Windmill Gift Shop**, 428 Fleur-de-Lys, has an eclectic mixture, mostly *brocante* and stencils. Mrs A. Vassallo, 'Patros', Wignacourt Street, sells old engravings, clocks and prints by appointment, © 440029.

Balzan: Benny's Antiques, 234 Main Street, has a small emporium of *brocante* and antiques. **Country Lane**, 24 Main Street, sells perfumed **oddments** and twee house decorations. The best **supermarket** outside St Julian's, **The Dolphin**, is just off the main street; you can't miss it.

Attard: near to the secondary entrance to Palace Gardens is **Ceramica Saracina**, 87–8 St Anthony Street. All kinds of handmade and home-fired oddments from vases to old-fashioned piggy banks. Prices from Lm1.

Lija: Melitensia Art Gallery, Transfiguration Avenue, is next to the old Villa Gourgion Tower, once a central part of its gardens and now a roundabout. A deceptively large gallery, it displays all kinds of pictures of Malta and is very browser-friendly.

Where to Stay

The Corinthia Palace Hotel★★★★★ (luxury), De Paule Avenue, Attard (opp. San Anton Palace), © 440302/440820. Just reopened after undergoing a major rebuilding programme, the Palace provides

220 rooms, a business centre, three restaurants, a tennis court and an interesting megalithic-shaped pool complex. **The Grosvenor Hotel★★★** (moderate), Pope Alexander VII Junction, Balzan, © 486916, is out of the way to the north of the San Anton Gardens. Like the swankier Corinthia Palace it's ideal if you want to dip your toes into Mdina, Valletta or Sliema but don't want to stay in a town. There's a decent-sized adults' and children's pool, good but spartan rooms, and two restaurants; don't let the garish entrance hall put you off.

Eating Out

Next to the main entrance to the San Anton Gardens is **Melita** (inexpensive), © 441077. There's a small bar, and the restaurant serves salads, pizzas, burgers and the like indoors or out. A little uninspiring, but the only place. For anything more substantial than snacks of fruit or *pastizzi* the selection in Birkirkara is larger but not always better; go to Mdina or to one of the new restaurants in the Corinthia. If you just want a drink, the **Three Villages Bar** at the north end of St Anthony Street is a small and friendly place with moody wood-panelling and about every conceivable liquor on its dusty shelves.

Żebbuġ

This is 'old banger country' where ancient vehicles and busted machinery are brought to be sold, or to die. If you want a second- or tenth-hand car, Żebbuġ is the place. It was not always so. Żebbuġ means olives, and the village grew from a handful of tiny *casals* knitted together around the common industries of olives and cotton. Żebbuġ cotton was weaved into a high-quality heavy sailcloth and exported all over Europe. Neither crop is farmed any more, but as one of the original 10 parishes recorded in 1436 it was and is a wealthy country village. Unfortunately, it has turned its gaze inwards: the village is well kept but the de Rohan arch signalling the entrance to the village is in a sad state.

Getting Around and Tourist Information

Żebbuġ is south of the Rabat–Qormi road, but the easiest and sign-posted route is via Attard. The *festa* of St Philip is held on the 2nd Sunday in June.

An Enlightened Grand Master

I can't be King; I won't be Duke: I am Rohan.

Motto of the noble de Rohan family

When de Rohan was elected to the magistracy in 1775, a spell was broken over the French *langues*, which had not provided a grand master since Adrien de Wignacourt in 1697. But the regal celebrations in the French *auberges* could not conceal the Order's troubles for a split second longer than the fireworks illuminated the bastions of Valletta—de Rohan had inherited a near-bankrupt Order in moral disarray. Nevertheless, his 22-year reign was to be an enlightened and reforming one. A cheery, optimistic, and by grand master standards young man of 57, he was not only popular with his peers but with the Maltese, 10 of whom—one-third of the entire Maltese nobility—he ennobled. He made himself accessible, revised taxes and abolished the more brutal acts of torture enshrined in the penal code; the Code Rohan still forms a part of Maltese common law. The Order's library in Valletta was completed the year before he died, and he was the first to admit women to court.

Nevertheless, his generosity of spirit and loyalty to his doomed monarch, Louis XVI, was to speed the Order's inevitable demise. Despite the parlous state of the knights' finances de Rohan sold silver plate to pay for the French royal family's disastrous flight to Varennes in 1791. Their capture brought on a near-terminal apoplectic fit, and he limped through Louis XVI's execution in 1793 to the summer of 1797, when he died, convinced he would be the last grand master to reign in Malta.

One year later Napoleon, with his elephant's memory, told de Rohan's successor von Hompesch that the knights could not plead with impunity that theirs was a neutral and religious order: had they not, seven years before, been strident Royalist sympathizers?

Grand Master de Rohan adopted Żebbuġ and elevated it to a city, renamed it *Citta Rohan*, and built what is today a sorry-looking **triumphal arch** at the entrance to the village. In its older streets off St Anthony Street and Hospital Square (Misrah L-Isptar and behind the church) are many generous old houses which serve to date it. Some of the cuboid buildings here go back to the 16th century.

The villagers and the nuns of Żebbuġ are devout; niches and churches prolif-erate. In the main square the **parish church of St Philip**, begun in 1599, was initially the work of Cassars, *père et fils*, but Dingli finished it 60 years later. It's far more ornate, even fussy than Gerolamo Cassar's most famous church, the striking St John's Co-Cathedral built over 25 years before. The two towers seem squeezed together in the screen façade, isolating the twin domes either side. For a lavish interior, study the north and south transepts and the coffered semi-circular vault.

On the northern outskirts of Żebbuġ is the little church of **Tal Ħlas**, dedicated to mothers in labour. In the early days of the Order it was on the main route between Mdina and the Three Cities, and was used by travelling knights. (*Today it's not so easy to find: 50 m before the roundabout to Siġġiewi on the Rabat–Qormi road, turn left down a hilly track at Raymond Auto Dealer, 700 m later by a field is Tal Ħlas.*) Partly shaded by a weaving old tree-climbing evergreen, the tiny church is charmingly simple. The original building dating from 1500 was destroyed by the 1693 earthquake, but in between rebuilding St Paul's Cathedral in Mdina, Lorenzo Gafa found time to rebuild it. It's said the organ came from the wreckage of St Paul's in Mdina. The unusual twin porti-coed loggias on either side were added in 1699 to provide shelter for pilgrims, and the escutcheon is that of Pope Clement XI. A good example of priestly self-preservation, common in many of the small churches, is the heavily barred windows in the façade; during corsair raids they enabled the priest to remain locked safely inside, and say mass to the congregation outside .

Where to Stay

Father Pio's House (moderate), 292 Main Street, Żebbuġ, is an old part-18th-century house to rent. It sleeps eight people, and a simply furnished cottage annexe accommodates four. Wide stone stairs lead to cool, high-ceilinged bedrooms, but only average bathrooms. Outside, as in many older Maltese houses, there are small and private shady courtyards overgrown by citrus and bougainvillea, and a private swimming pool.

Gozo and Comino

'Gozo is different', concluded the priest Dun Salvatore.
Nicholas Monsarrat, *The Kappillan of Malta*

Gozo is further in spirit from Malta than the 8-km channel *Il-Fliegu* which separates the two islands would suggest. Some visitors to the comparative fast lane of Malta cannot comprehend the idea of spending more than one day in sleepy Gozo, while Gozo's visitors, an eclectic mixture of discerning wealthy Europeans and divers on a budget, would never contemplate setting foot in Malta.

The island's proud emblem of three green hills (said to be Żebbuġ, Xagħra and Nadur) over a blue sea is the first silhouette of landfall; peaceful villages cling like limpets onto the sides of the fertile and flat-topped hills. The greens of the landscape and valleys are a welcome surprise after the summer has baked Malta into a dusty brick. This is not a place for a wild Bacchic party; it's about first gear, a slow pace. To a Gozitan, *pace* (prounounced par-chey) is a common surname, not something that governs anyone's life.

Like most peaceful islands Gozo is diminutive—14 km by 6.5 km at best, 67 square kilometres in all—and its population of 26,000 is little more than that of Sliema and St Julian's combined. Yet the bathing and diving are superb, and the walks are peaceful; as Edward Lear said in 1866, 'Gozo's coast scenery may truly be called pomskizillious and grophibberous, being as no words can describe its magnificence'.

There are a handful of good restaurants, some pretty handmade lace to buy, and the finest hotel on the Maltese islands.

The community is primarily agricultural. This is Malta's fruit and vegetable basket. The farmers, most of whom double as fishermen, have used traditional implements to work the blue clay soil of the hillside fields for generations. Their weathered and leathery faces are coarser than those of the Maltese, but they are a lot more house proud; the whole island is neater and cleaner than Malta.

Gozo's landscape has made it vulnerable to invasion, and over the centuries the islanders have developed a healthy suspicion of foreigners—and that includes the Maltese. This insularity has coalesced the community into a proud and traditional one, and slowed down the rate of change. (Being a few steps back in time is the island's charm.) Fortunately, over the past 30 years the Gozitans' natural wariness has eased into friendliness. They have now accepted that not all tourists are direct descendants of 16th-century Turkish slave-traders, but just people who have come to mosey around *their* island.

Centuries of self-sufficiency have bred a culture built around folklore, and the villagers have countless tales to tell—from the legend of Calypso ensnaring Odysseus in her cave above the red sand of Ramla Bay, to the metamorphosis of an altarpiece of San Dimitri in Għarb. This capacity for faith is manifested in the islanders' energetic devotion to their church. For weeks before the lively local *festas* they wind themselves up with a torque wrench of anticipation, then celebrate with more gusto and warmth than anywhere else.

History

Gozo has been inhabited by a self-sustaining agricultural community for about 5,500 years (as evidenced by the ancient temples of Ġgantija). Because it lacks a natural harbour it held no attraction for the seafaring nations that roamed the Mediterranean, all of whom gave it a cursory name. The Phoenicians called it *Gwl* meaning 'round ship' (the Greeks and the Romans chose something similar). The Byzantines called it *Gaudos* and, finally, the Arabs in the 9th century settled on Ghudash (*Ghawdex* in Malti), a name which is still used today. It was the Aragonese and the knights who christened it Gozo.

The island's fate has, not surprisingly, always been linked with Malta's. Largely undefended, for a while its sole and unwitting purpose was to be the provider of a steady flow of slaves to passing Barbary Coast pirates or Turks; the bays of Marsalforn, Xlendi and Ramla being safe enough to anchor in while a few villagers were rounded up to be sold in the markets of Tripoli or Constantinople or, if lucky, ransomed. (Until 1637 every inhabitant had to be within the walls of the citadel at Victoria by sundown.)

The scourge of the central Mediterranean, **Dragut Rais**, was attracted to Gozo like a magpie to silver, his raids providing recreation in between serious missions like devastating Naples or Sicilian shipping. There was, however, a reason for his spite. During an attack in 1544—only 14 years after the the Order had arrived in Malta—his brother was captured and killed. The governor of Gozo refused to return the body and burned the corpse. Dragut, a man who thought revenge was a dish best eaten cold, waited before he hit back. In July 1551, he and Sinan Pasha besieged the citadel. The islanders finally surrendered on 27 July, but not before desperate action had been taken by some survivors—the soldier Bernardo Duopuo put his wife and two daughters to death rather than allow them to be captured. Almost the entire island's population of 6,000 was then hauled away into slavery. The only survivors were the infirm, who could not be sold, and those who had escaped over the citadel's walls. The island was only resettled three years later, by Grand Master de Sengle who bribed many Maltese to cross the channel by waiving their last four years debts.

The island endured six more raids during the latter half of the 16th century. It was only in the early 17th century, when the Order realized how potentially destructive a Gozo-based Turkish army could be, that they grudgingly took action. St Mary's Tower (1618) on Comino was the first link in what was to become a chain of defences that stretched from Gozo across Malta. It took a century before the island was sufficiently well fortified to ward off incursions— the last pirating raid the Gozitans had to endure was as late as 1708.

When the **French** invaded in June 1798 they met with little resistance from the enfeebled garrison of knights. But soon after, the Gozitans rebelled against French rule, recaptured the countryside, and besieged the 50-strong French garrison in the citadel until its surrender in 1800. Ironically, it was during this brief two-year period of French rule that the Gozitans enjoyed their only spell of political independence from Malta.

The **British** had little use for the island which they regarded as a nuisance, another Scotland; with little to contribute and there only to be protected. However, during the siege years of **World War II** their approach changed when Gozo provided food and accommodation for many of Malta's evacuees.

Gozo's Stockpile

During World War II the failure of convoys to provide adequate foodstuffs during the hot summer of 1942 brought an already desperate situation to a head. The newly appointed governor Lord Gort calculated a target date at the end of August when starvation alone would force him to replace the Union Jack with the white flag of surrender. (As it was, subsistence rations for a family of *five* were four 300-g tins of corned beef and four 100 g tins of fish *per month,* and a daily bread ration of 1,375 g.) But, the Gozitans had, like squirrels for winter, stockpiled much of their produce. Furthermore, many are said to have sailed in small boats at night across the 100-km channel to enemy-occupied Sicily to barter for provisions. Only after a direct appeal to the bishop of Gozo, Michael Gonzi, did the Gozitans open their cache—enabling Lord Gort to move his pencilled date back a few weeks in anticipation of the next convoy.

The Constitution. Politically, Gozo is part of Malta. The Romans organized both islands as separate *municipia* and until the arrival of the Order in 1530 Gozo's self-governing local council, the *Università*, was headed by the *Hakem* or Captain of the Rod. After another of Dragut's raids in 1551 the Order perceived Gozo as a security risk and brought the island under its jurisdiction. Since 1987 the island has had its own ministry, sending five representatives to the 65-seat House of Representatives. It has been a separate diocese with its own bishop since 1864.

The Future. Progress in the *concrete* sense of the word has yet to arrive in Gozo, but talk in the bars and offices of Malta and Gozo of 'enlarging the bedstock' has intensified of late; large-scale developments are being planned.

Gozo's ecology, environment and infrastructure are as fragile as Meissen china, its beauty still unspoiled. The island's docile temperament and low profile have endeared it to many; Sag Harbour, Long Island it isn't, but it's as near to a writers' colony as the Mediterranean has. If parts of Malta's northern coastline were replicated here, the emigré and wealthy tourist would head for the hills—and they wouldn't be Gozo's, however many 5-star hotels were built on them.

All Gozo's legends warn of the blindness of greed that leads to the inevitable comeuppance. Ironically, the moral is going unheeded now. That's more than unfortunate, for Gozo's magic stems from being outside the world it has hitherto so successfully avoided becoming a part of. See it soon.

Getting to and Around Gozo

In this chapter the island has been divided into five areas: the capital Victoria, and the north, west, south and east. Victoria is at the centre and with one or two exceptions all points lead from it, to it and through it. It is often referred to by its pre-1897 name of Rabat and the main street is known officially as Republic Street, more popularly as Racecourse Street.

By Sea

The **Gozo Channel Company**, © Mġarr 556114 or 580435/6, runs a 24-hour, 365-day ro-ro car ferry service from Ċirkewwa and Pieta in Malta to Mġarr harbour (the service is more frequent in summer). Its 30-minute **hover-marine** service to and from Sliema runs only in summer.

By Air

Malta Air Charter operates the 12-minute **helicopter** link from Luqa to Xewkija, April to October. Reservations © 557905. (*See* pp. 8–9 for times and fares.) Schedules have a twitchy habit of altering, so check in advance.

By Road

A car is not vital, but is recommended. The driving is marginally less nerve-wracking here than on Malta and the signposting is better. **Petrol** is only available in Mġarr or Victoria. For **hire cars** try Mayjo in Victoria, © 556678 and Marsalforn, © 555650 or Gozo United Rent-a-Car in Victoria, © 556291. Also in Marsalforn, Grace rents **bikes** from Lm1.50 a day and **mopeds** from Lm3. You can find her opposite the Marsalforn Hotel, © 561503. **Taxis** line up at the ferry and bus terminus and sometimes in It-Tokk, Victoria, otherwise contact Harry 'Fixit' Debono, the best independent driver, © 553499/551950 or the Belmont Garage (which operates from 'Wombat Maison' in Nadur), © 556962.

By Bus

Buses are all painted civil service grey with a spruce red stripe, and their prime concession to the tourist industry is to meet most of the summer ferries from

Mġarr harbour. You will be deposited at the central terminus in Victoria, from where all the buses originate, depart and often stop. The service ceases early in the evening; stops anywhere other than the main villages are about as frequent as Halley's Comet.

On Foot

Walking is not a hardship and much less dangerous than on Malta—in rural Gozo a donkey and cart reaches about 10 kph. There are excellent walks, the most fragrant time being spring when the island is at its most colourful.

Tourist Information

The **NTOM** has two offices. Mġarr Harbour, Mon–Sat 0900–1900 in summer and –1800 in winter, and Sun 0900–1300, ✆ 553343. Hours are sometimes Gozitan, i.e. erratic. The very helpful principal office is on the corner of Republic Street and Palm Street in Victoria, open Mon–Sat 0700–1900 and –1800 in winter, Sun 0900–1300, ✆ 558106/557407.

Gozo General Hospital, ✆ 556851, is signposted on the Xewkija road just outside Victoria. There is a **clinic** for minor complaints 100 m out of St Francis Square in Enrico Mizzi Street; and a small private **health and beauty** centre in San Lawrenz, the Head-to-Toe, ✆ 552014. The new **sports complex** in Victoria has excellent amenities, free: tennis, squash, basketball, volleyball, gym; Mon–Fri 0800–2100, Sat 0900–1900 and Sun 0900–1700, ✆ 560677/8.

Shopping

Shops tend to shut for the weekend at Saturday lunchtime. Even if they post notices of opening and closing times, it should be remembered that these are Gozitan times and therefore elastic.

Each village has a **grocer** for essential items, the larger ones have a butcher and baker. If you are staying in one of the villages buy all you can from **local farmers**, their produce will be the freshest and best. Victoria is well stocked with provisions and hosts a **daily market** in It-Tokk, meaning literally 'the meeting place' (early morning until 1300-ish). It's basically a **clothes** market, displaying bolts of gaudy cloth destined to be fashioned into expressive Sunday dresses. Shops in the square sell fresh **fruit and vegetables**. Beside the Banca Giuratale at the west of It-Tokk a couple of **fish hawkers** always set up a stall. Better still, go to Pescolina behind the shops past the Gozo Heritage, or in **Mġarr Harbour** look out for a fisherman called Palalu who sits underneath the balcony of the Gleneagles Bar, and normally has a catch. Ta'Bendu at the main roundabout before Victoria sell **chickens** and **rabbits**. Foreign **wines and spirits** and local **cheroots** can be bought from one of three shops in St George's Square. One of the most drinkable local wines is Razzett, which can be sampled and purchased at 4 Fosse Street in the citadel. Next to the NTOM office is the reputable **Palm Pharmacy. Tower Bakery** at the east end of Republic Street is not the only one, but the easiest to find. English **books and newspapers** can be obtained from Bookrose in Republic Street near the junction with Capuchin Street. In a typical example of eccentric Gozitan charm English Sunday newspapers are available on Sunday morning only from the back of Bezzina's Confectionery in Main Gate Street, near the bus terminus.

Three kilometres to the south in Kerċem, an Italian called Carlo has set up a tiny shop making delicious fresh **pasta**: Casa Atzori, Ġuze Flores Street, ℂ 555411. On the outskirts of Kerċem opposite the old knights' wash-house is a **souvenir emporium** full of products from the knitting and lacemaking cottage industry. **Handmade lace**, for which Gozo is famous, is harder to find. (Beware, sometimes there are 'handmade' labels on what is machine made.) The Ulysses Boutique at the junction of Capuchin Street and Republic Street has both handmade lace and chunky winter knitwear, although prising open a wallet for a heavy sweater in 35° heat is hard. (For some of the best handmade lace, *see* p. 315.)

The **Cittadella Centre**, 14–16 Sir Adrian Dingli Street (a continuation of Republic Street) is a refurbished new mall with a jewellers, a souvenir shop and a perfumery as well as a bar and a restaurant. Prestige Gifts a few doors along at no.2 also has a good selection of **souvenirs**. Seventy metres away in Savina Square is a *brocante* stall (open every day except Monday) where all the old merchandise—some good and some tat—is hung from the outside walls. Two hundred metres along the Xlendi road out of St Francis Square is another **antiques dealer,** who keeps idiosyncratic hours. In **Meylak Jewellery** at 24 Republic Street there is a tiny cupboard of a place with good stock, both old and new. Some of the simplest and best of the local souvenirs are hand-carved **stone** objects by Joe Xuereb at 'Ta Peppi', Baħħara Street, Għajnsielem, ℂ 553559. In Bieb il-Imdina Street in the citadel, Mrs Grech at **The Candlemaker**, ℂ 553686, has handmade souvenirs (and not just in wax). Also in the citadel, at 4 Fosse Street among the souvenirs is local wine, anisette and **honey**. For something truly unique the Sacred Heart Bazaar in Sir Arturo Mercieca Street, Victoria has **religious icons** and paraphernalia.

En route to Għarb is the **Ta'Dbiegi Craft Village** (winter 0800–1645 summer 0830–1845)—the usual mixture of disappointing tourist merchandise set in a row of ex-British forces huts. **Gozo Glass** is before the craft village next to Jeffrey's Restaurant and the souvenirs are more original, but the local garishly coloured glass is not to everyone's taste.

Where to Stay

For the time being Gozo has a mercifully small number of hotels and guest houses, 17 in all, 7 of which are in Marsalforn on the north coast. One of the the finest hotels south of Messina is the **Hotel Ta'Ċenċ★★★★★** in Sannat. The oldest, the **Duke of Edinburgh** in Victoria, reopened in July 1993 with three stars. For divers or the budget-minded the **Ritz** or the **Marsalforn** are okay, but the **Atlantis★★★** is worth the extra. For countryside tranquility the **Cornucopia★★★★** in Xagħra is recommended. The **Grand Guest House** in Mġarr is also noteworthy and reasonably priced. For **self-catering**, Gozo Farmhouses have 18 superb houses dotted over the island, ✆ 553106/552540 or try Meon in the UK, ✆ 0730 266561. Other **agencies** for flats and houses are Dahlia, 49b Republic Street, Victoria, ✆ 551984, Ta'frenc in Capuchin Street, Victoria, or Mayjo in Marsalforn, ✆ 555650. (*See under destinations.*)

Eating Out

The best way to eat well in Gozo is to **stay with the fish** and any of the following can be trusted to provide good food: Il-Kċina tal Barrakka (simply known as **Sammy's**) and the **Seaview** in Mġarr, **Jeffrey's** and **Salvina** in Għarb, the **Oleander** and **Gesther's** (lunch only) in Xagħra, **Il Kartell** or the **Pink Panther** in Marsalforn, and the **It-Tmun** in Xlendi. The **Hotel Ta'Ċenċ** restaurant in Sannat is especially good at lunchtime. The island's two heavy-weights, **Ta'frenc** outside Marsalforn and **Chez Armand** in Għarb serve sound but not always justifiably expensive fare. On the road to Xlendi is **Il-Grotta** a wild and exceptionally good **discotheque**, half in a cave and half *al fresco*, over-looking the mysterious bamboo floor of Xlendi Valley. (*See under destinations.*)

Victoria (Rabat)

To celebrate Queen Victoria's Diamond Jubilee of 1897 the capital of Gozo, Rabat, changed its name in her honour (although to hear the Gozitans talk you would never know, it is still Rabat to the majority).

This Lilliputian capital of 6,200 people is lively in the mornings, gently nods off in the afternoons, twitches with energy again from about 1800 to the sound of birdsong from the trees of It-Tokk and St Francis Square, before retiring early.

The old quarter behind It-Tokk began to take shape more than 350 years ago and is made up of narrow alleys that mould themselves into a cohesive little maze of dark angular shadows and bright sunlight, distorting the delightful local balconies out of proportion. All is made more mysterious by the mix of aromas that waft through the nameless streets.

The **citadel**, with its patriarchal history, four museums, cathedral and panoramas of the whole island is well worth visiting, as is the Collegiate Basilica of St George behind It-Tokk.

Getting Around and Tourist Information

All **buses** go from the terminus in **Main Gate Street**, but times coincide with school and work hours, not the whims of tourists. There is a large map depicting the different routes, and a ferry company board warns of delays. **Bus 25** goes to and from Mġarr—in summer, the last one leaves around 2100.

Between 0730 and 1700 part of Republic Street and Sir Adrian Dingli Street is one-way adding to Victoria's already confusing one-way system. **Park** your **car** behind the terminus in the free car park; the 3-minute walk to the centre of town is less aggravating than trying to find a space.

The **NTOM**, © 558106/557407, is on the corner of Palm and Republic Streets. Impossible to miss and grouped together on both sides of Rebulic Street are **Telemalta**, the main **post office**, the **police station** and **the banks**. The **library** is next to the Gozo Ministry Building in St Francis Square. Victoria has two **cinemas**, the Aurora and the Astra in Republic Street. These enormous emporia belong to their respective band clubs and show films only from autumn to spring. There are **public conveniences** under Banca Giuratale in It-Tokk and next to the bus terminus and the Archaeological Museum in the citadel.

Victoria has two very excited and rivalrous feasts: the cathedral's *festa* of the Assumption (Santa Marija) on 15 August, when half Malta invades Gozo; and the *festa* to St George on the 3rd Sunday in July. The battlements of the citadel make the ideal launching pad for an increasingly colourful palette of fireworks. In Republic Street (also known as Racecourse Street) there are horse races the day after.

The Citadel

Victoria's citadel, like Mdina's, sits on a high ledge. From the semicircular battlements running from east to west there is an unrivalled panorama of Gozo, each of the pocket-sized villages being identifiable by their anything but pocket-sized churches. The immense dome of the Xewkija rotunda to the east looks even more splendidly over-the-top from this eyrie. Apart from its dramatic vantage-point, the citadel's attraction lies in the colour of its old limestone buildings, whose pallor has warmed with age. There is a diversity of styles within the fortifications: the baroque cathedral, diminutive Palazzo Bondi, the derelict Norman area, the bastions and the gutted little alleys.

The original citadel dates back to the Romans, who probably used the 150-m high bluff at the heart of the island as an acropolis for their settlement below. But hardly any traces of this or the 9th-century Arab occupation have survived. The 12th-century Norman citadel or *Gran Castello* was destroyed by Dragut during the disastrous short siege of 1551 (Until 1637 this was a town in which the island's population had to pass the night in order to avoid being captured by pirates). The town, within its fortified walls, was rebuilt by fits and starts on the existing plan by a series of grand masters. The present entrance to the citadel was cut through into Cathedral Square in 1957; the original and much smaller one 25 m further on and known as the Mdina Door, is marked by a Roman inscription dating back to the 2nd century AD.

Victoria (Rabat)

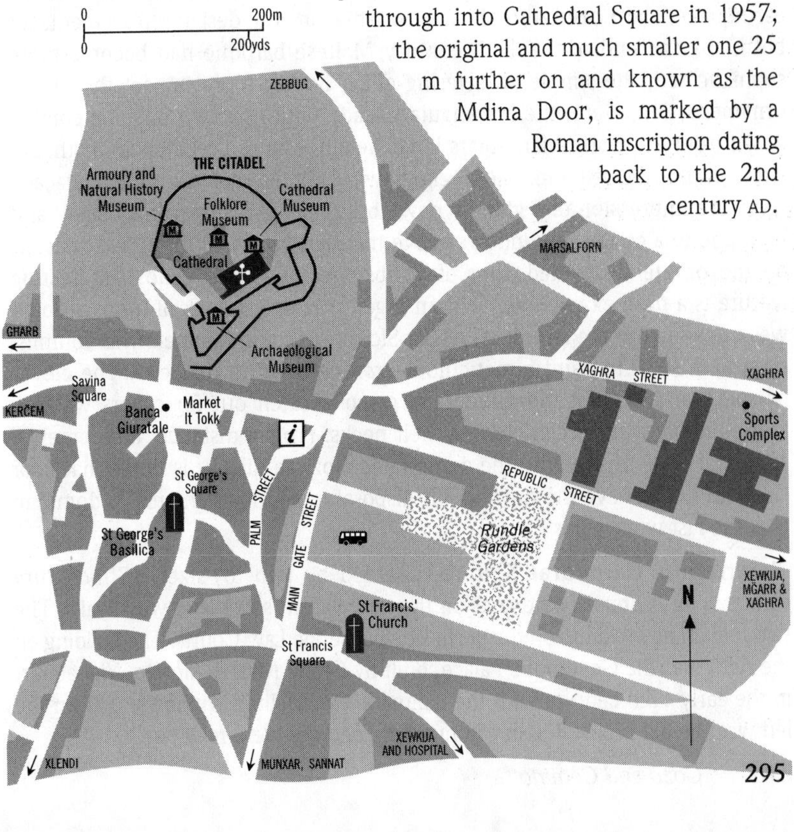

Map labels: ZEBBUG; THE CITADEL; Armoury and Natural History Museum; Folklore Museum; Cathedral Museum; Cathedral; Archaeological Museum; MARSALFORN; GHARB; Savina Square; KERĊEM; Banca Giuratale; Market It Tokk; XAGHRA STREET; XAGHRA; Sports Complex; St George's Square; PALM STREET; REPUBLIC STREET; St George's Basilica; MAIN GATE STREET; Rundle Gardens; XEWKIJA, MĠARR & XAGHRA; St Francis' Church; St Francis Square; N; XEWKIJA AND HOSPITAL; XLENDI; MUNXAR, SANNAT

0   200m
0   200yds

The Cathedral of the Assumption

The cathedral, originally the matrice until Gozo became a separate diocese in 1864, is built on the site of three or more older places of worship, including Roman and Phoenician temples. Construction commenced in 1697, four years after the 1693 earthquake had damaged its predecessor and destroyed large tracts of southeast Sicily. (The cathedral at Mdina was another victim of the earthquake, and **Lorenzo Gafa** was commissioned to design replacements for both.) By the end of the 17th century Maltese baroque had become more sophisticated, the simple swaggering effect having more impact than mere ornamentation. Here, the rectangular façade with its gown of stairs coming down from the Corinthian pillars lends height, and the escutcheon is that of Grand Master Perrellos in whose reign it was built. From the outside the façade gives the impression of a gloomy nave, but inside it's surprisingly small and light due to a course of windows above the high vault and distended pilasters on the ornate tessellated floor of tombstones. The single-most interesting feature is a pure example of Gozitan ingenuity: due to lack of funds a dome was not added to the structure, so the Sicilian Antonio Manuele was commissioned in 1739 to paint a meticulous *trompe l'oeil* in its stead. The clever perspective is at first too difficult to grasp—watch out for others walking around in dizzying circles craning their necks. From a distance, the domeless cathedral oddly fits in with the decapitated Gozitan hills. It is ironic that poor Gafa did not to have the funds at his disposal to add his signature, a dome, in this, the last work of his life.

The irregular **Cathedral Square**, guarded by two toy-sized 17th-century cannons, once housed dwellings on the now vacant south and west walls. The two remaining buildings on the north side house the Law Courts. The building on the right was the Governor's Palace, built by Grand Master Alof de Wignacourt in the early 17th century with the hallmark 'fat' Melitan windows; that on the left was the old Public Registry from where decrees were read out.

The Museums

The citadel has four museums: the **Archaeological, Folklore, Natural History** and **Cathedral**. A one-day ticket costs Lm3 and allows entrance to the first three and the prehistoric temples of Ġgantija and Il Mithna both in Xaghra; otherwise entrance is Lm1 per museum, except Sun when all are free. The Cathedral Museum is the least interesting, and cheapest (20c). *All museums and Ġgantija open: 1 Oct–31 Mar, Mon–Sat 0830–1630, Sun 0830–1500. 1 Apr–15 June, Mon–Sat 0830–1830, Sun 0830–1500. 16 June–15 Sept, 0830–1900, Sun 0830–1500. 16 Sept–30 Sept 0830–1830, Sun 0830–1500.*

The **Cathedral Museum** is 70 m up Fosse Street. The vault in the basement displays ecclesiastical silverware, on the ground floor there is the bishop's British-made landau of 1860 and clerical oddments. On the first floor, take a look at the expressions of Gozo's influential bishops and dignitaries in the picture gallery. Bishop Cassar with his viciously stern expression led the local insurrection against the French; nearby Dr Nicola Mahnuk, a prosperous 17th-century merchant, is portrayed as comically smug. Note also the early 16th-century cathedral altarpiece, a gentle polyptych of tempera on wood to St Maria.

Housed in a row of three well-restored 15th-century buildings (the windows display the Siculo-Norman influence) is the excellent little **Folklore Museum**, and opposite the entrance is where Bernardo Duopuo fell in 1551 (*see* p. 288) at the end of the Dragut's siege. The exhibits reflect the simple yet hard Gozitan life through the ages: a blacksmith's and carpenter's workshop, looms, and primitive grain-milling and grape-pressing equipment. The social and sporting side of Gozo is also well documented with 18th-century guns, fishing paraphernalia, mortars for the *festas* and costumes.

The new **Natural History Museum** is opposite the old granary, the British garrison's headquarters in World War II and now the Armoury. (The **Armoury** is a frustration—displays of the knights' weaponry are behind permanently barred gates.) In the museum, is the tragic display of birds which innocently strayed into local airspace; it's possible the once-proud Mediterranean peregrine falcon on display was one of the very last pair to nest under the Ta'Ċenċ cliffs.

Sir Harry Luke, lieutenant governor 1930–38, was responsible for the restoration of the Palazzo Bondi which has since 1959 housed the impressive little **Archaeological Museum**, a small but grand building with a fine carved stone balcony in Mdina Door Street near the citadel's old entrance. (In the same street are small **crafts shops** and at the end of it, in what was the old prison, is a centre with displays of Maltese- and Gozitan-manufactured products.)

The Maltese Falcon

In 1980 the Maltese falcon was declared a protected species, yet here it has been hunted, trapped and shot into extinction. There is an irony to this tragedy, for the Act of Donation of 24 March 1530 (preserved and displayed in the Bibliotheca Valletta) by which the Spanish Emperor Charles V ceded Malta to the Order states the none-too-onerous annual rent for the islands—a single *live* falcon was to be presented on All Saints Day to the viceroy in Sicily.

The ground floor of the museum is dedicated to **prehistory**. In the right-hand room are relics from **Ġgantija**; a model and watercolours of the temples help bring these extraordinary structures to life. A carved relief of a snake (hard to discern) is among a sparse collection found when the first, and badly executed, excavation took place in 1827. The room on the left houses earlier neolithic shards and pottery discovered in the Xaghra area to the north. **Punic, Roman and Arabic** relics are on the first floor: the Xlendi room (on the left) is named after the deceptively treacherous and narrow bay to the south where two merchant ships sank, one in the 2nd century BC, the other in the 5th century AD; the anchors, countless wine jars and amphorae on display were uncovered in 1961. On the landing tucked away in a niche is a beautiful Majmuna tombstone (1174), inscribed with the pitiful yet sad Cufic (early Arabic) lament of a distraught father at the death of his 12-year-old daughter. The largest room is reserved for Gozo's Punic and Roman finds including: pottery and tiles from the old Roman villa in Ramla; the grisly remains of a split Punic burial amphora found underneath stones in Santa Marija Bay, Comino; and a **coin collection** found in 1937 near St George's, an old part of Victoria that is believed to have fallen within the boundary of the Roman *municipium*. On the coins **Nero** (AD 54–68) is depicted in lampooning profile, with a boxer's neck, weak jaw and pusillanimous nose. The unflattering image of the despotic and insane emperor (apart from playing a fiddle while Rome burned he put St Paul to death), raises the question as to the unknown artist's fate.

Outside the Citadel

The **Banca Giuratale** (1733), a pretty bow-fronted baroque building in It-Tokk, was Grand Master de Vilhena's present to the people of Gozo after his visit in 1723. The 'civil building' (the knights referred to them grandly as

Municipal Palaces or Banca Giuratale), became the seat of the *Università*, the almost powerless local governing body, whose authority amounted to the ability to lend money to the poor, collect taxes and conscript able-bodied farmers into the diminutive 90-strong garrison. The *jurat's* (officers of the *Università*) privileges were equally hollow—the right to a special pew and incense at high mass. *It is still a government building, and houses the occasional local art exhibition. Adm. free.*

Behind It-Tokk is the **Basilica of St George**, the original parish church, built in 1678 as no more than a simple nave. The façade was altered in 1818 and the aisles, dome and transepts were all added between 1935 and 1945. Despite architectural meddling the church has remained a pleasing structure. Its interior, however, is the product of a contemporary and somewhat over-enthusiastic baroque school, and is only muted when the sunlight filters through the stained-glass windows. The bronze and black canopied altar with its barley-twist columns is a small copy of Bernini's in St Peter's, Rome and the ornate vaulted ceiling and dome show colourful episodes from Saint George's dramatic life. Hidden amongst the remodelled exuberance of its interior, the church possesses some important paintings. **Mattia Preti's** *St George* (1678) in an heroic pose differs greatly from the artist's version which hangs in St John's Co-Cathedral, Valletta. In this composition the saint is diminutive to the point of harmlessness, with cherubic cheeks and a slight pot-belly. His foot rests cautiously on the freshly severed and extinguished dragon's head while his sword flashes mysteriously clean. (Ten years later the church received another Preti, *The Virgin of Mercy with Souls in Purgatory.*) **Francesco Zahra**, one of the finest of 18th-century Maltese painters shows yet another interpretation of St George with two equally powerful works, one of which includes his beheading. The 150-year-old statue of the saint by another local artist was carved in one piece from a tree trunk. Finally, the bells of St George's, unlike those of other Gozitan churches, chime at 1100—tradition states this was to remind the women to begin kindling the fire under the *kenur* for lunch.

Rundle Gardens at the bottom of Republic Street next to the Duke of Edinburgh Hotel, were planted in the last two years of Sir Leslie Rundle's governorship (1909–15), and have remained Gozo's main public gardens. Formally laid out, they have, apart from the indigenous *ficus nitida* tree, an avenue of olives, tall Canary Palms, and an aviary of noisy chirping birds. The annual **agricultural fair** is held here on 14–15 August, the feast day of Santa Marija or the Assumption.

The oldest hotel in Gozo, the **Duke of Edinburgh Hotel★★★** (moderate), 85–9 Republic Street, ✆ 556392, has been run by the same family for more than 80 years. A major refit should, by the time you read this, be complete. 20 new rooms, and 8 renovated old-style rooms with high ceilings and whirring fans. There is a bar, restaurant with good English breakfasts, and a pool. Also family run, the **Three Hills Guest House** (Class III), Sir Luigi Camilleri Street, ✆ 551895, is tucked away behind Republic Street and has 10 perfectly adequate rooms.

Eating Out

Victoria is not a gourmet's mecca. Around noon you can't do better than go to **4 Fosse Street** (cheap) up from the cathedral in the citadel, where at the back of the conventional souvenir shop there are a few stools and a couple of tables. Here you can eat aromatic local tomatoes, fresh bread, olives and Gozitan *ġbejniet* (peppered goat's cheese) washed down with a glass of heady local red wine, all for less than 60c. Opposite It-Tokk is the **Cittadella Centre** (inexpensive), 14–16 Sir Adrian Dingli Street, ✆ 556628, which has a restaurant and bar/pizzeria. The restaurant has a secluded terrace and serves the usual pseudo-Italian fare—but well. The **Silver Jubilee** café next to the Cittadella Centre is open in the early hours for *pastizzi* and sweet tea. All the other bars around It-Tokk serve *pastizzi* but sell out by about 1130. Don't be put off by the bear-pit interior of the **Ginevra Bar** behind the Banca Giuratale. A hefty glass of its homemade, almost black, red wine at mid-morning will fuel you around the island till sunset.

North of Victoria

Xagħra

Xagħra, meaning 'a large open place', boasts the most enchanting village square on the island and the twisty hairpin road up to the plateau is lined with pink and white oleander trees. Xagħra was probably the *de facto* capital of the island in ancient times and was certainly the site of man's first efforts to cultivate Gozo. It now has 3,300 inhabitants and is the second-largest village after Nadur. The **Ġgantija** temples are nearby, as is the major non-event of the island—the boulder-strewn hole that is alleged to be **Calypso's Cave**.

The village is easy to find, midway between Mġarr and Victoria. There is a good short cut out of Victoria past the sports complex. **Victory Day**, 8 September, is a national holiday so the Xagħra *festa* is held on the Sunday closest to the 8th. Xagħra has a friendly rivalry with Nadur, and both their festive pyrotechnics can be elaborately daft.

Ġgantija

The two prehistoric structures known as **Ġgantija** are the most impressive and well preserved of all the 'temples' in the Maltese islands. Along with Ta Haġrat and Skorba in Malta they are believed to be the oldest free-standing monuments in the world. And although they lack the fine artistic treasures of the later Tarxien temples they make up for it with brute size—poised at the edge of a plateau, they're a daunting sight. In keeping with everything else on Gozo, the complex itself is well kept and colourful; the wild bougainvillea and the flower beds contrast gently with the massive deep-honey coloured stones.

The temples date back to the Ġgantija phase (3600–3200 BC of the Copper Age) and were first formally and badly excavated in 1827. The site comprises two similar structures (one with five apses the other with four) and the whole is enclosed by a shared outer wall of megalithic proportions. The outer walls were made from hard coralline limestone; softer, more versatile, globigerina

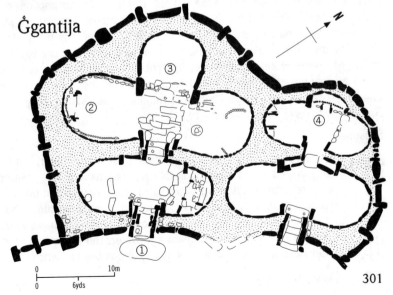

Ġgantija

limestone was used for the inside walls. A roof, which has not survived, would have covered the structures.

Walk across the threshold of each and there is a sensation of being 'inside', contained by the concave walls. The larger, and as you face it left-hand, temple is the older of the two, and like Mnajdra and Ħaġar Qim is orientated southeast (the significance of this is unknown). The southerly five-apse temple has, in contrast to any similar structure on the islands, smaller outer than inner apses. It also has the largest threshold slab [1] of the temples. The left-hand of the two inner apses (which together span 23.5 m) is stirring, with its 6 m-high walls curving inward; it was here [2] that the **snake relief-carving** now on display in the Gozo Archaeological Museum was found. The central apse is raised higher and has similar pitted decoration to that at Tarxien. To the rear [3], two stone heads believed to belong to the **headless female 'Fat' deities**, were discovered in the niche. These are on display in Valletta's Archaeological Museum.

On the right in the smaller temple (19.5 m long) there is little of note other than the small raised altar [4] in the central niche at the end. But the single-most striking element of Ġgantija is the perimeter wall. The stone wall reaches 6 m high in places, the largest of the slabs measures 6 m by 6.5 m.

As with all the megalithic structures in the islands the nature of the god or gods worshipped here can only be guessed at. The dramatic shape of Ġgantija (and others on Malta) has often been likened to an obese female form, with the threshold marking the entrance to the 'womb'. This has led to assumptions that prehistoric man worshipped deities of fertility and symbols of rebirth, an idea that is carried forward by the obese little figurines discovered in many of the sites. But the theory has no material basis, and assumes that the figurines *preceded* the structures and therefore influenced their form, whereas in fact they *post-date* the structures. That said, the supposition *could* be correct, even though the evidence is missing. Keep an open mind—who is to say they never contained a series of market stalls?

Sansuna

Copper Age man was an extraordinarily talented builder, but it must have taken decades, possibly generations to move, position and erect the boulders for Ġgantija's perimeter wall and the temples. Legend tells of a giantess from Qala named Sansuna who built the temples 5,500 years ago and owed her gargantuan stature to an awesome diet of broad beans and water. Her job was to carry on her head the stones from the quarry site at the Ta'Ċenċ cliffs.

The settlers were apparently an ungrateful lot, and Sansuna ended her days sapped of strength by a dearth of beans, and living alone and unwanted in a cave.

Between Ġgantija and Xagħra's square is the prominent **Il Miṭħna** or windmill, now restored as the latest government museum. All the various implements a miller or farmer would use are displayed, but it's rotten value at Lm1.

For a hoot visit **Nino's** and **Xerri's grottoes** (to the north and south of the square respectively), two underground caves of stalactites and stalagmites, which are often found in limestone strata. The entrance to Nino's, the smaller of the two, is through the owner's front room and the cave is not deep. But the descent to the much more substantial Xerri's Grotto, through a house called 'God Bless Australia', is more precarious: 10 m down a tiny spiral staircase off another sitting room. It costs 20c and a member of the family gives a 5-minute guided tour. (The entrance fee is justified on the grounds that 24 light bulbs are needed to illuminate the rock formations, not by the more enticing fact that it takes 1,000 years for a single centimetre to form.)

The church in Xagħra, like everything and everybody in Gozo, has a nickname—*Il Bambina*—after the church's 19th-century French statue. The large church, **Our Lady of Victory** (1815) has an interior with wide columns and ten small chapels and follows the idiom of the day, the marble work being rich and ornate. Apart from Christian scenes of victory over heathen enemies there is an apse painting of the *Nativity of the Virgin* by **Guiseppe Cali**.

Calypso's Cave

> *'The cave was sheltered by a copse of alders and fragrant cypresses, which was the roosting place of wide-winged birds, horned owls and falcons and cormorants with long tongues, birds of the coast, whose business takes them down to the sea. Trailing around the mouth of the cavern was a thriving garden vine, with great bunches of grapes; from four separate neighbouring springs four crystal rivulets were channelled to run this way and that; and in soft meadows on either side iris and wild celery flourished. It was indeed a spot where even an immortal visitor must pause to gaze in wonder and delight.'*
>
> *The Odyssey*, Verses 63–74, Book 5, Homer

Either Homer was a daydreamer *extraordinaire* or time has been unkind in its treatment of what is purported to have been Calypso's Cave. Despite her many charms it is highly unlikely Calypso enticed Odysseus to remain here for

7 minutes, let alone as many years. Although it's set promisingly on a craggy bluff, with a panorama of the Mediterranean, the fertile Ramla Valley and red sandy beach of Ramla below, the cave is no more than a grubby cramped hollow caused by a rock slide in the Xaghra cliffs. A loud youth is always on hand to light a candle, drip wax on his and other people's feet, and receive a tip. *Signposted from Xaghra, and all over the north and east of the island.*

Where to Stay and Eating Out

Originally a farmhouse, **The Cornucopia** ★★★★ (Expensive), 10 Gnien Imrik Street, © 556486, on the edge of the valley looking down to Marsalforn, has 44 comfortable, air-conditioned rooms. The two pools in the garden can become crowded and cramped, but the rooms are generously equipped and quiet. Two adjoining farmhouses offer larger or more private accommodation as well as use of the hotel's facilities.

Mario is a victim of his own success at the **Oleander** (inexpensive), 10 Victory Square, © 557230, and the service here is politely spasmodic. The menu changes regularly but old favourites such as pasta with rabbit sauce, pouched [*sic*] local fish, and chicken stuffed with all manner of things are always on. During the summer, dine outside under the oleander trees and bougainvillea. Open for lunch and dinner. In 8 September Avenue (off Victory Square) is tiny **Gesther's** (cheap), © 556621, with traditional Gozitan cooking by two sisters Gemma and Esther. Forget about the rudimentary tables and decor and try their *bragioli*. Good homemade pickles, spiced peels, etc. for sale.

Marsalforn

Marsalforn is an old fishing community which has evolved into Gozo's main summer destination—apart from seven hotels there are numerous rental apartments. A mixed bag of tourists head here: diving enthusiasts, people over from Malta for a few days and Europeans wishing to escape.

In the height of the season it never quite jumps (nowhere does in Gozo), but it becomes touristy and the seafront, overrun with cafés and shops, is the forum for the evening and Sunday *passeggiata*. Out of season, the hotels remain open and the esplanade has the eerie calm of an English seaside town in winter. Sometimes the strong north wind causes the waves to crash over the sea wall leaving snakes of seaweed on the slippery road, and the sea spray welds the shops' shutters with rust.

At Victoria turn right and head straight down the Marsalforn Valley to the sea—4 km approximately. There is ample **parking** behind the bus terminus. St Paul is the village's patron saint and he is said to have preached here, but as yet Marsalforn is not a parish and does not have a *festa*.

Marsalforn is a base, somewhere to return to in the evening, not somewhere to linger. The small beach underneath the seafront is not very attractive, cramped and more often than not untidy; there is much better swimming elsewhere. **Calypso Diving Centre**, next door to the Calypso Hotel, is licensed for beginners and experienced divers. There's free diving along the coast and off the salt pans at Qbajjar and Xwieni. The nearest organised dive site is 3 km away off **Reqqa Point**, the most northerly point on the islands. It's not a dive for the inexperienced but the clear waters and caves are good for fish-spotters. In nearby **Xwieni**, Paradise Water Sports, © 561949, teach **water-skiing**, have an equipped parakite boat and other more sedate **boats for hire**.

In the tiny harbour, **Il Menqa**, again in front of the Calypso Hotel, there is normally a fisherman who is willing to take visitors fishing. The **Xlendi Pleasure Cruise** boat, *Midas II*, leaves from here on a circuit via San Blas Bay and the Blue Lagoon in Comino. It alternates its departure point for trips around Gozo and Comino between here and Xlendi. Once a week it goes to **Popeye Village** in Anchor Bay, Malta—a total waste of time.

Where to Stay

The **Calypso Hotel★★★** (moderate), Marsalforn Bay, © 562000, dominates the east side of the bay. Built in the hazy 1960s, it now looks tired, and the rooms are rudimentary and in need of modernization. Half overlook the sea, but the inland accommodation has a gloomy aspect. It does have three restaurants, including a Chinese, and a small pool on the roof terrace. The **Atlantis Hotel★★★** (moderate), Qolla Street, Marsalforn Bay, © 554685, has neither position nor views, but much better and larger rooms, as well as a decent-size pool. Situated on the west of the bay 5 minutes walk from the seafront, it's small (only 46 rooms), family run and modern. For more basic accommodation the **Marsalforn Hotel★** (inexpensive), © 556147, is the most central option, just behind the seafront on an island site. Most of the rooms have balconies and there is a small restaurant on the ground floor; it's clean and unpretentious. Nearby is a block of six two-bedroom apartments under the same management. The immodestly named **Ritz Hotel★** (inexpensive), Xagħra Road, © 556143, is popular with divers who don't want to spend much time in an hotel and has 18 small and simple bedrooms. It also owns a block of less commodious flats and the **Ritz Café**, popular with tourists and local *cognoscenti* for late-night/early-morning breakfasts.

Eating Out

The choice of where to eat is split between those who require 'fuel' before another day's diving and those who require something more than pasta or pizza; 'downtown' Marsalforn is full of the former. The roof garden of the **Gauleon** (cheap), © 556107, on the seafront bravely offers as much pasta as you can eat for Lm1.50. On the first floor of Il Kartell, above a good and inexpensive pizzeria, is an excellent restaurant, **Il Kartell** (moderate), © 556918. The choice is limited to fresh fish and meat, simply grilled or baked. Reserve a balcony table overlooking the bay if it's a balmy summer evening. Walk out on the Xagħra Road for 0.5 km and under twitching neon and peeling paint you will find the **Pink Panther** (inexpensive), © 556149. Don't be put off, inside is a decent kitchen and a fun bar, with a suspiciously long cocktail list (beware a vile concoction called 'Scotch Frog' which is 'guaranteed to make you croak'). The menu is lost somewhere between Gozo and Sicily, but Noel the owner provides a good dinner made with fresh ingredients. In summer the charmingly ramshackle garden is open. Much further up the hill towards Xagħra the **Raj Mahal** (inexpensive), © 551675, is the only place to assuage a craving for a curry in Gozo; sometimes the food is not as good as the view overlooking the valley. About 1.5 km out of Marsalforn on the Victoria road is one of Gozo's two upscale eateries, the **Auberge Ta'frenc** (expensive), © 553888, but this isn't the cutting edge of local cuisine. Although the farmhouse setting is charming, the food hovers between competent and pretentious. Stay with meat, the lobster is invariably dry. Not far away is **Il Maxtura** (inexpensive), © 557617, which started as a large barn but now houses a conventional but small à la carte restaurant and a fast and furious pizzeria and bar. It's popular with Gozitans and tourists alike.

Żebbuġ

Żebbuġ, meaning 'olives' is one of the highest of the villages straddling the spine of a ridge; it's Gozo's windy city, where it is said the people live longest.

Żebbuġ has wide running views but there isn't much to see in the village itself, apart from the rich marble interior of the early 18th-century parish **church of the Assumption**. The local inhabitants were fortunate enough to have had a rich seam of marble, now exhausted, which not only covers the walls of their church but was used in parts of St John's Co-Cathedral.

This part of the exposed northern coastline is pock-marked with **saltpans** (squares carved in the hard coralline rock) which yield coarse sea salt. Salt is still harvested today and has long been a source of both income and legend. The lip of soft limestone rock stretching from unattractive Xwieni to the Għasri valley provides somewhere to sunbathe and clamber into the sea.

Getting There and Tourist information

By **car** you can ascend via Xwieni and along the saltpans or by turning north off the first main road west out of Victoria. Żebbuġ is one of Gozo's six original parishes and *festa* of the Assumption is celebrated on the 1st Sunday after 15 August.

The Clockmaker's Saltpans

Legend tells of a clockmaker from Żebbuġ whose greed propelled him to think of new and devious methods of fulfilling his lust for money. Blinded by avarice, he cut new saltpans on the cliff-top far above the sea. Then, in order to harness the thundering winter waves and so fill his pans with seawater, he dug a steep shaft down to the water's edge. When the winter came the seawater shot up through his man-made funnel and filled his salt-pans. But the mercenary clockmaker had cut them into soft, porous globigerina limestone not the hard coralline limestone and the seawater disappeared long before the valuable crystals could form. Worse—the saltwater spray continued to erupt through the funnel and destroyed his neighbour's crops until the clockmaker was sued into bankruptcy.

West of Victoria

San Lawrenz

You are likely to pass through the little village of **San Lawrenz** en route to the wholesome scenery and cliff walks around **Dwerja** and the **Inland Sea**, areas which offer some of the best diving in the central Mediterranean. San Lawrenz is the westernmost settlement, where the late author Nicholas Monsarrat once lived. It's the only village in Gozo to take its name from its patron saint (whose emblem is a palmfrond on a gridiron; poor St Lawrence was roasted to death in AD 258).

Getting Around and Tourist Information

If you go **walking**, the landscape demands stout shoes and care should be taken near the cliffs' edge. **Head-to-Toe**, Tower Street, San Lawrenz, © 552014, is a sauna, gym, spa and beauty salon in a converted farmhouse. Open 0930–2130 six days a week. St Lawrenz *festa* is held on the 2nd Sunday in August.

The Inland Sea

Also known as Qawra, the Inland Sea is a geological fault, similar to but much more spectacular than Il Maqluba (*see* p. 217). It was created when the roof of what must have been an immense cave collapsed some 80–100 m, leaving a land-locked basin of seawater opening into the Mediterranean via a massive gothicky arch. This is a quiet and not too touristified spot with little to do other than let the day evaporate: soak up the sun, swim in the clear water and watch the fishermen toying with their *luzzus*. You could haggle for the short trip out through the arch and the **Azure Window**, or simply sit in the shade of the one café and read; on windy days the swallow-hole formation turns into an effective windbreak.

Most days, tourists on whistle-stop day trips from Malta are disgorged from their coaches in the late morning, shatter the peace and spend 10 minutes photographing everything in sight before a guide hauls them off.

Fungus Rock and Dwejra Bay

Fungus Rock is the affectionate nickname for *Il-Ġebla tal-Ġeneral*, 'the General's Rock'. This 60 m-high monolith guards the entrance to an almost circular black lagoon with a spooky seaweed-covered bed. Apparently a general of the knights' galleys discovered a rare tuber plant *fucus coccineus melitensis* which grew on the rock's flat top. The knights believed the repulsive-smelling plant had medicinal properties when brewed into an even more foul-smelling concoction; it was used as a styptic dressing for wounds and a cure for dysentery. Grand Master Pinto decreed the rock out of bounds in 1746—trespassers were punished with a three-year spell in the galleys—posted a permanent guard and built a precarious cable-car basket to the mainland 50 m away. Later it was discovered that all Pinto's efforts were for nought; *fucus coccineus melitensis* has no medicinal properties whatsoever. The climb to the top is only for aspiring mountaineers.

If dark waters don't target the spectral side of your imagination, Dwerja is a placid place to swim. There are two small grottoes, and plenty of fish for divers to spot off Fungus Rock. In calm weather the bay (5 m–7 m deep) is an idyllic spot to anchor for the night. You will be awoken in the early morning by goats on the cliff-top, as their shepherd leads them away from the weather-devoured Dwerja Tower to another meagre patch.

Diving and Snorkelling

It is often said that the diving between Dwerja Point (by the Inland Sea) and Wardija Point (the southwestern tip of Gozo) is the finest in the Mediterranean, with the blue hole dive off Fungus Rock one of the best. All dives here are for experienced and team divers only.

Among other dives are: a 35-m tunnel dive from the Inland Sea out into the open sea where the floor falls away dramatically, a dive under the Azure Window, a blue hole dive, and a long drift-type dive off Crocodile Rock, named after the shape of its back jutting out above the surface. There are caves, groupers and all manner of marine fauna in the clear waters.

The clear but dark sea and deserted, ragged coastline make this ideal territory for keen **snorkellers**. Care should be taken on anything other than calm days: getting into the water with a swell is easy, getting out can be treacherous. The points of ingress over the battered coralline are laceratingly sharp under foot.

Gharb

Gharb, meaning 'west', is the oldest and main western village, with its own unintelligible dialect. Tourists are as ubiquitous as legends in the west, and Gharb is where they both meet. So much building and refurbishment is going on that it's beginning to resemble the suburbs of the late-1980s. Fortunately, the village itself has remained tranquil and unspoiled; essentially this is still hard farming country. On their way to the unforgiving fields, you still see elderly farmers creaking their laden and ancient single-geared bicycles through the square.

Gharb has the tastiest and most aromatic tomatoes in Gozo, an **exquisite parish church**, fine old carved stone balconies and **two good restaurants**.

Getting There and Tourist Information

The west road to Gharb, 4 km from Victoria, goes past the remains of the 19th-century Victoria aqueduct and is clearly flagged. The Visitation of Our Lady to St Elisabeth on the 1st Sunday in July is Gharb's *festa*. A celebratory mass is said at San Dimitri on the Sunday after 9 October.

The foundation stone of the **parish church of the Immaculate Conception** was laid in 1699, 20 years after Gharb had become a parish and had outgrown its older church of St Mary's, known as Taz-Zejt. One of the many narcissistic elements baroque needs in order to thrive is space for admiration, and here three old boundary tracks have neatly formed a wide sweeping square leaving the church isolated on an island site at one end. In a fit of immodesty the villagers instructed their architect Guiseppi Azzopardo to model the design on the Santa Agnese in Piazza Navona, Rome. Azzopardo's more parochial work does have the obvious Roman baroque swathes of the day, but otherwise can hardly be said to resemble Santa Agnese. The concave façade is split by a razor of a balustrade and the two dominant bell-towers are set back from it. The upper façade neatly hides the drumless dome collecting the whole into a uniform and manageable size; notice how the church works with the village houses and not against them by following the contours of the square. The three statues of Faith (middle), Hope and Charity on either side complete the fine building. Inside, the plan is circular and the main altarpiece, the *Visitation of Our Lady to her cousin St Elisabeth*, was a gift from Grand Master de Vilhena in the early 18th century. An inscription on the right-hand clock face reads 'heed precious time'.

A Tale of Greed

Still in use today and shaded at the bottom of its own pastoral little valley is the 16th-century church of St Mary known as **Tas-Żejt**, 'of the oil' (*600 m from the village square towards Birbuba*). The legend and its simple moral tells of an old spinster, conveniently named Marija, whose only solace in her abject poverty was two daily visits to the church. Her sorrow deepened each winter because she was unable to earn enough money to replenish oil in the lamp in front of the church's Madonna to whom she prayed. One night, the Madonna appeared to her and mysteriously told her to take a jar to the 4 am mass. When Marija arrived at the church she glimpsed, coming from underneath it, a spring of oil glistening in the dawn light—the answer to her prayers. But once the miracle became known, people came from all over Malta and Gozo to bottle and profit from the oil which was intended to illuminate the Madonna's statue. The priest's protestations and warnings went unheeded, and one day Marija's river of oil dried up as quickly and miraculously as it had flowed.

The Loneliest Chapel on Gozo

Right in the middle of a field is the loneliest chapel on Gozo, **San Dimitri** (*1.5 km to the west of Għarb and signposted*). The beauty of the little square building, like the Magdalene chapel on Dingli Cliffs, lies in its windswept isolation. The front door is always open. Behind the security bars is the altarpiece of San Dimitri on his white steed, keeper of probably the best and certainly the dottiest of Gozitan legends.

Back in the time of savage corsair raids there was a pious woman called Zgugina, who had a son, and prayed every day to San Dimitri. One day a pirate ship hove into view, and finding nothing worth plundering in the village the corsairs seized as many able young lads as they could find, including Zgugina's son. Zgugina immediately crept back to the chapel, where she prayed to San Dimitri. As she did so the altarpiece came to life and San Dimitri rode out of the chapel towards the sea, galloped across the water and returned with her son. Zgugina vowed to keep an oil lamp alight in front of the altarpiece for the rest of her life.

Nearly two hundred years later the original chapel fell victim to an earthquake and sank to the bottom of the sea. Years passed, until one day a ship anchored in the vicinity of the cliffs. The ship's anchor became snagged and divers were sent down to free it. But all of them disappeared beneath the waves, and were assumed to have been drowned. Then, miraculously, they surfaced unharmed and told of a beautiful chapel lying intact on the seabed and how they had walked into it, breathed in fresh air and seen an altarpiece to San Dimitri illuminated by an oil lamp. Fishermen say that on especially calm days you can still see the glow from the seabed, and farmers believe that two indentations in the hard rock near the present chapel were those made by the hooves of San Dimitri's horse as he galloped back from the slavers' boat with Zgugina's son.

Eating Out

At the turning into Għarb is **Jeffrey's** (inexpensive), 10 Għarb Street, ✆ 561006, a simple rustic restaurant, serving good food from a short and idiosyncratic menu in a small converted farmhouse. Nothing has changed since Joe, the owner, won the National Lottery in 1992—a good omen. The service is friendly; in summer the courtyard at the rear is open and in winter there is a cosy bistro atmosphere. Dinner only. A couple of hundred metres beyond the parish church in Għarb is **Salvina** (moderate), 21 Rock Street, ✆ 552505, in a little townhouse with a fine balcony. It's bigger and swankier than Jeffrey's, with a busy bar, but there is still a family mood. Flies make the terrace a no-go area for lunch in summer, but it's ideal for dinner when the insects have gone to bed. Stay with the time-honoured local dishes, such as fish or *bragoli*.

Għasri, Għammar and Ta'Pinu

Għasri is Gozo's smallest village with 350 people, and Għammar is no more than a hamlet in between Għasri and Għarb. One of the best-kept secrets of the island is at the bottom of the Għasri valley, a minuscule gem of a **beach**. The national shrine of **Ta'Pinu** underneath evergreen Għammar hill, and the views from the top of the **Gordan Lighthouse** are other reasons for prowling around this agricultural area. Like Għarb many of the farmhouses on either side of the Għasri valley have become holiday homes. The farmers continue to be bewildered as to why northern Europeans should wish to come to this picturesque but comparatively barren spot and pay exorbitant prices for rubbly old animal sheds. Being Gozitan they don't question it, they bank it.

Getting Around and Tourist Information

By **car** from Victoria all routes are clearly signposted; for **Għasri** just turn right by the large tree and derelict watchtower on the Victoria road. If you are staying in one of the many **farmhouses** unravel a ball of string in your imagination as you go, or you will never find your way home—asking is invariably of no use, as the villagers don't know the house by its smart brochure name. The *festa* is Christ the Eucharist on the 1st Sunday in June.

Ta'Pinu

The huge basilica of **Ta'Pinu** with its solitary 47 m-high campanile is the national shrine and a church of pilgrimage, not a parish church. Built in a neo-Romanesque style, at an architecturally uninspiring time between the two world wars, the taut exterior stands in austere isolation amid the surrounding cultivated fields. By direct contrast the interior is plain, reverential and moving.

A place of worship has existed on the site since the early 16th century. In 1575 the original structure was condemned, but the demolition never took place; according to folklore the first hammer strike broke the wrecker's arm. The original church remained, and lurched between repair and disrepair until the late 17th century when the family of Fillipino Gauci—abbreviated to Pinu—repaired it for the last time. Today the old structure is incorporated into a small chapel behind the apse.

On 22 June 1883 a peasant woman from Għarb, Carmela Grima, heard a voice calling to her from the isolated chapel. The same voice requested that she say three Hail Marys, 'In memory of the three days My Body rested in the sepulchre.' She told only one person, Francesco Portelli, who admitted that he too had heard a voice on six occasions. Three years later both attested to their experiences at the insistence of Bishop Pace. Since then, miracles and narrow escapes have been attributed to the grace and intercession of Our Lady of Pinu. There are numerous votive offerings in the church. In the groves of Għammar hill overlooking Ta'Pinu is a **Way of the Cross**, with 12 lifesize marble statues. *Ta'Pinu closes between 1230–1300 every day and during the numerous packed masses. Visitors must wear long trousers or knee-length skirts. Guides and multilingual information machines are available.*

From dozy one-horse Għasri village square, turn right down a shocking road for the mini-**beach** at the bottom of the Għasri Valley. The track peters out and you can park on the coralline outcrops at the top of a precipitous fjord. At the end of this 400 m-long and needle-thin fjord between the cliff faces is the often deserted fine-pebble beach—no bigger than 5 m by 6 m. Some rudimentary steps have been cut for the steep climb down to sea level. Bring an air bed if you are too lazy to swim to the mouth, and a picnic. Sometimes the whole day passes here without interlopers. Swimming and access are suitable for children.

Over the other side of the valley and past Ta'Pinu is **Gordan Lighthouse**, 145 m above sea level; on clear nights the powerful beam can be seen from more than 40 km away. The final third of the road is too steep to drive up but the hike is worth it for the panoramic views.

South of Victoria

Kerċem

Approximately 1,500 people live in the villages of Kerċem and Santa Lucija, 2 km and 2.5 km southwest of Victoria respectively. The two *festas* are: St Gregory the Great on the 2nd Sunday in March, and on the 2nd Sunday in July, Our Lady of Perpetual Succour.

Two Walks

The **Lunzjata Valley** peels away on the left as you come into Kerċem. There is a pleasant **15-minute walk** through this, the most fertile part of the island. The valley was a game preserve of the knights who built several, now decayed watchtowers for hunting (grand masters erroneously believed sport exorcized the impure thoughts of young knights). The walk begins at an old arched entrance and guardhouse and opens into a verdant oasis of plants and fruit trees. Part of the small **chapel of the Annunciation** (half in a cave and still in use) dates back to 1347; most of the present structure dates from the early 17th century. As you walk the dusty track the rustle of bamboo on the valley floor amplifies the sound of running water, the rarest of sounds on the Maltese islands. Fat and vivid dragonflies buzz around pools of water in the sadly forgotten remains of a public spring over which Grand Master Perellos built an arch in 1698. On the way back up the path past the chapel, tempting plump figs dangle from a tree overhanging the dry-stone wall.

For a much **longer walk**, with a destination in mind, drive west out of Kerċem past the daftly positioned parish church, to a small car park where the path begins. The cliff walk towards an old tower near **Wardija Point**, not quite the westernmost point of Gozo, is one of solitude above what is a higher continuation of the Ta'Ċenċ cliffs. The desolate peace of the countryside is sometimes shattered by the *kaċċatur*, or hunters, shooting blindly at migrant birds, in and out of the so-called season. Nevertheless, it is an enjoyable walk.

Sannat and Munxar

Sannat is Gozo's most southerly village, close to the Ta'Ċenċ cliffs. **Munxar**, a small village of 500 people perches between Sannat and Xlendi on the eastern slope of the valley.

Sannat's attractions include the 145 m-high **layercake cliffs** with their breathtaking scenery, an energetic and **long track walk** down to the sea at Mġarr ix-Xini, the famous **Hotel Ta'Ċenċ**, and at least two places to buy handmade traditional **Gozitan lace**. Sannat was the traditional centre of the island's **lacemaking** cottage industry and on rare occasions you still see women nesting on their stumpy chairs in the shade of the 18th-century parish church of St Margaret, their fingers working the bobbins with fury and precision.

Getting Around and Tourist Information

By **car** the road for Sannat leaves Victoria through St Francis Square and is well signposted. For the **Hotel Ta'Ċenċ**, head southeast round the village square, where the hotel's own signposts take over. For Munxar, the easiest route is to take the Xlendi road and turn left onto a terrible road 500 m after Fontana. In **Sannat** the *festa* of St Margaret is held on the 4th Sunday in July. **Munxar's** *festa* to St Paul is on the last Sunday in May.

Ta'Ċenċ cliffs and San Dimitri Point were once the breeding grounds of the Mediterranean peregrine falcon, the Maltese falcon. The species, despite a 1980 declaration of protection, is now—as far as the Maltese islands are concerned—extinct. The last-known pair 'disappeared' from these cliffs in the mid-1980s. Apart from shooting or trapping the birds, the *kaċċatur* would let themselves down the cliff face by rope, some 145 m, in order to steal the young or the eggs. This sad story now means there are tranquil **walks** along the cliffs. Two tracks out of Sannat lead down to the beach at **Mġarr ix-Xini**; take the first turning left out of the square for the more direct route or follow the track past the hotel. Along the way there are a few cart ruts, two dolmens and the meagre plan of the old temple-period site of Borġ il-Mramma. If you leave the track, the lip of the limestone cliffs should be treated with great respect—the sea is 145 m below.

Lace

8 x 12 pairs long and 8 x 12 pairs short mits, besides a scarf.
An order from Queen Victoria, 1838

Sannat lace is a creamy off-white colour and very hard-wearing. Nearly all the patterns are traditional and are laid over the *trajbu* or lace pillow. Pins are placed in the pillow and the bobbins are thrown over them to produce the weave. Black lace, the type worn by Queen Victoria, isn't found anymore: working with black thread strains the eyes.

In the tiny square behind Sannat church and next to Main Street is the **Old Lace House** where many of the skilled women worked. It is now a private house but there is a plaque commemorating the visit of Princess Elizabeth and the Duke of Edinburgh on 2 April 1951.

When you buy, try to resist the temptation to haggle. A tablecloth for Lm400 represents over 12 months work and a set of napkins can cost as little as Lm6. Both women listed below have various items for sale and distinctive styles. Mornings or early evenings are good times to visit. **Rosina** sometimes weaves and sells lace in Xlendi and her house, which is not named or numbered, is opposite the main entrance to the school on the way into Sannat. Persevere, her work has a fine edge. She is an ebullient woman, the eldest of 17 children, and learnt to weave at the age of four. If **Marianne Cordina**, 140 Ta'Ċenċ Street, Sannat (50 m past the church on the left) isn't working in her garage workshop, knock on the front door. Marianne has a large selection of lace and locally made knitted goods.

Munxar has its own brand new and very pleasant 33-room hotel, the **Andar Hotel★★★★** (expensive), Munxar, © 560736/7. Set in the countryside it's a family-run establishment with a decent pool, generous public rooms, bar and restaurant and games room. The rooms are air-conditioned and each has satellite TV. Only the noise of the church bells will detract from its appeal if all you want is to escape and recharge. The hotel is not clearly flagged and is best approached from the Xlendi road.

Hotel Ta'Ċenċ★★★★★ (luxury), Sannat, © 556830, is owned by an Italian family who came to Gozo more than 20 years ago to construct the breakwater in Mġarr Harbour. In 1992 it was enlarged to more than 240 beds. Its skilled one-storey design, the originality of the handful of *trullos* (beehive-shaped suites) scattered about, and Italian decorating touches make it an infinitely flexible hotel: a base for a family holiday, a businessman's retreat, or a honeymoon idyll. Facilities include two large pools, tennis and volleyball courts, and a restaurant which sprawls under the sinewy branches of a magnificent 150-year-old carob tree. At dusk, the long walk back from its private lido as the apricot sun flops into the sea over the cliff's edge is a singular attraction. But if you like dancing under fairy lights to a cover version of 'The Lady in Red' it's not for you. The best rooms are 32, 35 and 36 in the old hotel, and 131–3 in the new.

Xlendi

The old fishing village of Xlendi used to have a peace, a magic, and was Gozo's most beguiling spot. Now, it's just another stop for the tourist bus, and has been well and truly trampled. From the head of the bay the entire left side as far as the knights' tower is a seamless colonization of characterless apartments. The right-hand side is safe only until an engineering wizard figures out a way to build on its craggy face. But there is a good **diving school**, an over-supply of reasonable **self-catering accommodation** and an **excellent nightclub**.

Yachtsmen should take note that the bay offers up on first impression deceptively safe shelter from all but westerlies. Tremendous care should be exercised as a shallow reef—1.5 m below the surface—straddles the mouth. Many ships have come to grief here, the relics of two, one from the 2nd century BC and another from the 5th century AD, are on display in the Gozo Archaeological Museum.

Xlendi is just over 3 km south of Victoria. The road is straight, downhill all the way, and there is a large car park at the bottom. En route, in Fontana, is an old arched **public wash-house** built by the knights; opposite is a comprehensive **souvenir store**.

Under the meagre shelter of the tamarisk trees at the head of the bay is a small but always crowded **beach**; the rocks going out to the tower (1658) are also staked out with tourists who leap in and out of the water like penguins. In front of the statue to St Andrew, the patron saint of fishermen, is a flight of steps cut into the limestone which lead up over a large rock to a small and secluded natural cove. The steps were cut to allow private bathing for the local nuns, who seldom use it today.

St Andrew's Diving School, St Simon Street, ✆ 551301, on the left of the bay, offers beginners' courses, and a full range of dives around the island, including night dives. They hire out equipment, and apartments from Lm5.50 per person per night in the peak season. Four days a week the **Xlendi Pleasure Cruise** boat leaves from Xlendi (from Marsalforn on the remaining alternate days) for trips round Gozo and Comino; ✆ 551909.

Where to Stay

Nearly all the cafés and restaurants have 'apartments to rent' signs for flats in improbable-sounding blocks such as the 'Xlendi Hilton'; take your pick. The new **St Patrick's Hotel**★★★★ (expensive), 12 Xlendi Seafront, ✆ 556598, or c/o Cornucopia Hotel, ✆ 556486, opened in the summer of 1993 with 50 rooms, 20 facing the sea, and a roof-top swimming pool. Owned and managed by the Cornucopia Hotel, it is likely to be run to the same high standards. The **Serena Aparthotel** (Class III) , Upper St Simon Street, ✆ 553719 has 12 well-maintained serviced apartments overlooking the bay, a large restaurant and terrace on the roof, a private pool and a mini-market. The top two floors have the best outlook.

Eating Out

The family-run **It-Tmun**, 'the Helmsman' (inexpensive), 3 Mt Carmel Street, ✆ 551571, is the best restaurant in Xlendi. Set way back from the seafront it serves and prepares local fish and meat dishes well. Like Xlendi itself, It-Tmun closes in the dead of winter. The **Stone Crab Pizzeria** (cheap), St Andrew Street, ✆ 556400, is at the water's edge yet far enough away from the bustle of the seafront. Try the Stone Crab pizza, it's got more ingredients than a Chinese feast. The owner has just opened a **bar** in the knights' tower at the mouth of the bay. The village's old seafront stalwart is the **Moby Dick** (inexpensive), Xlendi Seafront, © 551616. Downstairs is an all-day snack and pizzeria and on the fifth-floor terrace overlooking the harbour there is a more formal barbeque restaurant (evenings only). They too have apartments.

If you can't face Xlendi's or Il-Grotta's parking problems (*see below*), try **Il-Kenur** (inexpensive), Xlendi Road, © 551583 (250 m past the nightclub on the road to Victoria). Inside it's somewhat uninspiring, but it has a terrific terrace overlooking the valley and the bay beyond. The food—both local and Italian—won't win any awards but it's competent and there is good bar to linger in.

Nightlife

The nightclub **Il-Grotta**, Xlendi Road (*adm. Lm1.50*) has a superb position above the bamboo floor of Xlendi valley. Half in a grotto and half *al fresco* it has everything a good summer resort nightclub needs: loud music, quiet nooks, and three bars. It's at its best on a Friday (Saturday is sardine night) and keeps its own hours—but a full head of steam is not reached until 2 am. Parking can be a nightmare: the line of cars along both sides of the valley road can sometimes stretch for 1.5 km.

Xewkija and Mġarr ix-Xini

Xewkija is famous for its contemporary parish church to St John the Baptist, known simply as '**the Rotunda**'. Not only does it dominate the village, it dominates the entire island. The village with its population fewer than 3,000 has an eccentrically suburban air for an agricultural community. Men on ancient lilac-coloured *vespas* roar noisily through the streets wearing soup-bowl helmets and shot guns slung across their backs; young boys goad a donkey and cart full of pungent manure through the main square; a handful of people too old to work the fields sit beside their bamboo-slatted front doors awaiting the cool of the day, while tourists gawp at their church.

Getting There and Tourist Information

The village sprawls along and off the main Victoria–Mġarr road, and is well signposted. On the 4th Sunday in June Xewkija celebrates its *festa* to St John the Baptist, patron saint of the knights of Malta.

The Rotunda Church

To understand the rationale behind building a cathedral-sized parish church that just happens to be marginally higher than Mosta's (though volumetrically smaller), is to begin to understand the intensity of Maltese-Gozitan rivalry.

The Rotunda does look a little eccentric stuck in the middle of the Gozitan countryside surrounded by diminutive cuboid village houses, but it's mightily impressive. It has the second highest dome, internally, in Europe (after St Peter's in Rome), is 6 m taller than St Paul's in London and can accommodate nearly three times the village's population. The villagers wanted such a church and it was constructed and paid for *entirely* by local volunteer labour and donations.

Construction began in 1951 around the structure of the existing 17th-century baroque church. The design, neither quixotic nor plagiaristic, is by Guiseppe Damato in homage to Santa Maria della Salute in Venice. The fanatical dedication and skill of the stone masons is remarkable but the single-most impressive feature is the dome, a 45,000-ton structure set on eight columns. Seen from within, the 16 clear-glass windows of the dome and 16 smaller windows in the lantern illuminate the milky limestone, invoking more space than actually exists. If you stand at a distance, in the fields opposite Għajnsielem at sunset, the dome presents a striking silhouette as the orange light powers through it.
The interior is restrained and simple in its execution. Above the six side altars are six paintings depicting the life of St John the Baptist, which culminate in another rendition of his martyrdom (for rebuking an adulterous King Herod, and at the behest of Salome). The image of the price he paid for speaking his mind is violent, without the temperance of Caravaggio's in St John's Co-Cathedral. Part of the rich interior of the old church has been dismantled like Lego, and rebuilt stone by stone in what is called the Museum of Sculpture to the left of the Carrara marble main altar.

Mġarr ix-Xini

From Xewkija it is 3 km to the pebbly beach at **Mġarr ix-Xini** (meaning 'the galley's landing place'). Fork left exactly 1 km out of Xewkija—the road is not for the drunk or fainthearted. The **swimming** in the small fjord at the bottom of the steep single track is clean and suitable for children. Gozo's south coast has the same topography as Dingli cliffs: the waters are dark, deep and clear against the sheer cliff face, offering good diving and snorkelling. **Fishing** lazily off Fessej Rock is a peaceful if not always fruitful way of passing the time and around the tiny headland to the west is the private **lido and bar** of Hotel Ta'Ċenċ.

Mġarr ix-Xini tower was built in 1658, more than a hundred years too late, for this was a favourite landing place for the Barbary slavers and the spot from which most of the population was carried away in Dragut's catastrophic raid of 1551 (*see* p. 288).

East of Victoria

Mġarr and Għajnsielem

Mġarr means simply 'a place to where goods are taken or a landing place' but today P.T. Barnum could be **Mġarr Harbour's** ringmaster. Under the big top of summer the shenanigans that take place here in Gozo's principal harbour, bottled-necked front door, tradesmen's entrance, yacht marina and emergency exit can be truly comical. Unfortunately, it is the sort of place that needs a second chance to make a good impression, for any sane person, tourist or local, will turn and flee from the dysfunctional world that greets them. Ferries barge, hoot and churn the waters in lopsided tussles with incompetent yachtsmen and obstinate fishermen 365 days a year. Tourists lost in the one-way maze of queues are ignored by mean-looking policemen, while Gozitan men in their stained singlets (which never quite stretch over their bellies to meet their over-tight shorts) gesticulate wildly and release a bonanza of obscenities that is only curbed when a priest ambles by.

Amidst the apparent chaos, fishermen tinker with their *luzzus* and mend their nets. And in the cool of the day, under the watchful eyes of the mock-gothic church, Fort Chambray and those on the balcony of the Gleneagles Bar (hub of the Mġarr cosmos), Gozitans tenderly bathe the fetlocks of their chestnut trotting horses in the shallows of the harbour (*see* p. 286). While on the slopes above the harbour, the village remains aloof, ignoring the circus below.

Getting There

The Gozo Channel Co. enjoys a highly profitable monopoly ferrying people and cars between Malta and Gozo. In daylight hours in the summer, ferries shuttle between Mġarr and Ċirkewwa once an hour; arrive at least 30 minutes before the advertised departure time. The less frequent **Hovermarine** service to Sliema is never full, so you can leave it to the last minute. Unlike most things in Gozo the services are punctual. The ticket office is on the quay next to two mobile canteens.

The road between Mġarr and Victoria is Gozo's main road, and the port is well signposted. At most times of the day **bus 25** greets the arriving ferries and goes only to Victoria. **Taxis** park on the quayside. The **heliport** is stuck in a field outside Għajnsielem 2 km west of Mġarr, down a lane by the St Cecilia Tower and opposite the Gozo Heritage. Unless you are being met, phone in advance for a taxi as none are ever on hand; the only alternative is to walk 500 m up to the main road and catch a bus into Victoria.

Tourist Information

The **NTOM** (*see* p. 291) has an office in the parade by the harbour car park. The Gleneagles Bar, 150 m up the hill from the harbour has an **international payphone**. In August and September take advantage of the van in the car park selling *bambinelli* (small sweet pears) available only in Sicily and Malta. There are excellent new **pontoon facilities** in Mġarr Harbour for up to 114 visiting boats (*see* Yachting pp. 45–8). Għajnsielem shares a *festa* on the last Sunday in August with Mġarr. Celebrations are in Għajnsielem's square in front of the huge mock-Gothic church to Our Lady of Loreto.

History

Mġarr is the closest shelter to Malta and a service linking the two islands dates back to the late 13th century. During the reign of the knights a communication of sorts was maintained despite the plundering attentions of pirates holed up in Comino. Until the advent of steam in the mid-19th century the islands relied upon the infrequent visits of sailing craft subject to the vagaries of the wind and strong currents of the channel. In June 1885 the first formal service was begun in a brand new 41 m-long iron steamer, *Gleneagles*, and with it came the beginning of the end of Gozo's isolationist ways. The jetty and breakwater was extended in the 1930s and again in 1970 to its present protective size.

Fort Chambrey, high above the harbour on the blue-clay Tafal Cliffs, was originally planned as far back as the mid-17th century as a mini-Valletta. In the 18th century when the project resurfaced, the knights finally accepted Gozo's need for somewhere more secure than the citadel. But the Order was by now in moral and financial decline and the fort proved to be its last major defence project. The original plan was scaled down by the prolific builder, Grand Master de Vilhena, but he was still forced to seek private funding.

Retired Admiral Jaques de Chambrey, a wealthy and disgruntled seadog fed up with the cancerous disintegration of the Order he had joined aged 13 as a page, offered to fund the new fortress town himself and so became the governor of Gozo. Work began in 1749 and was completed in 1761, but few Gozitans were willing to buy plots of land as the threat of the Barbary corsairs no longer existed. Since then, apart from a brief and spirited defence against the French on 10 June 1798, Fort Chambrey has had a chequered and miserable life: first as an unpopular British garrison post, then as a mental institution and, imminently, as a tourist village. All but the outer structure is closed to the public.

Mġarr Harbour is an interesting microcosm of local life. In 1992 the government lassoed the fishermen's *luzzus* and yachts and coralled them into order. Locally, unmitigated disaster was predicted as no Gozitan, least of all a fisherman, was going to be told where to moor. Moreover, they predicted, the harbour's unique charm would be gone forever. Fortunately, the harbingers of doom have been proved wrong: Gozitans and yachtsmen have taken to the new pontoon facilities and the harbour has lost none of its quirky charm.

The Gozo Heritage, Ghajnsielem, © 551475, *Mon–Sat 1000–1630, Adm. Lm1.50*, is an excellent thematic walk—in five languages—through Gozitan history. The tour starts with neolithic man and wanders colourfully through more than 5,000 years of local history, aided by cleverly designed audio-visual techniques and static sets on themes including the legend of Calypso, the Romans, Dragut Rais, World War II and a contemporary harbour scene—all well worth seeing. There is a bar and a good souvenir shop.

Where to Stay

Terminus hotels can invoke grimy nightmares; not so with either of Mġarr's. The **L-Imġarr Hotel★★★★** (luxury), © 560455, is Gozo's recently opened (1992) second 5-star hotel, a terracotta-coloured Moorish confection overlooking the harbour. Great effort has been expended and it's big on creature comforts, with huge rooms and bathrooms and mountains of marble, but very short on style: this could be a plush Holiday Inn in Little Rock, Arkansas. The awful open-air disco next door—not the hotel's—is a major detraction. Quieter, and 250 m away, is the immodestly named **Grand** (Class III), 56 St Anthony Street, © 556183, with six rooms. This is probably the best guest house in Gozo, a friendly homespun place with a welcoming bar and restaurant. (There are plans to floor the Grand, so check before turning up.)

Bars and Eating Out

Almost as famous as Calypso herself is Tony, the proprietor of the **Gleneagles Bar**, also known as 'Tony's', 150 m up the hill from the harbour. Everyone meets here. The drinks are generous, the decor is 'eclectic fishermen' with old lobster pots and taxidermed fish, and the balcony overlooking the harbour is a perfect *tal-barrakka* or look-out. Only fearless swimmers should ask Tony for the photos he keeps behind the bar of the 7-m Great White shark caught in local waters. His over-worked brother Sammy runs the restaurant called **Kċina tal-Barrakka**, but known to all as **Sammy's** (moderate), underneath Tony's at the waterfront, © 556543. The menu consists of whatever the fishermen hauled in that day and a few staple items such as pastas and steak. Tables are shoe-horned in place resulting in Gozitan service, but more often than not the food is excellent—try the king prawns. In summer dinner is *al fresco* under a bamboo canopy; in winter it's cosy inside and full of warm kitchen aromas. Highly recommended, book in advance. Right next door, a new restaurant called **Manoels** was about to open at the time of writing. It's owned by Noel from the Pink Panther in Marsalforn so will be reliable. As yet there is no telephone; call the Pink Panther for a reservation. The **Seaview** (moderate) Mġarr Harbour, © 553985, is next door to the police station and is another restaurant often referred to after its owner, Lino. He offers plain grilled fish and a few Italian meat dishes in more ordered surroundings, and has a surprisingly varied wine list. In summer you can sit outside on the balcony and wolf down local garlic bread. Booking is advisable.

Qala

Not a lot goes on in Qala, but there are two places to swim nearby. It's Gozo's most eastern settlement, with 1,300 inhabitants. The winds, especially the northeastern *gregale*, whip across the headland of Qala Point and the exposed village. The knights built many windmills, a couple of which remain in use. Nowhere is further from the citadel than Qala, and as befits what must have been a desolate part of the island many legends are woven into the village's history.

By **car** the easiest way to get there is to take the road north out of Mġarr or follow the signposts from Xewkija. St Joseph's *festa* is on the 1st Sunday in August.

Kerrew the Hermit

One of the oldest legends involves the trials of a hermit, Kerrew, and the part-13th-century little **chapel of the Immaculate Conception**. Kerrew was an unassuming and religious chap from Mosta who, like most hermits, lived in a cave. When a jealous prank was devised to induce him to break his holy ways, he fled from the doomed village. Arriving at the northern channel separating Gozo and Malta, he threw his moth-eaten old cloak onto the water and miraculously floated across to Hondoq ir-Rummien, Qala's sandy cove. Here, in a new cave on the Qala to Hondoq ir-Rummien road, he continued his holy ways until he died a venerated and peaceful death.

Tucked away just inside the front door of the chapel is a basement shrine to Kerrew. His bones lie in a pile on the small altar which, like the grotto in Mellieħa, is visited by families with unwell children. (*1.5 km east of Qala, and usually open during the day*.)

There are two entirely different **places to swim** on the southern channel coast below Qala. The easiest and therefore less rewarding is **Hondoq ir-Rummien**, signposted but none too clearly from Qala. A small sandy beach suitable for children, it faces the bays of Santa Marija and San Nicklaw on Comino. The sea runs up through the channel and is always clean, but it can become crowded at weekends with families of picnicking Gozitans.

The clear and sheltered waters off **Qala Point**, with its lone and now crumbling redoubt, are tantalizingly visible from Comino's northern headland. But it is hard to reach. There is a rudimentary footpath in an old quarry area, which peters out into a scramble ending west of the rock, Ġebel tal-Ħalfa, but it's an infinitely easier journey by boat. (On foot this is a destination for the day, not a dip.) The swimming and snorkelling in the inlets are superb; the seabed shelves away in sand and rocks. In any weather other than a strong *gregale* or *sirocco* Qala Point is a sheltered and often deserted place to drop anchor for the night.

Where to Stay and Eating Out

Not far from St Joseph Square is a five-room guest house, **St Joseph** (Class III), Immaculate Conception Street, © 556573. The owners, the Bartolo family, also run a small and very popular restaurant on the ground floor which is open for lunch and dinner.

Nadur

From Nadur ('look-out point') the knights were able to keep vigil over the Malta–Gozo channel at all times. The village, with its imposing houses, is the largest and wealthiest of Gozo's settlements after Victoria, with 3,500 inhabitants including many immigrants. (Come the *festa*, probably the island's best, half of the roof-top flags are American, Australian or Canadian.) The Nadurese themselves may have emigrated to seek their fortune, but invariably they return with at least a part of it. Those who remain farm the fertile fields and slopes which fall away to the northern beaches of Ramla, San Blas and Daħlet Qorrot, where once Grand Master Alof de Wignacourt came to hunt and now much of the island's fresh fruit grows.

Getting There and Tourist Information

The road out of Victoria to Xagħra winds its way up past the Kenuna Tower to the village of Nadur, a journey of 6 km. Alternatively, from Mġarr the village is only 2.5 km up the hill. Nadur's main *festa,* on the Sunday following 29 June, is not to be missed; it has sometimes been known to run on literally for days. A procession to commemorate St Coronatus is held on the 2nd Sunday in November.

It would be surprising if Nadur did not have a powerful and edifying church to complement its affluence. Folklore says the position of the original church was determined by a holyman's donkey laden with stones which would not budge from the site, and that the foundation stone was taken from those on the donkey's back. The present church, dedicated to **Saints Peter and Paul** and nicknamed *iż-Żewġ*, 'the twins', was begun in 1760 and designed by Guiseppe

Bonnici. The wide, robust and symmetrical building took 20 years to complete. The façade, and the dome with stained-glass windows were added in the mid-19th century (alterations are easy to detect by contrasting the colour of the ageing stones). The interior is splendidly ornate with extravagant marble inlaid floors, walls and pillars. Around the turn of the century the Maltese painter Lazzaro Pisani painted 150 canvases to be attached to the vaulted ceiling; the images and the stories told are the liveliest of many such ecclesiastical works on the islands. In the right-hand aisle is a twinned processional statue of the saints, made in 1881 in Marseille for the then huge sum of Lm50. Also on the right, in the transept is the macabre skeleton of **St Coronatus**, brought here intact along with a cup of his blood soon after he was martyred in AD 100. His skeleton is now, thankfully, clothed save for the peepholes.

Where to Swim

Side by side and to the north of Nadur lie three good bays: **Ramla**, **San Blas**, and **Daħlet Qorrot**. The most accessible and best for children is Ramla with its wide red-sand beach, but the most rewarding swimming is off the rocks of San Blas.

Ramla, meaning 'sandy beach', is Gozo's largest beach and it's here that the nymph Calypso and Odysseus are supposed to have played out their one-sided seven-year affair (*see* pp. 303–4). The beach can be approached from both Nadur and Xagħra, although the Nadur road is easiest. Both routes are steep—if you hoof it down the bamboo valley road around 1600 a taxi normally appears to save you making the long trek back up. The coarse sand, the colour of burnt almonds, the watersports concessions, three cafés and a stall selling everything from English newspapers to inflatable sharks have made it too touristy for many and at weekends it gets crowded. There is a strong undertow in rough weather, and scratch any notion of a picnic when the wind is from the north unless you like sand sandwiches. The very few campers who visit the Maltese islands pitch their tents on the bay's western ridge or beside the cafés.

San Blas bay is named after St Blaise. Along with the miniature fjord at Wied Għasri it affords the best bathing in Gozo, but access is poor. The road down the valley is narrow and steep, with less than half a dozen places to park at the end. From there it's a scramble down to the rocks and gravelly sand. Arrive early with a picnic, and like a seal secure yourself a rock for the day; because of San Blas's position and unsuitability for children, it is unlikely you will be disturbed. **Daħlet Qorrot**, to the east of San Blas is popular with the Gozitans. It's a small sandy beach devoid of honeypot concessions, and easier to get to than San Blas; an ideal place for a quick dip. There's plenty of parking space, and a cold drinks vendor.

Not with a Bang but a Whimper

An unknown Roman citizen built a large villa on the western edge of Ramla Bay (some of the finds are in the Gozo Archaeological Museum). In the 18th century the knights wished to make the beach as impregnable as possible; the remains of some of the interlinked defences are still clearly visible: a redoubt (a few courses of brickwork remain above the site of the Roman villa); and an undersea wall linked, on the east headland with a *fougasse*, a fiendishly clever device which resembles a deep and primitive mortar hewn out of living rock which was packed with explosives, shrapnel, rocks and anything else that would decimate the enemy. The Order's military engineers dreamed up the theory that an invader would enter the bay and ram into the unseen wall, thereby leaving the soldiers time to detonate the *fougasse* and attack the dazed enemy with cannon and musket fire from the redoubt. However, when the French landed in the bay in 1798, the only time the theory was put to the test, the soldiers fled and surrendered without firing a shot, and to quote the historian Dr Trump, 'so ended ingloriously the knights' rule of Gozo'.

Eating Out

Apart from the none-too-appetizing food at the **beach concessions** in Ramla Bay, Nadur has three **bars** in the village square and one of the best **bakers** in Gozo.

Comino (Kemmuna)

Comino takes its name from the cummin herb, one of the few plants that grow wild in the inhospitable topsoil of this basically uninhabitable island. For centuries Comino sat orphaned in the middle of the channel separating Malta and Gozo. Now it's a prized jewel, albeit sun-baked and barren; one of the few places left in the Mediterranean where there are no cars or roads and the land, including its airspace, is a wildlife sanctuary. The indigenous population remains in single figures, and with the exception of the residents of the one hotel all visitors and day-trippers depart before sunset, leaving only yachtsmen to linger for the night in the bays where 400 years ago Saracen pirates lay in wait.

Time your visit correctly—before 1030 or after 1600—and Comino offers the finest bathing, snorkelling and diving for hundreds of miles around. Time it incorrectly and parts of the island, especially the translucent waters of the Blue Lagoon, can be more unpleasant, noisy and populous than Bognor Regis or Coney Island on a hot August weekend.

Yet despite its daily invasions, Comino has retained that rarest of commodities—an unhurried temperament in a hurried world. It's a kindly and gentle island where even the sinister prickly pear seems to cast long defeated shadows.

Getting There

There are three different ways of getting to Comino from Malta, and one from Gozo. The schedules are for an extended summer period (April–Oct); no service exists when the Comino Hotel is shut (Nov–Mar). Anyone wishing to visit in winter should enquire of the fishermen in Mġarr Harbour, Gozo.

From Marfa, 1.5 km before Ċirkewwa, '**Gozo Charlie**' runs a service every day in summer on the hour every hour in the *Royal 1* for the 15-minute trip to the Blue Lagoon (Lm2 return). The **Comino Hotel** operates its own service from Ċirkewwa seven times a day, starting at 0730 with the last departure at 1830; and seven times a day from Mġarr Harbour from 0630–2300 (Lm1.50 return from either Ċirkewwa or Mġarr). The *Captain Morgan* fleet has day-trips from the Sliema Ferries: departing at 0945, arriving in the Blue Lagoon 1½ hours later and returning at 1530 for Sliema (Lm7.50 including a good buffet lunch).

However temptingly close the shores of Comino look from Gozo, do not attempt to swim across the 1.5-km channel; the strong currents are likely to wash your corpse up in Sicily.

Tourist Information

Comino's **police station** is unusually attractive—a cream-painted one-man outpost, set above a boathouse at the water's edge in Santa Marija Bay and proudly flying the Maltese flag. The only **telephones** are at the

Comino Hotel and Club Nautico and their use is at the owners' not always helpful discretion. The only **public convenience** is 50 m above the Blue Lagoon. There is no shade anywhere on the island, other than at Santa Marija Bay, so bring protective clothing and a bottle of water.

Festa

The island's small *festa* is organised by the parish priest from Qala. Attended by both Maltese and Gozitans, it takes place on the 4th Sunday in July and is dedicated to the **Sacred Heart of Jesus**.

History

A 3rd-century BC Phoenician amphora containing an adult skeleton and anointment oils has been uncovered in Santa Marija Bay. There is no logical explanation for the find (the Phoenicians were far too wise to colonize Comino) and it's now on display in the Gozo Archaeological Museum. Almost the only individual who is known to have survived a troglodytic life here was the 13th-century author and prophet **Abraham ben Samuel Abulafia**, otherwise known as 'the Spanish Messiah'. Selfless and harmlessly unhinged, his quest in life was to be at the vanguard of a new religion, uniting in one faith Christianity, Judaism and Islam. Abraham tried to convert Pope Nicholas III (who died of an apoplectic stroke the day Abraham espoused the idea), and had to flee Rome as his execution pyre was lit. The poor man eked out a subsistence on Comino until the end of his days. Here he wrote up his *Kabbala* philosophy and best-known work, the *Book of the Sign*.

Even after the arrival of the **knights** in 1530 the island was no more than a pirate's lair with corsairs laying in wait under the lee of the southwestern cliffs for ships crossing the channel. In 1618 Grand Master Alof de Wignacourt finally built St Mary's Tower, which linked a line of defence and communication from Valletta to the citadel in Victoria. Doomed efforts were made during the Order's reign to populate the island and Comino remained no more than another game preserve, where a trespasser 'armed with gun, dog, ferret or net' could be sentenced to three years as a galley slave.

The **British** legacy to Comino (and Filfla) was not a proud one. In 1800, after Nelson saw off the French, some 2,000 prisoners-of-war were interned on the island before being sent home. At the begining of World War I the British built an isolation hospital, now the village, in an effort to contain the many frightful diseases imported with the sick and dying servicemen of the Crimean campaign. During and after World War II their imperialistic habits continued, as the Royal Navy fired torpedos at it for practice; the waters were so clear that the unexploded torpedos could be retrieved from the seabed. Their final act in 1961, was to sell the island to a British development company who subsequently built both the Comino Hotel and Club Nautico. Their 150-year lease was surrendered back to the independent Malta government in the 1970s.

What to See

A tower on Comino to guard the troublesome channel was first mooted in the early 15th century when King Alphonso V of Aragon levied a local wine tax to pay for it, but having collected the money he squandered it elsewhere. Nearly two hundred years later, in 1618, Grand Master Alof de Wignacourt built **St Mary's Tower** to the design of Vittorio Cassar. As a partnership they had already beefed up the coastal defences with the Wignacourt Tower, and Forts St Lucien and St Thomas; St Mary's Tower was their final and most costly effort. Commanding the high ground on the southwestern cliffs, St Mary's is smaller but no less robust and fierce than its Maltese forerunners; Cassar had by now perfected his technique. The classical four square fort has a commanding presence of both channels from its raised podium and it housed a permanent garrison of 30 men.

Today it's a lookout post for the Armed Forces of Malta and a snoop around it to see its far-reaching rooftop views is at their friendly discretion. The crumbling escutcheon above the makeshift drawbridge is de Wignacourt's. The fort has struggled with the elements for nearly 400 years and is not in good condition, but when crossing the channel at night the powerful uplighting imposes its strength on the channel once more.

The old isolation hospital 300 m away, now the village, is only worth visiting if the **Comino grocery** is open; you won't find an older or more rural bar anywhere. Scattered around in front of what is daftly known as Liberty Square, is the detritus of bygone conflicts and ancient rusty machinery which no one has bothered to cart away.

Along the oleander-lined solitary dirt-track to **Santa Marija Bay** (named Congreve Street after a British governor who died in office in 1927 and was buried at sea off Filfla), is the island's **chapel**, dedicated to Our Lady's Return from Egypt. Comino falls under the parish of Għajnsielem on Gozo but has had its own chapel dating back to the 13th century. Its setting is more Greek than

Maltese; the small white-fronted building with its little picket gate, tamarisk trees, three hooped bells and snout-like water spouts was built not long after the fort. Mass is said at weekends, when the priest comes over from Qala.

Activities

Comino is justly famous for the colour of its water, bathing, diving and general aquatic recreations. With no cars the island, especially in spring, is good for lazy **walks**; the rugged landscape is tranquil but botanically dull. Temperatures can soar in summer, so bring a bottle of water and a hat.

The stretch of water between the leaf-sized beach on Comino and Cominotto, the **Blue Lagoon**, has a South Pacific quality; limpid crystal turquoise water over a white-sand seabed. In June 1993 the very core of the lagoon was roped off to the flotillas of small boats; you will be safe from the lunatic fringe of speedboat show-off here. The day-trippers' boats and other yachtsmen can still anchor *outside* the area. The best time to visit is before 1030 and after 1600. If you drop anchor for the night (the holding is good) swim at dawn and flee after breakfast.

Past the little hideaway caves of uninhabited Cominotto, and under the lee of the fort, the swimming is less frantic and the snorkelling more rewarding. The **caves** in the cliff face are worth a look, but can become fouled with boats' exhaust fumes. When the wind comes from any direction but the southwest the deep bay is perfect for **water-skiing**, especially in the late afternoon.

Round the headland from the Blue Lagoon and approximately 15 minutes walk away, are the **San Nicklaw** and **Santa Marija** beaches. The immediate foreshore and beach in front of the Comino Hotel in San Nicklaw Bay is **private** and the management guard their unique (for Malta) territorial rights vociferously. Use of all the hotel's facilities for the day, such as the pool and the beach, are available to non-residents for an expensive Lm9 per person, excluding the ferry crossing but including a decent buffet lunch; © 529827–9 and book in advance. The beach by Club Nautico in Santa Marija Bay is not private. The swimming, providing a few underwater rocks and seaweed don't put you off, is excellent, and the tamarisk trees provide privacy and shade. It's a picnic beach and one of the best sand beaches in Malta, and not least because there aren't any water or food concessions. Also idiotic speedboat drivers rarely venture in. Even more secluded is **Smugglers Cove**, a small pleasant cove on the south channel. Head for the fort and walk downhill in a southeasterly direction in order to get there.

There are three good **diving** locations in Comino's waters. The southwestern tip of the island is called Ras I-Irqieqa, and the deep dive is sheer down to 40 m. The fast currents running through the channel keep the area well-stocked with fish. Among the easiest and most exciting dives are the cave dives off Ghiemieri, around the Santa Marija headland. A good dive for photographers, since the caves are full of fish as well as the occasional moray eel. The easiest dive in Comino is the slow relaxing plod along the sea floor and the reef off the west in between Għar Għana and the Blue Lagoon. The Comino Hotel has its own diving school.

Snorkellers should swim in pairs and take extra precautions with a marker buoy; all the dive and snorkelling areas are in the speedboats' line of fire.

Where to Stay

The Comino Hotel★★★★ (expensive) © 529827–9, closed Nov–Mar, encompasses what was two hotels: the Comino Hotel (San Nicklaw Bay) and the bungalow-style Club Nautico (Santa Marija Bay). Both were built during the bleak architectural period of the early 1960s with lashings of cheap cement and acres of aluminium windows. The present Swiss owners have done a commendable job with the old carcasses. The Comino Hotel has more than 90 rooms, unfortunately their decor is still locked in the regrettable 60s time capsule, but the Club Nautico has been very well modernized, air-conditioned and now comprises 45 suites in three grades set in a cleverly landscaped garden at the water's edge. It positively bristles with facilities, many of which are extremely expensive. There is a Club Med atmosphere but you are a captive; it's fine for young children but teenagers can 'go tropo'.

Between the two hotels there are no less than 10 sand tennis courts, three swimming pools, a windsurfing and diving school, a large children's play area, skiing off the private sandy beach as well as a private boat service to Malta and Gozo. Residents of both the hotel and Club Nautico can use each other's facilities. The management can be authoritarian at times but for a get-away-from-it-all destination it has few peers.

Trips to Ionian Sicily

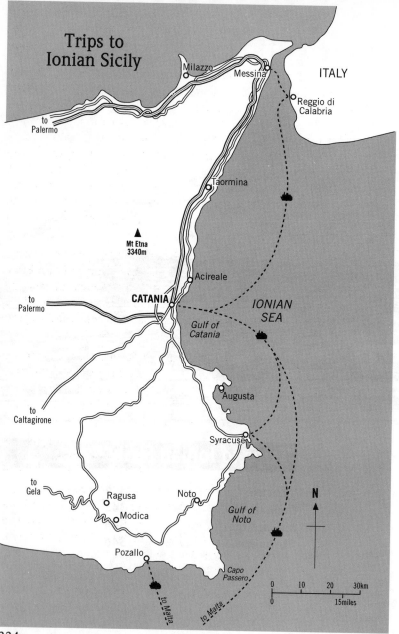

Trips to
Ionian Sicily

Milazzo

Messina

ITALY

Reggio di
Calabria

to
Palermo

Taormina

▲ Mt Etna
3340m

Acireale

CATANIA

to
Palermo

*IONIAN
SEA*

*Gulf of
Catania*

Augusta

to
Caltagirone

Syracuse

to
Gela

Ragusa

Noto

Modica

*Gulf of
Noto*

N

Pozzallo

*Capo
Passero*

to Malta

to Malta

0   10   20   30km

0   15miles

*'Like Sicily extremely—a good on-the-brink feeling—
one hop and you're out of Europe: nice, that.'*

D.H. Lawrence, 1920.

Sicily is the largest island in the Mediterranean; beautiful, stirring, mysterious and crammed to the very peak of Mount Etna with history and myth. Malta once formed a part of the Sicilian landmass from which it is now separated— Grand Harbour to Capo Passero—by a comparatively shallow 93-km channel, only 90 minutes by boat. The Sicilians and the Maltese share an Arabic sense of fatalism and solemnity; the cultural, topographical, and anthropological similarities are easy to discern. That said, when you visit you will find an entirely different country. Sicily is not really like anywhere else. An island surrounded by three seas—Ionian, Tyrrhenian and Mediterranean—and set in between the two republics of Italy and Malta, it has a character quite different from that of mainland Italy.

Along the Ionian coast of Sicily are the superb Greek and Roman archaeological treasures of **Syracuse**, the menacing anger of the active volcano **Mount Etna**, the idyllic beauty and romance (especially in spring) of **Taormina**, and the exciting market in the forever nervous city of **Catania**. The signposting of the sites, hotels and towns is faultless, a welcome change from Malta, enabling you to explore freely and without frustration.

The press has rightly publicized the horror of the *mafia's* tentacular grip and has begun the slow process of its deglamourization. For the tourist (even the most independent backpackers), the *mafia* poses very little threat; its enemies are specific and its attacks are not indiscriminate. The sun set 35 years ago on the days of coach hi-jacks in the island's central plains. Except in Catania, you won't feel the chill of its shadowy cloak.

Getting There and Around

The **Virtu Ferry Co.** runs a year-round service to **Pozzallo** (90 mins), **Catania** (3 hours) and **Licata** (2 hours 30 mins) in its 300-seat high-speed catamaran, SES *San Frangisk*. From June to Oct there are five sailings a week to Pozzallo and four to Catania. The Licata sevice (primarily for Sicilians visiting Malta, but ideal for people who wish to explore the wild west of Sicily), runs twice a week from July to Sept only.

Two different 1-day **excursions** via Pozzallo are organized by Virtu; one takes in Mount Etna and Taormina and the other Syracuse. Both depart at 0700 and arrive back in Malta at 2300 and cost Lm29 (inc. departure tax). Virtu has 1–3-**night breaks** in Taormina at the excellent Hotel Jolly Diodoro from Lm74, and a **sea-drive** arrangement with Europcar who will deliver and collect from the embarkation points.

SES *San Frangisk* leaves from Pinto Wharf in the Grand Harbour and all departures are subject to a punitively high 'departure' tax of Lm4 per person. The 'VIP upgrade' to first class at Lm8 is good value if you hate queuing; apart from more comfortable seats you are allowed to disembark first, and when the ferry is full and there are only two immigration officers on duty at 2300 it's worth every cent.

If you are travelling independently, **Catania** is the better disembarkation and embarkation point: not a lot happens in **Pozzallo** and the new quay is a nightmare to find. The local *carabinieri* are quite used to providing an escort for those who get seriously lost.

Malta–Pozzallo: Monday, Wednesday, Friday and Sunday, 0700 and 1930.

Malta–Catania: Tuesday, Friday, Saturday, and Sunday, 0530 and 1530.

Malta–Licata: Wednesday and Sunday, 0830 and 1130.

Timetables are always being tinkered with and there are a myriad of fares but up-to-date times and prices can obtained from Virtu Ferries Ltd, 3 Princess Elizabeth Terrace, Ta'Xbiex, © 318854, fax 314533.

If you hate the sea, **Air Malta** flies 16 times a week to Fontanarossa, Catania's airport and five times a week to Palermo in the high season, call © 234397 for times and fares.

Syracuse

The most beautiful and noble of the Greek cities

Livy (59 BC–AD 17)

The rubber stamp of tourism has yet to be printed on the wobbly faded terracotta streets of Syracuse. It's strange to think that this sleepy old southern Sicilian town divorced from violent headlines was the centre of the civilized world 2,000 years ago. The archaeological treasures found and lodged here rank among the finest in central Europe; the new **Museo Archeologico Paolo Orsi** (1988) and the **Neapolis Archaeological Park** alone are worth a special trip. The original centre of ancient Syracuse, the tethered island of **Ortygia**, is a maze of narrow and twisted streets where the baroque and medieval buildings are cleansed by the sea air and bleached by the diffused Mediterranean light. Here the less site-minded can eat well, sip an *espresso* or meditate. Plato walked the same streets 2,350 years ago; as did Archimedes, who was born here 130 years later.

History

The city of Syracuse was founded by **Corinthians** in 733 BC. Like Malta its destiny was foretold by its position and its protected harbour, **Porto Grande**, as well as by the sometimes calamitous underground twitches from Mount Etna 60 km to the north.

The nearby southern coastal town of Gela had a tyrannical leader called **Gelon**, who after a victory over the Carthaginians in 480 BC at Himera in the northwest of Sicily declared himself master of Syracuse. Gelon's influence extended over half of Sicily and the golden era of his adopted power-base began. Syracuse's rise eclipsed Athens and lasted until it fell—in spite of **General Archimedes'** ingenious weapons—to the Romans in the Second Punic War of 211 BC. In those 270 years Syracuse was governed both by wise rulers and by monstrous tyrants, during whose reigns the ancient monuments that can be seen today were built. **Hieron I** (478–466 BC) and the paranoid and black-hearted **Dionysius I** (405–367 BC) stand out as shining examples of tyrants. Dionysius I had a wastrel son and heir, **Dionysius II**, who in spite of being tutored by Plato, ended his days, according to Plutarch, 'loitering about the fish market, or sitting in a perfumer's shop drinking the diluted wine of the taverns, or squabbling with common women'. Only Syracuse's last two rulers, **Timoleon** and **Hieron II** (who died in 216 BC), displayed peaceful and democratic intentions.

Under the Roman governorship of **Verres**, 73–70 BC, a master of Roman-Maltese relations (see pp. 233–4), Syracuse reached its nadir; 90 years later **St Paul** stayed here for three days en route to Rome from Malta. Except for the **Byzantines** who briefly made Syracuse their capital from AD 663–8, it was largely ignored by the Arabs, normans, and other north European powers.

During the **Great Siege**, on 25 August 1565 the Spanish viceroy, Don Garcia, finally embarked his relief force of 8,000 men and 58 galleys from Syracuse to

Malta. When the long overdue force arrived in Malta on 7 September Grand Master de la Valette had all but claimed victory over the Turks.

The earthquake of 1693 wiped out the town **Noto Antico** and destroyed much of the city. In so doing it provided a clean sheet for the embryonic Sicilian baroque. In 1865 the city once again became the provincial capital. **World War II** saw bomb damage inflicted by both sides. After the most recent **earthquake** of December 1990, many of the old buildings are being restored.

Tourist Information

The **AAST**, the tourist office, has a small office in the railway station; the main one is in via Maestranza 33, Ortygia. There are **APT Information Offices** in the archaeological park and opposite the catacombs of St John. All have free maps, and hotel and transport information, as well as details of festivals, the regular local puppet shows and cultural programmes.

The town of Syracuse is divided into five areas: the principal attractions are in **Tyche, Neapolis**, and **Ortygia. Achradina** is the commercial centre and in the suburb of **Epipolae** 8 km to the west are the remnants of **Euryalus Fort,** the last important Greek fortification in the Mediterranean. Further afield is the **River Cyane** with its banks of withering Egyptian papyrus.

The archaeological park is in **Neopolis** (*Adm. L2,000. Tues–Sun 0900–sunset. Keep your ticket until the last site*). The park comprises four very different sites. By the main entrance is the **Greek Theatre**, bigger than the theatres at both Delphi and Athens, and still in use today; plays and concerts are performed here biannually in even-numbered years from May to August, check with AAST. It was hewn out of the rock in the 5th century BC and was enlarged by Hieron II to accommodate an audience of 15,000. At the top of the auditorium is the Street of Tombs and an artificial *nymphaeum* of cascading waterfalls to clarify the actors' orations.

Further along the same path is the **Latomia del Paradiso**, Paradise Quarry, a warped misnomer in English, where Dionysius I kept 7,000 Athenian prisoners hacking away at the rocks for seven years to build Syracuse's fortifications, after the calamitous **Great Expedition**. (The so-called Great Expedition was Athens' bungled but heroic attempt to wrest control of Syracuse from Dionisius I, in 413 BC, with one of the most impressive fleets ever assembled.) Part of the quarry is a 23 m-high cave, called the **Ear of Dionysius** by the painter Caravaggio in the 16th century due to its shape. According to legend, the remarkable acoustics—still evident today—enabled Dionysius I to indulge his paranoid delusions by eavesdropping from the small hole at the top on the scheming whispers of his prisoners below. The neighbouring cavern, visible but closed for safety reasons, is the **Grotta dei Cordari** or 'ropemakers' cavern'. Until recently its damp air afforded ropemakers who worked here the constant moist temperature they needed to twist the hemp. Further along is the **altar of Hieron II** and the **Roman amphitheatre**, the entrance to both is almost hidden behind the tacky souvenir stalls, a café and an information office. Only the outline remains of the 199 m-long **altar of Hieron II** which consequently resembles an elongated football pitch. Built in the latter half of the 3rd century BC its sole purpose was the ritual and sacrificial slaughter of animals. (The historian Diordorus records that on one occasion 450 oxen were put to the knife between flaming pyres—to celebrate democracy.) A row of nine sarcophagi leads to the even more gory early 3rd century AD **Roman amphitheatre**. The huge 140 m by 119 m elliptical theatre assuaged the Romans' appetite for circus-style games of death. The arena itself is out of bounds, but stand amongst what would have been the cheap seats at the top and appreciate the sheer scale of it. By the expensive front ringside seats and under the centre of the *cavea* is the *vomitorium* or corridor through which the animals would enter the fray. At the end of a contest, spectators would crowd around the animal carcasses to drink the warm blood and eat the raw livers (an early holistic remedy?).

On the east of town in **Tyche** and visible from everywhere in Syracuse is the **Santurio della Madonnina delle Lacrime** looking like an immense concrete rocket. This bizarre structure houses a statue of the Madonna which apparently wept for five days in 1953. It has been fitfully constructed over the last two decades and is due to be opened sometime in 1993 by the Pope.

Opposite and subtly concealed in its own gardens is the famous **Museo Archeologico Paolo Orsi** (*L2,000. Tues–Sun 0900–1300 and 1530–1830; allow at least 2 hours*). Spectacular relics from the many archaeological sites in Sicily are displayed in three sections: from the prehistoric to the Roman/Greek eras up to early-Christian times. Among the almost too numerous exhibits are the dreamy, almost marshmallow soft, white marble statue *Venus Anadyomene* coming out of the sea with a playful dolphin at her ankles, another headless statue, suckling twin babies, an ornate Roman marble sarcophagus from the 4th century BC, and a collection of vases from Camarina and Gela.

A few hundred metres west along the via Teocrito and grouped together are the **basilica and catacombs of St John** (San Giovanni) and the crypt of **St Marcianus** (San Marziano). The basilica has been a ruin since the 1693 quake and is pleasantly overrun with flowers but you still need to go through it to reach the underground crypt where **St Paul** preached. Under Roman rule, Tyche was outside the Ortygia city limits and Roman law provided that all burials had to take place outside the city limits. Consequently, the catacombs are a vast Christian necropolis of more than 4,000 sq m, and not in the least bit spooky. (*L2,000. Closed Wed. Accompanied tours only, on the hour from 1000–1200 and 1600–1800.*)

Ortygia Island

Ortygia is tenuously joined to the mainland by two very short bridges, but it always appears eager to drift out to sea. The main bridge opens onto the **Piazza Pancali** and the sparse remains of the temple of Apollo (6th century BC), the oldest Doric temple in Sicily. The **morning market** stretches off the piazza and down the via Trento to the sea.

Even if you have feasted on (or drowned under) baroque churches in Malta, do not miss the different Sicilian-baroque buildings in the **Piazza del Duomo**. The Greeks built a temple to the goddess Athena on the present site of the **Duomo**—the Doric columns still form part of it—and the whole edifice nearly tumbled down in the 1693 earthquake which destroyed the cathedral in Mdina, Malta. The entire contents, including the huge doors of gold and ivory, were thieved by the governor, Verres in 73–70 BC. The ornate baroque façade is magnificent and contrasts with the austere and voluminous interior. But there is much to see inside, including early Renaissance statues by Antonello Gagini (the most notable being the Madonna of the Snows, 1512). Also, peer into the interesting three chapels in the right-hand aisle. The **Palazzo Beneventano del Bosco** (1779), in an open courtyard, has an imposing staircase rising up from the ground; it became the local headquarters of the knights of Malta as the Order was disintegrating.

South of the Piazza del Duomo, 200 m away, is the **Palazzo Bellomo**, the finest of the buildings to be temporarily shut as a result of the 1990 earthquake. Constructed around a small courtyard, this hybrid building houses the regional art museum. Within its 13–15th-century walls are the world-famous 15th-century *Annunciation* by Antonello da Messina and one of Caravaggio's last paintings, *The Burial of St Lucia*, Syracuse's patron saint. He painted it in

1608–9 just after his escape from Malta and two years before his death (*see* pp. 101–2). This darkly evocative depiction of the saint's burial shows Caravaggio's talents at their zenith. The museum's director promises to reopen in September 1993. Take that with a pinch of Sicilian salt.

A Love Story

A few hundred metres away from the Palazzo Bellomo at the water's edge is the **Fonte Arethusa**, guardian to a delightful myth and love story.

In ancient Greece, the nymph **Arethusa** swam in the clear flowing waters of the river Alpheus. She was so beautiful that Alpheus, the river god, fell hopelessly in love. Artemis, the guardian of all virgins, rudely interrupted Alpheus's advances just as Arethusa was about to succumb to his charms. Artemis commanded the earth to open and the nymph vanished into the ground. Swiftly, she crossed underneath the Ionian Sea and metamorphosed as a fresh-water spring, the **Fonte Arethusa**, in Ortygia. A distraught (and possibly frustrated) Alpheus disappeared under the Ionian Sea and joined her, and here their waters have mingled ever since. Today comical ducks play among the papyrus in the lovers' water and the fountain in Ortygia's **Piazza Archimede** romances Arethusa's transformation into the spring.

Below the Fonte Arethusa, the **Foro Italico** (where the car ferry for Malta embarks) was, according to Cicero, Governor Verres's 'den of iniquity'. Today, lined with a handful of cafés, trinket and nut vendors, it's the stage for the evening *passeggiata*.

If you want to **swim**, the **Fontane Bianchi** 15 km to the south has a long sandy beach. Further away and through Cassibile, a one-horse village where the Italians surrendered to the Allies on 3 September 1943, is **Noto Marina** and an even longer stretch of gently shelving hot sand. Don't swim north of Syracuse, the foul pollution of Augusta finished off those beaches ages ago.

Where to Stay and Eating Out

The **Jolly Hotel**★★★★(expensive), Corso Gelone 45, ℂ (0931) 64744, is modern, central and dull. **Villa Politi**★★★ (moderate), via Politi 2, ℂ (0931) 412121, is not so central (Tyche) but has a pool; Churchill stayed there. The **Grand Bretagne**★ (inexpensive), via Savoia 21,

© (0931) 68765, is the only hotel open in Ortygia and is run by a gruff individual. The much friendlier **Grand Hotel** was another victim of the earthquake and is temporarily shut.

You will eat well at **Al Gambero Rosso**, **Archimede** and **Arlecchino**, all in **Ortygia** (all inexpensive–moderate). Overlooking the sea within **Tyche**, the imposingly named **Jonico-a Ruttae Ciauli** (moderate), © (0931) 65540, conjures up Sicilian specialities and good pasta dishes on a terrace somewhat less imposing than the restaurant's name. The **La Tavernetta del Porto** (inexpensive), © (0931) 842494, in the tiny fishing harbour of **Portopalo**, 55 km away on the southernmost tip of Sicily, is definitely worth the trip for Sicilian cooking at its simplest and very best.

Catania

Etna looked like a toy, but a rather dangerous one.

Lawrence Durrell, *Sicilian Carousel*, 1977

Mount Etna is a consistently violent and psychopathic neighbour. Yet, paradoxically, the Catanese put up with it and in their own way mock it. Most aspects of life in this city of more than 400,000 inhabitants openly flout the powerful superiority of the volcano. Life is loud and never pauses, lest it be caught unawares—hence the horns, the market catcalls, the traffic, the capricious humour, the *mafia* and its Machiavellian manoeuvring. Why conform, the people here seem to say, when you are sitting on a lit fuse?

History

Catanese history is one long **horror story** beginning with Syracusan tyrants and followed by death and destruction from a succession of pirates, Normans, Angevins, plagues and volcanic eruptions. The most spectacular **eruption** began on 11 March 1669 in the Nicolisi area, when the earth opened up into a 15 km-wide fissure. Molten lava flowed through and past the city and out into the sea continiously for eight weeks. Charles II, with the magnanimity of a caring monarch, exempted what was left of the barbecued city from taxes for 10 years. In 1693, their tax holiday having barely ended, a Mount Etna-inspired earthquake wiped out two-thirds of the remaining inhabitants. In the 20th century alone there have been six major eruptions; one in 1950 lasted 380 days and produced in excess of 800 million cubic metres of lava. The last major eruption was in 1992.

The main **APT Information Office** in Largo Paisello 5 is too complicated to find; go to the smaller one at the train station. **Fontanarossa**
airport has an office providing free maps, cultural information and transport timetables.

Catania has been rebuilt many times. Today, the city may look like it's
constantly being repaired, but it's not: it's just in a permanent state of propped-
up-ness. Much of what you see was built after 1693, when a widely spaced
grid-plan was laid over the network of narrow streets; a lot of what remains
from before 1693 is lava-encrusted.

For sightseeing, the **Piazza del Duomo** with the city's totemic emblem, a
fopishly grinning elephant carved from lava, is a handy reference point—everything worth seeing is within walking distance.

Unlike the more exuberant gold of Maltese stone, the greyish tones of the
city's volcanic stone tends to suffuse the richly ornamental baroque style of
Giovanni Vaccarini's post-1693 buildings. Parts of the **Duomo** have
survived since it was first built in the 11th century, but the exaggerated façade
is mainly Vaccarini's handiwork. Inside, the fine baroque chapel of the city's
patron Saint Agatha is to the right of the choir. (She is also one of Malta's
patron saints.) In the sacristy is a good snapshot painting of the 1669 disaster
completed only eight years after the event. Catania's favourite son, **Vincenzo
Bellini**, is buried next to the second pillar on the right which has a musical
inscription from his opera *La Sonnambula*. Perhaps an even greater accolade is
the naming of a pasta dish *spaghetti Norma* (a Sicilian speciality), after his
opera, *Norma*.

The **Porta Uzeda** leads down a few steps from the Duomo to the most
enthralling open-air **market** in the Mediterranean. Stall-holders with hoarse
voices, who sound as if they have gargled *grappa* and gravel all night, sell every
kind of thing that's edible. The crowded market with its aromas and incredible
displays of meat and fish—locally caught 165-kg tuna with flesh redder than
steak, writhing displays of seafood, lambs sheared in half from head to tail—is
not for vegetarians or the faint-hearted. See it, smell it and live it, but hang on
tightly to your wallet.

Further south, the entire area of land around the forebidding smut-grey 13th-
century **Castello Ursino**, once Frederick II's cliff-edge fortress, was
reclaimed by lava flows after the eruption of 1669. The Museo Civico inside

the fortress is closed and no one expects it to reopen for years, despite promises to the contrary.

The two **Roman** sites are the theatre (400 m west of the Duomo in via Vittorio Emanuele II) and Amphitheatre (650 m north along via Etnea) both built from blocks of the ubiquitous lava. The latter, which is railed off, seated roughly 16,000 and lies unexcavated under many buildings, but you can see its impressive shape from the steps of the church. The theatre and the *odeon* next door are also 2nd century AD and are accessible (*0900–sunset and free*).

Vincenzo Bellini died in 1835 at the early age of 34; his birthplace is now the little **Museo Bellini** (*300 m along via Vittorio Emanuele II, open Mon–Fri 0830–1330, Sun 0830–1230. Adm. free*). Crammed with memorabilia, including original scores, models of theatrical sets, his piano, and macabre death mask and coffin, it's worth looking in on. The acoustic properties of the ornate neo-classical **Teatro Bellini** (1890) are said to be the third-finest in the world. (*Back across the via Etnea in Piazza Bellini, open on Mondays only.*)

Mount Etna

Practical Information

From the centre of Catania, the first few hundred metres of the via Etna are one-way, against you. Ask permission from the policeman in the Piazza del Duomo with all the effusiveness your stammering Italian can muster and he will invariably let you proceed; it saves an age. Follow the signposts for Nicolosi (700 m) and the **Museo Vulcanologico Etneo**. Nicolosi Nord, the 'base camp' (1910 m) and **Silvestri Craters** are signposted. An easier (but longer) way is to take the road to Zafferana past Acireale, heading north on the motorway to **Taormina**, from where the 'base camp' is flagged. From the Silvestri Craters you can take a cable car (in winter you can ski down), then a jeep and finally a guide to as close to the central crater at the summit as safety permits, (approx. 3200 m). The trip to the summit is L37,000 per person.

A couple of **restaurants** and an information and **tourist office** are at the 'base camp'. *Bring stout shoes and a sweater; it can be very windy at the summit and the temperature falls 2° F every 325 m above sea level.*

The Volcano

Etna spat out a mouthful of hot coals and then dribbled a small string of blazing diamonds down her chin.

Lawrence Durrell, *Sicilian Carousel*, 1977

Look at any map and you will see how Mount Etna, like an industrial-size burbling pimple, dominates the face of Sicily. The volcano was originally formed by a massive undersea eruption that forced its way up from the seabed. It now has three craters and is the largest volcano in Europe, and one of the most active in the world: more than 135 fatal eruptions have been recorded.

From the summit the views are extraordinary (on rare occasions you can see Malta); the odours are sulphurous and the winds fierce, although the land-scape of once-vicious igneous lava is now benignly lunar. At the summit the strangest sensation of all comes through your feet: this is, a tap into the earth's core, or even possibly one of the brimstone gateways to hell. Mount Etna's satanic power is hypnotic. Ignore your heart's quickened pace and the conse-quences that an immodest burp from below might have, the ascent should not be missed.

Mount Etna has always held a powerful fascination. The **Greeks** believed its quakes were the attempts of the giant **Enceladus** to free himself from his prison underneath Sicily. **Vulcan**, the lame son of **Jupiter** and armourer of the gods, is believed to have had one of his forges in the mouth of crater, with branch offices in the **Aeolian Islands** off Sicily's north coast. Legend also tells how the mighty cyclops **Polifemus**, having been blinded by **Odysseus** (who paused here while on his way home from seven years on Calypso's Isle, **Gozo**), heaved three of Mount Etna's immense rocks at Odysseus's fleeing ships. Not surprisingly, he missed and thereby created the three rocks of Aci Trezza. The demented 5th-century BC philosopher **Empedocles** came from Agricento on the south coast. He was so convinced he was a god that he threw himself into the crater, in the belief he would float on the gases and prove his divinity. The only traces of him that remained were his golden sandals, melting on Mount Etna's lip.

With true Sicilian perversity, the volcano has always symbolized Catania's inherent contradictions: it threatens the city below yet provides for it. The citrus fruits and vineyards of olives and grapes that grow in the fertile volcanic ash of the vast lower slopes are the finest to be found anywhere in the central Mediterranean. Patrick Brydone's words of 1773 still hold true: 'If

Aetna resembles hell within, it may with equal justice be said to resemble paradise without.'

Where to Stay and Eating Out

The **Jolly Hotel★★★★**(expensive), Piazza Trento 13, © (095) 316933, is the most reliable but is in the north of the town. The **Central Palace★★★**(moderate), via Etnea 218, © (095) 325344, is central but noiser. Those with a strong constitution should try eating at the lively **Trattoria Tipoli** (inexpensive) right in the heart of the heaving market; lunch only. A good *tavola calda* in via Etnea is **Al Caprice** (inexpensive). **La Siciliana** (expensive), via Marco Polo 52, © (095) 376400, is a fine local restaurant with a cool garden. But the best place to eat lunch or dinner is 4 km north in Ognina—the **Costa Azzura** (expensive), via De Cristofaro 4, © (095) 494920, overlooks a small port and serves excellent fish; it's very *mafiosi*.

Taormina

> *Taormina should be let out by the Italian government, as an open-air asylum for Anglo-Saxons who live their lives according to the adage 'time is money'. It would cure their restless efficiency. Nobody ever looks at a clock in Taormina.*

Walter Starkie, *The Waveless Plain*, 1938

Without its views, Taormina might just have slipped by unnoticed like so many other hill-top Sicilian villages. Even the hundred or more hotels that share the craggy 213 m-high lair in the Peloritani Mountains with the locals have not diminished the almost too-lyrical beauty of the place.

Taormina is touristy and only *mafia* scares can empty the place (as they did in 1992). In August it can be an Anglo-Saxon jungle, but in the mellow golden light of late September, or the crisper days of April–May, when the bougainvillea tumbles like a purple waterfall, it becomes a moocher's nirvana.

Getting Around

Taormina is 52 km equidistant from Catania in the south and Messina in the north. Forget the car. Most of the town is pedestrianized and you are better off driving up and parking wherever you can on the outskirts.

Alternatively, the **cable car**, which like most things Sicilian has been undergoing repairs for the last couple of years, is due to recommence its almost continuous service from Mazzaro to town. The **bus stop** is in via Luigi Pirandello. **Taxis** are in the Piazza Vittorio Emanuele and the Piazza del Duomo.

Tourist Information

The **AAST tourist office** is in the Palazzo Corvaja at the junction of Corso Umberto and Piazza Vittorio Emanuele. Half-heartedly multilingual but very helpful, they can tell you anything from where to rent a *vespa* to an how to track down an hotel room in August. The free large-scale map is excellent.

History

Nearby Naxos was the first Greek colony in Sicily and foolishly allied itself to Athens during the Great Expedition, which forced the ill-tempered and conquering Syracusan **Dionysius I** to reduce it to rubble in 403 BC. Led by Andomachus in 358 BC the few survivors settled in Tauromenium on Monte Tauro, and since then Taormina's fortunes have been tied to those of **Syracuse**. By 215 BC it was a *civitas foedecata*, a **Roman** federated city, and when Syracuse fell it became capital of Byzantine Sicily until the Saracen **Arabs** sacked it in AD 902. The town was slowly rebuilt and by the 11th century it flourished again under the **Norman, Count Roger**; many of the buildings bear the Norman hallmark. During the **Sicilian Vespers** (1282), the town sided luckily with the victorious Aragonese. In 1410 the Sicilian parliament sat in the Palazzo Corvaja to elect a successor to the extinct line of Aragon. The town remained **Spanish**—except for a brief French interlude when Spain was short of funds—until the 1860 arrival of the **Bourbons**.

It remained undiscovered as a tourist destination until the 19th century. A German, Baron von Gloeden, put it on the map when he returned to the chilly climes of northern Europe with an armful of sepia photographs depicting hot-blooded young Sicilian men and boys demurely naked save for laurels of ivy (you can buy reproduction postcards anywhere in town.) While not quite becoming an early Club 18–30, it was firmly positioned on the itinerary of the Grand Tour where it has remained ever since. Field Marshall Kesselring had the unfortunate good taste to turn The San Domenico Palace into his headquarters during **World War II**, resulting in Allied bomb damage both for itself and the town in July 1943.

What to See

Taormina is the archetypal picture-postcard subject and the town itself is the main attraction. Whether you look down from the old Saracen fort beneath Castelmola or up from the beach at Giardini-Naxos, its pedestrianized streets, alleys and piazzas have a self-conscious charm; Taormina is just meant to be admired.

No wonder that the ancient Greeks ruled the civilised world, their eye for a site was faultless. From the top of the *cavea* of the **Greek Theatre** (*0900–half an hour before sunset. Adm. L2,00*), you can frame the smouldering spire of Mount Etna, the Ionian Sea, terracotta roofs, the mountains and valley through a camera's viewfinder. The position of the theatre is Greek, but the fabric is Roman. It was built in the middle of the 3rd century BC by **Hieron II** and like all Greek theatres it functioned as their omnipotent media forum. Partly by hewing out the rock the **Romans** enlarged it to its present size to cater for their more gladiatorial tastes in the 2nd century AD. Their changes were drastic, the new arched openings and columns obscuring much of the natural view, with the obvious intention of keeping the audience focused on the slaughter at hand. The semicircular theatre, the second largest in Sicily after the one in Syracuse, is 109 m in diameter. It held approximately 6,000 and is still used today during the summer arts festival. For romantics, the best time to go is just before sunset, otherwise go at 0900 for the morning light. Like many other museums along this coast the small museum here is 'closed for restoration'. Don't hold your breath.

The main *corso*, **Umberto I**, begins at Porta Messina and ends at the Porta Catania. Everything of note is on it or off it. Inside the Porta Messina, by the old forum, the Piazza Vittorio Emanuele, is the **Palazzo Corvaja** (1372), a handsome but somewhat frigid Norman building with lancet windows and inlays of black lava and white stone. The public rooms off the courtyard staircase house local art exhibitions. The Sicilian parliament met here in 1410 and now, more prosaically, the tourist office occupies part of the ground floor. Next door are the submerged, dull remains of a 2nd century AD Roman *odeon* which crops out through the floor of the church of Santa Caterina. Further up the hill (via Cappuccini and via Fontana Vecchia) is the old villa where **D.H. Lawrence** lived from 1920–23, now a private house marked by a plaque and a pair of cypress trees.

The evening fun is played out in the large open terrace of the **Piazza Aprile IX**. On a clear windy day look up above the skull-and-crossbones escutcheon over the main door of the 17th-century church of San Guiseppe at the clouds racing through the sky, and the backdrop of Castelmola appears to move while all around is stationary. It seems to confirm the sense of time suspended. If the night-time views don't bowl you over, you can have a cartoon drawn for L10,000 or sit in the Café Wunderbar under the watchful eye of the **Torre dell'orologico**, the 12th-century clock tower built above the Porta di Mezzo, and people-watch during the evening *passeggiata*.

Through the Porta di Mezzo lies the medieval part of town. Down to the left is the old monastery, now the **San Domenico Palace** hotel. The many nook-like piazzas are sheltered, colourful in spring and cool in summer. The **Piazza del Duomo** is typically discreet and shares its insignificant piazza with cafés and a spluttering early 17th-century fountain, the steps of which are still a rendezvous. The Duomo (dating from the 13th century, but completely remodelled during the Renaissance), is restrained and unexciting save for its lofty wooden beamed ceiling and a 15th-century alabaster statue of the Madonna by Montinini. Before you reach the Porta Catania with its Aragonese coat of arms is, on the left, the **Palace of the Dukes of St Stephen** (1330).

The 2nd floor mullioned lancet windows with intarsia decorations, and the lava and limestone frieze above are the best remnants of the Norman period. (*Open 0900–1300 and 1600–1900 for exhibitions. Adm. free.*)

The **Public Gardens**, laid out at the turn of the century by an eccentric Englishwoman, are worth a look. Among the follies is an extraordinarily bizarre monument: a reconditioned *mezzo d'assolto della marina* or two-man submarine with a 300-kg warhead of the type used by the Italian navy during the siege of Malta in World War II. Somehow, it doesn't blend in with the trees and noisy *ciccadas*. For would-be mountaineers there is a long-stepped climb (allow 35 mins) from the via Circovallazione up to **Sancturio Madonna della Rocco**. A further 200 steps leads up to the remains of the seemingly impenetrable Saracen fort or *castello*. Higher still is **Castelmola**, a real Gilbert and Sullivan village. In 1912 a donkey ride (return) to Castelmola was the equivalent of 6p or 9 cents, today you can take a bus or a taxi from Taormina. Lick an ice cream from the Café San Giorgio as you digest the stupendous panorama.

Beaches

The cable car—when it works—goes down to the beaches of **Mazzaro** and **Isola Bella**, separated by the headland of Capo Sant'Andrea. Five kilometres further afield is the long sandy beach of **Naxos**, with a younger crowd.

There are over one hundred hotels and *pensiones* in and around Taormina (*dialling code © 0942*). The **San Domenico Palace★★★★★** (expensive), Piazza San Domenico 5, © 23701), is very, very special and stupendously expensive. The **Jolly Diodoro★★★** (expensive), via Bagnoli Croce 75, © 23312, enjoys a good position beneath it. An excellent value hotel with sound plumbing and views is the **Pensione Svizzera★** (inexpensive), via Pirandello 26, © 23790.

Among the restaurants that lurk everywhere are the expensive but good old-timer **La Giara**, © 23360, the **Ristorante Luraleo** (moderate), © 24279, with a secluded terrace and fresh fish. The **Ristorante La Venere** (moderate), © 23367, by the Porta Catania is pleasant for lunches but if it is views you crave **Il Maniero**, © 28139, at the top of Castelmola is worth a visit. Cafés and *gelaterias* are everywhere; take your pick.

Languages are the pedigree of nations.

Samuel Johnson (1709–84)

If Samuel Johnson is to be believed, the Maltese nation is a true hybrid, a Heinz 57 country. The language of the Maltese islands, Malti, is a unique Semitic tongue woven from the linguistic threads of those who came in peace or in war; the Phoenicians, Arabs, Italians, Spanish, French, and latterly the English have all corrupted and influenced spoken Malti.

To the visitor, it's particularly hard on the ear—like Turkish but without the chewy, gravelly noises. And it becomes even more incomprehensible when spoken at speed, as it often is—then it's like the koranic incantations of a fanatical *mullah*. You will notice above all else, that the Maltese speak like they drive—loudly, and with windmilling arms and hands, imbuing everyday life with a true sense of Latin drama.

Getting around the islands is not a problem. The Maltese are talented linguists, for until this century Malti was purely a spoken language; the script with its modified Roman characters only evolved early this century. Italian was the official language of Malta until 1934, when it was replaced by English. Nearly all Maltese speak English, and many speak Italian. Menus are all in English, but road signs are for the most part in Malti. Problems usually only occur with bold attempts at pronunciation, which follow rules few people will be familiar with.

Ground Rules

Dispel any notion of trying to learn the language, it's nigh on impossible. Almost every word conjugates byzantinely *and* has a gender; by comparison English is spectacularly simple. As an indication of the gurning skills required to master its complexities, try saying something as prosaic as 'What's the time, please?'—*Xhin hu jekk joghġbok?*—or the even more tongue-twisting, 'Which way to?'—*Minn liema triq ngħaddi għal?* The acquisition of a basic

Language

vocabulary and a few correctly pronounced place names is a solid accomplishment, and one the Maltese will appreciate.

The **alphabet** consists of 29 characters, 24 consonants and 5 vowels:

a, b, ċ, d, e, f, ġ, g, h, ħ, i, j, k, l, m, n, għ, o, p, q, r, s, t, u, v, w, x, ż, z.

Of the 24 consonants, 14 sound similar to English; the other 10 are trickier and are therefore keys to correct **pronunciation**.

ċ—as in 'ch' e.g. chapel, ġ is softer than an undotted g; j is soft like a 'y', e.g. Għajn (well) 'ein'; ħ is spoken openly as in 'house' as opposed to 'hour' which is how the unlined 'h' is used; għ is a single letter and is usually silent. It has tonal variations when followed by an i or u and if it's found at the end of a word. The safest bet is a silent 'ahr', e.g. Għar (cave) is pronounced 'ahrr'; q is usually a clipped 'k' except for when followed by a vowel when it's silent, e.g. Qala is 'arla'; s is hissed, sssnake-like; x is a key letter. As in Chinese it's pronounced 'sch', e.g. Xlendi is 'Schlendi'; ż is soft while the unaccented z is a germanic 'tz': try Żejtun.

Il or *I* (or any of its other numerous manifestations) precedes many words and means simply, 'the'.

Basic Vocabulary

Notice the French and Italian phonetic influences, especially on 'thank you' and 'good night'.

English	Malti	Pronunciation	English	Malti	Pronunciation
Yes	*iva*	eva	Yesterday	*il-bierah*	ill-bee-rahh
No	*le*	leh	Street	*triq*	trik
Please	*jekk*	eekk-y-ojbok	Square	*misrah*	miss-rahh
	joghġbok		Where is?	*fejn hu*	fey-noo
Thank you	*grazzi*	grat-see	Bread	*hobż*	hobsz
Goodbye or	*sahha*	sah-har	Wine	*imbid*	im-biit
ciao			Water	*ilma*	as written
Excuse me	*skuzzi*	skoossi	Ice	*silġ*	silch
How much?	*kemm*	kehm	Church	*knisja*	k-neesya
Good	*bonġu*	bon-jew	Cliff	*irdum*	ir-duum
Morning			Beach	*plajja/*	plai-ya/
Good Night	*bonswa*	bon-swa		*spjaġgdoja*	spe-ajja
Today	*illum*	ill-loom	Valley	*wied*	we-ed
Tomorrow	*għada*	ahrda	Harbour	*marsa*	marssa

Numbers

Zero	*xejn*	shayn	Four	*erbgħa*	airba
One	*wiehed*	weehehd	Five	*hamsa*	hum-sah
Two	*tnejn*	tn-ayn	Six	*sitta*	as written
Three	*tlieta*	tlee-tah	Seven	*sebgħa*	sehbah

English	Malti	Pronunciation	English	Malti	Pronunciation
Eight	*tmienja*	tmee-eyn-ya	**Fifty**	*ħamsin*	hamm-seen
Nine	*disgħa*	dissah	**Hundred**	*mija*	meeja
Ten	*għaxra*	ash-rah	**Thousand**	*elf*	as written
Twenty	*għoxrin*	osch-rin			

Place Names

Most of the villages and towns are pronounced as written, with the following exceptions:

Location	Pronunciation	Location	Pronunciation
Balzan	*Bal-tsan*	**Mġarr-ix-Xini**	*Imjarr-ish-sheeney*
Birżebbuġa	*Beer-zee-booja*	**Mnajdra**	*Im-nigh-dra*
Buġibba	*Buj-ibba*	**Mqabba**	*Im-abba*
Ċirkewwa	*Chir-kewwa*	**Msida**	*Im-seed-ah*
Dwejra	*Dweyrah*	**Nadur**	*Na-dour*
Ġgantija	*Jagan-teeya*	**Naxxar**	*Naschar*
Ghainsielem	*Ein-seey-lemm*	**Pieta**	*Pe-etah*
Għajn Tuffieha	*Ein-tofeeah*	**Qala**	*Ala*
Għarb	*Arb*	**Qawra**	*Owwra*
Gharghur	*Gargour*	**Qrendi**	*Rendi*
Ġnejna	*Je-nayna*	**Siġġiewi**	*Si-jee-wee*
Gudja	*Goodya*	**Ta'Ċenċ**	*Ta-chench*
Gzira	*Ge-zeera*	**Ta'Pinu**	*Ta-pee-noo*
Ħaġar Qim	*Hajar-eem*	**Tarxien**	*Tar-sheen*
Kerċem	*Ker-chem*	**Ta'Xbiex**	*Tash-beesh*
Lija	*Leeya*	**Xagħra**	*Shahh-ra*
Luqa	*Loo-ar*	**Xewkija**	*Scher-keya*
Marsamxett	*Mar-sam-schett*	**Xlendi**	*Schlendi*
Marsaxlokk	*Marsa-schlok*	**Żebbuġ**	*Ze-booje*
Mdina	*Imdeena*	**Żejtun**	*Tzay-toon*
Mġarr	*Imjarr*	**Żurrieq**	*Zur-rea*

Belli, Andrea (1705–72). Little-known baroque architect from Valletta who probably remodelled the Auberge de Castile et Leon and designed the Cathedral Museum in Mdina.

Bonici, Guiseppe (1707–79). Maltese architect responsible for Castellania, Valletta Customs House and Nadur church, Gozo.

Buonamici, Francesco. The Order's resident engineer between 1635–59 who was probably responsible for the introduction of an early-baroque style of architecture in major buildings. The Hostel de Verdelin, the Jesuit church in Valletta and the church of St Paul at Rabat are among his works.

Cachia, Domenico (c.1700–90). Maltese architect of St Helen's at Birkirkara, and Selmun Palace on the outskirts of Mellieħa. The other, but less likely candidate, for the remodelling of the Auberge de Castile et Leon.

Cali, Guiseppe (1846–1930). A portrait and ecclesiastical painter born to Neapolitan parents in Malta. Many of his works are to be found in parish churches.

Caravaggio, Michelangelo Merisi da (1571–1610). Regarded as the greatest Italian painter of the 17th century; a master of realism, his paintings are chromatically stunning.

Cassar, Gerolamo (1520–86). Famed Maltese architect and engineer who designed most of Valletta's buildings; his prodigious oeuvre includes the Grand Master's Palace, St John's Co-Cathedral, and all the *auberges*.

Cassar, Vittorio (d.1605/7). Son of Gerolamo, and like his father an architect and an engineer. Formed a formidable partnership with Grand Master Alof de Wignacourt: together they built Forts St Lucian and St Thomas on Malta, and St Mary on Comino.

Dingli, Tommaso (1591–1666). Maltese architect who built many fine

churches with certain Renaissance flourishes, notably St Mary's in Attard, and the Assumption in Birkirkara.

Favray, Antoine de (1706–98). French painter who adopted Malta; best known for his evocation of late 18th-century grand masters, especially Grand Master Pinto in the sacristy of St John's Co-Cathedral.

Ferramolino, Antonio (??-1550). Italian military engineer who worked for the emperor of Spain, Charles V. He advised Grand Master de Homedes on the vital fortifications of St Angelo and was the first to suggest building fortifications on Mount Sceberras (where Valletta now stands).

Firenzuola, Vincenzo Maculano da (*b.* 1578). An Italian engineer and Dominican friar who served the Pope and built the Margherita Lines around the Three Cities in the mid-17th century.

Floriani, Pietro Paolo (1585–1638). Italian military engineer responsible for the immense Floriana Lines.

Gafa, Lorenzo (1630–1710). Doyen of Maltese baroque architects. Trained in Rome and famed for his light touch; the dome is his signature. The cathedrals of Mdina and Victoria, and the parish churches of Siġġiewi, Vittoriosa and Żejtun are among the most notable of his works.

Gafa, Melchiorre (1635–67). Noted sculptor brother of Lorenzo.

Gruenenberg, Don Carlos de. The emperor of Spain's engineer, who first came to Malta in the late 17th century at the request of Grand Master Perellos to advise on the Valletta Harbour fortifications. He built (and paid for) the batteries still standing at St Angelo, and was made a Knight of Grace.

Laparelli da Cortona, Francesco (1521–70). Italian architect and engineer who conceived and oversaw the masterplan for the new city of Valletta. He died in Crete just before the battle of Lepanto.

Mondion, Charles Francois de. Outstanding French military engineer and architect, the Order's resident designer from 1715–33. Apart from his work on the magnificent Fort Manoel (with de Tigne) he rebuilt much of Mdina after the 1693 earthquake for Grand Master de Vilhena, including the Main Gate and Banca Giuratale.

Perez d'Aleccio, Matteo (1547–1616). Rome-based Spanish painter who arrived in Malta in the wake of the Great Siege celebrations (1565). His most noted works are the cycles of frescoes in the Grand Master's Palace including 12 events of the Great Siege. He died in Peru.

Preti, Mattia (1613–99). Southern Italian baroque artist who embellished many of the islands' churches and is best known for his work on the vault of St John's in Valletta and the influence his ecclesiastical paintings left behind. The Order made him a Knight of Grace.

De Tigne. French military engineer who came to Malta in 1715 to aid the works to what became Fort Manoel. Not to be confused with Chevalier Tigne who designed, built and paid for the fort which bears his name.

Zahra, Francesco (1710–73). Gifted Maltese painter some of whose works can be seen in St Catherine's in Zejtun.

Bastion. A fortified stone wall, often backed with earth, that thrusts out from the main fortifications at angles.

Cavalier. Defence work inside the *enceinte* and higher than the first line of defence. e.g. a bastion. Sometimes used as a gun platform and to store arms (*see* St John's *and* St James's Cavaliers, Valletta).

Counterguard. An acutely angled polygonal stonework built to protect a bastion (set lower than and in front of it).

Curtain. A sheer stone wall, bordered by a parapet, which usually joins two bastions.

Demi-bastion. A half bastion built to protect a curtain wall.

Enceinte. A wall enclosing a fortified area, and/or the area enclosed (e.g. the fortifications that surround Valletta).

Hornwork. A defence work independent of the main fortifications.

Melitian (or fat) mouldings. A triple roll of mouldings around windows and doors which get progressively fatter (the inner being thinner than the outer). They were typical to Malta in the 16th century.

Parapet. A low, and sometimes indented wall at the top of a rampart, built to protect the besieged.

Essential Glossary

Pasha. A senior Ottoman rank (not a surname, as in Mustapha Pasha) of admiral or general or governor; itself subdivided into three grades.

Ravelin. A V-shaped defence built outside the main fortifications in front of a curtain wall and with open access for the defenders at the rear.

Before 4,000	Arrival of man.
Circa 3,600	Introduction of copper.
Circa 2,500	First arrival of bronze-using people.
Circa 1,500	Second arrival of bronze-using people.
Circa 900-800	The Iron Age.
Circa 800–480	Phoenician period.
Circa 480–218	Carthaginian period.
264–241	First Punic War.
218–201	Second Punic War.
218	Malta incorporated in Republic of Rome.
149–146	Third Punic War.

AD

60	Shipwreck of St Paul.
117–138	Islands made municipalities during reign of Hadrian.
395	Final division of Roman Empire.
395–870	Byzantine period.
870	Invasion by Aghlabite Arabs.
1048	Byzantine bid to recapture the islands.
1090	Norman invasion.
1122	Uprising of the Arabs.
1144	Byzantines again attempt to recapture the islands.
1154	Bishops of Malta under the jurisdiction of the See of Palermo.
1194–1266	Swabians (Germans).
1266–1283	Angevins (French).
1283–1412	Aragonese (Spanish).
1350	Establishment of Maltese nobility by King Ludwig of Sicily.
1350–1357	First Incorporation of Islands in Royal Domain.
1397–1420	Second Incorporation of Islands in Royal Domain.
1397	Establishment of *Università* (Commune).
1425	Revolt against Don Gonsalvo Monroy.
1429	Saracens from Tunis try to capture Malta.
1428–1530	Third (and final) Incorporation of Islands in Royal Domain.
1530	Order of St John takes formal possession of the islands.
1535	First known date of celebration of carnival in Malta.
1561	Holy Inquisition officially established in Malta.
1565	Great Siege.

Chronology

1566	Founding of Valletta.
1578	Inauguration of St John's Co-Cathedral.
1593	Inauguration of Jesuits' College.
1768	Jesuits expelled from Malta.

1775	Rising of the Priests.
1784	Promulgation of the *Diritto Municipale* by Grand Master de Rohan.
End of 18th Century	General decline of the Order of St John.
1798	The French, under Napoleon, occupy Malta.
	Abolition of the Inquisition
1799	Britain takes Malta under its protection *in the name* of the king of the Two Sicilies.
1800	The French capitulate. Major General H. Pigot is instructed to place Malta under the protection of the British Crown.
1802	Peace of Amiens by which Malta was to have been returned to the Order of St John. Declaration of Rights.
1813	The Bathurst Constitution. First issue of *Gazzetta del Governo di Malta* (changed in 1816 to *Malta Government Gazette*).
1814	Treaty of Paris by which Malta is granted to Britain.
1819	Dissolution of *Università*.
1828	Proclamation regulating state-church relations.
1831	See of Malta becomes independent of See of Palermo.
1834	Opening of Malta Government Savings Bank.
1835	First Council of Government.
1839	Abolition of press censorship and introduction of law of libel.
1840	Council of Government with elected members.
1864	Diocese of Gozo separated from See of Malta .
1869	Opening of Suez Canal.
1880	Malta Railway Company founded.
1881	Executive Council—an entirely official body.
1887	The Stickland-Mizzi Constitution.
1903	Council of Government—largely a return to the 1840 Constitution.
1914–1918	World War I.
1919	*Sette Giugno* riots.
1921	The Amery-Milner Constitution granting self-government. Opening of first Malta parliament.
1930	Constitution suspended.
1931	End of Malta Railway Company.
1932	Constitution restored.
1933	Constitution withdrawn. Crown Colony government as in 1813.
1936	Constitution providing for nominated members to Executive Council.
1939	Macdonald Constitution: Council of Government to be elected. Lord Strickland's Constitutional Party returned.
1939–1945	World War II.
1940	First air raids on Malta (11 June).
1942	Award of the George Cross for Gallantry to the People of Malta by King George VI (15 April).
1943	Italians surrender (8 September).
1946	National Assembly resulting in 1947 Constitution.
1947	Restoration of self-government: Dr Paul Boffa's Malta Labour Party returned.

1958	Dom Mintoff resigns as prime minister. Dr G. Borg Olivier declines invitation to form alternative government and the governor takes over direct administration of the islands.
1959	Interim constitution providing for Executive Council.
1961	Blood Constitution published by Order-in-Council, providing a measure of self-government for the 'State' of Malta.
1964	Malta becomes a sovereign and independent state within the British Commonwealth.
1968	Establishment of Central Bank of Malta.
1971	Sir Anthony Mamo becomes first Maltese governor general.
1972	Military base agreement with Britain and other NATO countries.
1974	Malta becomes a republic.
1979	Termination of military base agreement. British Services leave Malta after 180 years.
1989	US President George Bush, and Soviet leader Mikhail Gorbachev meet at Marsaxlokk for Summit (1–3 December).
1990	Pope John Paul II visits Malta (25–27 May).
1990	Prof. Guido de Marco elected president of 45th Annual UN General Assembly.
1992	Her Majesty Queen Elizabeth II visits Malta for George Cross 50th anniversary celebrations (28–30 May).

Maltese Rule—Grand Masters to Prime Ministers

Grand Masters of the Order of St John

1530–1534	Philippe Villiers de L'Isle Adam (*French*)
1534–1535	Pierino de Ponte (*Italian*)
1535–1536	Didier de Saint Jaille (*French*)
1536–1553	Juan de Homedes (*Spanish*)
1553–1557	Claude de la Sengle (*French*)
1557–1568	Jean Parisot de la Valette (*French*)
1568–1572	Pietro de Monte (*Italian*)
1572–1581	Jean L'Evesque de la Cassiere (*French*)
1581–1595	Hugues Loubenx de Verdalle (*French*)
1595–1601	Martin Garzes (*Spanish*)
1601–1622	Alof de Wignacourt (*French*)
1622–1623	Luis Mendez de Vasconcellos (*Portuguese*)
1623–1636	Antoine de Paule (*French*)
1636–1657	Jean Paul de Lascaris Castellar (*French*)
1657–1660	Martin de Redin (*Spanish*)
1660	Annet de Clermont de Chattes Gessan (*French*)
1660–1663	Rafael Cotoner (*Spanish*)
1663–1680	Nicolas Cotoner (*Spanish*)
1680–1690	Gregorio Carafa (*Italian*)

1690–1697	Adrien de Wignacourt (*French*)
1697–1720	Ramon Perellos y Roccaful (*Spanish*)
1720–1722	Marc'Antonio Zondadari (*Italian*)
1722–1736	Antonio Manoel de Vilhena (*Portuguese*)
1736–1741	Ramon Despuig (*Spanish*)
1741–1773	Manoel Pinto de Fonseca (*Portuguese*)
1773–1775	Francisco Ximenes de Texada (*Spanish*)
1775–1797	Emmanuel de Rohan Polduc (*French*)
1797–1798	Ferdinand von Hompesch (*German*)

French Rule

| 1798–1799 | Napoleon Bonaparte |
| 1799 | General Vaubois |

British Rule

Civil Commissioners

1799–1801	Captain Alexander Ball, RN president of the provisional government
1801	Major General Henry Pigot, in charge of the troops and of the government
1801–1802	Sir Charles Cameron
1802–1809	Rear Admiral Sir Alexander Ball, Bart
1810–1813	Lieutenant General Sir Hildebrand Oakes

Governors

1813–1824	Lieut. Gen. The Hon. Sir Thomas Maitland
1824–1826	General the Marquess of Hastings
1827–1836	Major General the Hon. Sir Frederic Ponsonby
1836–1843	Lieutenant General Sir Henry Bouverie
1843–1847	Lieutenant General Sir Patrick Stuart
1847–1851	The Right Hon. Richard More O'Farrell
1851–1858	Major General Sir William Reid
1858–1864	Lieutenant General Sir John Gaspard le Marchant
1864–1867	Lieutenant General Sir Henry Storks
1867–1872	General Sir Patrick Grant
1872–1878	General Sir Charles van Straubenzee
1878–1884	General Sir Arthur Borton
1884–1888	General Sir Lintorn Simmonds
1888–1890	Lieutenant General Sir Henry Torrens
1890–1893	Lieutenant General Sir Henry Smyth
1893–1899	General Sir Arthur Freemantle
1899–1903	Lieutenant General Lord Grenfell
1903–1907	General Sir Mansfield Clarke, Bart
1907–1909	Lieutenant General Sir Henry Grant
1909–1915	General Sir Leslie Rundle
1915–1919	Field Marshal Lord Methuen

1919–1924	Field Marshal Viscount Plumer
1924–1927	General Sir Walter N. Congreve, VC
1927–1931	General Sir John du Cane
1931–1936	General Sir David Campbell
1936–1940	General Sir Charles Bonham-Carter
1940–1942	Lieutenant General Sir William Dobbie
1942–1944	Field Marshal Viscount Gort, VC
1944–1946	Lieutenant General Sir Edmond Schreiber
1946–1949	Sir Francis (later Lord) Douglas
1949–1954	Sir Gerald Creasy
1954–1959	Major General Sir Robert Laycock
1959–1962	Admiral Sir Guy Grantham
1962–1964	Sir Maurice Dorman

Governors General after Independence

| 1964–1971 | Sir Maurice Dorman |
| 1971–1974 | Sir Anthony Mamo |

Presidents of the Republic

1974–1976	Sir Anthony Mamo
1976–1981	Dr Anton Buttigieg
1981–1982	Dr Albert V. Hyzler (acting, 27 Dec–15 Feb)
1982–1987	Miss Agatha Barbara
1987–1989	Mr Paul Zuereb (acting, 16 Feb–3 Apr)
1989–	Dr Vincent Tabone

Prime Ministers

1921–1923	Hon. Joseph Howard, OBE
1923–1924	Hon. Sir Francesco Buhagiar, LLD
1924–1927	Hon. Sir Ugo P. Mifsud, KB
1927–1932	Hon. Sir Gerald Strickland, GCMG (later Lord Strickland)
1932–1933	Hon. Sir Ugo P. Mifsud, KB
1947–1950	Hon. Dr (later Sir) Paul Boffa, OBE
1950 (Sept–Dec)	Hon. Dr Enrico Mizzi, LLD
1950–1955	Hon. Dr Giorgio Borg Olivier, LLD
1955–1958	Hon. Dom Mintoff, MA (Oxon)
1962–1971	Hon. Dr Giorgio Borg Olivier, LLD
1971–1976	Hon. Dom Mintoff, MA (Oxon)
1976–1981	Hon. Dom Mintoff, MA (Oxon)
1981–1984	Hon. Dom Mintoff, MA (Oxon)
1984–1987	Hon. Dr Carmelo Mifsud Bonnici, BA LLD
1987–1992	Hon. Dr Eddie Fenech Adami, LLD
1992–	Hon. Dr Eddie Fenech Adami, LLD

Books marked ★ are either out of print or probably only available at a library. Those marked ★★ are in print but may only be available in Malta.

Malta: History, Biography and Culture

Attard, Joseph, *Britain and Malta*★★ (PEG). The 180-year British ocupation told from the Maltese viewpoint.

Balbi, Francisco, *The Siege of Malta*★ (Folio Society). Remarkable day-by-day diary account written by a humble foot-soldier who survived the 5-month Turkish siege in the summer of 1565.

Baldacchino, Alfred, *Discovering Nature in the Maltese Islands*★★ (Merlin Library). Out of 100 pages, 8 deal with birds not yet extinct.

Blouet, Brian, *The Story of Malta*★★ (Progress Press). An enjoyable brief history from prehistoric times to the 1980s—no index.

Borg, Joseph, *The Public Gardens of Malta and Gozo*★★ (Media Centre). A detailed horticultural guide with photographs.

Bradford, Ernle, *The Great Siege*★★ (Penguin). A highly readable history of the Turks' attempt to wrest Malta from the knights in 1565; many references are taken from Balbi's account, *(see above)*.

Bradford, Ernle, *Siege: Malta 1940–1943*★★ (Penguin). Written with insight, and clearly demonstrates how little siege warfare has evolved over the centuries.

Buhagiar, Mario, *The Iconography of the Maltese Islands 1400–1900* (Progress Press). A comprehensive title for an equally comprehensive illustrated book. An excellent guide for those who wish to snoop around Malta's churches.

Cheetham, Simon, *Byron in Europe* (Equation). The hedonistic Lord's wanderings in Childe Harold's footsteps before he died of marsh fever in Missolonghi. Entertaining and not too academic.

Cini, Charles, *Gozo: The Roots of an Island*★★ (Said). A lively coffee-table book with both written and photographic essays on Malta's sister island.

Elliott, Peter, *The Cross and The Ensign*★★ (Grafton). A riveting history of Britain's naval affair with Malta from 1798–1979; reads like a good novel.

Further Reading

Galea, Michael, *Sir Alexander John Ball*★★ (PEG). Thorough biography of the island's first British administration.

Galizia, Anne & Helen, *Recipes from Malta* (Progress Press). Not just rabbit and *lampuka* dishes.

Hughes, Quentin, *The Building of Malta 1530–1795*★★ (Progress Press). Illustrated and primarily architectural guide to the islands.

Lucas, Laddie, *Malta, the Thorn in Rommel's side* (Stanley Paul). An engaging recent (1992) biography of a 26-year-old Allied Spitfire pilot stationed in Malta.

Luke, Sir Harry, *Malta*★ (Harrap). The lieutenant governor (1930–8) paints an erudite and affectionate portrait of the islands and its people.

Mahoney, Leonard, *A History of Maltese Architecture*★★ (Author). Masterful and detailed. A superb illustrated book for the architecture buff.

Niven, David, *The Moon's a Balloon* (Hamish Hamilton). The late star was posted to Malta and his memoirs dwell amusingly on his less than hard army sojourn on the islands.

Schermerhorn, Elizabeth, *Malta of the Knights*★★ (AMS Press New York). Wonderfully written in 1929, with tremendous understanding and sympathy of the Order's reign in Malta; it brings the knights into sharp focus.

Sultana, Donald, *The Journey of Sir Walter Scott to Malta* (Alan Sutton). Heavy going but detailed account of the dying writer's last year and last work.

Trump, Dr David, *Malta: An Archaeological Guide*★★ (Progress Press). Pithy and readable illustrated guide to the mysteries and complexities of prehistory.

Vella, Philip, *Malta: Blitzed But Not Beaten*★★ (Progress Press). Thorough and gripping account of Malta's role in World War II; excellent archive photos used throughout.

Waugh, Evelyn, *Labels* (Methuen). No back-pack for the 29-year-old Waugh as he takes a pleasure cruise and pauses at the great Mediterranean ports in the late 1920s.

Malta in Literature

Burgess, Anthony, *Earthly Powers* (Penguin). The aged protagonist lives in Lija; a phenomenal book.

Monsarrat, Nicholas, *The Kapillan of Malta* (Pan). The author, one of the great contemporary storytellers, lived in Gozo. This is a love story set in World War II and intertwined with the island's history; a great read.

Quinell, A.J., *Man on Fire* (Fontana). Another of Gozo's literary alumni. A terrific yarn which begins and ends on Gozo and involves kidnapping and a rite of passage.

Quinell, A.J., *The Perfect Kill* (Chapmans). Somehow it features Gozo, the Lockerbie 747 disaster, and a DIY survival course for life on Comino.

Sicily

The largest island in the Mediterranean has caused more printer's ink to be spilled than anywhere else in the region. The books listed exclude titles in *The Godfather* genre which, although good reads, offer little more than background vignettes.

Blunt, Anthony, *Sicilian Baroque*★ (Zwemmer). The late spy's cleverly anecdotal and witty walk through the intricacies of baroque.

Cronin, Vincent, *The Golden Honeycomb* (Collins Harvill). What starts off as a search for Daedalus's proffered gift to Aphrodite ends up as the most eloquent of travelogues.

Durrell, Lawrence, *Sicilian Carousel*★ (Faber). For some reason this excellent 1970s book is out of print.

Fallowell, Duncan, *To Noto* (Bloomsbury). An amusing and raucous tale of the author's journey from London to Sicily in an old Ford. Racy.

Gilmour, David, *The Last Leopard* (Collins Harvill). Not only a biography of di Lampedusa (*see below*) but a sympathetic record of a bygone era.

Guido, Margaret, *Sicily: An Archaeological Guide*★ (Faber). Hard to find and a little out of date (mid 1970s); the best guide of its kind and worth tracking down.

di Lampedusa, Giuseppe Tomasi, *The Leopard* (Collins Harvill). A desert island book; if you only pack one book make it this one.

Lewis, Norman, *The Honoured Society* (Elland Books). An account of the *real* post-war Sicilian *mafia*, as observed by one of the greatest travel writers.

Maxwell, Gavin, *God Protect me from my Friends*★ (Longmans). One of the very few Europeans to have a true grasp of Sicily. This book is about the famous 1950s bandit Salvatore Guiliano. His other book about the poverty-striken west of the island, *The Ten Pains of Death* (Alan Sutton) might be easier to find.

Pirandello, Luigi, *Short Stories* (Dedalus). One of the island's most famous poets, playwrights and novelists, Pirandello was born at Agrigento in 1867.

Sciascia, Leonardo, *The Day of the Owl* (Paladin/Carcanet). Another Sicilian writer, who lived under the skin of the island's tortured psyche; his works are mostly short stories and political thrillers. Try also, *The Wine Dark Sea*.

Simeti, Mary Taylor, *Sicilian Cooking* (Century). Countless ways to stuff vegetables and make the most of *melanzane* from an American who married a Sicilian.

Places in Gozo, Comino and Sicily are followed by (G), (C), or (S). Otherwise they may be assumed to be on the island of Malta itself. Entries in **bold** indicate chapter titles. Entries in *italics* indicate maps. The abbreviation, GM, stands for Grand Master. In the case of locations, it may be assumed that all relevant information on travel, tourist offices, *festas*, sports, nightlife, accommodation and restaurants is included within the page reference given.

Index